John Knox and the British Reformations

John Knox
and the British Reformations

Edited by

ROGER A. MASON

Ashgate

Aldershot • Brookfield USA • Singapore • Sydney

Published by
Ashgate Publishing Limited
Gower House
Croft Road
Aldershot
Hants
GU11 3HR
England

Ashgate Publishing Company
Old Post Road
Brookfield
Vermont 05036–9704
USA

British Library Cataloguing in Publication Data

John Knox and the British Reformations.
(St Andrews Studies in Reformation History)
    1. Knox, John, 1505–72.   2. Reformation—Great Britain—
Congresses.
    I. Mason, Roger A.
    285.2'092

Library of Congress Cataloging-in-Publication Data

John Knox and the British Reformations/edited by Roger
   A. Mason.
    (St Andrews Studies in Reformation History)
    Includes index.
    ISBN 1–84014–600–1 (alk. paper)
    1. Knox, John, c. 1514–72—Congresses.
  2. Reformation—Great Britain—Congresses.   3. Great
Britain—Church history—16th century—Congresses.
    I. Mason, Roger A.   II. Series.
    BX9223.J893   1999
    285'.2'092—dc21   98–35720
                                              CIP

ISBN 1 84014 600 1

This book is printed on acid free paper

Typeset in Sabon by Manton Typesetters, 5–7 Eastfield Road, Louth, Lincolnshire, LN11 7AJ and printed in Great Britain by Bookcraft (Bath) Ltd.

Contents

Part Three   The Scottish Reformation

St Andrews Studies in Reformation History

*The Shaping of a Community: The Rise and Reformation of the
English Parish c. 1400–1560*
Beat Kümin

*Seminary or University? The Genevan Academy and
Reformed Higher Education, 1560–1620*
Karin Maag

Marian Protestantism: Six Studies
Andrew Pettegree

Protestant History and Identity in Sixteenth-Century Europe
(2 volumes) edited by Bruce Gordon

*Antifraternalism and Anticlericalism in the German Reformation:
Johann Eberlin von Günzburg and the Campaign against the Friars*
Geoffrey Dipple

*Reformations Old and New: Essays on the Socio-Economic
Impact of Religious Change c. 1470–1630*
edited by Beat Kümin

Piety and the People: Religious Printing in French, 1511–1551
Francis M. Higman

The Reformation in Eastern and Central Europe
edited by Karin Maag

John Foxe and the English Reformation
edited by David Loades

The Reformation and the Book
Jean-François Gilmont, edited and translated by Karin Maag

Notes on Contributors

Stephen Alford is a British Academy Postdoctoral Research Fellow at Fitzwilliam College, University of Cambridge. He is the author of *The Early Elizabethan Polity: William Cecil and the British Succession Crisis 1558–1569* (1998) as well as articles on William Cecil and Anglo-Scottish relations. He is currently researching aspects of political culture in the reign of Edward VI.

J.H. Burns is Professor Emeritus of the History of Political Thought at the University of London and is an Honorary Research Fellow, University College, London. His recent major publications include *The True Law of Kingship: Concepts of Monarchy in Early Modern Scotland* (1996) and he is currently working on aspects of fifteenth- and sixteenth-century conciliarism and papalism.

Euan Cameron is Professor of Early Modern History in the University of Newcastle upon Tyne. He is the author of *The European Reformation* (1991) and editor of *Early Modern Europe* (1998). He is currently researching popular superstition in the late medieval and early modern periods and writing a general history of the Waldensian heresies between the twelfth and seventeenth centuries.

Patrick Collinson retired as Regius Professor of Modern History at the University of Cambridge in 1996. A renowned authority on sixteenth-century religious history, his many publications include *The Elizabethan Puritan Movement* (1967), *Archbishop Grindal* (1979), *The Religion of Protestants* (1982) and *Elizabethan Essays* (1994).

Jane E.A. Dawson is John Laing Lecturer in the History and Theology of the Reformation in the Department of Ecclesiastical History at the University of Edinburgh. The author of many articles on sixteenth-century British political and religious thought, she is the editor of the forthcoming Scottish History Society volume of *Campbell Letters, 1550–83*, and is completing a political biography of the 5th Earl of Argyll, *c.* 1530–73.

Carol Edington was formerly a British Academy Postdoctoral Research Fellow at the University of St Andrews and is the author of *Court and Culture in Renaissance Scotland: Sir David Lindsay of the Mount* (1994). She has published several articles on the cult of chivalry in late medieval Scotland as well as on various aspects of the Scottish Reformation.

Michael F. Graham is Assistant Professor of History at the University of Akron. He is the author of *The Uses of Reform: 'Godly Discipline' and Popular Behavior in Scotland and Beyond 1560–1610* (1996) as well as of several essays and articles on medieval and early modern Scottish, English and French history. He is currently researching the history of crime and law enforcement in early modern Britain.

W. Ian P. Hazlett is Senior Lecturer in Ecclesiastical History at the University of Glasgow. As well as publishing extensively on the thought of Bucer, Calvin and Knox, he has edited *Early Christianity to 600 AD* (1991) and *Traditions of Theology at Glasgow 1450–1990: A Miscellany* (1994). Current research includes the completion of a critical edition of a tract by Bucer for the series *Martini Buceri opera latini*.

James Kirk is Reader in Scottish History at the University of Glasgow. He is the author of *Patterns of Reform: Continuity and Change in the Reformation Kirk* (1989) and his more recent publications include editions of *The Books of Assumption of the Thirds of Benefices: Scottish Ecclesiastical Rentals at the Reformation* (1995) and *Calendar of Scottish Supplications to Rome, vol. 5, 1447–71* (1997).

Michael Lynch is Professor of Scottish History at the University of Edinburgh. The author of *Scotland: A New History* (1991) and *Edinburgh and the Reformation* (1981), he is an authority on Scottish urban history and has published extensively on the Reformation period. His current research interests include the royal court in the sixteenth century and he is the editor of a forthcoming collection of essays on the reign of James VI and I.

Roger A. Mason is Reader in Scottish History at the University of St Andrews. He is the author of *Kingship and the Commonweal: Political Thought in Renaissance and Reformation Scotland* (1998) and editor of *John Knox On Rebellion* (1994). He is currently working on an edition of George Buchanan's *De Jure Regni apud Scotos Dialogus* and writing a book entitled *Kingship and Tyranny: Scotland in the Age of Reform 1513–1603*.

Jenny Wormald is a Fellow and Tutor at St Hilda's College, University of Oxford. She is the author of *Lords and Men: Bonds of Manrent 1442–1603* (1985), *Court, Kirk and Community: Scotland 1470–1625* (1981) and *Mary Queen of Scots: A Study in Failure* (1987) as well as of many articles on late medieval and early modern Scottish and British history. She is currently working on a book on James VI and I.

David F. Wright is Senior Lecturer in Ecclesiastical History at the University of Edinburgh and a former Dean of the Faculty of Divinity. The chief general editor of the *Dictionary of Scottish Church History and Theology* (1993), he has also translated *The Common Places of Martin Bucer* (1972) and edited *Martin Bucer: Reforming Church and Community* (1994).

Preface

This collection of essays constitutes the proceedings of a conference held at St Andrews University from 30 June to 3 July 1997 to mark the 450th anniversary of John Knox's debut as a Protestant preacher. No more appropriate occasion or setting could be imagined for an academic gathering designed to reassess Knox's career and his impact on the processes of reform in Britain. It was while under siege in St Andrews Castle that Knox first received his call to the Protestant ministry and it was in April 1547 that he delivered his first sermon from the pulpit of the parish Church of the Holy Trinity in the town. If for late twentieth-century Scots Knox has lost much of the iconic status he once possessed, his enduring significance to historians of the sixteenth-century Reformations is amply borne out by the enthusiastic response to the conference and the high calibre of those who agreed to address it.

In enabling me to assemble such a cast of speakers, I am indebted above all to the trustees of the John Jamieson Trust whose remarkable generosity not only helped to ensure a successful conference but also eased the transition from the spoken to the printed word. I also owe an enormous debt to the St Andrews Scottish Studies Institute for officially hosting the conference, to its director, Douglas Dunn, for his support, and particularly to its secretary, Frances Mullan, for handling an inordinate administrative burden with her customary assurance and calm. In planning the conference, I was able to draw freely on the experience of the St Andrews Reformation Studies Institute, and I am extremely grateful to Andrew Pettegree and Bruce Gordon for their advice and encouragement and for facilitating publication of the proceedings in the Institute's prestigious series, St Andrews Studies in Reformation History. To Bruce Gordon again, as well as to John Guy, Keith Brown and James K. Cameron, thanks are due for their skilful chairing of the conference sessions, while Colin Vincent, Vice-Principal of the University, lent the proceedings gracious institutional support. Uniquely among British universities, St Andrews is an affiliate of the Folger Institute in Washington DC, and I am grateful to Kathleen Lynch for her willing collaboration in establishing a competitive scholarship which allowed a graduate student from the United States to participate in the conference.

Whatever Knox's reputation as a Puritan killjoy, it did nothing to inhibit the conviviality of an occasion designed to commemorate his name. A more sober but no less memorable contribution to the conference was made by Jamie Reid Baxter who, at very short notice, organized a concert of choral music of the Scottish Reformation which was performed in Holy Trinity Kirk by the St Rule Singers under the direction of Angela Bell. Based on the great St Andrews Psalter of the 1560s, this was the first public performance since the sixteenth century of a body of work which deserves to be much better known than it is. Those who attended the performance, conference-goers and general public alike, are greatly indebted to the Minister and Kirk Session of Holy Trinity Kirk, to Jamie Reid Baxter, and above all to Angela Bell and her group of accomplished singers, for bringing the music and language of the reformed Scots liturgy so vividly to life.

Finally, as the proceedings of the conference go to press, it is a great pleasure to acknowledge the good-humoured efficiency with which Nancy Bailey has prepared the typescript for publication and, in the process, greatly eased my own editorial responsibilities. Those responsibilities were themselves made much easier to shoulder through the generosity of the British Academy Humanities Research Board and the freedom to complete the editorial work on the volume afforded by their Research Leave scheme. I am also indebted to Alec McAulay and Caroline Cornish of Ashgate Publishing for their advice and support throughout. Above all, however, I am grateful to the contributors for their enthusiastic participation in the conference, and their ready co-operation in preparing their papers for publication.

Roger A. Mason
St Andrews

Abbreviations

APS	*Acts of the Parliaments of Scotland*, ed. Thomas Thomson and Cosmo Innes (12 vols, Edinburgh, 1814–75)
BIHR	*Bulletin of the Institute of Historical Research*
BL	British Library
BUK	*The Buke of the Universall Kirk: Acts and Proceedings of the General Assemblies of the Kirk of Scotland from the Year MDLX*, ed. Thomas Thomson (3 vols, Edinburgh, 1839–45)
Calderwood, *History*	David Calderwood, *The History of the Kirk of Scotland*, ed. Thomas Thomson (8 vols, Wodrow Society, Edinburgh, 1842–49)
CR	*Corpus Reformatorum*
CSP Scot.	*Calendar of State Papers Relating to Scotland and Mary Queen of Scots 1547–1603*, ed. J. Bain et al. (13 vols, Edinburgh, 1898–1969)
DNB	*Dictionary of National Biography*
Edin. Recs	*Extracts from the Records of the Burgh of Edinburgh 1403–1589*, ed. J.D. Marwick (4 vols, Edinburgh, 1869–82)
EHR	*English Historical Review*
JEH	*Journal of Ecclesiastical History*
Knox, *Works*	*The Works of John Knox*, ed. David Laing (6 vols, Edinburgh, Wodrow Society, 1846–64)
Knox, *History*	*John Knox's History of the Reformation in Scotland*, ed. William Croft Dickinson (2 vols, London and Edinburgh, 1949)
Knox, *On Rebellion*	*John Knox On Rebellion*, ed. Roger A. Mason (Cambridge, 1994)
L&P Henry VIII	*Calendar of Letters and Papers, Foreign and Domestic, Henry VIII*, ed. J.S. Brewer et al. (21 vols, London, 1864–1932)
NLS	National Library of Scotland
PRO	Public Record Office (London)
RPC	*The Register of the Privy Council of Scotland 1545–1625*, ed. J.H. Burton et al., first series (14 vols, Edinburgh, 1877–98)

RSCHS	*Records of the Scottish Church History Society*
SHR	*Scottish Historical Review*
SHS	Scottish History Society
SP Henry VIII	*State Papers of Henry VIII* (11 vols, London, 1830–52)
SRO	Scottish Record Office (Edinburgh)
STC	*A Short-Title Catalogue of Books Printed in England, Scotland and Ireland and of English Books Printed Abroad 1475–1640*, ed. A.W. Pollard, G.R. Redgrave et al. (3 vols, London, 1976–91)
STS	Scottish Text Society

Introduction

Roger A. Mason

> I cannot apologize for Knox. To him it is very indifferent ... what
> men say of him. But we, having got above all those details of his
> battle, and living now in clearness on the fruits of his victory, we
> for our own sake ought to look through the rumours and contro-
> versies enveloping the man, into the man himself.[1]

So wrote Thomas Carlyle in his lectures *On Heroes, Hero-Worship and
the Heroic in History*, first published in 1841. Carlyle was a great
Knoxian enthusiast. For him John Knox was not so much the Scottish
hero *par excellence* as the *only* Scottish hero. 'In the history of Scotland
... ', he wrote in the same lecture, 'I can find properly but one epoch:
we may say, it [Scottish history] contains nothing of world-interest at all
but this Reformation by Knox.'[2] This is not a judgement to which many
modern historians of Scotland in general or the Scottish Reformation in
particular would readily subscribe. It is well over twenty years since the
last substantial scholarly biography of Knox appeared and, in so far as
he retains any iconic status in the popular imagination of late twentieth-
century Scots, it is as a Puritan killjoy whose contribution to Scottish
history was to confine its culture within a Calvinist strait-jacket from
which it is only now beginning to escape. Carlyle's Protestant hero, the
prophet and patriarch of the Scottish Reformation, has few of the
resonances in the secular world of post-modern Scots that he did in the
world of their Victorian ancestors. It may well be that attempts to enlist
him in the tired disputes between Presbyterians and Episcopalians may
still arouse some (rather muted) passion; but for the majority of professional historians this is simply to belabour issues which, in the trenchant
words of one student of the period, 'have little beyond their longevity to
recommend them'.[3]

If Knox as the stuff of myth and legend has outlived his usefulness,
no longer commanding respect or inciting passion as once he did, then
modern historians are all the better placed to follow Carlyle's advice
and 'look through the rumours and controversies enveloping the man,
into the man himself'. They are also much better placed than ever

---

[1] Thomas Carlyle, *On Heroes, Hero-Worship, and the Heroic in History*, ed. Michael
K. Goldberg, Joel J. Brattin and Mark Engel (Berkeley and Los Angeles, 1993), p. 125.

[2] Ibid., p. 123.

[3] Arthur Williamson, *Scottish National Consciousness in the Age of James VI* (Edinburgh, 1979), p. vii.

before to place the man against the complex backdrop, not just of sixteenth-century Scotland, but of the wider world of Reformation Britain and Europe. It was in this spirit that the present volume, and the conference on which it is based, were conceived. The year 1997 marked the 450th anniversary of the occasion on which Knox preached his first Protestant sermon in the Holy Trinity Kirk in St Andrews. It was thought appropriate to commemorate that event by re-evaluating Knox's career in the light of the considerable advances in Reformation scholarship made over the past two decades and more. Much important recent literature relating to Knox himself is succinctly surveyed by James Kirk in the opening chapter of this collection, and it would be superfluous to revisit here the historiographical debates which have long surrounded the Scottish reformer. However, it is worth highlighting the fact that, as Kirk points out, no very significant new evidence relating directly to Knox's career has been unearthed for over a century. It is in the reinterpretation of existing evidence, and the exploration from different perspectives of the contexts in which his career and thought took shape, that this volume can claim to mark a significant advance in our understanding of Knox and his contribution to the Reformation movement in England as well as Scotland.

Following James Kirk's introductory chapter, the volume falls into three distinct but overlapping parts. The first focuses on Knox's early career from his debut on the public stage in 1547 through his years in England and the Continent up to his final return to Scotland in 1559. Very little is known of Knox's upbringing and education at Haddington, his university studies at St Andrews in the 1530s or his subsequent life as an ordained priest and public notary, a period of his life when (as he later put it) he languished in 'the puddle of papistrie',[4] and which he seems deliberately to have suppressed. His own account of his calling to the Protestant ministry, however, and the circumstances in which he delivered his first Protestant sermon, provide a wholly appropriate starting-point for Carol Edington's investigation of the network of Protestant believers and sympathizers with whom Knox was associated in the Scotland of the mid-1540s. But Knox was not, of course, destined to remain long in Scotland and the two remaining chapters in Part One follow him to England and the Continent. Thus Euan Cameron places the liturgical conflicts which beset the English exiles in Frankfurt and Geneva on a broad European canvas, while Patrick Collinson focuses more narrowly but no less luminously on the nature of Knox's often fraught relationship with both the Church of England and the women of England.

---

[4] Knox, *Works*, IV, p. 439.

It is in his relationships with women, and particularly in his correspondence with his mother in law, Mrs Bowes, and with female members
of his congregations such as Mrs Locke, that we gain a rare glimpse of
the private Knox, the man behind the public *persona* of the preacher
and the prophet. Not surprisingly, however, it is with Knox's role as
God's trumpet and instrument that the majority of chapters in this
volume are primarily concerned. In 1972, as part of the somewhat low-
key commemoration of the 400th anniversary of Knox's death, the late
Gordon Donaldson delivered a lecture in which he sought to recover
'the reality and the humanity' of Knox lurking behind the body of
principles and abstract theory attached to his name.[5] The result was a
portrait – at times indeed a caricature – of a vain and loud-mouthed
bigot whose impact on events was much less profound than Knox
himself liked to think. While this had the desired effect of cutting Knox
down to size, it was based on a misleadingly rigid distinction between
ideas and reality, principles and practice. Fortunately, late twentieth-
century historians are much less inclined than scholars of Donaldson's
era to see ideas as somehow distinct from reality rather than as an
integral part of it. As a result, though few of the chapters here are
wholly sympathetic to Knox – many of the contributors would no
doubt agree that he was a vain and loud-mouthed bigot – they are
nevertheless much more sensitive than was Donaldson to the complex
thought-world Knox inhabited and to the ideas which animated his
private as well as his public *personae*.

The decision to devote Part Two of this collection specifically to his
ideas was therefore a quite deliberate one. Knox was never a systematic
thinker and left no coherent body of theology or political theory. The
six substantial volumes of his collected works read more like sermons
pursued by other means than academic tracts or treatises. A preacher
and a prophet rather than a scholar or a lawyer, Knox's thought is
characterized above all else by an intense commitment to the primacy of
the Word of God as revealed in the Bible over other sources of knowledge and learning. It is perhaps not surprising, then, that David Wright's
analysis of the extent of Knox's familiarity with the early Church Fathers reveals his interest in them to be sporadic and half-hearted. Yet
that Knox's university education, and particularly his legal practice, did
leave some imprint on his thought is teased out by J.H. Burns, who
detects significant examples of scholastic and canonistic influence in his
later writings, and not least in his political theory. Knox's modern
biographers have frequently focused on his political ideas – the

---

[5] Gordon Donaldson, 'Knox the Man', in Duncan Shaw (ed.), *John Knox: A
Quatercentenary Reappraisal* (Edinburgh, 1975), pp. 18–32.

allegedly constitutionalist and even democratic bent of his thought – as a means of lending Knox contemporary relevance and of making more acceptable to modern ears his often rebarbative biblical rhetoric.[6] Yet as Jane Dawson's chapter makes clear, Knox's political thought was not only a good deal less radical than that of his colleague and friend, the Englishman, Christopher Goodman, but is liable to be seriously mis-construed if detached from the covenanting ideology, derived from Old Testament sources, in which it is invariably couched.

The same point is made in my own contribution, where the focus shifts from the development of Knox's resistance theory to his under-standing of the relationship between the spiritual and temporal realms, and his initially ambivalent but ultimately hostile attitude to the idea of the royal supremacy. Like most sixteenth-century reformers, Knox's aim was the creation of a godly Protestant commonwealth ruled by a godly Protestant prince, and it was only the failure of the civil powers to live up to his expectations of them that drove him to develop theories of resistance to what he construed as Roman Catholic tyranny. At times, indeed, his frustration at the apparent unwillingness of the secular authorities to fulfil the Word and the Will of God led him to contem-plate withdrawal from an ill-reformed national Church into the purer 'small flock' of the elect. One such occasion is examined by Ian Hazlett who for the first time subjects Knox's little known tract on fasting, dating from 1566, to detailed scrutiny. The idea of a general fast, a public display of repentance in the face of God's plagues and punish-ments, was to become part and parcel of the Scottish Protestant tradition.[7] In the mid-1560s, at a time when the reformed Scottish Kirk appeared to be in danger not just from a Catholic Queen but from the backsliding and apostasy of the Protestant nobility, the need for penitential purifica-tion in the face of a wrathful God was, in Knox's view, overwhelming.

Hazlett's chapter returns Knox to Scotland and to the complexities of his role in the Scottish Reformation with which the final part of this volume is primarily concerned. Even as he threw himself wholeheart-edly into promoting God's cause in his native land, however, Knox did not lose sight of the wider context in which the processes of reform were necessarily played out. Thus Stephen Alford draws attention to the British dimension of the Scottish Reformation, exploring the different

---

[6] Thus Jasper Ridley, *John Knox* (Oxford, 1968), pp. 527–30, not only describes him as 'one of the most ruthless and successful revolutionary leaders in history', but con-cludes that 'Knox, despite his intolerance ... was a great contributor to the struggle for human freedom'.

[7] See Leigh Eric Schmidt, *Holy Fairs: Scottish Communions and American Revivals in the Early Modern Period* (Princeton, 1989).

ways in which Knox and William Cecil conceptualized and sought to realize a new Protestant Britain. Yet for all the attention that modern historians now lavish on British history, Knox's Britishness remains oddly elusive: if (like many of his contemporaries) he saw dynastic union between the Scottish and English kingdoms as the key to safeguarding Protestantism in both, his sense of what being British might mean is much less easy to discern than his sense of being English or Scottish. Many of the chapters that follow lay emphasis on the extent to which Knox identified with his adopted English homeland both during the reign of Edward VI and subsequently during his years of exile on the Continent. Others prefer to highlight what are sometimes seen as the characteristically Scottish aspects of his thought. Perhaps ultimately, however, it is Patrick Collinson who comes closest to encapsulating the reformer when he writes that: 'For all his forthright patriotic self-consciousness, Knox was not so much either Scots or English as a Protestant internationalist, with no continuing city' (below, p. 88).

It was Knox's sense of himself as part of a Protestant international, as (above all) a preacher and a prophet engaged in a cosmic struggle between the forces of Christ and Antichrist, which lend his activities in Scotland in the 1560s a decidedly unreal air. Jenny Wormald, in discussing Knox's relations with Mary Queen of Scots, highlights Knox's apparent inability to come to terms with the fact that Mary refused to act out the role of a persecuting Jezebel which he assigned to her. Likewise, the black-and-white terms in which Knox characteristically articulated the struggle between God and the Devil contrasts markedly with Michael Lynch's detailed analysis of the religious complexion of contemporary Edinburgh where confessional loyalties were anything but clear-cut. Moreover, just as Knox's religious imperatives need to be set against the economic realities of a trade slump, so the vision of a godly commonwealth adumbrated in *The First Book of Discipline* must be tempered by the reality of the painfully slow spread of Christian discipline in the Scottish localities. Michael Graham's concluding chapter shows how, even in urban areas such as Edinburgh, St Andrews and Aberdeen, the imposition of discipline, with all that this implied in terms of behavioural reform and spiritual regeneration, was fitful and only sporadically effective.

Knox in the late 1560s and early 1570s was only too well aware of the fragile nature of the reform movement he had helped to nurture in Scotland. Politically sidelined, however, and suffering from increasingly poor health,[8] there was little he could do about it. On his death in

---

[8] J. Wilkinson, 'The Medical History of John Knox', *Proceedings of the Royal College of Physicians of Edinburgh*, 28 (1998), pp. 81–101. I am grateful to T.C. Smout for bringing this article to my attention.

November 1572, the work of the Lord to which he had devoted his life was anything but finished. The same is true of what has become Knox's most enduring memorial, his *History of the Reformation of Religion within the Realm of Scotland*, a brilliant Protestant polemic which remained incomplete and unpublished on its author's death. It is one of the many paradoxes associated with Knox that responses to the *History* vary so greatly, and that (as James Kirk points out) historians cannot even agree on whether it is essentially an autobiography, a memoir or a history. It would be surprising indeed if consensus on this or many other aspects of Knox's career emerged from a volume such as this. Like Thomas Carlyle before them, though for somewhat different reasons, the contributors to it would make no apology for Knox. Yet if they succeed in penetrating the 'rumours and controversies' that surround Knox, if they bring us closer to 'the man himself', they will have served the simple but salutory purpose of revealing what a complex and contradictory man he was.

CHAPTER ONE

John Knox and the Historians

James Kirk

'What I have bene to my countrie, albeit, this unthankfull aige will not knowe, yet the aiges to come wilbe compelled to beare witnes to the trueth.'[1] This attestation, uttered by John Knox from the pulpit towards the end of his life, when traduced by anonymous libellers, strikes an appropriately prophetic note from a man who saw his destiny in blowing his Master's trumpet. Quite simply, both in life and in death, Knox has attracted controversy. Over the centuries, he has been subjected to the familiar process of historical re-evaluation, reassessment and revision, a thoroughly legitimate and potentially refreshing exercise: it keeps historians in business and is a healthy sign of a flourishing historiography – though sometimes the revisions seem less profound than the interpretations they seek to revise. With Knox, however, the historiographical problem assumes a rather unusual dimension. No significant primary evidence on Knox has come to light since the appearance of Peter Lorimer's *John Knox and the Church of England*, in 1875;[2] and one recent discovery, slender though it is, is the snippet of information uncovered by Gordon Donaldson that Knox was on Queen Mary's payroll.[3] Yet the absence of fresh source material can scarcely be said to have served as a disincentive to potential investigators: the torrent of publications on Knox, far from diminishing, continues to grow apace, far outstripping those on all other Scottish historical figures, except, of course, Mary Queen of Scots, Bonnie Prince Charlie and Robert Burns.[4]

---

[1] Richard Bannatyne, *Journal of the Transactions in Scotland* (Edinburgh, 1806), p. 119.

[2] Lorimer uncovered material attributable to Knox in the Morrice MSS, Dr Williams's Library, London, including a letter from Knox to his Berwick congregation and other writings on aspects of worship criticizing kneeling at communion. *John Knox and the Church of England* (London, 1875), pp. 245–301.

[3] Gordon Donaldson, *Scotland's History: Approaches and Reflections*, ed. James Kirk (Edinburgh, 1995), pp. 63–4.

[4] See James Kirk, 'The Scottish Reformation and the Reign of James VI: A Select Critical Bibliography', *RSCHS*, 23 (1987), pp. 113–55, at pp. 135–9. Later contributions include Richard Kyle, 'John Knox and the Purification of Religion: The Intellectual Aspects of his Crusade against Idolatry', *Archiv für Reformationsgeschichte*, 77 (1986), pp. 265–80; Richard Kyle, 'John Knox's Methods of Biblical Interpretation: An Important

This imbalance, which still afflicts Scottish history, is apt to give the subject a faintly peculiar image. Even within the limited field of Scottish Reformation studies, concentration on Knox, whose words and actions precisely because they are so accessible[5] and so memorable are cited in preference to those of his contemporaries, inevitably leads to some distortion and certainly to a narrowing of horizons.

It took not a Scot but an American historian to point the way ahead in 1953 by producing a study of Knox's contemporary Lord James Stewart, Earl of Moray, Mary's half-brother, and surely a key figure in the Reformation struggle and ensuing settlement.[6] Unpopular though it

---

Source of his Intellectual Radicalness', *Journal of Religious Studies*, 12 (1986), pp. 57–70; Richard Kyle, 'John Knox's Concept of Divine Providence and its Influence on his Thought', *Albion*, 18 (1986), pp. 395–410; A. Daniel Frankforter, 'Elizabeth Bowes and John Knox: A Woman and Reformation Theology', *Church History*, 56 (1987), pp. 333–47; W. Stanford Reid, 'John Knox's Theology of Political Government', *The Sixteenth-Century Journal*, 19 (1988), pp. 529–40; James K. Cameron, 'John Knox (*c.* 1514–1572)', in Gerhard Müller (ed.), *Theologische Realenzyklopädie*, (Berlin and New York, 1976–), XIX, pp. 281–7; Richard Kyle, 'The Major Concepts in John Knox's Baptismal Thought', *Fides et Historia* (1989), pp. 20–30; P.-A. Lee, '"A bodye politique to governe": Aylmer, Knox and the Debate on Queenship', *The Historian* [USA], 52 (1990), pp. 242–61; Stuart Lamont, *The Swordbearer: John Knox and the European Reformation* (London, 1991); Jane E.A. Dawson, 'The Two John Knoxes: England, Scotland and the 1558 Tracts', *JEH*, 42 (1991), pp. 123–40; Richard Kyle, 'The Christian Commonwealth: John Knox's Vision for Scotland', *Journal of Religious History*, 16 (1991), pp. 247–59; Robert M. Kingdon, 'Knox and the Anti-Marian Resistance', in J.H. Burns (ed.), *The Cambridge History of Political Thought, 1450–1700* (Cambridge, 1991), pp. 194–200; Richard Kyle, 'John Knox', *Encyclopedia of the Reformed Faith*, ed. D.K. McKim (Louisville and Edinburgh, 1992), pp. 208–9; R.M. Healey, 'John Knox's "History": A "compleat" Sermon on Christian Duty', *Church History*, 61 (1992), pp. 319–33; Richard Kyle, 'John Knox', *Dictionary of Scottish Church History and Theology* [hereafter *DSCHT*], ed. N. de S. Cameron (Edinburgh, 1993), pp. 465–6; Henry R. Sefton, *John Knox: An Account of his Spirituality* (Edinburgh, 1993); John Knox, *On Rebellion*, ed. Roger A. Mason (Cambridge, 1994); R.M. Healey, 'Waiting for Deborah: John Knox and Four Ruling Queens', *The Sixteenth-Century Journal*, 25 (1994), pp. 371–86; Amanda Shephard, *Gender and Authority in Sixteenth-Century England: The Knox Debate* (Keele, 1994); Susan M. Felch, '"Deir Sister": The Letters of John Knox to Anne Vaughan Lok', *Renaissance and Reformation*, 19 (4) (1995), pp. 47–68; Susan M. Felch, 'The Rhetoric of Biblical Authority: John Knox and the Question of Women', *The Sixteenth-Century Journal*, 26 (1995), pp. 805–22; A.N. McLaren, 'Delineating the Elizabethan Body Politic: Knox, Aylmer and the Definition of Counsel 1558–88', *History of Political Thought*, 17 (1996), pp. 224–52; Jenny Wormald, 'John Knox', *The Oxford Encyclopedia of the Reformation*, ed. H.J. Hillerbrand (4 vols, New York and Oxford, 1996), II, pp. 380–81.

[5] For lists of Knox's own writings, see Thomas McCrie, *Life of John Knox* (Edinburgh, 1855), pp. 411–16; W. Ian P. Hazlett, 'A Working Bibliography of Writings by John Knox', in R.V. Schnucker (ed.), *Calviniana : Ideas and Influence of Jean Calvin* (Kirksville, MO, 1988), pp. 185–93.

[6] Maurice Lee, Jr, *James Stewart, Earl of Moray: A Political Study of the Reformation in Scotland* (New York, 1953).

may be, one conclusion to be drawn is that Scottish history might be in rather better shape if historians of the period abandoned their preoccupation with Knox in preference for an appreciation of the contribution of Knox's contemporaries – contemporaries who still, all too often, remain rather shadowy figures. If, over the last two centuries, half the energy expended on a mass of largely contradictory publications on Knox had been devoted to some of Knox's associates, the subject would surely be on a firmer footing. But, that said, already there are some encouraging signs, with modern scholarly studies, for example, of Alexander Alane (or Alesius),[7] Sir David Lindsay,[8] George Buchanan,[9] Christopher Goodman[10] and Maitland of Lethington;[11] with Archibald, 5th Earl of Argyll[12] and John Winram[13] in St Andrews currently under investigation. Even the activities of a subsidiary figure like Clement Little[14] and his circle can prove illuminating. Yet how remarkably little we still know of influential individuals like John Douglas, David Lindsay (of South Leith), John Row, John Spottiswoode and John Willock – all men who were Knox's colleagues and, more importantly, men who had travelled to other lands.[15] And what of the godly matrons of the Scottish Reformation, of whom we have heard next to nothing?[16]

With Knox, the historiographical tradition – if that is what it is – has been refined to such perfection that it has become almost obligatory for the latest writer to present an account of Knox's career which as nearly

---

[7] G. Wiedermann, 'Der Reformator Alexander Alesius als Ausleger der Psalmen' (unpublished Erlangen PhD thesis, 1988); G. Wiedermann, 'Alexander Alesius' Lectures on the Psalms at Cambridge, 1536', *JEH*, 37 (1986), pp. 15–41.

[8] Carol Edington, *Court and Culture in Renaissance Scotland: Sir David Lindsay of the Mount (1486–1555)* (East Linton, 1994).

[9] I.D. McFarlane, *Buchanan* (London, 1981); John Durkan, *George Buchanan (1506–1582) Renaissance Scholar* (Glasgow, 1982).

[10] Jane E.A. Dawson, 'The Early Career of Christopher Goodman and his Place in the Development of English Political Thought' (unpublished Durham PhD thesis, 1978); Jane E.A. Dawson, 'Revolutionary Conclusions: The Case of the Marian Exiles', *History of Political Thought*, 11 (1990), pp. 257–72.

[11] W. Blake, *William Maitland of Lethington, 1528–1573: A Study of the Policy of Moderation in the Scottish Reformation* (Lampeter, 1990); and, for a more fully researched study, Mark Loughlin, 'The Career of Maitland of Lethington c. 1526–1573' (unpublished University of Edinburgh PhD thesis, 1991).

[12] Dr Jane Dawson is presently examining the career of Argyll.

[13] By Linda Dunbar. See her forthcoming contribution on Winram as superintendent in *RSCHS*, 26 (1997).

[14] James Kirk, 'Clement Little's Edinburgh', in J.R. Guild and A. Law (eds), *Edinburgh University Library, 1580–1980: A Collection of Historical Essays* (Edinburgh, 1982), pp. 1–42.

[15] *DSCHT*, pp. 254, 486, 732, 788–9, 874.

[16] For England, see Patrick Collinson, *Godly People* (London, 1983), pp. 273–87.

as possible contradicts previous assessments of the subject. Accordingly, Knox the one-time founder of Scottish Presbyterianism[17] is reappraised as an enthusiast for Episcopacy.[18] Knox, the symbol of a certain type of Scottishness,[19] is seen to have been more at home as a good Church of England man, deferential to the higher powers,[20] preaching to his congregations at Berwick and Newcastle, or at the court of Edward VI, or in Buckinghamshire or against the Anabaptists of Kent, within an Episcopal Church whose form of worship centred on the Prayer Book – the man who became a Marian exile at Frankfurt and Geneva, and who acted as a focus for English Puritanism[21] – the man who was so thoroughly at home in an English setting that on returning to Scotland was duly criticized by his opponents for adopting English manners and, worse, an English accent.[22] And, of course, he even took an Englishwoman – a literate one – as his first bride.[23]

Knox, who invariably is portrayed as the Scot who established the ideal of a school in every parish and who lent his name to a scheme for reforming the Scottish universities,[24] is also the man who, as minister in Edinburgh, allowed his sons – both born in Geneva – to be educated in the very English environment of Durham or Richmond, and Cambridge University.[25] Sometimes it is said that this shows Knox valued the benefits of a superior English education. Gordon Donaldson has spoken of how Knox 'insisted that both his sons should have a sound Anglican

[17] J.G. Macgregor, The Scottish Presbyterian Polity (Edinburgh, 1926), 21 ff.; Lorimer, Knox and the Church of England, p. 34; S.J. Knox, John Knox's Genevan Congregation (London, 1956), pp. 5–6; W. Stanford Reid, 'Knox's Attitude to the English Reformation', Westminster Theological Journal, 25 (1963), pp. 1–32; Jasper Ridley, John Knox (Oxford, 1968), p. 528; W. Stanford Reid, Trumpeter of God (New York, 1974), p. 290.

[18] Gordon Donaldson, The Scottish Reformation (Cambridge, 1960), pp. 167–70.

[19] Peter Hume Brown, John Knox: A Biography (2 vols, London, 1895), II, pp. 115, 117, 295; William Croft Dickinson, The Scottish Reformation and its Influence upon Scottish Life and Character (Edinburgh, 1960), p. 19; Reid, Trumpeter of God, pp. 291–2; J.D. Mackie, John Knox (London, 1951), pp. 23–4; cf. Gordon Donaldson, 'John Knox: The First Puritan or the Victim of Puritan Mythology?', New Edinburgh Review, 3 (August 1969), pp. 20–23.

[20] Gordon Donaldson, The Making of the Scottish Prayer Book of 1637 (Edinburgh, 1954), pp. 9 ff.; Donaldson, Scottish Reformation, pp. 132–5.

[21] Knox, History, I, pp. 110–11, 123–4, 283; Knox, Works, III, pp. 157–216; IV, pp. 3–68; V, pp. 211–16, 469–94; Lorimer, Knox and the Church of England, pp. 15 ff., 98 ff., 146 ff., 162 ff., 201 ff., 251 ff., 290 ff.

[22] Ninian Winzet, Certane Tractatis for Reformatioun of Doctryne and Maneris in Scotland (Maitland Club, 1835), p. 118; Knox, Works, IV, p. 439.

[23] Knox, History, I, pp. 123, 351; Knox, Works, V, pp. 5–6.

[24] The First Book of Discipline, ed. J.K. Cameron (Edinburgh, 1972), pp. 129–55.

[25] Knox, Works, VI, pp. lxiii–lxiv.

upbringing, and sent them to school in England'.[26] Such an emphasis, however, seems not altogether well-placed. After all, Knox's two sons had left Edinburgh when they were five and six years old to be brought up by their grandmother in England, eventually entering St John's College, Cambridge, eight days after Knox's death. All along, Knox's contact with his sons was exceedingly remote; he is known to have visited them only once; and the truth would seem to be that from afar he exercised very little personal supervision over them.

Knox himself, who had been born just 40 miles or so from the English border, certainly succeeded in casting aside traditional Scottish animosities towards the English. His early links were with East Lothian lairds, who as 'assured Scots' were sufficiently well-disposed towards the English to accept the money Henry VIII offered them. Indeed, such is seen to be Knox's solicitude for England that the reformer, who once believed no other realm could displace Scotland in his affections, by 1554 had come to regard the troubles in England under Mary Tudor to be 'double more dolorous unto my hert than ever were the troubles of Scotland'.[27] Yet he is also portrayed as one who frustrated English efforts to export 'Anglicanism' – the official standards of Elizabethan Protestantism – to Scotland at the Reformation. Thus the Scottish Church ended up with the Genevan-inspired Book of Common Order instead of the English Book of Common Prayer in establishing patterns of worship for centuries to come.[28]

At a popular level, Knox is too readily dismissed as a figure of fun. This grim ayatollah-like figure might now be ridiculed safely at 400 years' distance and be treated as a joke, even as a bad joke at that – the culprit, the killjoy, responsible for imposing on Scotland a Calvinism from which the majority of Scots have suffered from that day to this. That, at any rate, is a prevailing image.[29] But Knox's emphasis on discipline, itself a reaction to the perceived laxity of the Middle Ages, was, of course, shared by many, including Pope Pius V and by John Hamilton, the last pre-Reformation Archbishop of St Andrews.[30] The

---

[26] Gordon Donaldson, *Scottish Church History* (Edinburgh, 1985), p. 149.

[27] Knox, *Works*, III, p. 133.

[28] McCrie, *Knox*, pp. 354–7; William D. Maxwell, *John Knox's Genevan Service Book, 1556* (Edinburgh, 1931), pp. 8–9; D. Macmillan, *John Knox, A Biography* (London, 1905), pp. 218–23; Eustace Percy, *John Knox* (London, 1937), p. 200; Reid, *Trumpeter of God*, pp. 161–2.

[29] Hugh MacDiarmid, Colin Maclean and Andrew Ross, *John Knox* (Edinburgh, 1976), *passim*.

[30] Gordon Donaldson, 'Knox the Man', in Duncan Shaw (ed.), *John Knox: A Quatercentenary Reappraisal* (Edinburgh, 1975), pp. 30–31; cf. Gordon Donaldson, *Church and Nation through Sixteen Centuries* (Edinburgh, 1960), p. 65.

difference with Knox was that he was rather more successful in helping to restore it – and, indeed, to apply it in Scotland.

For those who take Knox more seriously, the Scots reformer has become a kind of slogan for a baffling diversity of attitudes and beliefs which were frequently alien to his outlook. He is dissected as a body of theories – one modern work even bears the title *The Mind of John Knox*;[31] he is presented as a kind of abstraction, in which the figure of Knox as an individual – as a human being with all that this implies – is all too often lost sight of.[32] Nowhere, perhaps, is this more evident than in assessments of Knox's ecclesiastical loyalties. These have been appraised in some surprisingly ingenious ways. It once seemed almost heretical to assert unequivocally that Knox was not a Presbyterian; but heresy in one generation is apt to become orthodoxy in another. There even may seem to be a simple and commendable logic in claiming that Knox could not have been a Presbyterian since the presbytery – or, at any rate, the Scottish presbytery – had not been invented in his day. But such a beguiling approach turns out to be too simple by half. Again, to advance the rival claim that Knox was really an Episcopalian in disguise has unsettled many and seems to stretch the evidence like a piece of elastic to no sound purpose. It leaves out Knox's own identity of parish minister with bishop. And the claim that Knox's farewell advice to the Scottish Church was that it should have bishops is at variance with Knox's own declared preference, just before his death in 1572, for the very different structure he had helped to create in 1560. In Knox's case, both labels are quite inapposite, and their application ought simply to be abandoned.[33]

'What does it matter?', it might be asked. For a start, it neatly illustrates how Knox has become the victim of writers whose ecclesiastical allegiances have coloured their historical perceptions. For those whose interests centre on the pre-Reformation Church, the unregenerate Knox as 'minister of the sacred altar'[34] has naturally little appeal, and the renegade priest who rejoiced in the complete collapse of the medieval system has proved for some to be an even less attractive proposition.[35] David Hay Fleming (who, in protest at the introduction

---

[31] Richard G. Kyle, *The Mind of John Knox* (Lawrence, KS, 1984).

[32] Donaldson, 'Knox the Man', pp. 18 ff.

[33] James Kirk, '"The Polities of the Best Reformed Kirks": Scottish Achievements and English Aspirations in Church Government after the Reformation', *SHR*, 59 (1980), pp. 22–53.

[34] William Fraser, *Memorials of the Earls of Haddington* (2 vols, Edinburgh, 1889), I, p. xlii.

[35] John McQuillan produced *John Knox* for the Catholic Truth Society of Scotland (Glasgow, 1960).

of instrumental music, left the Free Church for the United Original Secession Church) complained in 1895 that Knox 'is still grossly misrepresented' by Roman Catholic writers and by apologists for Queen Mary.[36] In similar vein, Gordon Donaldson averred in 1969 that 'Knox's detractors have in the main been High Episcopalians and Roman Catholics, who, because they were unsympathetic to his theological premises, thought any stick good enough to beat him with'.[37] In practice, however, the sheer volume of literature produced by Knox's admirers heavily outweighs that of his detractors; and merely reflects the comparative paucity of detached and critical assessments. One writer, a Dominican (whose early upbringing had been within the Free Presbyterian Kirk), ventured into the debate some 40 years ago when he vigorously reviewed a slender work entitled, aptly enough, *John Knox in Controversy* by a professor of Ecclesiastical History who was also Principal of New College, Edinburgh.[38] The reviewer tersely concluded: 'the book, in brief, is so unscholarly, so clearly partisan in its treatment of material, that we would have let it pass in silence had it not been presented with such authority'.[39] Possibly the reviewer was right, though there are probably more charitable ways of saying so. Knox, it almost seems, has this kind of effect on writers – in bringing out qualities less than best. In that instance, however, controversy centred not on Knox himself but on how Knox ought to be assessed.

The year 1972, of course, saw the quatercentenary of Knox's death. Some were only too ready to celebrate the reformer's death; others saw the occasion as an opportunity to reflect on Knox's life; but even that ended in a kind of verbal punch-up. In an entertaining newspaper article, Gordon Donaldson considered the greatest compliment paid to Knox, and the measure of his success, had been the way 'in which almost all the churches sooner or later have come to adopt the practices he advocated and put his principles into effect'. With characteristically lawyer-like precision, Donaldson drew attention to the 'possibility', as he put it, that if Knox returned today, he 'would now support the Roman Catholic church, which has adopted so many of the things he strove in vain to persuade it to accept in his own day'. And he patiently explained how

> some modern Roman Catholic churches are every bit as naked and unadorned as Knox wanted churches to be; Rome has authorized

---

[36] David Hay Fleming, *Critical Reviews Relating Chiefly to Scotland* (London, 1902), p. 166.

[37] Donaldson, 'John Knox: The First Puritan', p. 20.

[38] Hugh Watt, *John Knox in Controversy* (Edinburgh, 1950).

[39] Anthony Ross, *Innes Review*, 1 (1950), p. 163.

services in the language of the people; and the participation of the laity in services; the altar against the east wall has been replaced by a table around which priest and people can gather; Communion is much more frequent; church life is based on Bible study. Knox would recognise the Church of Rome as a reformed church.[40]

What, however, the professor omitted from this selection was any mention either of the papacy or the Mass, the two issues against which Knox had relentlessly thundered in exceedingly lurid and vitriolic outbursts, even by the standards of his age.

Donaldson, whose article was written tongue in cheek, enjoyed being Devil's advocate, and his piece probably had the desired effect. A professorial thunderbolt descended from the Free Kirk, condemning the Scottish history professor's failed attempts at historical objectivity, for it was claimed that 'it is not the John Knox of Scottish history that Professor Donaldson is reassessing but the product of history richly mixed with fantasy and ecclesiastical bias'.[41] *The Scotsman* newspaper which thought it newsworthy to carry the article also published the letter. One can scarcely imagine newspapers in the south giving similar prominent coverage, say, to Cranmer, Hooper, Grindal or Whitgift. That may say something about both Knox and the Scots, and possibly something about the English, too. The upshot was that the Free Kirk professor did not quite appreciate the Scottish history professor's idea of a joke – of having a rather mischievous joke at the expense of Knox, and those who take Knox too seriously. In that instance, however, the attempt at dispelling prevailing preconceptions had merely the effect of reinforcing them.

A decade later, in 1981, Knox was still causing controversy. This time professorial lightning from the west of Scotland hit the pages of *The Glasgow Herald* in defence of a book which had been attacked in an idiosyncratic review by Elizabeth Whitley, author of *Plain Mr Knox*, who complained in the review that Knox had not been given sufficient credit for his achievements. The professorial onslaught, on this occasion, stigmatized the review as 'illiterate' and made the point, among others, that historians refuse 'to assess Knox at his own well written estimate'.[42] But what *was* Knox's estimate of himself? That is less than clear. He did, of course, write (though he declined to have published) his classic *History of the Reformation in Scotland*,[43] a masterly and vivid narrative, in which inaccuracies, misconceptions and even

---

[40] *The Scotsman*, 25 November 1972.
[41] R.A. Finlayson, *The Scotsman*, 1 December 1972.
[42] A.A.M. Duncan, *The Glasgow Herald*, 30 June 1981.
[43] Maurice Lee, Jr, 'John Knox and his *History*', SHR, 45 (1966), pp. 79–88.

deceptions are to be found.[44] At the same time, Knox was curiously reluctant to assess his own role in the Reformation movement. He might be ever-ready to blow his Master's trumpet, as he put it, but he was remarkably reticent in much of his *History* about blowing his own. This may come as something of a surprise. It does not quite fit in with stereotyped ideas about Knox the tub-thumper, the big-mouthed and loud-mouthed boaster; the man who was always right and, therefore, allowed no room for dialogue; the man with his almost innate disregard for earthly authority, who lectured Queen Mary in his hectoring pulpit style, and reduced her to tears of frustration and rage when he insisted that princes possessed no absolute power and were directly responsible for their actions to their subjects. Historians, it seems, cannot even agree about the nature of Knox's *History*. Peter Hume Brown's verdict was that Knox's *History* was 'his own biography writ large'; Gordon Donaldson insisted that it ought to be regarded as Knox's memoirs; J.D. Mackie thought that in the *History* 'Knox the autobiographer is secondary to Knox the historian'; and Jasper Ridley concluded that it must be considered a 'chronicle of a movement, not a personal biography'.[45]

If the *History* does consist essentially of Knox's memoirs, it is surely odd that its author, who was not exactly self-effacing, did not introduce himself until half-way through Book I; he says nothing about his parentage and background; he does not portray himself as the principal actor in the unfolding drama of the Reformation; and he is at pains to retain a degree of anonymity throughout the proceedings. Knox, of course, enters the pages of his *History* in dramatic enough fashion as the bodyguard of George Wishart in 1546, carrying for his master's defence a great two-handed sword – a rather unusual entry in history for a renegade priest and notary. But his appearance as a minor character takes up less than six lines in the narrative and he soon fades from the scene, later to emerge with greater clarity as one of the Castilians at St Andrews, loosely associated with the murderers of Cardinal Beaton. Yet he hardly mentions the subsequent 'torment' he sustained for 19 months in the French galleys, and merely alludes to his activities as a preacher in England and elsewhere in Europe.[46]

Besides, among Protestant preachers who returned to Scotland in the mid-1550s, Knox places himself last and frequently gives precedence to the views and actions of ministers other than himself. He comes into his own, of course, in his famous face-to-face encounters with Queen Mary,

---

[44] See Andrew Lang, *John Knox and the Reformation* (London, 1905), *passim*.

[45] Hume Brown, *Knox*, I, p. 31 (see also Macmillan, *Knox*, p. 13); Donaldson, 'Knox the Man', p. 18; Mackie, *Knox*, p. 4; Ridley, *Knox*, p. 454.

[46] Knox, *History*, I, pp. 67–9, 81–93, 107, 182, 110–11.

interviews apparently arranged at the Queen's request, and narrated in considerable detail. Yet it is really only in Book V, written by another author after Knox's death, that Knox's own name, on occasion, is allowed to take precedence over other ministers. Throughout the *History*, Knox speaks of himself in the third person, which is hardly characteristic of memoirs or an autobiography. In short, Knox's assessment of himself is not forthcoming from the pages of his *History*. That masterly work is nothing less than 'the odyssey of the people of God'[47] – to adopt Jenny Wormald's admirable depiction of it – or, more precisely, an odyssey of *some* of the people of God, for Knox was conscious of his limited source material, and sought 'farther helpe then is to be had in thys countrie, for more assured knowledge of thyngs passed than he hath hymself, or can come bye here'.[48]

Yet, the more an appeal is made to historians for appraisals of Knox's career and personality, the more it becomes plain that the enigma of Knox remains as impenetrable as ever. So often, he has been presented in terms of a series of perplexing paradoxes: Knox, the hard man of the Kirk who bayed for the execution of practising priests, witches and adulterers and who is yet depicted as 'not a man of blood'; the fearless leader who led from behind; the ruthless coward; the hesitant revolutionary and timid deposer of princes; the confident doubter; the principled trimmer and intransigent opportunist; the man who wrote a 'dreary'[49] book on predestination but supposedly did not really believe what he wrote; the endearing rabble-rouser; the cautious extremist; the authoritarian democrat; the man who urged the abolition of patronage in the Church but who acted as arbiter between two patrons in 1561; the Puritan who enjoyed his Sunday dinner parties and a good play as well, and who let it be known he did not 'utterly condemn' dancing; the uncompromising hypocrite; the anti-feminist womanizer; the Old Testament prophetic figure who turned to the New Testament and to the Gospel of St John in 1547 when teaching his pupils in St Andrews Castle, the 'anchor' to which he returned, and had his wife read him, on his deathbed in 1572.

Possibly historians have felt an obligation to cut Knox down to size. After all, is he not to be found on the run from women – from Mary Tudor, from Mary of Guise and, by 1566, from Mary Queen of Scots? Where better for historians to begin than by reappraising Knox as a courageous coward? The first obstacle to be overcome is the Earl of Morton's memorable tribute at Knox's funeral when he declared that

---

[47] *The Oxford Encyclopedia of the Reformation*, II, p. 381.
[48] Knox, *Works*, VI, p. 121.
[49] Percy, *Knox*, p. 59.

Knox 'nather fearit nor flatterit anie fleche'.[50] There can be little doubt that Knox was not exactly over-given to flattery. After all, he had attacked as a 'folishe presumption', Queen Elizabeth's belief that as a woman she had a natural right to rule; he told Elizabeth's chief minister that he deserved to roast in hell; he warned that his letter to Elizabeth would be 'smelling nothing of flattery'; he fell out with the Earl of Moray on account of his plain-speaking; and much earlier Northumberland, who had offered him the bishopric of Rochester, found him 'neither grateful nor pleasable'.[51] These had been Knox's political allies, not his enemies. On another, more private occasion in 1572, when a woman began to sing his praises, Knox severely scolded her: 'tongue, tongue, ladie, flesh of it self is too proud, and needeth no meanes to esteeme the self'. He told her firmly to 'cast away stinking pride', warning her 'never to puffe up flesh'.[52]

This seems to have been characteristic of Knox's austere and rigorous approach throughout. What Morton had to say about Knox's distaste for flattery seems consistent with the evidence. But what of the other claim – the claim regarding Knox's boldness, his intrepidity, his ability to stand up to princes and people? How does Knox fare here? Knox's own judgement was not so very different from Morton's. He once observed, 'I have looked in the faces of many angry men and yet have not been afraid above measure',[53] a revealing remark and qualification. He claimed to have been 'not afraid above measure', and yet had the courage, or rashness, of his convictions not to flinch when duty called. Or had he?

Knox – who was Wishart's bodyguard – has been criticized by historians for displaying timidity in 1546 when he obeyed Wishart's instructions to leave his company when Wishart's arrest was imminent.[54] Gordon Donaldson detected, if not exactly cowardice, a 'prudential regard for his own safety' in Knox's action. Knox shrank from danger. Certainly, as a fugitive priest and defector from 'the puddle of Papistrie',[55] he had no wish for premature martyrdom, though he can hardly be justly criticized for that. He wanted to live to fight another day. His behaviour here, of course, was no different from that of Alexander Alane, Katherine Hamilton (sister of martyred Patrick),

---

[50] *The Autobiography and Diary of Mr James Melvill*, ed. R. Pitcairn (Edinburgh, 1842), p. 60.
[51] Knox, *Works*, VI, pp. 19, 16, 31; Knox, *History*, II, pp. 78–9, 134; Knox, *Works*, III, 83*.
[52] Calderwood, *History*, III, p. 235; Bannatyne, *Journal*, p. 423.
[53] Knox, *History*, II, p. 46.
[54] Ibid., II, pp. 67–9.
[55] Knox, *Works*, IV, p. 439.

Henry Hamilton (advocate), Adam Dayes (shipwright), Henry Cairns (skipper), John Willock, John Macdowell, Alexander Seton, John Macalpine, John Craig, George Buchanan, James Wedderburn, John Rough, Robert Richardson, John MacBrair, Andrew Charteris and John Borthwick, all of whom had earlier left Scotland when danger threatened.[56] Their example was an obvious one for Knox to follow.

Again, some modern writers have observed that Knox was quick off the mark to leave England when Mary Tudor came to the throne;[57] but so too were several hundred English Protestants who sought safety overseas. Anyone like Knox who had experienced life as a galley slave would not want to be caught a second time. His 'faint-heartedness' or 'prudence', at any rate, saved him from the fate of Cranmer, Ridley, Latimer and Hooper. This at least can be said in Knox's defence: he did not leave England immediately on Mary Tudor's accession in July 1553 but continued to preach in London, Kent and in the north against Catholicism and against a foreign marriage for Mary, until January 1554, when, with the expulsion of foreign Protestants, Knox decided he ought to go – even though that might entail leaving behind his English fiancée.[58] He was anxious, however, to justify his actions; he declared himself to be 'readie to suffer more than either povertie or exyle' for his faith. Yet,

> why did I flie? Assuredlie I can not tell; but of one thing I am sure, the feir of death was not the chief cause of my flieing. ... And albeit that I haif in the begynning of this battell, appeired to play the faynt-heartit and febill souldeour (the cause I remit to God), yit my prayer is that I may be restorit to the battell agane.[59]

Knox, who was prepared to take calculated risks, also knew when to beat a strategic retreat. From the relative safety of exile, he urged those who remained at home to prefer death to the Mass.[60] In practice, the prevailing situation – at least in Scotland – was one in which 'very few' people even in populous parishes troubled to attend Mass, so the Church authorities noted in 1552.[61] Any prospect, therefore, for the exaction of an exemplary penalty for mere abstinence from Mass was somewhat remote. Yet there is surely something distasteful in Knox's conduct here.

---

[56] James Kirk, 'The Religion of Early Scottish Protestants', in James Kirk (ed.), *Humanism and Reform: The Church in Europe, England and Scotland, 1400–1643* (Oxford, 1991), pp. 361–411, at pp. 373, 377, 379–84.

[57] Lang, *Knox and the Reformation*, p. 40; Donaldson, 'Knox the Man', p. 21.

[58] Lorimer, *Knox and the Church of England*, pp. 180 ff.; Ridley, *Knox*, pp. 146–65.

[59] Knox, *Works*, III, pp. 120, 154–5.

[60] Ibid., III, pp. 166–330; V, pp. 475–94.

[61] David Patrick (ed.) *Statutes of the Scottish Church, 1225–1559* (SHS, 1907), p. 138.

He himself felt conscience-stricken over the episode; and, when called upon to do so, he abandoned 'the den of my awin ease',[62] as he described his stay in Geneva, and came to Scotland, 'contrarious to my own judgement', to undertake a difficult and potentially dangerous preaching mission.[63] Then, as he returned to Geneva to become a minister to the English congregation, the bishops summoned him to Edinburgh and burned his effigy in his absence.[64] Earlier, too, at Frankfurt, in his dispute with Cox who accused him of treason against the Emperor, the King of Spain and Queen of England, Knox had taken advice from friends and left for Geneva.[65]

Later in Scotland, Knox left his ministry in Edinburgh when the going got rough. This also has been represented as evidence of his timidity.[66] What has not been so readily observed is that in two instances the decision to leave was not his own. In 1559, the Protestant lords, fearing for Knox's safety, are on record as insisting that they 'would not suffer John Knox to remain in Edinburgh'; and so when they withdrew from Edinburgh, they urged him to accompany them, leaving John Willock as a replacement.[67] That was a reasonable enough request, for Knox was already acting as secretary to the Lords of the Congregation and was involved in secret negotiations with the English government.

Again, in 1571, during a bitter civil war which hit Edinburgh particularly hard, Knox was reported to have 'departed the toun sore against his will, being compellit by the brethren of the kirk and toun, becaus that his tarie wold be ane occasione of farther truble unto them, and ane occasione of the schedding of blood for his defence'.[68] Knox realistically accepted the advice; his departure was motivated by reasons other than simple cowardice. There was even a third occasion in 1566, after Riccio's murder, when Knox decided to leave Edinburgh, first for Ayrshire, where he stayed for nine months, before going off to England, with the General Assembly's blessing, for another six months. Like his colleague John Craig, he arguably had heard in advance the outlines of the plot to kill Riccio, though neither minister figured among the conspirators denounced as rebels by the government. On the day preceding Mary's arrival in Edinburgh with some 8 000 troops, so it was said,

---

[62] Knox, *Works*, IV, p. 217.
[63] Ibid.; Knox, *History*, I, pp. 118–23.
[64] Knox, *History*, I, pp. 123–4.
[65] Knox, *Works*, IV, pp. 39, 47; Knox, *History*, I, pp. 110–11.
[66] Donaldson, 'Knox the Man', p. 22.
[67] David Laing (ed.), *Wodrow Society Miscellany I* (Wodrow Society, 1844), p. 65; cf. Knox, *History*, I, p. 211.
[68] Bannatyne, *Journal*, p. 144; Knox, *Works*, VI, p. 651.

Knox departed for Kyle. Yet John Craig stayed on in Edinburgh. We know next to nothing of Knox's actions, far less his motives, at this point, but it is hard to resist the conclusion that his instinct for self-preservation helped shape his conduct here.[69]

Elsewhere, Knox's determination not to compromise on issues which he saw as matters of principle is evident in his approach to discipline, which he and his associates elevated to one of the marks of the true Church.[70] Remarkably, the Scottish reformers, from the outset, succeeded in exercising a distinctive disciplinary jurisdiction, with power to excommunicate, without the protracted struggle experienced by Calvin in Geneva. Not only had Knox and his associates insisted that even the prince was subject to the Church's discipline, administered by ministers and elders, but they proceeded to deny the prince – any prince – supremacy over the Church. In any event, if, as Knox contended, the prince's rule in civil government was firmly curtailed by human and divine law alike, it was hardly surprising that a no less critical attitude should emerge towards claims by the Crown to supremacy, precisely by denying to the civil magistrate control of ecclesiastical affairs.[71]

Knox, of course, was most at home in the pulpit, where he saw himself as God's mouthpiece and he described his preaching as 'blowing the trumpet'. His voice, thundering from the pulpit – so the English agent in Edinburgh reported in 1561 – 'is hable in one hower to put more lyf in us than 500 trompettes contynually blusteringe in our eares'.[72] He was good at trumpet-blowing: 'we doe nothing', Knox wrote in 1559, 'but goe about Jericho, blowing with trumpets, as God giveth strenth.'[73] His pulpit rhetoric was powerful and effective. Where he acquired the technique is less obvious. The ex-friar Thomas Guillaume, also a native of East Lothian, is said to be 'the first man frome whome Mr Knox receaved anie taste of the truthe'; and Knox himself considered Guillaume's preaching 'wholesome' and 'of a prompt and good

---

[69] Knox, *History*, II, p. 183; T. Thomson (ed.), *Diurnal of Remarkable Occurrents* (Edinburgh, 1833), p. 183; *CSP Scot.*, I, pp. 270, 351; Hume Brown, *Knox*, II, pp. 231–2, 304–10; and Hay Fleming, *Critical Reviews*, p. 179, and his *Mary Queen of Scots* (London, 1898), p. 398, argue against Knox's foreknowledge of the deed. Ridley, *Knox*, p. 448, considered Knox was 'a party to the conspiracy'. Lang, *Knox and the Reformation*, pp. 251–3, found the evidence inconclusive, but added: 'Knox, whether privy to the murder or not, did not, when he ran away, take the best means of disarming suspicion.'

[70] Knox, *History*, II, p. 266.

[71] James Kirk, *Patterns of Reform: Continuity and Change in the Reformation Kirk* (Edinburgh, 1989), pp. 232–79; James Kirk (ed.), *The Second Book of Discipline* (Edinburgh, 1980), pp. 57–65.

[72] *CSP Scot.*, I, pp. 551, 548.

[73] Knox, *Works*, VI, p. 78.

utterance'.[74] Yet the man whose impact on Knox was greater than any other was surely George Wishart, whose praises Knox sang as 'singularly learned as well in godly knowledge as in all honest human science' and 'clearly illuminated with the spirit of prophecy', and whose preaching left Knox spellbound.[75] Knox's own first sermon at St Andrews in 1547, preached in the presence of John Mair on the apocalyptic theme of Daniel and the four monarchies, provoked lively responses; and by the time of his first English ministry at Berwick and Newcastle he had become an accomplished orator.[76] The eloquence of his preaching at Dieppe, presumably in French, also won converts to his cause.[77]

On returning to Scotland a seasoned preacher, he once told Mary (whom he left in 'a vehement fume') that, when he stepped inside the pulpit, 'I am not master of myself, but must obey Him who commands me to speak plain'.[78] And he saw himself 'appointed by God to rebuke the sins and vices of all';[79] hence his reputation as a firm disciplinarian. 'Stern and severe' was how one contemporary described his countenance.[80] Even in old age he retained his special gifts as preacher: 'the threatnings of his sermonts', it was felt, 'war verie soar'; and at St Andrews, in 1571, he had to be 'lifted upe to the pulpit, whar he behovit to lean at his first entrie; bot or he haid done with his sermont, he was sa active and vigorus that he was lyk to ding that pulpit in blads, and fly out of it'. The spectacle certainly impressed a student at the university there.[81]

Knox's tactlessness, his breath-taking frankness, his vehemence and austerity are often contrasted with the milder approach of some other ministers like the 'meek and gentle' John Erskine of Dun, who comforted Mary when Knox reduced her to tears.[82] What is usually forgotten is that the gentle Erskine (with his courtly manners) as a young man in the 1530s had killed a priest in Montrose; he was also a hard-line exponent of the 'two kingdoms' theory in 1559; whereas the early Knox in the late 1540s had argued that it was lawful for Scottish Protestants to escape from prison in France only if they avoided killing their jailers.[83] Knox also refrained from reporting to the authorities in England

---

[74] Calderwood, *History*, I, pp. 155–6; Knox, *History*, I, p. 42.

[75] Knox, *History*, I, pp. 60 ff.

[76] Ibid., I, p. 86; Knox, *Works*, III, pp. 167–8.

[77] Hume Brown, *Knox*, I, pp. 215–21.

[78] Knox, *History*, II, p. 82.

[79] Ibid., II, p. 45.

[80] Peter Young quoted in Hume Brown, *Knox*, II, p. 323.

[81] Melville, *Diary*, p. 33.

[82] Knox, *History*, II, p. 83.

[83] J. Stuart (ed.), *Spalding Club Miscellany IV* (Spalding Club, 1849), pp. 26, 88–92; Knox, *History*, I, pp. 109–10.

an Anabaptist, whose views he abhorred, and so saved the Anabaptist from death at the stake, unlike the gentler Cranmer who upheld the law; and, years later, Knox still refused to reveal the identity of that Anabaptist who had approached him in trust.[84]

When it comes to assessing his complex character, Knox is often accused of conceit and self-importance and of lacking humility.[85] Certainly, some of his public actions and extravagant utterances would justify such a belief: the 'runagate' Scot in England who meddled with matters too high for him; the man who proposed that if Queen Elizabeth would accept his theories on unnatural government by women, he would recognize her as an exception to the rule; the man who interviewed Queen Mary and explained that as 'a subject of this realm', he had the right to oppose her marriage to an infidel, and who informed her that if only she attended his sermons, she would then 'fully understand both what I like and mislike as well in your Majesty as in all others'. Thereafter, when he was accused of convoking the lieges illegally, an exasperated Mary, who laughed at Knox, where once she had wept, dismissed him as an 'old fool'.[86] But he could also be a dangerous old fool.

Yet, when we turn from Knox the radical reformer to Knox the private individual and family man, his modesty and gentler qualities become apparent. He once remarked that 'of nature I am churlish and in conditions different from many'; and in valuing his friendship with others, he readily acknowledged that 'I have rather need of all then that any hath need of me'.[87] There is scarcely a trace of vanity or self-esteem in any of this. Besides, he wrote with modesty of his days on the galleys, only referring briefly, without elaboration, to 'the torment I sustained in the galleys'. In his private correspondence, too, he often showed humility and was remarkably frank in his reappraisal of his actions. He confessed in 1553:

> I am no man-killer with my handis; but I help not my needie brother sa liberallie as I may and aucht. I steill not hors, money, nor claithis fra my nychtbour; but that smaller portioun of worldlie substance I bestow not sa rychtlie as his halie law requyreth. ... I speik not the treuth of God sa boldlie as it becumeth his trew messinger to do.[88]

---

84 Knox, *Works*, V, pp. 420–21.
85 Donaldson, 'Knox the Man', p. 24.
86 Knox, *History*, I, pp. 282–7, 291–4; Knox, *Works*, IV, pp. 363–420; Knox, *History*, II, pp. 45–6, 82–100.
87 Knox, *Works*, VI, p. 11.
88 Ibid., III, p. 339.

Again, he confided to a friend in 1558 how he could offer no excuse for 'my rude vehemencie and inconsidered affirmations'.[89] None of this, of course, quite adds up to the conventional picture of Knox.

A rare glimpse of the paternal Knox is afforded in his admission to Queen Mary that he could 'scarcely well abide the tears of my own boys whom my own hand corrects'.[90] Again, as Knox the public figure (who could preach against a witch before her execution and affirm that Mary herself deserved death[91]) gave way to Knox the private man, removed from public glare, his gentler, more affectionate, even self-effacing qualities become more evident, not least in his relations with women – his 'sisters in Edinburgh'; his wife Marjory; his mother-in-law, Elizabeth Bowes; Elizabeth Adamson, Anne Locke (whose second husband was Edward Dering), Mrs Hickman – whose friendship and company he valued and in whom he confided.[92] Conscious of his 'awn wreachit infirmitie', he admitted to Mrs Bowes how he felt 'woundit' at being 'compellit to thounder out the threattnyngis of God aganis obstinat rebellaris' and to rebuke in others sins of which he knew himself to be 'criminall and giltie'.[93]

Gordon Donaldson once speculated how far 'Knox, who blasted against the monstrous regiment of women, was hen-pecked at home', and rather fancied that 'Knox was the kind of man who would have taken his mother-in-law on his honeymoon'.[94] Exile in Geneva may have been no honeymoon, but Knox put up with his mother-in-law – trial that she sometimes was – where others might not; there was even a phase when she moved into the manse of St Giles' for a spell; and she returned there to look after Knox's children after Marjory's death in 1560. When he married for a second time in 1564, Knox did not make the mistake of taking his new mother-in-law along on the honeymoon, though some thought the marriage itself to the seventeen-year-old daughter of Lord Ochiltree was ill-advised and mistaken.[95] That episode alone, however, ought to dispel the image of Knox as a misogynist.

How, then, might Knox's contribution be assessed? His career – indeed his notoriety – in England, Geneva, Frankfurt and Scotland ensured for him a European reputation. In essentials, his stature remains intact, regardless of tinkering or refinement on the periphery; and

---

[89] Ibid., V, p. 5.

[90] Knox, *History*, II, p. 83.

[91] Melville, *Diary*, p. 58; Knox, *History*, II, pp. 120–21.

[92] Knox, *Works*, III, pp. 337–402; IV, pp. 217–41, 244–53; VI, pp. 11–27, 30, 77–9, 100–104, 107–9, 129–31, 140–41; Knox, *History*, I, pp. 119–20.

[93] Knox, *Works*, III, p. 338.

[94] Donaldson, *Scotland's History*, pp. 100–101; Donaldson, 'Knox the Man', p. 29.

[95] *CSP Scot.*, II, p. 54.

there is substance in the claim that Knox was a founding father of English Puritanism. Not the least of his gifts was his ability to act as a pamphleteer and propagandist. His views made international news. Through his writings, of course, Knox achieved a kind of immortality. He has found his way into all the works on early-modern political thought,[96] and has attracted biographers in German, French and Dutch as well as English.[97] As a contributor to the *Scots Confession of Faith* and *Book of Discipline* in 1560, he had a strategic role at a crucial moment in shaping priorities for the reformed Church. Again, his sermon on building the house of the Lord at a point when the Reformation Parliament assembled in Edinburgh in July 1560 was apposite as a rallying call to the faithful,[98] and it serves as a reminder both of his rousing work as a preacher (a preacher whose sermons curiously have not survived) and as minister in Edinburgh (by far the largest Scottish town with many of the attributes of a capital). He was even assigned the right to summon the General Assembly (accustomed as it was to meet in or near Edinburgh), if danger threatened, a privilege accorded to no other minister.[99] In the eyes of Edinburgh town council, he was their 'chief minister' and so the council supplemented his top salary, approximating to 300 merks a year, with a rent-free manse (complete with a cosy study, fireplace, furnishings and, thoughtfully, a new lock for the front door), together with travelling expenses and other perks. Whatever problems confronted John Knox, they were not financial ones. In his testament, he had no outstanding debts, and left assets of just over £1 500.[100]

---

[96] E.g. J.W. Allen, *A History of Political Thought in the Sixteenth Century* (London, 1957); G.H. Sabine, *A History of Political Thought* (London, 1944); Quentin Skinner, *The Foundations of Modern Political Thought* (Cambridge, 1978); J.H. Burns (ed.), *The Cambridge History of Political Thought, 1450–1700* (Cambridge, 1991); J.H. Burns, *The True Law of Kingship: Concepts of Monarchy in Early Modern Scotland* (Oxford, 1996).

[97] E.g. R. Mulot, *John Knox, 1505–1572: ein Erinnerungsblatt zur vierten Zentenarfeier* (Halle, 1904); E. Huraut, *John Knox et ses relations avec les Églises reformées du continent* (Cahors, 1902); A. Mezger, *John Knox et ses rapports avec Calvin* (Montauban, 1905); P. Janton, *John Knox: l'homme et l'oeuvre* (Didier, 1967); P. Janton, *Concept et Sentiment de l'Église chez John Knox, le reformateur ecossais* (Paris, 1972); P.J. Kronisigt, *John Knox als Kerkhervormer* (Utrecht, 1895); G. Douwmeester, J*ohn Knox de Hervormer van Schotland* ('s-Gravenhage, 1964).

[98] Knox, *History*, I, p. 335.

[99] *BUK*, I, pp. 38–9.

[100] G. Donaldson (ed.), *Accounts of the Collectors of Thirds of Benefices* (Edinburgh, 1949), pp. 54, 61, 72, 128, 131, 141, 180, 191, 212, 297; J.D. Marwick (ed.), *Extracts from the Records of the Burgh of Edinburgh, 1557–1571* (Edinburgh, 1875), pp. 63, 76, 87, 97, 99, 104, 115, 128, 135, 154, 174, 177, 191, 210, 219, 245, 258, 260; Knox, *Works*, VI, p. liv.

An unintended tribute to Knox's standing is supplied by some of his Catholic opponents who considered him 'principal patriarch of the Calvinian court'; and his colleague, John Willock, who is also depicted as 'primate of their religion', is none the less presented as 'the loon [fool] who pulled the plough that Knox steered'. Even a contemporary ballad spoke of how 'Knox is grown a king'; and, in 1561, Mary considered him 'the most dangerous man in all her realm'.[101] For a spell, Knox benefited from contacts with English diplomats – diplomats who were sometimes of Puritan inclination.

Knox's influence, of course, was by no means constant. English diplomatic reports for the years between 1559 and 1563 are testimony to Knox's prominence – they fail even to mention John Craig, his fellow minister in Edinburgh. This was the period when Knox was at his most active in Scottish affairs as a propagandist, justifying the action of the Protestant lords who had attempted to depose the Queen Regent and who eventually wrested the government into their own hands. He was at his best in a confrontation of this sort. But later he became an embarrassment when he declined to moderate his language. In 1561, the English envoy in Edinburgh reported how Knox 'thonderethe owte of the pulpet. ... He rulethe the roste, and of hym all men stonde in feare – wolde God you knewe howe myche'. That may be seen as a measure of Knox's strength. But the diplomat added: 'I feare no thynge so myche that one daye he wyll marre all'; and that was surely Knox's weakness.[102] He fell out with the English ambassador who complained that Knox had upset plans to induce Mary to become a Protestant.[103] He broke off his friendship with the Earl of Moray who considered him more of a liability than an asset. For the next six years, Knox figured less prominently in English dispatches. For the politicians Knox's usefulness was over – at least until the revolution of 1567 when he justified Mary's deposition and preached at her son's coronation. In effect, however, he had tasted real power merely for a few months in 1559.

All in all, any picture presented of Knox would be immeasurably enhanced if the spotlight focused less on Knox and more exactly on the activities and contributions of others – both Knox's associates and his opponents. That task is much harder, of course, for there is no convenient corpus of material on which to draw, as there undoubtedly is for Knox himself. Yet something of a parallel may be drawn with recent

---

101 Winzet, *Certane Tractatis*, p. 56; *Wodrow Society Miscellany I*, p. 267; J. Cranstoun (ed.), *Satirical Poems of the Time of the Reformation* (2 vols, STS, Edinburgh, 1891–93), I, p. 337; Hume Brown, *Knox*, II, p. 162.

102 *CSP Scot.*, I, p. 548.

103 Ibid., I, pp. 597, 603.

literature on Mary. The anniversary of Mary's execution in 1987 saw a plethora of assorted publications. One work stood out from the rest, and it did so precisely because it was a book not on Mary but on *Mary Stewart's People*,[104] examining the contrasting lives and circumstances of seven men and three women in Mary's Scotland, drawing heavily from unpublished manuscript sources. The outcome was a welcome and illuminating insight into society in Mary's Scotland. Among the *desiderata* surely to be sought is a study of 'John Knox's people' – not just his fellow ministers but those who worked with him as elders in Edinburgh,[105] and those commissioned from the localities to attend the General Assembly[106] at the centre, men who remain largely names and not people. That, for a start, would serve as a purposeful and promising approach which *inter alia* might clarify Knox's own role and standing within the Scottish Church.

---

[104] M.H.B. Sanderson, *Mary Stewart's People: Life in Mary Stewart's Scotland* (Edinburgh, 1987).

[105] The fragmentary records of Edinburgh general session survive for 1574–75 (SRO, CH2/450/1; extracts from which were published in J. Dennistoun and A. Macdonald (eds), *Maitland Club Miscellany I* [Edinburgh, 1833]). In 1989, I drew attention to an unnoticed list of members of Edinburgh's kirk session for 1561–62 in Kirk, *Patterns of Reform*, p. 110 and n. 56.

[106] *BUK*, I, *passim*.

PART ONE
Early Years and Exile

CHAPTER TWO

John Knox and the Castilians: A Crucible of Reforming Opinion?

*Carol Edington**

> In the name of God, and of his Sone Jesus Christ, and in the name
> of these that presentlie calles yow by my mouth, I charge yow, that
> ye refuise not this holy vocatioun, but that as ye tender the glorie
> of God, the encrease of Christ his kingdome, the edification of
> your brethrene, and the conforte of me ... that ye tack upoun yow
> the publict office and charge of preaching, evin as ye looke to
> avoid Goddis heavye displeasur, and desyre that he shall multiplye
> his graces with yow.[1]

With these stirring words was John Knox called to the ministry shortly
after Easter 1547. Confronted with such passion, he responded in kind,
bursting into noisy tears and seeking the sanctuary of his room. There
he spent several fraught days examining his conscience and considering
the direction his future should take. Eventually he emerged to refute the
teachings of that 'rottin Papist', John Annand, and, on being challenged
to explain his attack, he himself climbed into the pulpit of Holy Trinity,
St Andrews, the following Sunday.[2] Thus, according to Knox, was he
called upon to acknowledge and accept his vocation. For a man whose
surviving works exceed 3 500 pages collected in six volumes, this two-
paragraph report is a remarkably brief account of what must have been
one of the central experiences of his life.[3] Certainly, we might expect
any account of the personal and defining episodes of his life to be – if
not altogether accurate – at least expansive. Indeed, it is Knox's unchar-
acteristic reticence on this matter which convinces. While this restraint
has not gone unnoticed by his biographers, few have felt able to enlarge
upon the episode and endow it with the importance it most surely

---

* Writing this paper in difficult circumstances would not have been possible without
help. In particular, I should like to thank Dr Roger Mason, Jaqueta White, and the staff
at Overton Library, Hampshire.

[1] Knox, *Works*, I, pp. 187–8.

[2] Ibid., I, p. 188.

[3] Cf. Roger A. Mason who refers to Knox's detailed treatment of the episode (admit-
tedly when comparing it with the even more cursory account of his conversion), Knox,
On Rebellion, p. ix.

deserves.[4] This is a great pity for the manner of Knox's calling to the ministry, the way in which he perceived his vocation and the nature of his first public appearances, all have a great deal to tell us concerning the character of Protestant thinking in Scotland during the 1540s. This in turn sheds valuable light on Knox himself, for although it remains true that the most formative influences on his thought were rooted in experiences outwith Scotland, his early career and association with other Scottish reformers provided the inspiration for his faith and the bedrock of many of his best known attitudes.[5] Obviously there are methodological problems in an uncritical acceptance of Knox's own version of this episode, written up in his *History* in the mid-1560s. Any account of the 1540s reflects not simply Knox's experiences of that decade but also the later years of his life and his overriding evangelical purpose. Nevertheless, historians are surely correct to conclude that, used with caution, his *History* represents an indispensable source for the events of the Scottish Reformation and, although independent corroboration for much of what Knox has to say concerning the early episodes of his career is scant, focusing on some of the other individuals associated with him at this time offers a potentially fruitful approach to the problem.[6]

The events leading up to John Knox's dramatic emergence into public life are well known. Less fully appreciated, however, is the complex network of Protestant sympathizers and the heterogeneous collection of reforming beliefs they espoused, which together had contributed to a situation in which a small group of political and religious rebels were able to assassinate the most powerful figure in the land and plot a *coup* intended to topple the ruling administration and – in the dreams of some – the established Catholic Church. Significantly, several of those associated with Knox at this critical period in his life had long been involved in Scotland's nascent Protestant movement. In particular, Henry Balnaves, John Rough and David Lindsay of the Mount, the three men whom Knox names as being instrumental in persuading him to preach,

---

[4] For example: Eustace Percy, *John Knox* (London, 1937), pp. 54–5; Jasper Ridley, *John Knox* (Oxford, 1968), pp. 55–6.

[5] Scholars such as Richard G. Kyle have commented on the fact that, 'Knox's thought can not be considered as highly developmental. His basic theology was established early (probably before his going to Geneva) and remained fairly constant throughout his public career'. Yet he focuses on Calvinist influences on Knox's thinking and fails to appreciate the earlier contribution made by the ideas of his fellow Scots: *The Mind of John Knox* (Lawrence, KS, 1984), p. 12.

[6] This problem has often been dealt with in print. For a recent discussion, see J.H. Burns, *The True Law of Kingship: Concepts of Monarchy in Early Modern Scotland* (Oxford, 1996), p. 122.

each had long-standing connections reaching back into the difficult, often dangerous, days of the 1530s and which, in the following decade, saw them propelled centre stage.[7]

The nature and extent of early Scottish Protestantism has been the subject of considerable academic debate.[8] However, whether one talks the numbers up or down, it seems clear that the movement – if that is not too elevated and specific a term – was geographically scattered and fragmentary. While the majority of early Scottish Protestants were clerics, there was at court a small yet significant number of influential laymen who in the course of the 1530s began to attack the established Church and religious *status quo*.[9] By no means all of these were confessed Protestants and, even amongst those who could be said to have embraced the reformed religion, views were often so diverse and contradictory that it is no wonder historians fall with relief upon the convenient concept of 'evangelicalism', a term now frequently used to denote that reforming impulse and attachment to the message of the Gospel which characterizes much early Reformation thinking and which helpfully precludes the use of over-precise definitions in an uncertain religious climate.[10] Thus, on the one hand, we can consider such future Castilians as Sir David Lindsay of the Mount, a Fife laird and royal herald, who combined a savage – and very public – criticism of clerical abuse and papal authority with a humanist-inspired call for renewed spirituality based on the Word of God and the uncorrupted teachings of the early

[7] Knox, *Works*, I, p. 186.

[8] Some of the most important works dealing with early Scottish Protestantism are: Ian B. Cowan, *The Scottish Reformation: Church and Society in Sixteenth Century Scotland* (London, 1982); Gordon Donaldson, *The Scottish Reformation* (Cambridge 1960); James Kirk, *Patterns of Reform: Continuity and Change in the Reformation Kirk* (Edinburgh, 1989); David McRoberts (ed.), *Essays on the Scottish Reformation 1513–1625* (Glasgow, 1962); Jenny Wormald, *Court, Kirk and Community: Scotland, 1470–1625* (London, 1981). See also the essays by Mark Dilworth, 'Canons Regular and the Reformation', and Michael Lynch, 'Preaching to the Converted? Perspectives on the Scottish Reformation', both in A.A. MacDonald, M. Lynch and I.B. Cowan (eds), *The Renaissance in Scotland: Studies in Literature, Religion, History and Culture Offered to John Durkan* (Leiden, 1994).

[9] For clerical involvement in the early Reformation, see James Kirk, 'The Religion of Early Scottish Protestants', in James Kirk (ed.), *Humanism and Reformation: The Church in Europe, England and Scotland, 1400–1643, Essays in Honour of James K. Cameron* (Oxford, 1991), pp. 361–412.

[10] See, for example, the discussion in Dairmaid MacCulloch, *Thomas Cranmer: A Life* (New Haven and London, 1996), p. 2; and, in a Scottish context, Carol Edington, *Court and Culture in Renaissance Scotland: Sir David Lindsay of the Mount* (East Linton, 1995), p. 44.

Church, yet who never embraced the central tenets of reformed theology. On the other hand, one who certainly took this path was Sir John Borthwick, who first seems to have made Lutheran contacts in France and whose outspoken criticisms of the Church led to accusations of heresy, flight to England, and the burning of his effigy in the marketplace at St Andrews.[11] Other evangelicals at the Scottish court included men such as James Kirkcaldy of Grange, the Royal Treasurer, reputed to have 'becom ane heretik and [to have] had alwayes a New Testament in his poutch'; and James Learmonth of Dairsie, the Master of the Household.[12] Another key figure in this respect was Henry Balnaves. Appointed earlier in his career as Procurator and spokesman in the consistorial courts, Balnaves was later made Treasurer's Clerk by Kirkcaldy of Grange. He also acted as advocate and Lord of Session, his service receiving recognition and reward in 1538 when he was created Lord Halhill.[13] The presence of such men at court should not be taken to indicate Crown support for the type of ideas they espoused. The actions of James V suggest a conventional enough piety and – for diplomatic reasons if no other – the Scottish king was anxious to be viewed as a stalwart guardian of Catholic orthodoxy in the face of English schism.

The religious tensions present at court during the 1530s were, of course, much more complex than this necessarily brief and overly simplistic sketch suggests.[14] Nevertheless, by the end of the reign, the evangelicals – be they moderate or more radical in their opinions – must have hoped that many of their most cherished aims were about to be realized for, with the unexpected death of James V in December 1542 and the accession of his infant daughter, power passed to James Hamilton, Earl of Arran. Persuaded that his family's interests were best served by the adoption of a more reforming, pro-English policy, Arran patronized Protestant preachers such as John Rough; he agreed to dynastic union between Scotland and schismatic England; and in March 1543, in response to a bill sponsored by, amongst others, Henry Balnaves, Parliament authorized the reading of Scripture 'in the vulgar toung'.[15] In the eyes of many, it must have seemed as if a religious settlement along the lines of that enacted in England was now a real possibility. And, in

---

[11] For further details of Borthwick's career, see below, and John Durkan, 'Scottish Evangelicals in the Patronage of Thomas Cromwell', *RSCHS*, 21 (1983), pp. 127–57.

[12] *Sir James Melville's Memoirs* (Bannatyne Club, Edinburgh, 1827), p. 65; Calderwood, *History*, I, p. 140.

[13] F.J. Grant, *The Faculty of Advocates in Scotland, 1532–1943* (Edinburgh, 1944), p. 10.

[14] For a more detailed analysis, see Edington, *Court and Culture*, pp. 42–57.

[15] *APS*, II, p. 415.

similar fashion, historians too have viewed 1543 as 'a natural moment for the Reformation in Scotland'.[16] Too much, however, lay with the political will of the supremely malleable Arran. By the end of the year the Governor was firmly under Cardinal David Beaton's pro-Catholic, pro-French, influence and Parliament was vigorously calling for the implementation of Scotland's anti-heresy legislation. At first sight, this may seem like the Reformation that foundered, a premature putsch which failed to accomplish for Lutheranism what the events of 1560 would later achieve for Calvinism, but we should not underestimate the influence that the ideas and events of the first two decades of Scottish Protestantism exercised over its later development.

By the early 1540s Protestantism in Scotland was a potentially influential creed yet, without clear leadership, it lacked unity or a sense of purpose. These vital, yet hitherto elusive qualities, seemed poised to emerge in the person of George Wishart whose return to Scotland and subsequent ministry did so much to alarm the ecclesiastical authorities. Arriving via England from Germany and Switzerland, Wishart's theology owed a great deal to the ideas of Zwingli (in 1536 he had completed an English translation of the *First Helvetic Confession of Faith*, published *circa* 1548). Wishart's energetic proselytizing, his charismatic personality and evangelical message appealed not only to the large crowds who flocked to listen to his open-air sermons in Angus and East Lothian but also, and more significantly, to a group of influential nobles and local lairds whose support offered the preacher temporary protection. At this time employed as a tutor by one of those lairds sympathetic to Wishart, Knox found himself caught up in the events surrounding this unorthodox mission.[17] Without doubt, Wishart made an enormous personal impression upon him and, as we shall see, both Wishart's ideas and the character of his ministry were echoed by several of those later holed up in St Andrews Castle, not least Knox himself.

The disturbing conflation of popular appeal and influential patronage generated by Wishart's ministry, together with the genuinely subversive challenge which his teaching posed to the Catholic faith, persuaded the authorities to act. He was arrested and tried before an ecclesiastical court convened at St Andrews and presided over by Cardinal Beaton. There was no doubt but that he would be found guilty and,

---

[16] Julian Goodare, 'Scotland', in R. Scribner, R. Porter and M. Teich (eds), *The Reformation in National Context* (Cambridge, 1994), pp. 95–110, at p. 95.

[17] At this point in his career he acted as tutor to Francis and George Douglas, the sons of Douglas of Longniddry, and Alexander Cockburn, son of the laird of Ormiston.

on 1 March 1546, George Wishart was duly executed. Possessing important consequences both immediate and long term, Wishart's death represents a crucial turning point in the history of the Reformation in Scotland. Not only was his teaching to have a significant effect on the developing theology of the reform movement, but the execution was one of the reasons behind the assassination of Beaton on 29 May 1546.[18] That it was not the only reason can be inferred from the fact that plots to kill the Cardinal had been circulating over a year earlier.[19] Reports of those implicated, and indeed of the actual murder, disagree on how many were involved: Knox says 16, another sixteenth-century source, the *Diurnal of Occurents*, adds a couple more, and Parliament was later to attaint some 34 individuals for the 'crewell and tressonable slauchter'.[20] The key conspirators included Norman Leslie, his uncle John Leslie of Parkhill, James Melville, Peter Carmichael and William Kirkcaldy, the son of Sir James Kirkcaldy of Grange (the former Treasurer and one of those implicated in previous plots). Together they broke into St Andrews Castle, murdered the Archbishop, strung his body from the tower and proceeded to hold the building in anticipation of English military assistance. In many ways the episode was intended to implement by violence what the reformers had failed to establish by persuasion in 1543.[21] This impression is reinforced by the arrival on the scene of several of those associated with the earlier reform programme, men like Henry Balnaves, John Rough and David Lindsay of the Mount.

Also making an appearance at St Andrews Castle was, of course, John Knox, who arrived with his three young charges during Easter 1547. While his action may have been designed to distance himself from the Governor's renewed assault on suspected heretics, the exact reasons for his decision to join the Castilians can only be a matter for speculation.[22] After all, the castle might have been temporarily beyond Arran's reach but, as a strategy aimed at escaping public notice, Knox's chosen course of action had little to commend it. The eyes of all Scotland – and many more besides – were firmly focused on the unfolding drama, and its consequences not only for Scotland but also for England, France and

---

[18] For a discussion of Zwinglian ideas in Scotland including the role of George Wishart, see Duncan Shaw, 'Zwinglian Influences on the Scottish Reformation', *RSCHS*, 22 (1986), pp. 119–39.

[19] *L&P Henry VIII*, XIX, pt 1, no. 350; *SP Henry VIII*, IV, p. 377.

[20] Knox, *Works*, I, p. 175; *A Diurnal of Remarkable Occurents that have passed within the country of Scotland since the death of King James the Fourth til the year 1575* (Bannatyne Club, Edinburgh, 1833), p. 42; *APS*, II, p. 479.

[21] Margaret H.B. Sanderson, *Cardinal of Scotland: David Beaton, c. 1494–1546* (Edinburgh, 1986), p. 229.

[22] Ridley, *Knox*, pp. 51–2.

Rome were anxiously awaited. The situation was a curious one, for though Beaton's removal granted Arran a degree of political independence, it nevertheless left him in an almost impossible position. Capitulation to the murderers was unthinkable, the resumption of friendly relations with England would jeopardize his own dynastic interests, and to call for French aid would only pave the way for increased French domination of Scottish affairs. Obliged for appearances' sake to conduct an ineffective siege of the castle, Arran's only realistic hope lay with a mediated solution. The man chosen to open negotiations was Sir David Lindsay of the Mount who, in December 1546, was sent to the castle 'frome the Governour and Counsale'.[23] Arran's choice here seems the deliberate selection of one who, himself a Fife laird, known to several of the Castilians, and with avowed evangelical sympathies, may have served to break the deadlock. Lindsay's sympathies were, however, more fully committed than Arran had appreciated and he maintained communications with the Castilians, even to the point of encouraging Knox in his vocation.

As this suggests, the 'siege' of St Andrews Castle was, militarily speaking, a fitful and rather futile business interspersed with protracted cease-fires. Although any communication with the rebels had been expressly forbidden by the Governor, many, like Lindsay, had access to the castle.[24] Conversely, those in the castle enjoyed considerable freedom of action. Henry Balnaves twice journeyed to London where he hammered out a deal with the English government, while John Rough, the Protestant preacher associated with the 1543 reform programme who had joined the Castilians from Ayrshire, was able to preach in Holy Trinity. In short, there was considerable contact between the Castilians and the Fife population – much to the latter's consternation. Local memories were of violent forays into the neighbouring countryside, of arson and slaughter and men who 'wssit thair bodyis in leichorie with fair wemen'.[25] For many of those living in or near St Andrews, these were troubled times. Not only was the country at war with England (and several Fife men including Norman Leslie had seen action at Ancrum Moor) but a run of poor harvests, an outbreak of plague just across the Tay in Dundee a few years previously and again amongst those besieged in the castle itself, all accentuated the mood of unease and foreboding.[26] In such a climate, the dramatic message preached by Knox in his first sermon found a receptive audience.

[23] *SP Henry VIII*, IV, pp. 581–82.

[24] *RPC*, I, p. 38.

[25] *The Historie and Cronicles of Scotland by Robert Lindsay of Pitscottie*, ed. A.E. Mackay (3 vols, STS, Edinburgh, 1899–1911), II, p. 86.

[26] Pitscottie, *Historie*, II, p. 37; Knox, *Works*, I, p. 204.

Knox was later to describe this episode – what he vividly termed the expression of his mind in the public preaching place – in considerable detail.[27] Choosing as his text the seventh chapter of the Book of Daniel which recounts the prophet's vision of the four beasts or kingdoms, and beginning by showing God's love towards His Church, Knox went on to describe the Babylonian captivity and the destruction of the four world monarchies by 'that last Beast ... the Romane Church'. He defended what he termed the 'trew kirk' built on the Word of God and expounded the Protestant doctrine of justification *sola fides*. Defending his contention that the Pope was an Antichrist, Knox sought to expose the false teachings of the Catholic Church: the doctrine of good works, pilgrimages, pardons, clerical celibacy, fasting, Purgatory and the Mass.

Further aspects of Knox's thinking at this time can be seen from the charges he faced when he and John Rough were later summoned to appear before John Winram, the subprior at St Andrews, where they were presented with a list of articles cataloguing the heretical opinions they had been preaching in St Andrews and were called upon to explain themselves.[28] These beliefs included the assertion that the Pope was an Antichrist, that nothing could be added by man to religion as laid down in the New Testament, that the Mass was 'abominable idolatrie, blasphemous to the death of Christ, and a profanation of the Lordis Suppar', that there was no Purgatory for 'heavin restis to the faythfull, and hell to the reprobat and unthankfull', that praying for the dead was vain and praying to the saints idolatrous, that bishops were not bishops unless they preached in person, and that tithes did not necessarily belong to churchmen. It has been suggested that the inspiration for this inaugural sermon, in particular Knox's ideas on the apocalypse, were derived principally from English sources – or at least from English translations of continental works.[29] While this is probably so, it is equally true that many of the basic assumptions used to justify this interpretation of world history were shared by his fellow Scots.

During the early days of his residence in St Andrews Castle, Knox seems to have been most closely associated with John Rough. Originally a Dominican friar of Stirling, educated at that notorious hotbed of

---

[27] Knox, *Works*, I, pp. 189–92.

[28] Ibid., I, pp. 193–200.

[29] Katharine Firth has offered some tentative suggestions as to the precise identity of these sources, including George Joyes's *Exposition of Daniel* (1545), Frith's translation of Luther's *De Antichristo* (1529), and possibly Barnes's *Vita Romanorum Pontificum* (1535); see K. Firth, *The Apocalyptic Tradition in Reformation Britain, 1530–1645* (Oxford, 1979), pp. 116–17. See also Kyle, *Mind of Knox*, pp. 219–21.

reforming opinion, St Leonard's College, Rough had risen to national
prominence as one of the two preachers patronized by the Earl of Arran
during the Governor's short-lived reforming policy. His fellow Dominican, Thomas Guillaume, has been identified as a one-time prior of
Inverness and an early influence on John Knox, possibly even introduc-
ing the future preacher to his mentor, George Wishart.[30] According to
Knox, Rough had joined the Castilians shortly after Beaton's assassination and had begun preaching in St Andrews. He was not, in Knox's
estimation, 'the most learned' of men, being regularly worsted by John
Annand, yet his doctrine he judged 'without corruptioun, and tharefor
weall lyiked of the people'.[31] Allegedly impressed by the way in which
Knox instructed his pupils, Rough several times urged him to preach in
public and, despite his initial refusal to do so, Knox did agree to help,
providing written material countering Catholic argument. That the two
men were closely identified with one another in contemporary opinion
can be seen from the fact that both were summoned to appear before
John Winram and his friars in St Leonard's yard. However, the account
of the subsequent disputation given by Knox, our only source for this
episode, deals exclusively with Knox's clever rebuttals of the charges
levied against them and mentions Rough not at all. In fact, little is
known of how the latter spent the rest of his time in St Andrews and
exactly what it was that caused him to leave the Castilians later that
year remains a matter for conjecture.

Unfortunately, beyond the fact that it earned Knox's approval, we
remain ignorant of the precise details of Rough's theological position.
We should, however, note that his earlier preaching was striking for its
advocacy of vernacular Scripture and it may be significant that in the
following century, his associate Guillaume would be credited – almost
certainly incorrectly – with a vernacular translation of the New Testament.[32] Above all, it was the doctrine of *sola scriptura* which marked
out the new Protestant faith and which in turn focused attention on the
need for accurate, accessible scriptural texts. Universal as this belief was
amongst the early reformers (both Catholic and Protestant), it is as well
to remember that it was Henry Balnaves, another future Castilian, who
in 1543 had put forward the legislation authorizing the reading of
Scripture in the vernacular, and that, throughout his career, David

---

[30] Sanderson, *Cardinal of Scotland*, p. 81; John Durkan, 'The Cultural Background in
Sixteenth-Century Scotland', in D. McRoberts (ed.), *Essays on the Scottish Reformation
1513–1625* (Glasgow, 1962), pp. 274–331, at pp. 296, 300.

[31] Knox, *Works*, I, pp. 184, 188.

[32] By Sir James Balfour, see Sanderson, *Cardinal of Scotland*, p. 276, and for Rough
and Guillaume's sermon at Dundee, ibid., p. 189.

Lindsay likewise condemned the incomprehensible Latin of the clergy, calling for the Bible to be 'Iustly translatit in our toung Uulgare'.[33] That this was a central feature of early Scottish Protestantism cannot be doubted. Indeed, as evidenced by the 1543 legislation, its appeal was more widespread than this alone. Many, however, would have taken issue with Knox and the reformers who rejected the interpretive role claimed by the Catholic Church. The passage of the English Act for the Advancement of True Religion (1543) which effectively limited access to Scripture to an upper-class élite, was reportedly received with disgust by those Scots 'such as do pretend ... to be professors of God's Word', but it should be noted that the Scottish act of the same year had carefully reaffirmed official opposition to disputation and heresy.[34] Yet, this evangelical impulse, the passionate desire that God's Word be heard by as many as possible, was something which informed both the ministry of George Wishart and the thinking of Knox and his associates in St Andrews Castle.

For Knox, of course, Scripture was synonymous with the Word of God.[35] As Luther expressed it: 'Christ can not be known except through his Word.'[36] Calvin's *Catechism* expresses the same idea: 'Where shall we seeke for ... His word? It is conteined in the holy Scripture'; and so too does the opening passage of the *First Helvetic Confession* which, through its translator George Wishart, probably helped confirm Knox in his beliefs even if it did not directly inspire them.[37] It has been argued that Wishart conceived of the Word of God only in this rather narrow sense, whereas Knox, possibly inspired in this instance by Balnaves, identified it not only with Scripture but also with the power of Christ.[38] This idea, no doubt much discussed by the Castilians during the course of the siege, would later receive dramatic expression in *Ane Satyre of the Thrie Estatis*, a play written by David Lindsay and first performed in Cupar, some ten miles from St Andrews, in June 1554. Here the

---

[33] Lindsay, *Ane Dialog betuix Experience and Ane Courteour, Off the Miserabyll Estait of the Warld, (The Monarche)* in Douglas Hamer (ed.), *The Works of Sir David Lindsay of the Mount, 1490–1555* (4 vols, STS, Edinburgh, 1931–36), II, p. 680. He also appeals for books necessary to the good government of the realm to be similarly translated.

[34] *The State Papers and Letters of Sir Ralph Sadler*, ed. A. Clifford (2 vols, Edinburgh, 1809), I, p. 265.

[35] Kyle, *Mind of Knox*, pp. 26–7.

[36] Quoted by P. Althaus, *The Theology of Martin Luther*, trans. R.C. Shultz (Philadelphia, 1966), p. 35.

[37] Richard L. Greaves, *Theology and Revolution in the Scottish Reformation: Studies in the Thought of John Knox* (Grand Rapids, MI, 1980), p. 18.

[38] Ibid., pp. 18–19.

character Veritie, carrying an English Bible and punished for her heresy, symbolizes not only the virtue of that name but also the Word of God found in Scripture: 'our Christs word, baith dulce and redolent, /Ane springing well of sinceir veritie'.[39] Unlike Luther, for example, who did on occasion question some of the Bible's textual contradictions, Knox was committed to the 'verie simplicitie and playne infallible trewthe of Godis Word'.[40] This conviction underpinned the biblical literalism which informed so much of his thinking and which, it has been argued, was 'the most fundamental feature of his thought'.[41] Certainly, without this crucial assumption, his understanding of issues such as idolatry, the Mass, and indeed the very development of world history and his role within it, would have been very different.

Concomitant with the reformers' emphasis on the Word was their elevation of the sermon and the emphasis laid upon the need to preach. The question of preaching – arguably the key issue of the pre-Reformation period – lay close to the hearts of Knox, Balnaves and Lindsay. As we have seen, Knox stood accused of claiming that a bishop who did not preach in person was no bishop at all. This view was shared by Balnaves, and Lindsay too reserved some of his fiercest verse criticism for those bishops who failed their flock in this respect.[42] Such condemnation was not without foundation. A lack of learning and failure to preach was recognized by the three Provincial Councils of the Scottish Church which met in 1549, 1552 and 1559, all of which prescribed measures to deal with the situation, 'seing that the preaching of the Gospel is no less necessary to Christian commonwealths than lecturing thereon'.[43] Of course, the preaching ideals of the Reformation extended beyond the bishops. The proselytizing mission of George Wishart, for example, vividly signalled the need to urge God's Word upon as wide an audience as possible. Certainly this was a lesson which would not be lost upon John Knox as he considered his own future career and, in the decades ahead, preaching lay at the very heart of his ministry, dictating not only the path of his future career but also the confrontational,

---

[39] Lindsay, *Ane Satyre of the Thrie Estatis*, lines 1150–51, in Hamer, *Works*.

[40] Knox, *Works*, III, p. 166.

[41] Knox, *On Rebellion*, p. x.

[42] Knox, *Works*, I, p. 194; III, pp. 460, 531–2.

[43] *Statutes of the Scottish Church, 1225–1559*, ed. David Patrick (SHS, Edinburgh, 1907), p. 253. While this 1549 statute went on to state that preaching was 'the principal duty of bishops', it permitted them to delegate the responsibility to 'fit persons'. Ten years later, however, the Council insisted that bishops preach in person at least four times a year with only the elderly, not hitherto accustomed to preaching, being exempt: ibid., pp. 274–5.

dramatic, and attention-grabbing rhetorical approach which informed his words, both written and spoken.[44]

If Rough's impact on Knox remains hard to pin down, assessing the contribution made by the ideas of Knox's other Castilian companions is a much less conjectural business. The poetry penned by David Lindsay of the Mount and Henry Balnaves's 1548 *Treatise on Justification* both shed considerable light on their thinking and merit further scrutiny. In addition, the charges levied against John Borthwick, another later addition to the ranks of the Castilians, repay consideration. Borthwick was a particularly interesting figure, able to combine his position as a trusted member of the court of James V with increasingly unorthodox religious views.[45] Unlike his associates Rough, Balnaves and Lindsay, Borthwick was not connected with the reforming policies of 1543. Instead, at this time, he was to be found in the service of the English government, assisting with plans for a Scottish invasion and praised as being 'singularly devoted to the King's service'.[46] While in London he appears to have been in contact with Sir John Melville of Raith and, through this Fife family, to have fostered links with the murderers of Cardinal Beaton.[47] Following the assassination, he joined the Castilians where he seems to have been associated with Balnaves in his dealings with the English administration.[48] It is the trial of 1540 conducted in Borthwick's absence that best reveals the cast of his thought.[49] Concerned less with theology and more with the need for a Henrician-inspired Reformation, he urged throwing off papal authority and transferring ecclesiastical wealth to the royal Treasury. He also attacked the monasteries, demanded that the religious life be dissolved, argued the case for clerical marriage, called for a vernacular New Testament, denied the legitimacy of pardons and declared canon law to be invalid. He was also accused of the possession of heretical books including works of Erasmus,

---

[44] Maurice Lee, 'John Knox and his History', *SHR*, 19 (1966), pp. 79–88, p. 87. See also Chapters 3 and 11 in this volume by Euan Cameron and Jenny Wormald.

[45] Durkan, 'Scottish Evangelicals', p. 132.

[46] Quoted, ibid., p. 152.

[47] Ibid., p. 153.

[48] Exactly when Borthwick joined the Castilians is not clear. He was certainly there by April 1547 at which date he accompanied Balnaves to Berwick: *RPC*, I, p. 43; *CSP Scot.*, I, p. 6.

[49] The charges against Borthwick are listed in the account of the reversal of his sentence passed in 1561 and recorded in the Register of the Kirk of St Andrews, 'The Ordour and Process deducit in the Declarator gevyn agains Schyre Jhon Borthwick of Cenerie, knycht, be umquill Dauid, Cardinall', in *Bannatyne Miscellany I* (Bannatyne Club, Edinburgh, 1827), pp. 255–63. Based on these articles, and incorporating parts of the defence Borthwick later made of his position as preserved by Foxe, is *L&P Henry VIII*, XV, no. 714.

Oecolampadius, Melanchthon and an English New Testament. Many of Borthwick's views were echoed in Knox's St Andrews sermon, predictably such matters as his condemnation of pardons and clerical celibacy and, most notably, his virulent antipapalism. This is not, of course, to argue that Borthwick was the preacher's immediate inspiration, but it does point to the community of interest which existed amongst those involved in the St Andrews siege, reinforcing the fact that Knox's first public exhortation did not emerge *ex nihilo*.

The inescapable fact that Knox was so clearly in sympathy with the attitudes of these early Scottish reformers raises a question central to this period of his life yet all too often underestimated – or even disregarded – in broader assessments of his career. His identification with Calvinist thinking, so firmly as to admit of no other influence and so indelibly engraved on the popular imagination, has not survived scholarly scrutiny unscathed.[50] And yet the influence of early Scottish Protestantism – of Lutheranism and, through Wishart, of the Swiss reformers – continues to be largely overlooked.[51] Of course, it cannot be denied that Calvinism was Knox's principal theological and social inspiration, but we must always remember that his understanding of Calvin's teaching was grafted on to his earlier Scottish experiences. His plans to visit the Protestant churches of Germany – jettisoned in favour of joining the Castilians – also suggest his interest in Lutheran theology at this time and, had he followed this inclination, his future might have been very different indeed.[52] As it is, it has been suggested that Lutheran influences can be traced in Knox's conception of the Atonement (which echoes that of Patrick Hamilton), of the Christian family and, possibly, also of education.[53]

Knox's strongest links to the Lutheran tradition and his most explicit commendation of Lutheran ideas are suggested by his relationship with Henry Balnaves. As we have seen, the two men were closely associated with one another during the course of a difficult and dangerous siege and each seems to have respected the talents of the other. At this point in their respective careers, their ideas appear to have been essentially compatible and when Balnaves, incarcerated in the castle of Rouen following the collapse of the siege, penned his *Treatise on Justification*, Knox was only

---

[50] Summarized in Greaves, *Theology and Revolution*, pp. 217–18.

[51] But see Durkan, 'The Cultural Background', pp. 295–7. For an introduction to Lutheran ideas in Scotland, see James K. Cameron, 'Aspects of the Lutheran Contribution to the Scottish Reformation', *RSCHS*, 22 (1984), pp. 1–12. A further discussion of Wishart's influence on Knox can be found in Shaw, 'Zwinglian Influences', pp. 130 ff.

[52] W. Stanford Reid, 'Lutheranism in the Scottish Reformation', *Westminster Theological Journal*, 7 (1944–45), pp. 91–111, at p. 109.

[53] Greaves, *Theology and Revolution*, pp. 210–11.

too happy to sanction the work. It has even been suggested (unconvincingly considering the circumstances in which it was written) that Knox contributed to it.[54] The treatise, more properly known as *The Confession of Faith, conteining how the troubled man should seeke refuge at his God, Thereto led by faith: with the declaratione of the article of justification at length. The order of good workes, which are the fruites of faith: And how the faithful, and iustified man, Should walke and liue, in the perfite, and true Christian religion, according to his vocation*, though first written in 1548, was not published in Scotland until 1584. Knox, himself a prisoner in the French galley *Notre Dame*, received a copy soon after its composition, and so greatly did it comfort his soul, that he prepared a summary of the work for 'the better memory of the Reader ... [and] the more instruction of the simple' (again emphasizing the importance of preaching God's Word to as many as possible).[55] Though the direct influence of Luther's teaching has been a matter for debate, the treatise is typically Lutheran in tone and content, a fact which may owe as much to the example of such Scottish reformers as Patrick Hamilton and Alexander Seton as to the schools of Germany.[56] Unsurprisingly, the assumption that Balnaves's work can be judged representative of Knox's thinking has also been challenged.[57] On balance, however, Knox's warm endorsement of its 'godly and perfect' doctrine seems approval enough, and though comparing Knox's summary with the original exposes some differences in opinion, this is largely a question of emphasis rather than a divergence of doctrine.[58] For example, while Knox faithfully reproduced many of Balnaves's Old Testament references and examples, those drawn from the New Testament were frequently omitted.[59]

When Knox later described his interrogation before John Winram, he explained that his answers were contained in 'a treatise that he wrate in the gallayis, conteanyng the some of his doctrin, and Confessioun of his fayth'. Although it is generally assumed that this refers to a document now lost, it has been suggested that Balnaves's *Treatise* is the work in question.[60] Certainly there are similarities between the topics addressed

---

[54] Hugh Watt, 'Henry Balnaves and the Scottish Reformation', *RSCHS*, 5 (1935), pp. 23–39, at p. 29.

[55] Knox, *Works*, I, pp. 226–7. The summary is printed in ibid., III, pp. 13–28, and the full treatise in ibid., III, pp. 431–542.

[56] Kyle, *Mind of Knox*, p. 98 and n. 13.

[57] See, for example, Ridley, *Knox*, pp. 76–7, and Kyle, *Mind of Knox*, p. 98.

[58] Knox, *Works*, III, p. 9.

[59] Greaves, *Theology and Revolution*, p. 2; Ridley, *Knox*, p. 77. For a discussion of the importance Knox attached to the Old Testament and the implications this had for his thinking, see Kyle, *Mind of Knox*, pp. 38–41.

[60] Knox, *Works*, I, p. 200; Watt, 'Henry Balnaves', pp. 28–9.

by Balnaves and the charges levelled against Knox, but this surely is only to be expected. For example, both attacked the Mass, Purgatory and prayers for and to the dead, both denied that man could add anything to religion as instituted by God, and both declared that bishops were only bishops if they preached in person. Balnaves's work, however, contains little of the virulent antipapalism associated with Knox's first sermon, and Knox, unlike Balnaves, says nothing on the nature of vocation (perhaps, given the circumstances, this was a question best left alone). Moreoever, when it comes to comparing Balnaves's work with Knox's account of the subsequent disputation before Winram, the differences are more pronounced, with Knox focusing almost exclusively on his condemnation of the idolatrous ceremonies of the Church. While it is true that this theme also concerns Balnaves, the latter's detailed commentary on the relationship between salvation, faith, the law and good works which lies at the heart of his treatise is not touched on by Knox at this point in his *History*.

In 28 chapters Balnaves's *Treatise on Justification* addresses two fundamental questions: what is rightly the study of man? And what should man do in times of adversity? The simple answer, delivered in the opening passage, is that man should 'adhear unto God; running to him in the time of tribulation ... with sure hope of deliverance by him allone'. Expounding this in greater detail, Balnaves offers an essentially Lutheran exposition of the doctrine of justification *sola fides*, attacking Satan's corruption of the Church and the introduction of 'vaine superstitions, the which they call good workes'. Like other reformers, Balnaves did not deny the value of works which 'ought and should by done of a Christian', but he stressed that they were 'but the witnessing of faith' and not the path to salvation: 'We should put all our trust and hope in him [God] and in his mercy only, and neither in the law nor workes'.[61] Asserting that works of man's invention only incur God's displeasure, Balnaves criticized the Church for allowing prayers to images and Masses for the saints.[62] Significantly, he went on to thank God that such matters were now so plainly discussed that he need not dwell on them, referring his readers instead to the 'godly declamations' found in Scripture against the worship of saints, pilgrimages, Purgatory, holy water, the Mass, dietary laws and clerical celibacy together with the 'abominable abuses of the whole Christian religion, by the shaven, oincted, or

---

[61] Knox, *Works*, III, pp. 432, 458, 481, 504, 493.

[62] Balnaves here echoes Wishart rather than Luther when he advocates the destruction of all worship and superstition contrary to the Word of God for nothing displeases him more than the invention of 'any maner of worshipping of him which he hath not commanded'; Greaves, *Theology and Revolution*, p. 13.

smeared preists, bishops, monkes, and friers'.[63] The open discussion to
which Balnaves refers is clearly an allusion to the heady days of 1547
when such matters were the subject not only of intense debate amongst
the like-minded men brought together in St Andrews Castle but also of
sermons preached publicly in the parish Church of Holy Trinity. Such
memories must have helped sustain him and his colleagues during the
reversals of the 1540s and 1550s, holding out a vision of what a
reformed Church in Scotland might become.

As we have seen, one of the principal objectives of Balnaves's *Treatise*
was to explain why God subjected his faithful followers to tribulation.
According to Balnaves, affliction was to be viewed as 'marveilous
necessarie', and persecution as 'a communion with the passion of Christ'.
As such, suffering was not to be taken as a sign of divine displeasure
but, on the contrary, as a token of God's good will: He punishes us 'not
that wee bee lost thereby, but to drawe and provoke us to repentance'.[64]
While Knox's summary reproduces the gist of this argument, one has to
conclude that he did not really concur with it. Significantly, his précis
omits Balnaves's point emphasizing that such troubles are not the consequence of human action, and goes on to stress that the cause of
misfortune is the neglect of God's Word.[65] This attitude is typical of
Knox's thinking both in 1547 and as it developed during the course of
his career. Citing plagues, blizzards and military defeat as evidence, his
History is littered with examples illustrating how God sought to punish
Scotland for her apostasy.[66] Some events, such as the death of the
Regent, Mary of Guise, Knox regarded as divine retribution meted out
against individual wickedness, but he was equally comfortable with the
idea of corporate retribution and perfectly able to accept that God
punished the whole nation, the godly as well as the ungodly.[67]

This outlook was the direct consequence of Knox's conviction that to
do nothing about sin was in itself sinful – an attitude which ultimately
possessed important implications for his ideas concerning resistance to
established – Catholic – authority. Although this aspect of Knox's thinking has been the topic of considerable study, the Castilian episode
demands further comment.[68] This was, after all, an occasion on which

---

[63] Knox, *Works*, III, p. 519.

[64] Ibid., III, pp. 447, 448, 443.

[65] Ibid., III, p. 15.

[66] Roger A. Mason, 'Usable Pasts: History and Identity in Reformation Scotland',
SHR, 76 (1997), pp. 54–68, at p. 59.

[67] Kyle, *Mind of Knox*, pp. 16, 208.

[68] Knox's ideas on resistance have received considerable attention, for example, Burns,
True Law of Kingship, pp. 122–84; Greaves, *Theology and Revolution*, pp. 126–56. But
see in particular Roger A. Mason's introduction to Knox, *On Rebellion*, and Chapter 7
by Jane E.A. Dawson in this volume.

he deliberately chose to associate himself with men in open rebellion against the secular authorities. In adopting such a course of action, Knox clearly bestowed his approval on the enterprise, but whether this was the manifestation of a carefully formulated doctrine of resistance has been a matter of dispute.[69] The systematic study of Knox's political writings suggests a much more hesitant progression from a position in which, stymied by the well-worn Pauline injunction to civil obedience (Romans 13:1–7), he could urge no more than passive disobedience, to a point at which he not only sanctioned resistance to an ungodly ruler but positively dictated it. Nevertheless, while it remains true that Knox did not have a mature doctrine of resistance in 1547, he was clearly prepared to go much further in person than he might otherwise have urged in theory. This all too human divergence between actions and words reflects the similar experience of Henry Balnaves whose *Treatise on Justification* reads in places like a *cri de coeur* for social order and harmony but who, in his treasonable dealings with the English government, actually went much further in his rebellion than Knox. His later conservatism might almost be read as an *apologia* as, in traditional enough fashion, Balnaves urged his readers to 'Give to thy prince and superiour his duetie; or whatever he chargeth thee with concerning temporall riches', and to obey him in all things not repugnant to God's command 'howbeit he bee evill and doe the wrong'. Above all, he entreated, 'Be not a perturber of the common weale'.[70] Languishing in a French prison, Balnaves might well have wished that he had heeded his own words.

While it is true that Knox's later account of the murder of Cardinal Beaton displays a grim delight in the slaughter, his principal concern was to illustrate not the legitimate actions of a lesser magistracy but rather the process of divinely wrought tyrannicide.[71] In this respect, the *History* closely resembles David Lindsay's poem, *The Tragedie of the Cardinal*, which was probably written sometime in 1547 shortly after the events it describes and when Lindsay was clearly reflecting the attitudes of those around him. Lindsay's depiction of the actual murder, though evocative, provides no incriminating details and yet his chosen poetic genre powerfully suggests the inevitability of the deed, something which Beaton himself is made to attribute to 'the hie power Divine' (line 139). Through the figure of Beaton's penitent ghost, Lindsay launches an impassioned plea for religious Reformation, urging prelates to

---

[69] Cf. Burns, *True Law of Kingship*, p. 127 (who argues that it was not), and Greaves, *Theology and Revolution*, p. 127 (who takes the opposing view).

[70] Knox, *Works*, III, p. 540.

[71] Ibid., I, p. 80.

attend to their flock, to preach the Old and New Testaments and to leave off harlotry, gaming and greed. As this suggests, in 1547 men such as Lindsay, Balnaves and Knox would have viewed themselves as part of an attempt – albeit an alarmingly violent one – not to overthrow the existing authorities but to convince them of the error of their ways and set them on the path to righteousness.[72] Such was the mirror that men like Balnaves and Lindsay had held up to the monarch (or regent) throughout their long association with the court. It has been suggested that Knox's concept of the godly prince eager to challenge the papacy and reform the Church was a legacy of his experiences both in the Edwardian Church and in exile.[73] However, it seems clear that such ideas constituted an important backdrop to events in Scotland.

Politics was not, however, the only factor to focus mens' minds on the implications of their actions. Even more compelling in this respect was the widespread belief that the upheavals of the sixteenth century formed part of the final drama of world history. It is well known that the Protestant Reformation provided a new stimulus to the apocalyptic ideas which had long coloured the medieval conception of divine action in world history.[74] By explaining history – and in particular the existence of the Catholic Church – the Apocalypse helped the reformers justify their actions, explaining their persecution and holding out hope of salvation and vindication alike. As such it was immensely attractive not only to those like Knox engaged in the hazardous business of rebellion but also to a great many of the Scottish population who in the last decade had seen their country devastated by war, plague and political crisis. For Knox, this could all be explained by reference to the Apocalypse. The sense of a cosmic struggle between the forces of good and evil, so typical of apocalyptic historiography, is vividly conveyed by his *History of the Reformation*. But the fact that this type of interpretation was not just a feature of his later thinking is amply illustrated by the text chosen for his important first sermon. As we have seen, this

---

[72] Ibid., III, p. 528.

[73] A.H. Williamson, *Scottish National Consciousness in the Age of James VI: The Apocalypse, the Union and the Shaping of Scotland's Public Culture* (Edinburgh, 1979), p. 3.

[74] Numerous studies of sixteenth-century apocalypticism include: Richard Bauckham, *Tudor Apocalypse: Sixteenth-Century Apocalypticism, Millenarianism and the English Reformation: From John Bale to John Foxe and Thomas Brightman* (Oxford, 1978); Paul Christianson, *Reformers and Babylon: English Apocalyptic Visions from the Reformation to the Eve of the Civil War* (Toronto, 1978); Firth, *Apocalyptic Tradition in Reformation Britain*; C.A. Patrides and J. Wittreich (eds), *The Apocalypse in English Renaissance Thought and Literature* (Manchester, 1984). See also Williamson, *Scottish National Consciousness*.

allowed Knox to put forward the claim that the last beast or kingdom prophesied in the Book of Daniel was to be understood as the Roman Church. Then, as he later recalled, 'he begane ... to dissipher the lyves of diverse Papes, and the lyves of all the scheavelynges for the most parte; thare doctrin and lawes he plainelie proved to repugne directlye to the doctrin and lawes of God the Father, and of Christ Jesus his Sone'.[75]

Although historians have tended to suggest that the first half of the sixteenth century saw little challenge to papal authority in Scotland, this is not the only evidence of antipapal sentiment.[76] One orthodox aspect of this was the attack on excessive claims to papal authority put forward by conciliarist theorists such as John Mair: it could be but a short step from rejection of the *ius divinum* of the papacy to rejection of the office as a whole. Indeed, this was a jump Patrick Hamilton made having previously been a pupil of Mair's.[77] At a more humble level, four Ayrshire Protestants sought refuge in England in 1537, declaring to anyone who would listen that the Bishop of Rome was not the Pope.[78] More significantly for our purposes, antipapal feeling can also be located at the royal court. Writing in 1543, the English ambassador, Ralph Sadler, noted that 'such as do pretend to favour God's Word, do like chiefly that part which confuteth the primacy of the bishop of Rome'.[79] Significantly, two of those with whom Sadler had spent time when in Scotland three years earlier were John Borthwick and David Lindsay.[80] Sure enough, Borthwick was especially vehement in his criticisms of the papacy and Lindsay's later works would display a similar approach. Clearly Knox did not need to look outwith Scotland to fuel his own hostility and his forthright condemnation of papal corruption and idolatry.

With typical lack of modesty, Knox was of the opinion that his brand of reformed apocalypticism offered the majority of Scots something new. Knox himself, however, was well aware of Scottish precedents and later attributed what he termed 'the spreat of prophesy' to George Wishart.[81] Indeed, to his supporters, Wishart's martyrdom represented

---

[75] Knox, *Works*, I, p. 191.

[76] For example, Wormald, *Court, Kirk and Community*, p. 79; Cameron, 'Aspects of the Lutheran Contribution to the Scottish Reformation', p. 10.

[77] G. Wiedermann, 'Martin Luther versus John Fisher: Some Ideas concerning the Debate on Lutheran Theology at the University of St Andrews, 1525–30', *RSCHS*, 22 (1984), pp. 13–34, at pp. 26–7.

[78] *L&P Henry VIII*, XII, pt 1, no. 703.

[79] Sadler, *Papers*, I, p. 265.

[80] Ibid., I, pp. 17–45.

[81] Knox, *Works*, I, p. 125.

an important episode in the final struggle with the forces of Antichrist. This identification is made explicit in a description of the preacher's trial and execution published in London a couple of years after his death.[82] Significantly, the volume also contains a copy of Lindsay's *Tragedie of the Cardinal*, and a clear connection is made between the two. Whether or not Lindsay had anything to do with the production of this volume is unknown – though unlikely. But several of the Castilians, for example Balnaves and the Melvilles, had links with London, and it is not unreasonable to suppose that they or their associates helped propagate such a view south of the border.

With the day of judgement seemingly imminent, the need to urge God's Word upon as wide an audience as possible became increasingly pressing and, in this respect, the example of Wishart's Scottish ministry and open-air sermons was crucially important. This urgent sense of evangelism was echoed and developed by Knox and his Castilian associates. It certainly informs the later work of David Lindsay. His *magnum opus*, *The Monarche*, clearly sought to address as wide an audience as possible, and *Ane Satyre of the Thrie Estatis*, a drama written for public performance, fulfils a similar function. Both these works are notable for their attacks on the established Church and, as well as a virulent attack on clerical abuses, they each represent a powerful piece of antipapal polemic explicitly presented within an apocalyptic framework.[83]

Of all the Castilians influenced by Wishart, it was John Knox who made the most significant contribution to the future development of the Scottish Reformation. However, his decision to assume the mantle of divine emissary was, as we have seen, not lightly taken. A crucial sticking point concerned the nature of his calling for, as Knox put it, 'he wold do nothing without a lauchfull vocatioun'.[84] Although he had never obtained a benefice, Knox had been ordained in the Catholic Church in 1536. If he is to believed, by 1547, he was already of the opinion that this had no force before God – though natural trepidation rather than theological conviction seems a more likely cause of his

---

[82] *The Tragicall death of D. Beaton, Bishippe of sainct Andrewes in Scotland: Whereunto is joyned the martyrdom of maister G. Wysehart ... for whose sake the aforesaid bishoppe was not long after slayne Wherein thai mainst learne what a burnynge charitie they shewed not only towardes him: but vnto al suche as come to their handes for the blessed Gospels sake* (London, 1548?).

[83] For a more detailed discussion, see Carol Edington, 'Repentance and Reform: Political and Religious Culture in Pre-Reformation Scotland', *Renaissance Studies*, 11 (1997), pp. 108–22, at pp. 116–22.

[84] Knox, *Works*, I, p. 186.

hesitation to climb into the pulpit. However, his fellow Castilians, Rough and Balnaves, were convinced of the legitimacy of his calling. As part of the attempt to persuade Knox likewise, Rough preached a sermon in which he expounded the Protestant belief in the authority of the congregation to elect their minister. Balnaves's views are to be found in his 1548 *Treatise*, in which he identifies three types of vocation: the general, the mediate and the immediate.[85] The first, 'by the which we ar called by Christ and His Word' applies to all the elect without distinction of person, but the others are of a special type such as Paul's calling of Timothy or God's revelation to the Old Testament prophets. It was clearly this latter concept which made such an impression on Knox as he confronted this, the most important decision of his life. Certainly, in the course of his clash with the Lords of the Congregation in 1559, he would attribute his call directly to God and not to the St Andrews congregation and it was this conception of his prophetic vocation which informed his entire ministry.[86]

In the short term, of course, the Castilian episode did nothing to further Knox's Scottish career. As is well known, the castle fell to the Governor's French allies in July 1547.[87] It was an outcome which Knox would have us believe he already viewed through the eyes of a divinely called prophet: all the Castilians' hopes of victory he repeatedly dashed, foretelling instead that they should be taken by their enemies and carried off into a strange land.[88] As Knox the retrospective chronicler clearly intended it should, the biblical allusion took on a personal slant when Knox and Balnaves were both taken prisoner; the former sent to the galleys, the latter incarcerated in Rouen. By the time of Knox's return to Scotland in 1555, the leaders of the Reformation movement were a different set of men entirely. The importance of those early contacts should not, however, be overlooked.

Knox may not have provided us with a detailed account of the arguments which exercised his mind as he confronted Rough's call to the ministry but, by examining the issues which chiefly concerned him at this point in his career, it has been possible to see why he opted to heed the summons. Such views were not produced by Knox like rabbits from a hat. Instead they were the product of past experiences, most notably his association with George Wishart, as well as his more recent contacts with the Castilians. The fact that Knox and his companions

---

[85] Ibid., III, pp. 522–5.

[86] Greaves, *Theology and Revolution*, pp. 72–4.

[87] Elizabeth Bonner, 'The Recovery of St Andrews Castle in 1547: French Naval Policy and Diplomacy in the British Isles', *EHR*, 111 (1996), pp. 578–98.

[88] Knox, *Works*, I, pp. 204–5.

shared so many beliefs should not, of course, be taken as proof either of direct influence or of amiable unanimity. Even where views neatly coincide, this often points simply – yet none the less significantly – to no more than a common cultural or intellectual heritage. For example, it has been suggested that David Lindsay is the source for Knox's well-known opposition to female authority but, while there is indeed evidence in Lindsay's work to support such a thesis, such attitudes were not uncommon and in Lindsay were never developed to reach the conclusion sought by Knox.[89] After all, in a time of such political and religious upheaval, ideas were fluid and hard to pin down. Nevertheless, as we have seen, it is possible to identify a strand of reforming zeal which can be traced from the court of James V to the siege of St Andrews. The experiences of men such as Balnaves, Rough and Lindsay had rendered them established public figures, accustomed to articulating their views on the national stage. No doubt hoping that, at their invitation, Knox would take on a similar role, they surely little dreamed of where such encouragement might lead.

---

[89] Greaves, *Theology and Revolution*, p. 221.

CHAPTER THREE

Frankfurt and Geneva: The European Context of John Knox's Reformation

*Euan Cameron**

At St Andrews, shortly after Easter 1547, the preacher John Rough gave his dramatic commission to John Knox: 'I charge you, that ... ye take upon you the public office and charge of preaching, even as ye look to avoid God's heavy displeasure, and desire that he shall multiply his graces with you.' At which 'the said John, abashed, burst forth in most abundant tears, and withdrew himself to his chamber'. Until he preached his first sermon, 'no man saw any sign of mirth in him, neither yet had he pleasure to accompany any man, many days together'.[1] Almost exactly 12 years later, Knox returned to Scotland at a critical moment in the dramatic revolution which was the Scottish Reformation, in which his now developed pulpit skills played a decisive role. In the intervening years, Knox had learned much of his craft as a reformer of religion. Though briefly in Scotland over 1555–56, he devoted most of his attention in those years to the affairs of England, and of English-speaking reformers in continental Europe. He learned much of the wiles of politicians, and of those clergy whose political instincts were more subtle than his own principles allowed. He also witnessed, or heard of, the bewildering shifts of fortune which afflicted the various strands of the Reformation. How far Knox was shaped by these events, or how far he brought his own pre-formed personality and downright theological character to them: that is a matter for the religious biographer. The general historian, on the other hand, can only understand Knox's impact on events by placing Knox in his context. How did the man and the churchman belong in the world of religion and Church politics in which he found himself? Was he a prophet for his age, or in spite of it?

This question becomes especially important in the light of later events. Knox exerted almost as much influence on some of the early reformed

* The author gratefully acknowledges the support given by the Leverhulme Trust in awarding the Research Fellowship which made the preparation of this paper possible.
[1] Knox, *History*, I, p. 83.

Churches of England as he did on those of Scotland. Yet the Churches in those two countries were to follow very different destinies. They embraced different attitudes to forms of worship, and to relations between Church and State, the consequences of which are still visible to this day. Both, moreover, appealed repeatedly to the continental reformers for support and endorsement. It has been traditional to trace some of the strife between the English and Scots attitudes to Church reform back to the struggles between Knox and his fellow exiles in the Europe of the 1550s. If this is so, Knox may have exerted even more influence on future events during his stay in Europe than he did after his final return to Scotland. Did the rift between Knox and the 'Anglicans' really happen because 'he was talking European and they English'?[2] If so, what does that say about the European way of Reformation?

It may be helpful to look back to several years before Knox preached his first reformed sermon, to see how the European religious picture changed during the 1540s and 1550s. In 1540 the reformed cause in Germany and the Swiss Confederation was in the ascendant. A series of significant defections from Rome strengthened the Lutheran position among the German princes. At the time of the religious conferences of 1540–41 the Catholic cause was in disarray. Liberal Catholics in Germany such as Johann Gropper and Julius Pflug negotiated themselves as close to the Protestant cause as they dared, with the encouragement of the curial diplomat and Venetian moderate Gasparo Contarini.[3] Archbishop Hermann von Wied of Cologne tried to reform his diocese along lines suggested by moderate Protestants, in a project destined to have influence as far away as Scotland.[4] In 1541 two leading theologians from the most progressive tendency in Catholicism defected to Protestantism, causing a sensation and nearly

---

[2] Eustace Percy, *John Knox* (London, 1937), p. 198.

[3] On the religious conferences of this period, see F. Lau and E. Bizer, *A History of the Reformation in Germany to 1555*, trans. B.A. Hardy (London, 1969), pp. 153–7, 151–61; H. Rabe, *Reichsband und Interim: Die Verfassungs- und Religionspolitik Karls V und der Reichstag zu Augsburg 1546/48* (Cologne, 1971), pp. 92–117; P. Matheson, *Cardinal Contarini at Regensburg* (Oxford, 1972); R. Braunisch, *Die Theologie der Rechtfertigung im 'Enchiridion' (1538) des Johannes Gropper: sein kritischer Dialog mit Philipp Melanchthon* (Münster, 1974); and most recently Athina Lexutt, *Rechtfertigung im Gespräch: Das Rechtfertigungsverständnis in den Religionsgesprächen von Hagenau, Worms und Regensburg 1540/41* (Forschungen zur Kirchen- und Dogmengeschichte, Bd. 64, Göttingen, 1996).

[4] On Cologne, see Lau and Bizer, *History of the Reformation*, pp. 178–80, 187–9, 193, 197, 200; on its influence in Scotland, see James K. Cameron, 'The Cologne Reformation and the Church of Scotland', *JEH*, 30 (1979), pp. 39–64.

destroying the Capuchin order.[5] Meanwhile the project for a General Council of the Church suffered seemingly perpetual delays, and it was by no means clear what sort of Catholicism it would seek to restore or reinvigorate in any case.

In this atmosphere one city, and one might even say one reformer, typified the style of the moment. It was to Strasbourg, rather than Wittenberg or Zurich, that the emergent reformed Churches of Europe looked for an example to follow, and especially to its prolix, verbose and incorrigibly peace-seeking reformer Martin Bucer. Bucer negotiated the Wittenberg accord in 1536, and thus papered over the rift among the German-speaking reformers which had yawned so dangerously at Marburg in 1529 and at Augsburg in 1530.[6] Bucer led the negotiating teams at the conferences with the German Catholic theologians, and helped produce most of the mediating draft documents.[7] Strasbourg attracted the largest contingent of French expatriates seeking a refuge and an education in the reformed ministry, including most famously, of course, John Calvin in 1538–41.[8] Strasbourg represented a type of Reformation which drew much of its theology from Zurich, but which embraced the League of Schmalkalden and sought accommodation and alliance with the Lutheran Churches to the north. It was the quintessential 'south-German' reformed city, seething and bubbling with ideas, with social tensions and pressures, with cultural activities of all kinds.[9] As such it influenced both the reformed cities named in the title of this chapter. Frankfurt-am-Main, although far to the north of the Swabian heartland of south-German Protestantism, was first reformed by Dionysius Melander from Ulm. Its book-fair surely contributed to the eclectic cultural outlook of its citizens, and their affinity with the ideas

---

[5] P. McNair, *Peter Martyr in Italy: An Anatomy of Apostasy* (Oxford, 1967), pp. 263 ff.; 277 ff.

[6] Lau and Bizer, *History of the Reformation*, pp. 108–22; see also W. Köhler, *Zwingli und Luther* (2 vols, Leipzig and Gütersloh, 1934–53), II, pp. 320–525; M.U. Edwards, *Luther and the False Brethren* (Stanford, CA, 1975), pp. 127–55.

[7] Lexutt, *Rechtfertigung im Gespräch*, pp. 40 ff.

[8] On Calvin's time in Strasbourg, see e.g. W.J. Bouwsma, *John Calvin: A Sixteenth-Century Portrait* (Oxford, 1988), pp. 21 ff.; on the attraction of Strasbourg for the French, see note 20 below; on the city's Reformation, see esp. L.J. Abray, *The People's Reformation: Magistrates, Clergy and Commons in Strasbourg 1500–1598* (Oxford, 1985); M.U. Chrisman, *Strasbourg and the Reform: A Study in the Process of Change* (New Haven, CT, 1967).

[9] On social tensions, see T.A. Brady, *Ruling Class, Regime and Reformation at Strasbourg, 1520–1555* (Leiden, 1978); on print culture, see M.U. Chrisman, *Lay Culture, Learned Culture: Books and Social Change in Strasbourg, 1480–1599* (New Haven, CT, 1982) and M.U. Chrisman, *Bibliography of Strasbourg Imprints, 1480–1599* (New Haven, CT, 1982).

of the urban south.[10] The influence of Strasbourg's reform on the still young Calvin, as he resided there between his first stay in Geneva and his recall in 1541, was quite decisive; most of all, perhaps, in that it convinced Calvin of the need for discipline as well as education, *Ordonnances* as well as *Institution*, in a reformed city-state.

Yet the weakness of Catholicism, and the contrasting ascendancy of the south-German city reformations, proved both to be merely temporary. Between 1540 and 1553 the religious scene in central Europe changed dramatically. The Emperor Charles V had through the 1520s and 1530s been largely absorbed in warfare; from the middle 1540s he finally devoted serious effort to the German question. With the ease of a skilful politician he exploited every personal weakness among the princes to break up the Protestant alliances, from Moritz of Saxony's jealousy of his fellow Wettins, to Philipp of Hesse's bigamous marriage to one of his ladies-in-waiting. In the short war of 1546–47 Charles achieved the total defeat of the Ernestine Saxon and Hessian armies. In the end, Charles's victory, won at the cost of alliance with the disgruntled but still implacably Lutheran Moritz of Saxony, descended into sheer fiasco as one after another of the north-German princes and cities simply refused to make more than token concessions towards a restoration of Catholicism. In 1551–52 the bizarre alliance of the Lutheran Moritz of Saxony and the persecuting Catholic Henri II of France would shatter even this fragile achievement.[11]

However, one clear result did ensue from this conflict. The distinctive identity of the south-German Reformation movement was largely destroyed. The cities of the *Confessio Tetrapolitana* had placed their hopes for their defence on membership of the League of Schmalkalden; this was, in historical and geographical terms, a thoroughly unnatural partnership of northern princes and southern city-states, who occupied different regions of the Empire and had traditionally been politically at odds.[12] The princes neither could nor would do anything to save the cities from Charles V in 1548–51. In the agreement eventually reached between the *Reichstag* and Ferdinand of Austria in 1555 free cities, unlike princes, were required to accept some restoration of Catholic worship within their domains; the only form of Protestantism which

---

[10] On Frankfurt's place among the cities in the reformed tradition, see G.W. Locher, *Die zwinglische Reformation im Rahmen der europäischen Kirchengeschichte* (Göttingen and Zürich, 1979), pp. 469–99; on the book-fair, see B. Recke, *Die Frankfurter Buchermesse 1462–1792* (Frankfurt, 1951).

[11] These events are summarized in Euan Cameron, *The European Reformation* (Oxford, 1991), pp. 345–8 and refs.

[12] See T.A. Brady, *Turning Swiss: Cities and Empire, 1450–1550* (Cambridge, 1985), pp. 194 ff. for the unnatural quality of the alliance.

they might practise was Lutheranism.[13] In consequence of this restriction, several leaders of south-German reform, including Martin Bucer, were driven into exile and, as it happened, into the waiting arms of Thomas Cranmer and the Edwardian Church of England. Frankfurt-am-Main was by the early 1550s a conscientiously, even militantly Lutheran city under its chief pastor, Hartmann Beyer.[14]

Within about a decade the religious map of Protestant Europe had changed. In the 1540s there had been a subtly graduated spectrum, from Lutheran Scandinavia and north Germany, through the moderate hues of south-western German 'reformed' Protestantism in Swabia and around Lake Constance, to where it met the Zwinglianism of the German-speaking Swiss. From the mid-1550s, in contrast, confessional Lutheranism reigned, theoretically, everywhere within the Empire covered by the provisions of the Peace of Augsburg. Geneva, meanwhile, was on the brink of attaining its legendary – and sometimes overstated – position as the beating heart of 'Calvinist' reformed Protestantism. Reformation Europe was on the way to becoming 'confessionalized': that is, divided into two relatively distinct camps, defined by their adherence to particular creeds, acutely sensitive to the issues which divided them from each other, and deeply distrustful of anyone who temporized or tried to mediate in those disputes.[15]

One issue embodied the strife between Lutheran and reformed, as it had done since the mid-1520s, namely the understanding of the presence of Christ in the Eucharist. While it is always dangerous to try to simplify this tangled topic of sixteenth-century theology, one may suggest that the issues had subtly changed, and become more sharply defined, since the days of Luther and Zwingli's first dispute in the mid-1520s. Luther had insisted that the presence of Christ's *body* in the Eucharistic wafer must mean something objective, but did not define consistently what that 'something' was.[16] Zwingli's whole approach to

---

[13] On the Peace of Augsburg and the cities, see P. Warmbrunn, *Zwei Konfessionen in einer Stadt* (Wiesbaden, 1983), pp. 69–130; H. Tüchle, 'The Peace of Augsburg: New Order or Lull in the Fighting', in H.J. Cohn (ed.), *Government in Reformation Europe 1520–1560* (London, 1971), pp. 145–60; note also the comment of A.G. Dickens on this period, that 'the services of Charles V to Catholicism had been great, but at this moment they were transcended by the splendour of his services to Lutheranism', in his *The German Nation and Martin Luther* (London, 1974), p. 197.

[14] On Beyer's Lutheranism see below, note 23.

[15] For an introduction to 'confessionalism' in Germany, where the tensions were most acute, see Heinz Schilling (ed.), *Die reformierte Konfessionalisierung in Deutschland – Das Problem der 'Zweiten Reformation': Wissenschaftliches Symposion des Vereins für Reformationsgeschichte 1985* (Gütersloh, 1986).

[16] An intriguing insight into either the ambiguity or the variability of Luther's thought on this issue is given by R.W. Quere, 'Changes and Constants: Structure in Luther's

the sacraments reflected a cool rationalism: he insisted on their role as human pledges of loyalty and remembrance, little more.[17] Because neither of the antagonists resolved the issue in an entirely satisfactory way, they left the field open to others. By the 1550s, in contrast, the lines of battle were drawn more firmly. Hard-line second-generation Lutherans like Johannes Brenz or, especially, Joachim Westphal of Hamburg insisted that Christ's risen body was physically, corporeally, objectively present in every true Eucharist, according to the doctrine of 'ubiquity'. Against them, John Calvin taught that Christ was *spiritually* present, but treated the idea of a physical body infinitely extended in space with some derision.[18] In due course the Lutherans' insistence on the necessary role of the sacraments would entail a range of further disagreements with 'Calvinist' teaching and practice.[19] By this point there was little more theology left to be worked out; it remained only for the antagonists to rail at each other with increasing bitterness, which they duly did.

Into this increasingly charged atmosphere of theological and confessional hostility, there arrived the most tangible and poignant expression of a residual belief that all Protestants ultimately belonged to the same cause: namely, the congregations of exiles and refugees. By the early 1550s there had been French exile congregations in Strasbourg, and also in Wesel and Frankfurt, for some time.[20] With the death of Edward VI in the early summer of 1553, those exile Churches which had settled in England, including Valérand Poullain's French Church at Glastonbury, were sent back across the Channel. Poullain found himself minister of the French congregation at Frankfurt when the English began to arrive there. Host communities which received

---

understanding of the Real Presence in the 1520s', *Sixteenth Century Journal*, 16 (1985), pp. 45 ff.

[17] On the principles underlying Zwingli's attitude to the sacraments, see e.g. W.P. Stephens, *The Theology of Huldrych Zwingli* (Oxford, 1986), pp. 180–93.

[18] The debate between Calvin and Joachim Westphal may be followed through Calvin, *Institutes*, IV, xvii, 20–34, and Westphal's tracts against Calvin, which are listed in P. Barth and W. Niesel (eds), *Ioannis Calvini Opera Selecta* (5 vols, Munich, 1926–52), V, xi; also Calvin's tracts in reply.

[19] On the disagreements between later Lutherans and Calvinists, see e.g. B. Nischan, *Prince, People and Confession: The Second Reformation in Brandenburg* (Philadelphia, PA, 1994), pp. 137 ff.; Jill Raitt, *The Colloquy of Montbéliard: Religion and Politics in the Sixteenth Century* (New York and Oxford, 1993), pp. 73 ff.

[20] On the French at Strasbourg, see Abray, *The People's Reformation*, pp. 131 ff.; Jean Rott, 'L'Église des refugiés de langue française à Strasbourg au xvie siècle', *Bulletin de la Société d'Histoire du Protestantisme français*, 122 (1976), pp. 525–50.

refugee Churches faced an acute version of the more general problem confronted by Protestant Churches which tried to show solidarity with one another. They had to be sure that they supported only 'true' reformed gospellers, not sectarians, Anabaptists, or those whose doctrine deviated too dangerously far from their own. Even something so simple as sending a diplomatic letter entailed serious soul-searching. In 1557 the theologians of Lutheran Württemberg needed much persuasion before they would write to Henri II of France to plead with him not to persecute the Waldensian congregations of Piedmont, who were then sheltering under the moral protection of Geneva.[21] The issue was entirely predictable: should a Lutheran principality support the cause of 'Calvinist' Protestants whose sacramental views were at variance with their own?

Even when an exile Church had been received into a German city, as the French were at Wesel and Frankfurt, anxieties over the theology of the Communion continued to trouble hosts and guests alike. Trouble broke out between the Frankfurt Lutherans under Hartmann Beyer and the French congregation settled there under Valérand Poullain in the autumn of 1555. Beyer and his colleagues tried to have the French expelled, because of their non-Lutheran Eucharistic theology and in particular because of the views of the *émigré* Pole, Jan Laski, who was then living with the exiles at Frankfurt. Only the patience of the magistracy, and, one suspects, the support of Johann von Glauburg, the unofficial patron of the exile Churches, protected them from stronger measures.[22] There was no protection, however, from the litigious hostility of Hartmann Beyer, whom Hubert Languet would later describe as an 'intimate' of the ultra-Lutheran polemicist Joachim Westphal.[23] The row between Lutherans and reformed French at Frankfurt dragged on through 1556 and into 1557, filling many columns of Calvin's correspondence. The increasingly desperate hope was to find some face-saving formula which would allow the French to represent themselves as adhering to the Lutheran Augsburg confession.[24] In

---

[21] On this incident, see Euan Cameron, 'One Reformation or Many: Protestant identities in the later Reformation in Germany', in O.P. Grell and R.W. Scribner (eds), *Tolerance and Intolerance in the European Reformation* (Cambridge, 1996), pp. 111–13.

[22] G. Baum, E. Cunitz and E. Reuss (eds), *Ioannis Calvini Opera Quae Supersunt Omnia* (59 vols, Braunschweig, Berlin, 1853–1900), in CR, vols XXIX–LXXXVII, XLIII, cols 819, 884, 891; XLIV, cols 21–2.

[23] C.G. Bretschneider et al., (eds), *Philippi Melanthonis Opera Quae Supersunt Omnia*, in CR, vols I–XXVIII (Halle, 1834–60), IX, col. 484: 'Hartmannum Baier, concionatorem, qui est intimus Vestphalo'.

[24] See the correspondence in CR, XLIV, cols 53–6, 58–65, 89–98, 201–13.

September 1556 Calvin even visited Frankfurt himself to try to calm matters.[25]

Meanwhile, the French Church at Wesel also suffered from similar pressure either to conform to Lutheran beliefs and practices or leave. In these straits the exiles made the extremely astute decision to appeal to the adjudication of Philipp Melanchthon, the leader of moderate Lutheran opinion, whose views on the Eucharist were closer to Calvin's than Westphal's.[26] Melanchthon consistently supported the exiles' cause as far as his influence extended.[27] A delicious piece of gossip on this topic was reported to Calvin by Hubert Languet in a letter of 15 March 1558. On a visit to Frankfurt, Philipp Melanchthon had summoned Hartmann Beyer to meet him:

> During dinner, conversation turned to the refugees, and [Philipp] severely criticized [Beyer], and warned him, that he and his colleagues ... should set aside their hatred towards the wretched exiles and refugees for Christ's sake; he said that anyone who was not moved by their misfortunes ought not to be called a human being, far less a Christian. They should imitate their magistracy's kindness, though they ought rather to have exceeded it. When Hartmann [Beyer] answered that neither he nor his colleagues were acting from hatred, but simply doing this to achieve concord and agreement in doctrine in the churches, Philipp, now even more agitated, said that there had always been in the Church people who would deceive the simple with guile and fair words of this sort, and disguise their cruelty and hatred towards God and man. There was an agreement between the German and exile churches in doctrine, save that the leaders of the exiles wished clarification on the Eucharist ... Hartmann ... wrote all these things to Westphal, who for that reason is now no less hostile to Master Philipp than he is to yourself [Calvin].[28]

This incident shows how the middle-ranking reformers – figures of essentially local importance such as Beyer and Westphal – who lacked the breadth of vision, and dare one say it, the humanity of their leaders, could drag whole Churches into disputes and uncertainty over issues of doctrine.

On the other hand, exile Churches could also make trouble for themselves without any help at all from the neighbouring indigenous Church. The French congregation at Frankfurt was riven by the most dreadful

---

[25] CR, XLIV, cols 280–82.

[26] CR, XLIV, cols 286–8, 307–13, 323–5, 341–2, 377–8, 395–9, 517–18.

[27] In CR, IX, cols 179–80, Melanchthon wrote to the Frankfurt magistrates that he thought that the exiles should not be driven out because of disagreements over doctrine, and he had already given the same advice to Wesel.

[28] CR, IX, cols 484–5.

discords before the departure of its pastor Valérand Poullain late in
1556. There was concern over the regularity of his election as pastor; he
had tried to promote his old allies from Glastonbury as elders; and he
had involved himself in a running feud with Augustin Legrand, a merchant of the French congregation, leading to a host of further
recriminations. The row eventually went to the arbitration of Calvin,
Laski, Robert Horne, Laurent de Normandie and others.[29] When we
turn to consider the quarrels and feuds within the English-speaking
Churches of the exile, we should remember that for the continental
reformers, the disputes of the English at Frankfurt paled into insignifi-
cance before those of their French brethren.

The story of the 'troubles at Frankfurt' has been told and retold, both
from the perspective of Knox's biography and from that of the later
controversies in Elizabethan Protestantism.[30] There has not, however,
been so full an exploration of the motives and attitudes of John Knox
and his antagonists in terms of the wider theological concerns of the
Reformation. From one point of view, no doubt, the troubles at
Frankfurt ought to be seen as a small local difficulty among the English,
barely related to wider European issues; yet from another, the arguments which they threw up had much broader references and
implications.

Knox arrived in Frankfurt from Geneva in the autumn of 1554 at the
request of the English exiles to serve as a minister to the congregation
which had settled there in the previous summer. The English congregation had been allowed to use the French exile Church in the city, on
condition that the two groups of exiles embraced more or less the same
beliefs and practised (approximately) the same rites. This first group of
English then revised their liturgy, based loosely on the 1552 Book of
Common Prayer, so as to bring it closer to the French reformed orders

---

[29] The most important documents of this scandal are found in CR, XLIV, cols 288–
300.

[30] The standard modern discussion of the troubles at Frankfurt is in A.G. Dickens,
The English Reformation (London, 1964), pp. 289–93; the controversial primary source
for this episode, published in the middle 1570s, is *A Brieff discours off the troubles
begonne at Franckford in Germany Anno Domini 1554* (n.p., 1575, but 1574 in some
copies); on the details of this, see P. Collinson, 'The Authorship of *A Brieff discours off
the troubles begonne at Franckford*', *JEH*, 9 (1958), pp. 188–208. Exhaustive discussion
of the text is found in M.A. Simpson, *John Knox and the Troubles begun at Frankfurt*
(West Linton, 1975), though this is flawed by a tendency to claim that nearly every
source-text has been falsified by later English disputants, even one which survives as an
autograph copy in Geneva.

devised by Calvin at Strasbourg and revised by Poullain.[31] Barely a month after Knox's arrival the English Church at Strasbourg began to put pressure on the Frankfurt congregation, through letters and a visit by Edmund Grindal and Richard Chambers, to conform more closely to the 1552 English Prayer Book. The implication is that Frankfurt was viewed as a more attractive place of refuge than the other cities, and that exiles based elsewhere wished to move there, and hoped to find a properly established Church of England in exile. The negotiations with Strasbourg ran into the sand in the winter of 1554–55. Meanwhile those at Frankfurt found themselves embroiled in controversy over what order of service to use. Knox found himself in a quandary: he would neither adopt the full Genevan liturgy without the consent of the other English congregations, nor would he submit to some unacceptable features of the Prayer Book.[32] After consultation with Calvin, a temporary revised version of the Book of Common Prayer was adopted, to be used until the end of April 1555.[33]

Into this tense but peaceful state of affairs arrived a new group of exiles led by the academic and future bishop Richard Cox, who immediately showed themselves impatient to restore some discarded elements of the Prayer Book. They began to say the versicles and responses, and one of them read the Litany from the pulpit on the following Sunday. Knox promptly preached against the breaking of earlier agreements, and used the occasion to criticize not only the Prayer Book but the whole Edwardian Reformation. Soon a rift opened up between Knox and Cox, which reached the ears of the magistrates.[34] The magistrates simply reiterated their earlier instructions that the English exiles use the French order of service. Knox's opponents then resorted to a line of attack better calculated to impress the city fathers. They pointed out that certain passages in his *A Faithful Admonition to the Professors of God's Truth in England*, published in 1554,[35] could be construed as treasonable against the Emperor Charles V. The magistracy, quite un-

---

[31] Knox, *Works*, IV, pp. 9–11; on Poullain's adaptations of Calvin's liturgy, see W.D. Maxwell, *John Knox's Genevan Service Book 1556: The Liturgical Portions of the Genevan Service Book* (Edinburgh, 1931), pp. 20 ff., and A.C. Honders (ed.), *Valerandus Pollanus Liturgia Sacra 1551–1555* (Leiden, 1970). A version of Poullain's liturgy was published for the exile Churches at Frankfurt in 1554, with the names of both French and English subscribers: see Knox, *Works*, IV, pp. 144–5.

[32] Knox, *Works*, IV, pp. 12–21; the Genevan liturgy in question was *The forme of common praiers used in the churches of Geneva: The mynystration of the sacramentes ... made by master John Calvyne*, trans. W. Huycke (n.p., but Whitchurch, London, 1550).

[33] Knox, *Works*, IV, pp. 21–31.

[34] Ibid., IV, pp. 31–7.

[35] The text of the *Faithful Admonition* is in ibid., III, pp. 251–330.

derstandably sensitive after the imperial attacks on the free cities' status mounted after 1548, suggested that Knox ought to leave rather than be expelled, which he duly did on 26 March 1555. Knox settled at Geneva, and used it as a base for visits to France and Scotland. That autumn his former ally William Whittingham and a segment of the Frankfurt Church followed him there and founded their own community, worshipping according to a version of the Genevan rite.[36] The English remaining at Frankfurt then agreed a revised version of the Book of Common Prayer for their own services, though neither this agreement nor Cox's departure from Zurich saved them from further dissension in the remaining three to four years of the exile.[37]

So, Knox broke with the English over the Prayer Book; or rather, Knox and one section of the English broke with another section of the English over particular elements in the Prayer Book, which none of them actually wished to keep entire. From the Scots perspective, the troubles at Frankfurt can be read as a prelude or foreshadowing of the epic struggle over the 1637 liturgy and the Covenants. From the English point of view, they were the first round in a battle for 'further Reformation' which would be fought out in Convocation, Parliament and the counsels of the great through the Elizabethan and early Jacobean periods. In haste to read history forwards into subsequent national events and movements, it is all too easy to overlook the *reasons*, the arguments, which animated the debate over the liturgies of the exile Churches of Frankfurt and Geneva. The disputants did not think that they were acting out the first scenes in the respective historical dramas of the Churches of England and Scotland. They were struggling to think their way to a reformed order appropriate to their circumstances as a cramped, tense, sensitive *émigré* community. They were balancing different priorities with an eye to those remaining in England, as well as to the wider international reformed communion. The remainder of this chapter is devoted to exploring further these arguments and priorities, as they emerge from the letters, liturgies, and other writings of the period.

John Knox left a strikingly coherent set of arguments for his preferences in the matter of worship, some of which can be traced back to his first major writings on Protestant theology from around 1550. In that

---

[36] Ibid., IV, pp. 50–51; for the service order, see Maxwell, *Knox's Genevan Service Book 1556*, *passim*, and Knox, *Works*, IV, pp. 141–214.

[37] The 1555 service order is edited in Robin A. Leaver (ed.), *The Liturgy of the Frankfurt Exiles 1555* (Bramcote Grove, 1984); see also Dickens, *English Reformation*, pp. 292–4.

year Knox had been summoned to explain the sermons which he had been preaching at Berwick. He appeared before the Council of the North at Newcastle on 4 April 1550 and delivered his *Vindication of the Doctrine that the Sacrifice of the Mass is Idolatry*.[38] In this he urged as one of the principal planks of his argument that 'all worship not commanded by God is idolatry'. Any 'human invention', no matter how good or laudable its inventors might think it to be, was idolatrous *unless* it had specific warrant in the Word of God.[39] In other words, Knox's position was exclusive, as was typical in the reformed rather than Lutheran tradition: one should allow only such worship as could be proved to be scriptural, rather than abolish only what was explicitly contrary to Scripture. More important for Knox, no doubt, was the need to resist the *Catholics'* argument that long-established forms of prayer should be retained unless something could be shown to be wrong with them. This same exclusiveness appears in the preface to the 1556 English service-book of Geneva, and in the explanatory rubric at the end of the Communion rite: 'without his woorde and warrante, there is nothyng in this holy action attempted'.[40] When English supporters of the Prayer Book would ask what was wrong with their liturgy, Knox's response was preordained.

This fear of the 'idolatry', which Knox saw in any worship devised and defended by merely human ingenuity, holds the key to Knox's otherwise rather surprising allergy to particular parts of the 1552 Prayer Book, above all the versicles and responses in Mattins and Evensong, and the Litany. It was these apparently innocuous set phrases of prayer and worship which proved the sticking-point at Frankfurt. On the third day of the last-ditch discussions between Cox, Lever, Whittingham and Knox in the house of Valérand Poullain, Cox insisted that 'I will have' ('Ego volo habeo') the opening versicles and responses. Knox replied by referring to the

> 'Domine labia', 'Deus in Adjutorium', and 'Deum laudamus' and other prescript words, not read in Scripture, [as] an Order borrowed of the Papists and Papistical; then began the tragedie, and our consultation ended. Who was most blame-worthy, God shall judge; and if I spake fervently, to God was I fervent.[41]

Already in describing the Prayer Book to Calvin, Whittingham and Knox had taken advantage of writing in Latin rather than English, to render the names of all the traditional versicles in their medieval forms,

---

[38] Knox, *Works*, III, pp. 29–70.
[39] Ibid., III, pp. 34–46.
[40] Ibid., IV, pp. 160, 197.
[41] Ibid., IV, pp. 34, 46.

including the *Kyries* in Greek, quietly omitting to mention that they were, in fact, said in English.[42] Had Knox not begun his career as a reformer with a sweeping denunciation of all non-scriptural set forms of worship as 'idolatry', he might not have shown such sensitivity. Would he have objected to the English Litany so much had he not preached at Newcastle that, the first time the Greater Litany was said in the time of Pope Gregory the Great, 80 people had forthwith died of the plague in the congregation where it was said?[43]

However, with Knox's objection to the Litany one comes to another important aspect of his religious aversion to set forms of words, which links Knox to a much wider trend in early modern religious thought. In reporting the 1552 Prayer Book Litany to Calvin, Knox and Whittingham slightingly described its '*conjuring* [of God] by the mystery of the incarnation, the holy nativity and circumcision, by his baptism and temptation'.[44] The reference to 'conjuring' was not gratuitous. It denoted the use of holy words as powerful things in themselves, a belief which was embedded in popular Catholicism in the Middle Ages, and was a primary target of the reformers. The establishing of any set pattern of words tended to imply that only those words had spiritual power embedded in them. Already in 1550, Knox had mocked the Catholic belief in the power of the 'five words', *Hoc est enim corpus meum*, at the heart of the Canon of the Mass: 'O Papists! is God a juglar? Useth he certane number of wordis in performing his intent?'[45] In the preface to the baptism rite in the 1556 Genevan Service order, the reader was warned 'that the sacraments are not ordeined of God to be used in privat corners *as charmes or sorceries*, but left to the congregation, and necessarely annexed to God's word'. Baptism was not necessary to salvation (despite what Lutherans would later insist).[46] In the rite itself the minister explicitly denied 'that we thinke any suche vertue or power to be included in the visible water or outward action'; the spiritual effects of baptism would follow 'in tyme convenient', not automatically or mechanically, or at once.[47] The point of all this is, that when Whittingham or Knox denounced the 'superstition' in traditional

---

[42] *CR*, XLIII, cols 340–41.

[43] Knox, *Works*, III, pp. 38–40.

[44] *CR*, XLIII, no. 2059, col 341; compare the version from the *Brieff Discours* in Knox, *Works*, IV, p. 23.

[45] Knox, *Works*, III, pp. 50–51; for traditional beliefs about the the consecration of the Eucharist, see e.g. Eamon Duffy, *The Stripping of the Altars: Traditional Religion in England, 1400–1580* (New Haven and London, 1992), pp. 95 ff.

[46] For the Lutheran position on emergency baptism, see the authorities noted above in note 19.

[47] Knox, *Works*, IV, pp. 186–8.

worship, they were not merely bandying words. They attacked the belief that particular non-scriptural forms of words ought to be used to secure the appropriate spiritual benefits. In other words, they applied the early modern critique of superstition, which was largely concerned with the power of words and symbols, to the Book of Common Prayer itself.[48]

One may press the analogy between Knox's attack on prescribed worship and the 'critique of superstition' just a little further. Superstition-writers in the late Middle Ages and Counter-Reformation argued that set formulae used to secure spiritual benefits, if they were not authorized by the Church, must have been taught by the Devil as signs to the demons to work their magic.[49] They were sometimes described as the antithesis or inversion of the true sacraments.[50] Similarly stark antitheses were drawn by Knox, in his *Godly Letter to the Faithful in London* of 1554, between trusting in God and His Word, as opposed to trusting human inventions: 'God may not abyd that our bodeis serve the devill in joyning our selves with ydolatrie.' 'Greater iniquitie was never frome the beginning, than is containit in worshipping of an abominabill ydoll; for it is *the seill of the league whilk the Devill hes maid* with the pestilent sons of the Antichryst.' The Mass, as a marginal note to this text said, was 'the devills sacrament and seale', like the 'tacit pact' of the sorcerer or witch.[51] The practical purpose of this rhetoric was simply to dissuade as many Protestants as possible in Mary Tudor's England from attending Mass. In arguing thus, however, Knox attacked the Mass with all the weight of early modern demonology: the Mass was, literally, diabolical.[52] No wonder

---

[48] Compare Heinrich Bullinger, *The Decades of Henry Bullinger*, trans. 'H.I.' and ed. T. Harding (4 vols, Parker Society, Cambridge, 1849–52), IV, pp. 254–60, for a characteristic reformed critique of 'superstitious' Catholic claims about the power of words.

[49] The idea that ritual observances not based on orthodox religion imply an implicit pact with the Devil is a late medieval commonplace: for a classic instance, see Jean Gerson's *De Erroribus circa Artem Magicam et Articulis Reprobatis*, in H. Institoris and J. Sprenger, *Malleus Maleficarum*, (3 vols, Lyon, 1669), II, pt ii, pp. 165–7, 172.

[50] The idea that superstitious rites, and magic in general, were 'inversions' of the true divine order is fully explored in Stuart Clark, *Thinking with Demons: The Idea of Witchcraft in Early Modern Europe* (Oxford, 1997), pp. 31–93.

[51] Knox, *Works*, III, pp. 196–7, 212. For the expression 'sacraments of the devil' compare its repeated use by the later Lutheran Johann Georg Godelmann in his *Tractatus de Magis, Veneficis et Lamiis, deque his recte cognoscendis et puniendis* (Frankfurt, 1601), p. 91: 'But when divine words and names, or holy sentences, are converted to other uses, and to superstitious cures of illnesses, then that will be an abuse of the word of God, and they will become the sacraments of the devil, to the utmost blasphemy of God.'

[52] See also e.g. Knox, *Works*, III, pp. 284–6.

that any verbal borrowings from the old liturgy in the Prayer Book were anathema.

In early modern thought, stark antitheses between the divine and the demonic and a critique of superstition went hand in hand (improbable as it may seem to modern eyes) with an unflinching rationalism.[53] Belief in the magical power of words was wrong, because it abused the purpose of words, which was to communicate and instruct. This attitude underlay Knox's insistence that baptism be a public ceremony, a 'visible sermon' rather than a quasi-magical rite performed in secret. It followed, therefore, that words must be used for their proper purpose, to teach and chasten. This explains why Knox found yet further fault with the 1552 Prayer Book, in that it contained a triflingly short Catechism, covering only two leaves of paper, and nothing that most Catholics could not accept.[54] It also fits in with his complaint that the 1552 book contained no provisions for discipline, and thus lacked an essential third 'mark' of the true Church.[55]

Knox's adversaries at Frankfurt, Richard Cox, Thomas Lever and the rest had their reasons for their own stubborn defence of the English liturgy, as emotive and compelling as those which inspired Knox, though not perhaps quite so consistent. The heart of their defence of the Prayer Book seems to have been sensitivity that a godly order devised by devout people was being attacked without good reason. The more the book was criticized, the more they defended it. Where Knox wished to have specific scriptural 'warrant' for every ceremony, the defenders of the Prayer Book sought good reasons before abolishing them. As their rather testy letter of self-justification argued to Calvin on 20 September 1555, Whittingham and his party had left the Church 'solely on account of ceremonies which even they themselves dare no longer affirm to be ungodly, or can prove to be at variance with the word of God, or in any way unprofitable'.[56] As Thomas Sampson had reported even earlier, those who wished to retain the ceremonies did so partly 'be-

---

[53] For the 'rational' quality of early modern demonology, see Clark, *Thinking with Demons*, pp. 151 ff.

[54] CR, XLIII, col. 343; Knox, *Works*, IV, p. 26.

[55] Knox, *Works*, IV, pp. 33, 44, and compare the Genevan order in ibid., 172 f., 203 ff.

[56] CR, XLIII, col. 781; translated in Hastings Robinson (ed.), *Original Letters relative to the English Reformation: Written during the Reigns of King Henry VIII, King Edward VI, and Queen Mary: chiefly from the archives of Zurich* (2 vols, Parker Society, Cambridge, 1846–47) [paginated as one vol.], p. 762.

cause the opposite party can assign no just reason why the form should be changed'.[57]

There was another reason, even less theological. The 1552 Prayer Book might have been cherished with the lukewarm enthusiasm usually reserved for the products of a committee, as long as Edward VI had lived. In Mary's reign, however, pastors and people began to suffer imprisonment and death for their adherence to the Reformation, and implicitly to the book which embodied it. If Cranmer upheld the book from prison, was it not a slight to him, in his mortal danger, to impugn its rightness? As early as November 1554 the English Church at Strasbourg called on Whittingham's group at Frankfurt to restore their order 'to its former *perfection* of the laste had in Englande, so farre as possiblie can be atteined, least by much alteringe of the same we shulde seeme to condemne the chief authors therof, who as they nowe suffer, so are they moste redie to confirme that facte with the price of their blouds'.[58] In the circumstances of exile for some and impending martyrdom for others, Knox's stubborn continuance of the liturgical disputes of 1550–52 must have seemed simply to be in bad taste. Yet neither he nor Calvin could see why any one step on the road to reformation should be privileged or canonized in this way.[59]

In this light, the famous demand of Cox and his allies to have the 'face of an English church' while settled in exile meant much more than the liturgical equivalent of afternoon tea and cucumber sandwiches in a foreign land.[60] To insist on preserving the rites and forms of Cranmer's Prayer Book was to show solidarity with a leader in chains. It was to stake the claim of the English order to be as 'perfect' a reformed Church as any of the continental models to which others, including Knox, routinely appealed. It led them to insist to Calvin, without any apparent authority from the Frankfurt magistrates, that they had been 'allowed to adopt the rites of our native country'[61] rather than those of the French Church, under whose wing they actually resided. The wish was father to the thought.

Yet the Coxians did not follow their avowed principles with any great consistency. As Cox himself pointed out to Calvin on 5 April 1555, they had for the sake of peace negotiated away surplices, crosses, private baptisms, confirmation, kneeling at Communion and the use of a ring

---

[57] CR, XLIII, col. 447; translated in Robinson (ed.), *Original Letters*, p. 171.

[58] Knox, *Works*, IV, pp. 15–16; cf. also Sampson in Robinson (ed.), *Original Letters*, pp. 170–71.

[59] Compare Calvin's response in CR, XLIII, col. 394.

[60] For the 'face of an English Church', see Knox, *Works*, IV, pp. 32, 42.

[61] CR, XLIII, col. 552; translated in Robinson (ed.), *Original Letters*, p. 754; and Knox, *Works*, IV, pp. 55–7.

in marriage, while still denying, rather unconvincingly, that they thought there was anything 'impure and papistical' in such details.[62] They resented being criticized by Calvin, in the matter of 'lights and crosses', as though they still used the full paraphernalia of the 1552 book.[63] To some extent, they tried to have things both ways. Nor did their accommodation to continental patterns stop with their initial simplifications of the 1552 book. In the summer of 1555, as it has been plausibly inferred, they produced a manuscript order of service based on the Book of Common Prayer, which leaned even closer to French 're-formed' practice.[64] By omitting several of the prayers and versicles, and possibly substituting metrical psalms for chanting, they turned their Eucharistic rite into something sufficiently close to Poullain's French order to satisfy the magistrates.[65] In other words, once Knox was out of the way, Cox and his group do not appear to have taken advantage of his absence to restore those ceremonies which they so cherished; on the contrary, they pared them away yet further. Moreover, they responded to some of Knox's criticisms. The sparse catechism of the 1552 book was enlarged with the addition of material from John Ponet's full and controversially Protestant Edwardian catechism, though still preserving the eccentric order of the 1552 version. Later, in March 1557, Calvin's own catechism was adopted, as it had already been by the Genevan congregation.[66] Secondly, the reformed 'discipline', which Edward's death had prevented Cranmer from realizing for the Church of England, was supplied by the exiles for their own circumstances, including provision for the receiving and disciplining of members, and the election of elders and deacons after the French and Genevan pattern.[67] After further dissensions at Frankfurt this discipline was revised and amplified early in 1557.[68] One must then conclude that the ideological differences between Knox and his Frankfurt adversaries were really fewer and

---

[62] CR, XLIII, col. 553; Robinson (ed.), Original Letters, p. 754.

[63] CR, XLIII, cols 777–8; translated in Robinson (ed.), Original Letters, pp. 757–8; Knox, Works, IV, pp. 62–6.

[64] Edited in Leaver, Liturgy (as above, note 37), based on BL MS. Egerton 2836.

[65] Ibid., pp. 5, 8–9, and for the reconstructed Eucharist, pp. 23–33.

[66] Ibid., pp. 12–17; the Ponet Catechism is in Joseph Ketley (ed.), The Two Liturgies, A.D. 1549, and A.D. 1552: with other documents set forth by authority in the reign of King Edward VI, viz. The Order of Communion, 1548. The Primer, 1553. The Catechism and Articles, 1553. Catechismus brevis, 1553 (Cambridge, 1844), pp. 493–525, 541–71; for the adoption of the Geneva Catechism, see Leaver, Liturgy, p. 18, n. 2, and for its use by Knox and Whittingham, see Maxwell, Knox's Genevan Service Book 1556, pp. 65, 79, 83.

[67] Leaver, Liturgy, pp. 17–20.

[68] Dickens, English Reformation, pp. 292–3; Collinson, 'Authorship', p. 189, summarizes the disputes which the disciplinary issue caused.

slighter than the rhetoric employed suggests. Cox, Lever, and the others were willing to make changes, without compulsion, once Knox was out of the way, to which they would not consent while still under his apocalyptic glare. There may well be something in the suggestion that Richard Cox had never forgiven Knox for persuading the Privy Council to insist on the insertion of the 'Black Rubric' which explained away kneeling at Communion, into the 1552 book. The appearance of this rubric, pasted into the book after binding in some of the early copies, must have been at best an embarrassment to its compilers.[69]

In a wider and longer context, the debates which so exercised Knox in the mid-1550s look even more rarified. If the great divide in continental Protestantism in the 1550s was between Lutheran and reformed doctrines of the Eucharist, that question was simply not an issue between Knox and Cox. There may be good reasons to debate when Thomas Cranmer had crossed the Rubicon which divided Lutheran from reformed Eucharistic theology;[70] there can be little doubt that all supporters of the 1552 book, and *a fortiori* those like Knox who wished to progress beyond it, held a spiritualizing, reformed sacramental theology. The strife over liturgy occurred between those who agreed on all the essentials, and many of the peripheral details, of doctrine.

Nor did the agreement and coincidence between Knox and his English colleagues stop there. In different circumstances the English reformers would become as frustrated by the insistence on ceremonies as Knox had been, though they did not express their feelings with the same rhetoric. In the early months of Elizabeth's reign the future bishops of Protestant England were largely excluded from the discussion of the 'scenic apparatus' of worship; John Jewel complained to Piermartire Vermigli that laughable trivia were now earnestly discussed, 'as though the Christian religion could not exist without rags'.[71] Having found

---

[69] For the pasting in of the Black Rubric after the 1552 book was printed, see Ketley, *Two Liturgies*, p. 283 and n. 4.

[70] For Cranmer's Eucharistic beliefs, see Peter Newman Brooks, *Thomas Cranmer's Doctrine of the Eucharist : An Essay in Historical Development* (London, 1965); Basil Hall's response to Brooks, in Paul Ayris and D.G. Selwyn (eds), *Thomas Cranmer: Churchman and Scholar* (London, 1993); Diarmaid MacCulloch, *Thomas Cranmer: A Life* (New Haven, CT, 1996), esp. pp. 398 ff. Note also the reference in Knox, *Works*, III, pp. 278–9.

[71] Hastings Robinson (ed.), *The Zurich letters, comprising the correspondence of several English bishops and others, with some of the Helvetian reformers, during the early part of the reign of Queen Elizabeth* (Parker Society, Cambridge, 1842), p. 23, and the original on p. 13 of the *Epistolae Tigurinae* (ibid., separately paginated).

themselves on the conservative wing of European reformed Protestantism, Cox and his allies soon discovered that they had an increasingly
vocal Roman Catholic opposition with which to contend both inside
and beyond England. In this debate the forthright adversarial arguments foreshadowed by John Knox began to reveal their usefulness.

Polemical pieces written to support the Church of England against its
adversaries adopted exactly the same arguments from the critique of
superstitious worship, and the antithesis between divine and devilish
religion, which underpinned Knox's treatises in the 1550s. John Bale,
who had been a signatory to the letters defending the Coxians' conduct
to Calvin, wrote in his *The Latter Examination of Mistress Anne Askew*
in terms identical to those used by Knox:

> the mass (which is, in all points, of all that filthy antichrist's
> creation) took she for the most execrable idol on earth. And rightly
> ... look what properties any idol hath had, or feats hath wrought
> yet since the world's beginning, the pope's prodigious mass hath
> had and wrought the same ... .

Bale equated the rituals of the Mass with pagan sacrifices and Jewish
rituals, noting that it was regularly used as a talisman by sorcerers and
necromancers.[72] In his *The Image of Both Churches*, written during the
exile, Bale looked forward with apocalyptic vision to the time when
'she [the great whore] shall be wholly turned over into the bottomless
pit again with all her heathenish ceremonies, superstitions and sorceries'.[73]
James Calfhill, an Oxford theologian who became Archdeacon of Col-
chester under Elizabeth, in his *A Treatise of the Crosse* of 1565 drew
parallels and antitheses between God and His prophets and the Devil
and his jugglers; he associated Catholicism with the diabolical subversion of true religion, and compared priests to 'witches and sorcerers'.[74]
These sorts of arguments adapted traditional demonology to the cause
of defending the Reformation in a conventionally Protestant way. The
irony lies in the fact that early Prayer Book enthusiasts would use such
arguments quite freely, while defending a service which contained many
traditional elements.

Knox was not even unique in the subversive and apocalyptic tone of
his political writing. The Coxian party contrived Knox's expulsion from
Frankfurt by pointing out that certain passages in his *Faithful Admoni-*

---

[72] John Bale, 'The Latter Examination of Mistress Anne Askew', in H. Christmas (ed.),
Select Works of John Bale, D.D., Bishop of Ossory (Parker Society, Cambridge, 1849),
pp. 235–7.

[73] Ibid., p. 260; there are many other such references in this work.

[74] J. Calfhill, *An Answer to John Martiall's Treatise of the Cross*, ed. R. Gibbings
(Parker Society, Cambridge, 1846), pp. 12 ff.

tion to the Professors of God's Truth were highly inflammatory against the Emperor and the Emperor's family, including, of course, his cousin and daughter-in-law Mary Tudor and his son Philip. Within at most about a year of Knox's expulsion, the former Edwardian bishop John Ponet was working on his *Treatise of Politike Power*, published at Strasbourg around the time of his death in late summer 1556.[75] The two works make for a most interesting comparison. Knox's treatise takes the form of a long sermon about the storm on the Sea of Galilee, and Jesus's appearance to the disciples walking on the water. Ponet's is a reasoned presentation of the origin of political power, its purpose and right use. That is, however, the largest difference between the two works. Knox the preacher, both in the *Faithful Admonition* and the earlier *Godly Letter*, made a wide range of political observations. He savaged Mary and her counsellors for bringing in foreign domination contrary to her promise and statute law,[76] just as Ponet accused Bishop Edmund Bonner of potential treason by advising the surrender of Calais and Berwick.[77] Ponet, the ostensibly political writer, included apocalyptic warnings of portents, plagues and misbirths which he believed announced God's coming judgement on England.[78]

Both treatises were essentially religious in character. They uttered prophetic denunciations of the Tudor government for restoring 'the beastly popyshe masse', likened to the golden calf made by Aaron at the people's behest (Ponet), and thereby allowing the Devil to reign 'by idolatry, superstition, and tyranny' (Knox).[79] Both Knox and Ponet warned their readers against the 'Nicodemite' solution, of attending Catholic services and showing outward loyalty to the Roman rite while cherishing their Protestant beliefs in secret: it was far better to flee into exile.[80] Both likened Mary to Jezebel, and took gruesome delight in recalling the dreadful judgements meted out by God sooner or later to tyrants in the Old Testament.[81]

Both writers treated the Catholic bishops and the *politique* counsellors who surrounded Mary with withering scorn. There was, however, a slight difference in style. Knox wrote an invective which was erudite, poetic, at times brilliantly epigraphic and sarcastic. The Devil raged in his 'obedient servaunts, wyly Winchester, dreaming Duresme, and bloudy

---

[75] [John Ponet], *A Shorte Treatise of Politike Power, and of the true Obedience which subiectes owe to kynges and other civile Governours* (n.p., 1556). STC, no. 20178.

[76] Knox, *Works*, III, pp. 294–7.

[77] Ponet, *Treatise*, sig. Eii^r.

[78] Ibid., sigs Kiii^v ff.

[79] Ibid., sig. Bii^r; Knox, *Works*, III, p. 285.

[80] Ponet, *Treatise*, sigs Eiv^v ff; cf. Knox, *Works*, III, pp. 195–6.

[81] Ibid., sig. Div^v; Knox, *Works*, III, pp. 185–6, 293–4.

Bonner'. Yet one of the worst offenders was Lord Treasurer William Paulet, brilliantly depicted in the role of Sobna or Shebna, the corrupt court official under King Hezekiah. He had denounced Mary as a bastard and papist in Edward's time, only to emerge as a Catholic himself under Mary: 'which of the counsel, I saye, had these and greater persuasions against Marye, to whom he now crouches and kneleth? Sobna the Treasurer'.[82] In contrast, Bishop Ponet insulted his opponents with every weapon to hand, some of them in none too good taste. He mocked Mary's phantom pregnancy, suggesting that midwives had been corrupted to declare that 'when [her] belly is puffed up with the dropsy' there was a child on the way.[83] Edmund Bonner, Bishop of London, was told that he had no right to be a priest, far less a bishop, since his father was a 'savage' and his mother an 'errante hoore'. Cardinal Reginald Pole, Archbishop of Canterbury, Ponet deftly transformed into 'Carnal Phoole'.[84]

Yet, of course, it was as an advocate of treason and tyrannicide that Knox was denounced to the Frankfurt magistrates. In fact, even in this John Ponet wrote rather more fiercely and freely than Knox. In the *Godly Letter* Knox so far restrained himself to say only that ordinary people should not set about the killing of idolaters; that belonged to the civil magistrates, whereas ordinary citizens should only 'avoid participation and company of their abominations'.[85] In the *Faithful Admonition*, Knox did include a prayer to God to 'stirre up some Phinees, Helias, or Jehu, that the bloude of abhominable idolaters may pacifie Goddes wrath'; but the emphasis, there and elsewhere, lay on the special judgement of God against idolatry, rather than indiscriminate encouragement to tyrannicide. Ponet appears to have been less wary: the law of nature taught that an 'incurable member' might be cut off; the ancients regarded those who killed tyrants as public benefactors; Jehu, the subject of Jezebel, brought about her downfall and death. Ehud killed his overlord King Eglon of Moab, though only a private individual, at the impulse of the Holy Spirit.[86]

To answer one of the questions posed at the beginning, it is probably too simple to say, with Eustace Percy, that in 1554–55 Knox was

---

[82] Knox, *Works*, III, pp. 285, 282–3. Shebna occurs in II Kings 18:18–19:2, and in Isaiah 22:15–19, 36:3–37:2.

[83] Ponet, *Treatise*, sig. Div[r].

[84] Ibid., sigs Dviii[r], Giii[r].

[85] Knox, *Works*, III, p. 194.

[86] Ponet, *Treatise*, sigs Gv[v]–Hvi[r]. The story of Ehud is a reference to Judges 3:12–30.

'talking European', while Cox and his allies were speaking in an English idiom. Knox's idiom, in theology as in language, was in fact a perfectly valid version of those current in the England of his day.[87] He was, in truth, an English reformer, albeit one in the mould of John Hooper or William Whittingham. His preoccupation with the minutiae of worship was really typically English. In continental countries the Mass was gradually revised out of recognition, in Lutheran and reformed Protestantism alike, without any of the anguish experienced in England. The differences between Knox's approach to Reformation and that of his adversaries at Frankfurt may be explained by the different routes by which they had arrived at that point. Knox, from that fateful commission 450 years ago, lived out his reforming vocation as a *preacher*. He challenged his hearers with the stark difference between opposite extremes. He exploited to the full the rhetoric of antitheses and contraries: God and the Devil, true worship and idolatry, reasoned faith and superstition.[88] To succeed in his ministry, he had to make these differences as strong and as clear as could be.

For the English reformers who worked in the tradition and the shadow of Thomas Cranmer, precisely the opposite was the case. They worked as members of committees for the revision of liturgy and doctrine, rather than as preachers. They sought to win over the ruling laity, from the king downwards. The whole project of reforming Henrician and Edwardian England depended on making the transition from medieval to reformed as gradual, as natural, as progressive as possible. Knox's logic of stark opposites was positively unhelpful to the diplomacy of the Tudor court. Nor would it be especially convenient in early Elizabethan England, until the obdurate resistance of the old Catholics revealed itself. Once it became clear that there was a battle for souls to be fought, English reformers, even the most episcopal of them, would find that the rhetoric of Knox was useful after all.

If Knox's ideas were really a fairly typical product of mid-sixteenth century English Protestantism, how then does one explain the very different destinies of the English and Scots reformed Churches? In this, too, the answer may lie with the very different roles of the English and Scots governments in their respective polities. In loyalist and centripetal England, a distinctive form of Reformation took shape which preserved the political and cultural cohesion of the nation above all, even at some cost in religious consistency and principle. For Elizabeth, but also for

---

[87] Even Knox's use of the English language was English rather than Scots, as remarked by the Scots Catholic Ninian Winzet: see Knox, *History*, I, pp. lxxviii–lxxix.

[88] Compare the rhetoric of contrariety as described in Clark, *Thinking with Demons*, pp. 53–61 and refs.

many clergy until the 1630s, partial Reformation was preferable to all-out religious war. In more fissile Scotland, a weaker monarchy found Reformation foisted upon it by the real holders of decisive political power, the secular nobility. As a result, the ideals of the Scottish reformers did not suffer the sort of political dilution which they underwent in England. Reformation stood out in all its stark, adversarial clarity. The Church of Scotland would never be the obedient servant of the State, even to the rather qualified degree that the Elizabethan Church of England became. Knox's preaching rhetoric, with its aggressive challenge to the conscience, would remain embedded in the Scots religious psyche.

CHAPTER FOUR

John Knox, the Church of England and the Women of England

Patrick Collinson

Should we take John Knox altogether seriously; or, to be more cautious, how seriously should we take John Knox? As he withdrew from his last audience with Mary Stewart (if audience is the right word) Knox found himself more or less obliged to be civil to the ladies of the court, 'who war thair sitting in all their gorgiouse apparell'. Knox chose to warn the courtesanes that, sooner than they might think or hope, worms would be busy with their flesh. 'And by suche meanes procured he the cumpany of women.' These ladies knew about Knox and no doubt would have been disappointed if he had talked about the weather. Knox is our source for this bizarre incident, worthy of Rasputin.[1] In April 1559, Knox wrote to his friend, Mrs Anne Locke, about the Book of Common Prayer, not one jot of which he would counsel any man to use. 'The whole Order of your Booke appeareth rather to be devised for upholding of massing priests, then for any good instruction which the simple people can thereof receive.' But then he wrote: 'I appear to jest with yow.'[2] Was the real John Knox (a risky formulation for any historian or biographer to use) a male chauvinist and misogynist? Was he not strongly attracted to women? Was the real John Knox a Puritan? Did he make no concessions to the Church of England and its imperfectly reformed institutions and liturgy? Other contributions to this volume leave me more than ever convinced that the Knox whose voice we hear was a histrionic Knox, a rhetorician drawn into those extreme reaches of the rhetorician's art which we call preaching, a Knox carried away, if not, like Mr Gladstone, 'a sophistical rhetorician, inebriated with the exuberance of his own verbosity'.

When I reviewed Jasper Ridley's biography, back in 1968, the *Spectator* headlined my piece 'Hard Knox'. As Maitland of Lethington wrote to William Cecil: 'You know the vehemence off Mr. Knox spriet, which cannot be brydled; and that doth sometymes uter soche sentences as can

---

[1] Knox, *Works*, II, p. 389.
[2] Knox to Mrs Locke, 6 April 1559, ibid., VI, pp. 11–15.

not easaly be dygested by a weake stomach.'[3] But at the last great Knox Festival, held in Edinburgh in 1972 and attended by representatives of all the reformed Churches in the world, the late Historiographer Royal, Gordon Donaldson, invited the congregation to reconsider the usual, stereotypical, image, presuming to present Knox as a human being, even, God help us, as 'an ordinary human being'![4] Donaldson's Knox was a Knox of inconsistencies and unresolved tensions. 'It is very human to be inconsistent.' It is these tensions and occasional inconsistencies which this chapter seeks to explore, with some indebtedness to Donaldson, who put his finger on the two areas which form its subject: Knox and womankind, and Knox and the English religion.

Nevertheless, my title may look like an artificial contrivance, a coupling of two distinct subjects. What did Knox's relations with the women of England have to do with his dealings with the Church of England? A sharp eye might detect a connection of an almost subliminal kind, for the Church is female, the Bride of Christ, and Knox's intrusive masculinity imposed itself on and engaged with equal force the Churches of England, as well as of Scotland, and women, especially the women of the Churches, 'loving sisters', together with those very special women with power over the Churches, the three royal Maries. And in both sets of male–female transactions, there was a soft centre to 'hard Knox', some tension between a harsh exterior and a softer inner man.

But there is a little more substance to my subject than subliminality or post-modernism, for it was in his 'familiar' letters to women, including, especially, those to two English women, that Knox revealed much about his deeper concerns in relation to the English Churches, as well as information about his own inner self which is otherwise inaccessible. That he should have chosen to do so, and that the sequence of letters to Mrs Bowes and Mrs Locke should have been preserved, when most other familiar letters were allowed to perish, is very striking, and perhaps significant, although significant of what is something which we shall have to discuss.

The two ends of my dumb-bell of a subject are joined by ecclesiology, what one is tempted to call circumstantial or practical ecclesiology. And with ecclesiology we encounter another contradiction, or at least paradox, a paradox by no means peculiar to Knox but built into the process and progress of the Protestant Reformation itself, a movement which began with ones and twos and holy huddles, but aspired to convert and subdue entire peoples. Knox the prophet addressed nations, and more

---

[3] Maitland of Lethington to Sir William Cecil, 25 October 1561, ibid., VI, pp. 136–7.
[4] Gordon Donaldson, 'Knox the Man', in Duncan Shaw (ed.), *John Knox: A Quatercentenary Reappraisal* (Edinburgh, 1975), pp. 18–32.

especially the nation, and national Church, of England. Knox was one
of the first generously bearded preachers to have prophetically apostrophized England in the exclamation of 'O England, England!', which
was to become a homiletical commonplace in Elizabethan and Jacobean
preaching, a regular feature of the sermons delivered from the national
pulpit of Paul's Cross.[5] This was one powerful means of imagining into
existence a national community, to borrow Benedict Anderson's idea.[6]

And yet, while Knox, with Old Testament in hand, presumed to
correct and direct nations and national Churches, his natural and circumstantial environment belonged to the imaginary world of the New
Testament, finding its home in the 'Privy Kirks' and still more in the
inchoate and unstructured house groups and conventicles which pre-
ceded the Privy Kirks; as well as armed camps and places of refuge, so
many Caves of Adullam: St Andrews, Berwick, Geneva. How could it
have been otherwise? Protestants were at first thin on the ground, in
both Scotland and England, and even when they became more numerous and acquired political clout, Christ's New Testament address to 'the
little flock', reinforced by Calvinist exclusive predestinarianism, tended
to perpetuate the self-fashioning of Protestants as an embattled minority or remnant. To Mrs Bowes, Knox wrote in 1553, with Edward VI
perhaps still alive and the Protestant regime intact: 'And theirfoir aught
ye greatlie to rejois, knawing your self to be ane of the small and
contempnit flok to whome it hes pleasit God our Father to give the
kingdome.'[7] Moreover, and this is of the essence, the faith and assurance not only of Knox's spiritual patients but of Knox himself depended
critically upon the support and fellowship of conventicling groups.
Knox tells us of Elizabeth Bowes that her troubled conscience was only
at rest 'in the company of the faithful'. This, rather than any ecclesiology
of a formal, dogmatic kind was what sustained and fuelled the controlled sectarianism of evangelical, Calvinist Protestants two or three
generations later, and what seems to have principally motivated the
creation of a new kind of society and Church in New England.[8]

It was to 'the faithful' in Berwick, Newcastle, London, as well as
Edinburgh, that Knox publicly addressed himself, when absent, and to

---

[5] Patrick Collinson, 'Biblical Rhetoric: The English Nation and National Sentiment in
the Prophetic Mode', in Claire McEachern and Debora Shuger (eds), *Religion and
Culture in Renaissance England* (Cambridge, 1997), pp. 15–45.

[6] Benedict Anderson, *Imagined Communities: Reflections on the Origins and Spread
of Nationalism* (London, 1983).

[7] Knox to Mrs Elizabeth Bowes, 1553; Knox, *Works*, III, p. 351.

[8] John Knox, *An Answer to a Letter of a Iesuit named Tyrie*, in *Works*, VI, p. 513;
Tom Webster, 'The Godly of Goshen Scattered: An Essex Clerical Conference in the
1620s and its Diaspora' (unpublished Cambridge PhD thesis, 1993).

whom he ministered when present. Prominent among these faithful were women, and the pastoral nexus with these 'sisters' was special and intense, given the conventions into which Knox's ministry comfortably fitted, conventions older than the Protestant Reformation, by which the man of God received material sustenance and comfort from women and, as it were in return, heard their confessions and wrote out spiritual prescriptions.[9]

Practical ecclesiology is equally the key to Knox's radical nonconformity. For all his prophetic utterances, which are most of what survives in the public record, Knox was naturally a sectarian leader, applying an uncompromisingly scriptural religion to 'faithful' groups which had no need to make political compromises; and who was consistently hostile to, or at least suspicious of, governments and their ecclesiastical and 'politic' pretensions and contrivances: hostile not only to the Catholic Maries but to those ruling in England in the name of Edward VI, and above all to the Duke of Northumberland, 'that wretched (alas!) and miserable Northumberland'.[10] Knox was not, of course, the last sectarian leader in history to find himself suddenly in charge, more or less, of a country. The twentieth century contains many such examples, from Lenin to Castro. As Ernst Troeltsch taught us in his elegantly schematic religious-sociological typology, sects and Churches, both making exclusive claims and uncompromising demands, are opposite sides of the same coin. Ecclesiological tension between Church and sect was of the essence of Puritanism, a force at once turned in upon itself and potentially world-conquering: a church within the Church with an imperative to become itself the Church, a cuckoo in the nest.

What follows can stake few claims to originality, or only the rather scanty claim which rests on casting a fresh eye over familiar stories and evidence: on the one hand, Knox's letters to Mrs Bowes and Mrs Locke, which are exploited by all his biographers; and, on the other, the documents printed and discussed by Peter Lorimer in a book published as long ago as the 1870s, dated in its denominational partisanship (Lorimer being the equivalent of those mock-Gothic Presbyterian Churches put up by Scots in English cities at about the same time) but not in its mostly sound scholarship, *John Knox and the Church of England* (London, 1875). But freshness of eye and originality of perception will not defend me against Sir Philip Sidney's wounding remarks about historians in his *Defence of Poetry*, especially what Sidney wrote

---

[9] Patrick Collinson, '"Not Sexual in the Ordinary Sense": Women, Men and Religious Transactions', in Patrick Collinson, *Elizabethan Essays* (London, 1994), pp. 119–50.

[10] Knox, *A Faithful Admonition to the Professors of God's Truth in England* (1554), *Works*, III, p. 277.

about the historian 'authorising himself (for the most part) upon other histories'.[11]

Let us begin with the women. It has always been known, and especially since Robert Louis Stevenson wrote his remarkable essay, 'John Knox and his Relations to Women',[12] that Knox had a soft spot for the other sex. More than one biographer has suggested that even those bruising, tear-provoking encounters with Mary Stewart compensated for some susceptibility to Mary's notorious charms. There is a similar tension in Knox's dealings with private women in his familiar letters.[13] These letters are not only familiar. They are suffused with a no-holds-barred emotional warmth which, while it is addressed to religious matters and spiritual conditions, implies, since these were beings of flesh and blood, more than that. As Marjorie Bowen put it so perfectly, this was 'not at all a sexual relationship in the ordinary sense, and yet it could only have existed between persons of different sexes'.[14]

And yet no one we know of in the sixteenth century, or in history, was more insistent, and to a modern ear offensively insistent, on the insurmountable inferiority of womankind. Knox's 'sisteris in Edinburgh', whose consciences were troubled by fashion, were told that 'the garmentis of wemen do declair their weaknes and unabilitie to execute the offices of men'.[15] As Jane Dawson and Roger Mason have taught us, *The First Blast of the Trumpet* had one particular woman in mind, Mary Tudor. The political issues it addressed were not general but specific to England's Queen. Yet the argument rests on a general definition of womankind as 'weak, frail, impatient, feeble and foolish'.[16] Yet it was only in letters to women that Knox owned up to that harsh, uncompromising personality which was so notorious to all who had dealings with him. 'Of nature I am churlish.'[17]

---

[11] Sir Philip Sidney, *An Apology for Poetry*, ed. Geoffrey Shepherd (London and Edinburgh, 1965), p. 105.

[12] R.L. Stevenson, 'John Knox and his Relations to Women', in his *Familiar Studies of Men and Books* (London, 1901).

[13] One is reminded of Huldreich Zwingli's hostility to any form of Church music. It was not that Zwingli hated music. Quite the contrary. He was an accomplished musician and knew, with John Calvin, what inflammatory power it has. Charles Garside, *Zwingli and the Arts* (New Haven and London, 1966); H.P. Clive, 'The Calvinist Attitude to Music', *Bibliotheque d'Humanisme et Renaissance*, 20 (1958), pp. 79–107.

[14] Marjorie Bowen, *Life of John Knox* (London, 1949), p. 48.

[15] Knox 'to his sisteris in Edinburgh', n.d., *Works*, IV, pp. 225–36.

[16] Jane E.A. Dawson, 'The Two John Knoxes: England, Scotland and the 1558 Tracts', *JEH*, 42 (1991), pp. 555–76; Knox, *On Rebellion*, pp. xv–xvi, xx, 9.

[17] Knox to Mrs Locke, 6 April 1559, *Works*, VI, p. 11.

More than the letters to individual women, the famous correspondences with Mrs Bowes and Mrs Locke, Knox's pastoral epistles to pairs and undifferentiated groups of 'sisters' suggest a particular penchant for a ministry among women. Writing to the Edinburgh housewives Janet Adamson and Janet Henderson, Knox referred to earlier letters 'whilk I trust be commoun betuixt yow and the rest of oure Sisteris ... I wische that baith consall, exhortatioun and admonitioun written to any ane of yow, do serve to yow all.' 'For to me ye ar all equall in Chryst.' In another letter, Mrs Henderson was told: 'I have many whome I beir in equall rememberance befoir God with yow.'[18] In London, Mrs Anne Locke and Mrs Rose Hickman were reminded of their 'sic familar acquaintance' with Knox, and of how 'your hartis war incensit and kendillit with a special care over me, as the mother used to be over hir naturall chyld'. 'With none I was so familiar.'[19] On 1 March 1553, Knox wrote from London to his future mother-in-law in Northumberland, telling her that just when her latest, anxious letters arrived, he had been sitting with 'thrie honest pure [poor] wemen', whose spiritual infirmities were very like those experienced by Mrs Bowes, whom these London housewives had never met. Whereupon 'all oure eis wypit at anis [wept at once]'.[20]

And yet, as Knox seems to be constantly admitting in these letters, some women were to him more equal than others, and none more so than Elizabeth Bowes, a north-country gentlewoman, and Anne Locke, a young, wealthy member of London's merchant aristocracy, 'poor' in only a spiritual sense and so well able to take good care of Knox.

There is perhaps no need to dwell on the Knox–Bowes correspondence. So much has been written already. But it is not easy to resist the temptation to quote from some of Knox's most magnificent pastoral utterances, written in response to Mrs Bowes's almost chronic fears about her soul's safety.

> Dispair not Mother, your synnis (albeit ye had commitit thousands ma) are remissabill. What! think ye that Gods gudnes, mercie and grace, is abill to be overcum with youre iniquitie? Will God, wha

---

[18] Knox 'to his loving sisters in Edinburgh, Janet Adamsone and Janet Henderson', 1557, ibid., IV, pp. 244–5; Knox 'to mistris Guthrie, Janet Hendersone', 16 March 1557, ibid., IV, p. 246.

[19] Knox 'to Mistress Locke and Mistress Hickman, merchandis wyffis in Londoun', 1556, ibid., IV, p. 220. For information about Rose Hickman, see Maria Dowling and Joy Shakespeare, 'Religion and Politics in Mid-Tudor England through the Eyes of an English Protestant Woman: The Recollections of Rose Hickman', *BIHR*, 55 (1982), pp. 94–102.

[20] Knox to Mrs Bowes, 1 March 1553, *Works*, III, pp. 379–80.

can not dissave, be a lier, and lose his awn glorie, becaus that ye ar a synner?

And sa, Sister, ye ar seik, but sall not die. Your faith is weak and sair trubillit, but ye ar not unfaithfull. ... Deir Mother, my dewtie compellis me to advertteis yow, that in comparing your synnis with the synnis of Sodome and Gomorre ye do not weill ... Ye knaw not what wer the synnis of Sodome and Gomore.

A tutorial on this interesting subject follows.[21] It is tempting to conclude from some passages in these letters that Knox's feeling for his mother-in-law was stronger and more tender than his love for her daughter, his wife; but risky, since we have only one letter to Marjory Bowes[22] and know very little about the quality of their relationship – although we have evidence that Marjory was her husband's secretary, as well as the mother of his sons. Knox wrote to Elizabeth, very properly, but revealingly, two or three years before his marriage was solemnized: 'God I take to recorde in my conscience, that nane is this day within the Realme of Ingland, with whome I wald mair gladlie speik (onlie sche whome God hath offrit unto me, and commandit me to lufe as my awn fleshe exceptit) than with you.'[23] It is not hard to see why Knox's Catholic enemies made a field day out of this odd *ménage a trois*, which took Mrs Bowes to Geneva, leaving behind a husband whom she was never to see again, and later to Scotland to care for her widowed son-in-law and grandsons; and why later generations have allowed their somewhat prurient imaginations to dwell upon just what it was that happened 'standing at the copbourd in Anwiki in verie deid I thought na creature had bene temptit as I wes'.[24] One Catholic pamphleteer accused Knox of incestuous adultery, 'making ane fleshe of himself, the mother and the dochter'.[25] However, not only the letter which Knox himself printed in the last months of his life to give the lie to the Jesuit Tyrie, but the correspondence in its entirety amply bears out the claim that these were not flesh and blood matters but spiritual, 'a troubled conscience upon her part'. Even some words in the first letter in the collection, 'since the first day that it pleasit the providence of God to

---

[21] Knox to Mrs Bowes, 1553, ibid., III, p. 381; Knox to Mrs Bowes, 26 February 1553, ibid., III, p. 349; Knox to Mrs Bowes, n.d., ibid., III, pp. 382–3.

[22] Ibid., III, pp. 394–5. *Mea culpa*! In Collinson, 'Women, Men and Religious Transactions', p. 183, I made Elizabeth Bowes the recipient of this, the only surviving letter from Knox to his wife, Marjory Bowes, ending, 'I think this be the first Letter that ever I wrait to you'.

[23] Knox to Mrs Bowes, 1553, *Works*, III, p. 370.

[24] Knox to Mrs Bowes, 26 February 1553, ibid., III, p. 350.

[25] 'Nicole Burne's Disputation' (Paris, 1581), in T.G. Law (ed.), *Catholic Tractates of the Sixteenth Century 1573–1600* (STS, Edinburgh, 1901), pp. 143–4.

bring yow and me in familiaritie, I have alwayis delytit in your company', need to be put in context. There is an implied 'but' which follows. But you taxed my pastoral energies to the limit. Knox might have said that he was 'sair trauchilled' with Mrs Bowes. What he did tell Tyrie was that her company was 'not without some cross'.[26]

From recent accounts of the Knox–Bowes relationship, some interesting as well as disputed points have emerged.[27] Christine Newman suggests that Elizabeth Bowes's spiritual malaise had much to do with her isolation. As one of the first, if not the very first, Protestant gentlewoman in the whole region, she had little in common with the soldiers and renegade Scots who made up Knox's congregation at Berwick: practical ecclesiology again. Daniel Frankforter believes that if the letters are reassembled in a more plausibly chronological sequence, it will appear that Mrs Bowes's religious condition, her doubts about her own salvation, was not chronic and incurable but progressive. The patient eventually recovered. But Newman, on the contrary, thinks that lack of spiritual confidence haunted the poor lady to the very end, citing a letter which she dates to the (presumably early) 1560s.[28] Newman reminds us that our understanding of this friendship is limited by the survival only of Knox's letters to Mrs Bowes: nothing from her to him. So we cannot help but see the situation only through his eyes.

That being the case, if Knox had merely assaulted the fragility of Mrs Bowes with the force of his masculine and professional authority, the correspondence would not be very interesting and could be interpreted (perhaps by a feminist religious historian) as a species of spiritual rape, or at least seduction. But that is not what we find at all. The most remarkable feature of Knox's letters to Mrs Bowes is that he used them (no doubt as a deliberate pastoral stratagem) to confess that he shared his patient's problems; and, in effect, that she had done almost as much for him as he for her, a case of what would now be called co-counselling. 'But ane thing I will baldlie speik, not flattering yow, that your infirmitie has bene unto me occasioun to serche and try the Scripture mair neir then ever I cold for my awn caus.'[29] Mrs Locke and Mrs Hickman were told

---

[26] Knox, *Works*, III, pp. 333, 337–8.

[27] A. Daniel Frankforter, 'Elizabeth Bowes and John Knox: A Woman and Reformation Theology', *Church History*, 56 (1987), pp. 333–47; Christine M. Newman, 'The Reformation and Elizabeth Bowes: A Study of a Sixteenth-Century Northern Gentlewoman', in W.J. Sheils and Diana Wood (eds), *Women in the Church*, Studies in Church History, 27 (Oxford, 1990), pp. 325–33.

[28] Knox, *Works*, III, pp. 392–4. In Laing's edition, this letter (no. XXIII in the numbered sequence) is dated '1554'. But from internal evidence it is clear that is was written after Mrs Bowes's return to England from Geneva.

[29] Knox to Mrs Bowes, 1 March 1553, *Works*, III, pp. 379–80.

much the same: 'My hart was opinit and compellit in your presence to be mair plane in suche matters as efter hath cum to pass, then ever I was to any.'[30] And, most telling of all, this to Mrs Bowes: 'The expositioun of your trubillis and acknawledging of your infirmities, war first unto me a verie mirrour and glass whairin I beheld myself sa rychtlie payntit furth, that nathing culd be mair evident to my awn eis.'[31] To be sure, there was not parity in these relationships, but I am not sure that Stevenson was entitled to say that 'many women came to learn from him, but he never condescended to become a learner in his turn'.[32] As Knox wrote to Mrs Locke: 'I have rather need of all then that any hath need of me.'[33]

Elsewhere I have discussed repetitive patterns of this kind, a continuum of male–female spiritual interdependence, from the days of St Jerome and his Roman and Bethlehem groupies, to Jacques de Vitry and Mary of Oignies in the twelfth century, St Catherine of Siena and Blessed Raymond of Capua, St Francis de Sales and Ste Jeanne de Chantal in the seventeenth century, and on to the twentieth century and the psychological and spiritual interpenetration of my predecessor as Regius Professor, Dom David Knowles, and the Swedish psychiatrist and Catholic convert, Elizabeth Kornerup.[34] It was really not at all strange that a member of a species 'weake, fraile, impacient, feble and foolishe' should have done what Elizabeth Bowes did for Knox: that he should have come to know himself through her.

Knox's feelings for Mrs Anne Locke were, if anything, more intense than for Elizabeth Bowes, especially as they were expressed in the letters of 1556, written at a time when he was enticing her (hardly too strong a word) to take refuge with him in Geneva.[35] On 19 November he wrote: 'Ye wryt that your desire is ernist to sie me. Deir Sister, yf I suld expres the thrist and langoure whilk I haif had for your presence, I suld appeir to pass measure.' But for the impediment of his ministerial charge in Geneva (which was how he chose to describe it) 'my presence suld prevent my

---

[30] Ibid., IV, p. 220.

[31] 'The first letter to his mother-in-law, Mistres Bowes'[sic], 23 June 1553, ibid., III, p. 338.

[32] Stevenson, 'John Knox and his Relations to Women', p. 275.

[33] Knox, Works, VI, p. 11.

[34] Collinson, 'Women, Men and Religious Transactions', passim.

[35] Patrick Collinson, 'The Role of Women in the English Reformation Illustrated by the Life and Friendships of Anne Locke', in G.J. Cuming (ed.), Studies in Church History, II (London, 1965), pp. 258–72, reprinted in Patrick Collinson, Godly People: Essays on English Protestantism and Puritanism (London, 1983), where many details of Mrs Locke's family and career will be found which cannot be accommodated here. See also Patrick Collinson, 'A Mirror of Elizabethan Puritanism: The Life and Letters of "Godly Master Dering"', in his Godly People, pp. 289–324.

letter'.[36] One of history's might-have-beens sees Knox hasting back to Mistress Locke's side, getting himself arrested and burned in the process.[37] Better that Mrs Locke should come to him. So, on 9 December 1556, Knox wrote the most frequently quoted of all his letters. He confessed that in his heart he desired that God would guide and conduct his friend to Geneva, 'wherin I nather feir nor eschame to say is the maist perfyt schoole of Chryst that ever was in the erth since the dayis of the Apostillis'.[38] And, five months later, to Geneva she came, with her two small children, one of whom she buried within four days of her arrival.[39]

But while this relationship (almost, one dares to say, 'affair') was, as with Mrs Bowes, ostensibly founded on Anne Locke's spiritual needs, it was at an intellectual level a more equal match. After all, Anne Locke, née Vaughan, was the daughter of an international wheeler and dealer, the financier and diplomat Stephen Vaughan, part of a web of families (for the most part mercers) as much at home in Antwerp as in London. She had been well educated according to the nostrums of More, Vives and Ascham, and was to publish translations from the French. Her approving husband, Henry Locke, a leading mercer, inscribed his copy of her translation of some Calvin sermons, employing an elegant Italianate hand, suggestive of his own erudition.[40] Henry Locke had 12 brothers, who included Michael Lok, the traveller and adventurer who translated Peter Martyr's *Historie of the West Indies*, and other members of the family had literary pretensions, including Anne Locke's son, Henry, the little boy she took to Geneva, who became a minor poet, mostly in a religious vein.[41] Knox asked Mrs Locke to send him books,

[36] Knox, *Works*, IV, pp. 237–9.

[37] In his *Exposition uppon the syxt Psalm of David*, written in Dieppe for Mrs Bowes in May 1554, Knox wrote: 'I can not expresse the payne which I thinke I might suffre to have the presence of you, and of others that be lyke trubled, but a few daies' (*Works*, III, pp. 132–3). Unlike the case of Martin Luther, there is no evidence that John Knox regretted failing to win the martyr's crown, and some to the contrary. See David Bagchi, 'Luther and the Problem of Martyrdom', in Diana Wood (ed.), *Martyrs and Martyrologies*, Studies in Church History, 30 (Oxford, 1993), pp. 209–19.

[38] Knox to Mrs Locke, 9 December 1556, *Works*, IV, pp. 239–41.

[39] 'Anne Locke, Harrie her sonne, and Anne her doughter, and Katheriune her maid' joined Knox's congregation in Geneva on 8 May 1557. Anne was buried on 12 May. Charles Martin, *Les protestants Anglais refugiés à Genève au temps de Calvin 1555–1560, leur église, leurs écrits* (Geneva, 1915), pp. 333, 338.

[40] Collinson, *Godly People*, pp. 212, 280–81; *DNB*, art. Henry Lok. The copy in question was in the possession of the nineteenth-century book collector, Bright.

[41] Henry Lok, *Sundry Christian Passions contained in Two Hundred Sonnets* (London, 1593) (*STC*, no. 16697), *Ecclesiastes, otherwise called the Preacher, Abridged and Dilated in English Poesie*, with a second edition of *Sundrie Sonets* (London, 1596) (*STC*, no. 16696).

including the latest version of Calvin's *Institutes*, not something Mrs Bowes would have been expected to do.[42] There were not many book-shops in the uplands of Northumberland.

Knox's letters to Mrs Locke, who after his return from Geneva was his principal contact with 'the faithful' in London, form the bridge between the private and public dimensions of this chapter, affairs with women and ecclesiastical and political negotiations. In April 1559, still no closer to either England or Scotland than Dieppe, Knox wrote (to Mrs Locke) that England had refused him as it had refused Jesus Christ. 'For to me it is written that my *First Blast* hath blowne from me all my friends in England.'[43] The man of the hour, William Cecil, was written to in the same month and rebuked for his 'horrible defection', and for having 'followede the worlde in the way of perdicioun', 'worthy of hell'. God, for reasons best known to Himself, had promoted Cecil to honours and dignity. This was hardly the best way to win friends and influence people.[44]

Three months later was a long time in Reformation politics, and in August 1559, with the Protestant revolution in Scotland fighting to preserve its improbable successes, Knox was embarking on his brief career as a high-level diplomat and middleman, writing more politely to Cecil and almost meeting him at his house outside Stamford; while Cecil was busy being Cecil, writing to Sir Ralph Sadler: 'Suerly I lyke not Knoxes audacitie ... His writings doe no good here; and therefore I doo rather suppresse them, and yet I meane not but that ye shuld contynue in sending of them.'[45]

But before, and especially after, Knox's brief appearance on the rap-idly revolving stage of British politics (in the later months of 1559), it was through Anne Locke that he hoped to get through, not so much to the English government as to those godly and well-heeled networks of 'the faithful' which he looked to for material as well as spiritual suc-cour. From the first day of his arrival in Edinburgh in early May 1559, these letters, in form, are newsletters, reading like a parallel text to Knox's *History of the Reformation* and almost as an early draft of the

---

[42] Knox, *Works*, VI, pp. 101, 108.

[43] Knox to Mrs Locke, 6 April 1559, ibid., VI, pp. 11–15.

[44] Knox to Cecil, 22 April 1559, ibid., VI, pp. 15–21. Lord Eustace Percy called this 'the most brazenly tactless of all his letters'. Eustace Percy, *John Knox* (2nd edn, London, 1964), p. 235.

[45] Cecil to Sadler, 3 November 1559; *The State Papers and Letters of Sir Ralph Sadler*, ed. A. Clifford (2 vols, Edinburgh, 1809), I, p. 535.

History. A letter of 23 June 1559, when Knox for the first time could be certain of Anne's presence in London, consists of 2 000 words of eventful news, beginning 10 May, and concluding: 'Communicate the contents heirof ... with all the faithfull, but especiallie, with the afflicted of that little flocke now dispersed and destitute of these pleasaunt pastures in which they sometime fed abundantlie.'[46]

Anne had written to Knox from London on 16 June, so that these references to 'the little flock' must be read as meaning that, back in England, the Genevan congregation preserved its coherent identity. Thus Knox wrote in early September, mentioning a newsletter sent to the Genevan elder Thomas Wood, which Wood was to communicate to Mrs Locke and 'other brethrein of Geneva'.[47] In October and November, with the outcome of events in Edinburgh and Leith still desperately uncertain, Cecil not yet ready or able to move, and Queen Elizabeth's purse strings tightly drawn together, Knox tried to tap the good will of the faithful, 'that they wold move such as have abundance to consider our estate, and to mak for us some provisioun of money, to keepe souldiours and our companie together'.[48] Here is a fascinating glimpse of the Calvinist international (as we have learned to call it), a mechanism for moving from country to country money, or at least credit, the essential fuel and lubricant for sustaining religiously inspired insurgency.[49] Mrs Locke was his main and even only contact for this purpose. 'I cannot weill write to anie other.' But by

---

[46] Knox to Mrs Locke, 3 May 1559, 23 June 1559, *Works*, VI, pp. 21–7.

[47] Ibid., VI, pp. 30, 77–9. This is the most plausible reading of evidence which has misled some writers into supposing that Anne Locke remained in Geneva throughout 1559. We cannot be sure when Mrs Locke reached London, although it is likely that she would have written to Knox as soon as she arrived. A letter sent from Frankfurt on 23 March 1559 only reached Knox in Dundee in mid-September. Only then would he have known that his letter written from Dieppe on 6 April had gone astray, so that on 17 October he was obliged to repeat the advice that that letter had contained (ibid., VI, pp. 83–5). In reading these letters, it is important not to forget that these correspondents did not enjoy the advantages (such as they are) of modern postal services, let alone of e-mail.

[48] Knox to Mrs Locke, 18 November 1559, ibid., VI, pp. 100–101.

[49] The 'privatization' of the Reformation in the hands of wealthy 'sustainers', notably in the city of London, is a topic deserving much more investigation. See P. Collinson, 'England, 1558–1640', in Menna Prestwich (ed.), *International Calvinism 1541–1715* (Oxford, 1985), pp. 197–223; and Ole Peter Grell, 'Merchants and Ministers: The Foundations of International Calvinism', in Andrew Pettegree, Alistair Duke, and Gillian Lewis (eds), *Calvinism in Europe 1540–1620* (Cambridge, 1994), pp. 254–73. This will prove to have been a significant factor not only in assisting religious insurgency and resistance, but in helping to establish Protestant settlements. I am informed by Mr Brett Usher that the wealthy London faithful advanced substantial sums of money to some of the first Elizabethan bishops.

mid-November, no aid had materialized and Knox was growing desperate. 'If we perishe in this our interprise, the limits of Londoun will be straiter than they are now, within few yeeres'.[50] Mrs Locke replied that she had done her best with those of both high and low degree, but that this was thought to be too large an undertaking for private charity.[51] Knox insisted that whatever might be done by the English government, 'that ought not to stay the liberall hands of the godlie to support us privatlie; for the publick support of an armie sall not make suche as now be superexpended able to serve without private support'. What Knox meant was that the Lords of the Congregation had funded the insurrection from private resources which were now nearly exhausted.[52] On 4 February 1560, still waiting for his copy of Calvin's *Institutes*, and hinting at his hopes of other 'liberality' at Mrs Locke's hands, Knox wrote:

> I know not what of our brethren of Geneva be with you; but to such as be there, I beseeche you to say, that I think that I myself doe now find the truth of that which oft I have said in their audience, to witt, that after our departure frome Geneva sould our dolour begin.[53]

Here was the voice of nostalgia for the Cave of Adullam and the conventicle.

John Knox the honorary Englishman is not quite the subject of this chapter. And Stephen Alford tells us in Chapter 10 about Knox's Britishness; about the Knox who commonly wrote of 'this yle', or, as in the first line of *The First Blast*, 'the Isle of Great Brittany',[54] and who told Cecil, 'my eie hath long looked to a perpetual concord betuixt these two Realmes'.[55] My subject in the second portion of this chapter is a small but significant part of this larger whole: Knox and the English Church and its ceremonies, the issues of conformity and nonconformity,

---

[50] Knox to Mrs Locke, 31 December 1559, *Works*, VI, pp. 103–4.

[51] Ibid., VI, p. 101.

[52] Ibid., VI.

[53] Knox to Mrs Locke, 4 February 1560, ibid., VI, pp. 107–9.

[54] Ibid., VI, pp. 529, 531; Knox, *On Rebellion*, p. 3.

[55] Knox to Cecil, 28 June 1559, *Works*, VI, 31–2. Thomas Randolph wrote of Knox to Cecil in December 1562: 'I knowe his good zeal and affection that he beareth to our nation. I knowe also that his travaile and care is great to unite the hartes of the princes and people of these two realmes in perpetuall love and hartie kyndness' (Ibid., VI, p. 146). According to Gordon Donaldson, Knox's place in history lies in the part he played in creating a Protestant Great Britain (*John Knox*, in a popular series called 'Pride of Britain' [1983]).

painstakingly, polemically and pastorally negotiated within the terms of the legislated liturgies of the Reformed Church of England.

But let us pause for a moment on Knox's Englishness which, but for three things – events in Scotland, the offence caused in England by his political writings, and his nonconformity (and I am directly concerned with only the third of these) – might have taken him over entirely. We have already heard the exclamatory apostrophe, 'O England!', which echoes through the exile pamphlets and which was heard at Amersham early in Mary's reign, a sermon punctuated with 'O Englande, Englande!'[56] Soon after this, on 6 January 1554, Knox was in Dieppe, telling Mrs Bowes in a little treatise which was to become more or less public property, transposed into English English:

> Somtyme I have thought that impossible it had bene, so to have removed my affection from the Realme of Scotland, that eny Realme or Nation could have been equall deare unto me. But God I take to recorde in my conscience, that the troubles present (and appearing to be) in the Realme of England, are double more dolorous unto my hert, then ever were the troubles of Scotland.[57]

It has not often been noticed that Knox added to his *Brief Exhortation to England*, printed at Geneva in 1559, his own (remarkably full if not complete) tally of 281 Marian martyrs, 'the names of some part of those most faithfull servantes and deare children of God, which lately in thee, and by thee, O England!, have bene most cruelly murthered by fyre and imprisonment'; and that he offered, in effect, to change his name from Knox to Foxe. He explained that he would gladly have provided much more information than these names and bare facts, 'which thing, nevertheles, we mynde hereafter more largely to performe'.[58] Did Knox not know what John Foxe had been up to for the past five years?

And yet there was ambivalence in Knox's attitude towards his semi-adopted country. England in its Marian apostasy was 'thou happie and most unhappie England'. The England which had scotched the

---

[56] Knox, *Works*, III, pp. 307–8. According to Roger Mason, one reason for this transference of critical allegiance was that England under Edward VI was a covenanted nation, a nation which could be identified, as Scotland as yet could not, with Israel or Judah. 'Consider, Deir Bretherne,' Knox wrote in *A Godly Letter sent to the Faythefull* (1554), 'gif all thingis be alyke betuene England and Juda befoir the destruction thairof. Yea gif England be worse than Juda was' (*Works*, III, p. 188). See further, Chapter 8 in this volume.

[57] *An exposition uppon the syxt Psalm of David*, in Knox, *Works*, III, p. 133. There were editions of this little book in 1566 (*A Percell of the vi Psalme*) and 1580 (*An Exposition uppon the Syxt Psalme*) (STC, nos. 15074.4 and 15074.6).

[58] Knox, *Works*, V, pp. 523–36.

Scottish snake, not killed her, was 'foolish England', a reference to the marginalia of the Geneva Bible, where King Asa was censured for his 'foolish pity' in failing to kill his mother, the wicked Queen Maacah (2 Chronicles 15:10), in clear breach of the unsentimental law of Deuteronomy.[59] For all his forthright patriotic self-consciousness, Knox was not so much either Scots or English as a Protestant international-ist, with no continuing city. His account of what he said at Frankfurt when Richard Cox insisted that their Church should have the face of an English Church is justly famous. 'The Lord grant it to have the face of Christ's Church.'[60] The inhabitants of Newcastle and Berwick were reminded in 1559 that in Edward VI's reign, under Knox's ministry, they had received the Lord's Supper 'not as man had devised, neither as the King's procedinges dyd alowe, but as Christ Jesus dyd insti-tute'.[61]

Although this has been obscured by the Episcopalian desire of the late Gordon Donaldson to stress the convergence of the Scottish and English Churches in Knox's time, and to present Knox as far from a Melvillian Presbyterian, there is no doubt that he was almost the first and certainly the most potent of nonconformist dissenters from the symbols and ceremonies of the Edwardian/Elizabethan Church: in Lorimer's ironical words, following Carlyle, 'the chief priest and founder of ... Puritanism'.[62] By comparison, Bishop Hooper was a damp squib, if one may dare so to describe a man who came to such a crackling, smoky end at Gloucester. And it all began at Berwick and Newcastle, where Knox established something rare if not unique: an alternative, publicly unauthorized religious rite, regularly celebrated in a public place. This was his own, home-grown liturgy, and it found its symbolic heart in the practice of seated Communion.[63]

The far north of England was sufficiently remote for this to be less than a total public scandal. And yet, among the Duke of Northumberland's

---

[59] Ibid., V, p. 505; Knox, *On Rebellion*, p. 26. For the topos of 'foolish pity', see Patrick Collinson, *The English Captivity of Mary Queen of Scots* (Historical Association pamphlet, London and Sheffield, 1987), p. 1.

[60] Ibid., IV, p. 42. He also said, notably, 'that though we had changed countries, God had not changed his nature': ibid., IV, p. 44.

[61] Ibid., V, p. 480. 'Let not the King and his proceadinges (whatsoever they be), not agreable to his Worde, be a snare to thy conscience': ibid., V, p. 515.

[62] Peter Lorimer, *John Knox and the Church of England* (London, 1875), p. 221.

[63] See Knox's *Epistle to the Inhabitants of Newcastle and Berwick* (1558): 'How oft have ye bene partakers of the Lord's Table, prepared, used and ministred in all simplicitie, not as man had devised, neither as the King's procedinges dyd alowe, but as Christ Jesus dyd institute, and as it is evident that Sainct Paule dyd practise?' (Knox, *Works*, V, p. 480).

somewhat devious and multiple motives for bringing Knox south to the bishopric of Rochester, or, failing that, a London living (killing all too many birds with one stone), was the intention to bring to an end 'the ministration in the North contrary to that set forth here'.[64] Lorimer was right to talk of Knox in Berwick and Newcastle presiding over a 'Puritan franchise'.[65] But among the documents which he discovered and for the first time printed was an epistle 'to the congregation of Berwick' which spells out the limits which Knox placed, as early as 1553, on this aberrant practice:

> But because I am but one, having in my contrair magistrates, commone order, and judgements of manye lerned, I am not mynded for maintenance of that one thing to gainstand the magistrates, in all other and cheif poynts of religion aggreing with Christ and with his true doctrine, nor yet to break nor truble common order, thought meet to be kept for unitie and peace in the congregation for a tyme.[66]

In this letter, written from London or somewhere in the south, Knox was appealing to his old congregation to accept and use the 1552 Prayer Book, with the safety valve of the so-called Black Rubric, which Knox had negotiated, and which was intended to make crystal clear the absence of any 'popish superstition' in the act of kneeling at the Lord's Supper, 'but onlye for uniforme order to be kept'.[67] The story of the Black Rubric is too familiar to require any rehearsal on this occasion. I note only that Diarmaid MacCulloch has recently challenged Lorimer and conventional wisdom on its significance. It has been seen as a victory for Knox. 'Given that Elizabeth disliked the declaration [MacCulloch writes] and Puritans liked it, perhaps it becomes more understandable why posterity may lazily have assumed that it was more to the taste of Knox than Cranmer.' In fact, it was a total vindication of Archbishop Cranmer's position. Soon after this affair, Knox as a royal chaplain subscribed to the Forty-two Articles, which included Article 35, affirming that the Book of Common Prayer and the Ordinal were 'godly as to the truth of doctrine, and as to their propriety of ceremonies in no way contrary to the wholesome fruit of the Gospel'. MacCulloch comments: 'Game, set and match to Cranmer.'[68] The

---

[64] Lorimer, *Knox and the Church of England*, pp. 77–8, 149–50.

[65] It could be said that the north of England, and especially Lancashire, remained 'a Puritan franchise' for much of Elizabeth's reign, or was so regarded, even by the most conformist of Elizabethan bishops.

[66] Lorimer, *Knox and the Church of England*, p. 261.

[67] Ibid.

[68] Diarmaid MacCulloch, *Thomas Cranmer: A Life* (New Haven and London, 1996), pp. 527–30.

Berwick epistle, advocating conformity, and Knox's refusal of the English preferments offered by Northumberland, were contrary reactions to the tennis match, both entirely in character.

What about those preferments? Gordon Donaldson suggested that Knox's refusal of the bishopric of Rochester had less to do with a principled prejudice against Episcopacy than with Knox's realistic gift of second sight, his 'foresight of troubles to come'.[69] 'Troubles' tended to send Donaldson's Knox in the direction of prudent safety. That was doubtless one factor in the calculation and the words are Knox's. But it would be episcopally partisan to suppose that that was the only reason for the *nolo episcopare*. When John Douglas was made Archbishop of St Andrews, Knox, in the last year of his life, made clear his distaste for Episcopacy on the traditional model.[70] The critical evidence exists in the 1559 *Exhortation to England*:

> Let no man be charged, in preaching of Christ Jesus, above that which one man may do; I mean, that your bishoprikes be so devided, that of every one as they be nowe (for the most part) be made ten; and so in everie citie and greate towne there may be placed a godly lerned man, with so many joyned with him, for preaching and instruction, as shalbe thought sufficient for the bondes committed to their charge.[71]

This statement has often been cited as proof of Knox's pre-Presbyterian, even anti-Presbyterian ecclesiology. But what it more clearly spells out is an aversion from Episcopacy as England had known it. Very near the end of his life, Knox sent a message to Cecil, suggesting that it was not Cecil's fault that he had never become a bishop, with the implication that it was Cecil who had tried to promote him. 'It was not long of your Lordship that he was not a great bischope in England.'[72] Nothing with Knox is certain. It so happens that Rochester, of all the English sees, a small sliver of west Kent, was the only diocese which could almost have met Knox's criteria. It was Italian rather than English in scale, less than a tenth the size of Lincoln or Norwich.

---

[69] Donaldson , 'Knox the Man', p. 21.

[70] Lorimer, *Knox and the Church of England*, pp. 153–4.

[71] Knox, *Works*, V, p. 518. For the ecclesiological contexts and implications of this model, see Patrick Collinson, 'Episcopacy and Reform in England in the Later Sixteenth Century', in his *Godly People*, pp. 155–89; and Patrick Collinson, 'Episcopacy and Pseudo-Episcopacy in England in the Later Sixteenth and Early Seventeenth Centuries', in *Proceedings of the Conference of the Commission d'Histoire Ecclésiastique Comparée, Revue d'Histoire Ecclésiastique* (Louvain, 1988).

[72] Henry Killigrew to Lord Burghley and the Earl of Leicester, 6 October 1572; Knox, *Works*, VI, p. 633.

Knox was known as 'the Duke's [i.e. Northumberland's] preacher'[73] and the collapse of the Northumberland regime and the accession of Mary could only have strengthened his rejection of the Edwardian religious dispensation, which he had briefly endorsed. That is how I read 'the Troubles of Frankfort'. In the conditions of exile, it was no longer expedient to make the concessions which Knox had made in 1553 in England. Not only were Knox and his congregation now free to abandon ceremonies which had never been to Knox's taste. He fully believed that those deadly concessions had provoked the divine wrath and had directly brought about the collapse of the regime which had made them. That calamity was not the end of the matter. God was still the same God and the English Protestants had not escaped from His vigilant justice by moving to Germany. Hence the extremity of Knox's opposition to the Coxian party which insisted on the continued use of 'the Book of England' in exile. In the sermon which brought matters to a head, Knox maintained that 'amonge manye thinges which provoked godds anger against England, slacknes to reforme religion (when tyme and place was graunted) was one'. Some of these things were in the Prayer Book, 'things superstitious, impure, unclean, and unperfect'.[74]

And so we come to Knox's negative reaction to the religious arrangements of 1559. Knox wrote as a casuist, addressing Mrs Locke's conscience. 'I know I shall be judged extreme and rigorous. But, Sister, now is no tyme to flatter, nor dissemble.' He found 'the mark of the Beast' in 'the dregges of Papistrie' which remained in the Prayer Book of 1559, 'one jote whereof will I never counsell any man to use'.[75] Anne Locke, contemplating her future as a prominent London matron, more or less obliged to accompany other wives to baptisms and churchings and the like, did not know what to do. Knox assured her that sacraments ministered without the Word were no sacraments, mass-priests no ministers.[76] His letter of 15 October was still more uncompromising. Speaking scornfully of 'a bastard religion', he ruled: 'We ought not to justifie with our presence such a mingle mangle as now is commaunded in your kirks.'[77]

On the evidence of this letter, Anne Locke was the very first, documented, Elizabethan separatist. 'Ye conceale not the cause why ye assist not to their assemblie, which I thinke ye doe not.' The context for Mrs

---

[73] MacCulloch, *Thomas Cranmer*, pp. 525–6.

[74] J. Petheram (ed.), *A Brieff Discourse of the Troubles Begun at Frankfort* (London, 1846), p. xxxix. According to Knox's own account of the sermon, he spoke of 'many sins that moved God to plague England': Knox, *Works*, IV, p. 44.

[75] Knox, *Works*, VI, pp. 11–15.

[76] Ibid., VI, p. 14.

[77] Ibid., VI, 83–5.

Locke's questions and Knox's Gordian resolution of them is provided
by Thomas Fuller's account of this historical moment, recorded in 1586
in his 'booke to the Queene'.[78] In 1559 most of the Genevans had made
haste to return to England. But Fuller was so discouraged by the early
signs of how Elizabeth intended to proceed in matters of religion, 'my
first good hope and great rejoysing was quite quenched', that he intended to stay in Geneva, until John Calvin himself urged him to return
and do what he could, 'seing thextreme perseqution was ceased'. Would
Knox have given contrary advice? His verdict on the Prayer Book was
more harsh than Calvin's. Calvin had written of 'vices', things 'triflinge
and childish', but had told the Frankfurt congregation that 'they were
for a season to be tollerated'. It was wrong to make such things a cause
of schism. In effect, a plague on both your houses, Coxians and Knoxians
(although Knox had been dealt with uncharitably). But please make
your two houses one.[79]

   This would become Knox's position too when the Frankfurt troubles,
or something like them, replicated themselves in the Elizabethan Church
in the so-called Vestiarian Controversy: the first beginnings of that split
between conformist and nonconformist tendencies in the Church of England, a slim crack destined to open up into the profound chasm which
would eventually divide Church and Chapel.[80] With the enforcement of
uniformity within the terms of Archbishop Matthew Parker's so-called
'Advertisements', nonconformity underwent progressive radicalization as
extremists and moderates parted company, according to what is probably
a rule of political life, under these sorts of pressures. In London in 1566
there was a major ecclesiastical crisis when, only a week or two before
the busy season of Easter, as many as 37 clergy initially refused to
conform (particularly in the wearing of the white linen surplice) and
found themselves suspended. There were repercussions among London's
godly, 'faithful' community, some of whom now reverted to their 'Privy
Churches', and to the use of Knox's own Genevan liturgy. These were
rejectionist separatists: according to their somewhat anachronistically
denominational historians, the first Congregationalists.[81]

---

[78] Albert Peel (ed.), *The Seconde Parte of a Register* (2 vols, Cambridge, 1915), II,
pp. 49–64.

[79] Petheram, *A Brieff Discourse*, pp. xxxv–xxxvi.

[80] J.H. Primus, *The Vestments Controversy: An Historical Study of the Earliest Tensions within the Church of England in the Reigns of Edward VI and Elizabeth* (Kampen,
1960); Patrick Collinson, *The Elizabethan Puritan Movement* (London and Berkeley,
1967); J.S. Coolidge, *The Pauline Renaissance in England: Puritanism and the Bible*
(Oxford, 1970).

[81] 'The Examination of Certain Londoners Before the Commissioners', 20 June 1567
(from *A Parte of a Register*, 1593); W. Nicholson (ed.), *Remains of Edmund Grindal*

There ought to be a story to tell about John Knox's part in all this. But, except for one remarkable piece of evidence, to try to tell it is a case of making bricks without any straw whatsoever. Apart from a single letter of 1562, there were to be no more letters to Mrs Locke after 1559: or at least, none has survived. In December 1566, ten leading members of the General Assembly meeting in Edinburgh petitioned the English bishops on behalf of their nonconformist brethren. Knox was not among the signatories. No doubt it was thought that his name would not help what in any case seems to have been a lost cause.[82]

But on the same day (and can this have been a coincidence?) Knox was licensed by the same Assembly to depart for England.[83] What Gordon Rupp called Knox's 'curious' six-month 'sabbatical'[84] is an undocumented and utterly mysterious episode. It left Knox's Edinburgh pulpit vacant just as the convulsive events of 1567 unfolded, from the murder of Darnley to that island prison on Loch Leven. Ostensibly, the purpose of the visit was to see his motherless sons. But it is inconceivable that Knox did not become involved in the developing vestiarian crisis in the English Church, and possible that that was the real purpose of the visit. Knox in England was, understandably, the invisible man, and all that we lack is the evidence.

But what we do have, among the Morrice MSS in Dr Williams's Library, is a letter sent to Knox by a member of the London separatist congregation. Knox had written to the separatists when they were in the Fleet Prison. Now he was back in Scotland, and the writer had visited him, returning with another letter.

> Our brethren do give harty thanks for your gentle letter written unto them; but, to be plain with you, it is not in all points liked; and for my part, if I had known the tenor of it, when I was with you, I would have said many words that I never spake.

For Knox had declined to endorse the separatist position, which would be to condemn 'the public ministry of England'. 'God forbid that we should damn all for false prophets and heretics that agree not with us in our apparel and other opinions, that teacheth the substance of doctrine and salvation in Christ Jesus.' Knox's correspondent remained defiant.[85]

(Parker Society, Cambridge, 1843); Albert Peel, *The First Congregational Churches: New Light on Separatist Congregations in London, 1567–1581* (Cambridge, 1920).

[82] Knox, *Works*, VI, pp. 438–40.

[83] Ibid., VI, p. 437.

[84] Gordon Rupp, 'The Europe of John Knox', in Shaw, *Knox: A Quatercentenary Reappraisal*, p. 5.

[85] Lorimer, *Knox and the Church of England*, pp. 298–300.

It could have been Knox himself speaking. But now he was on the receiving end of this heady rhetoric and on the other side of the argument. He had parted company, definitively, with sectarianism.

And that is almost the end of the story. However, there is a coda, which concerns some of the documentation on which this chapter has depended, and the circumstances of its preservation. In spite of Knox's apparent defection from the most extreme puritan cause, he continued to be a role model and source of inspiration for radical English Puritans who stopped short of separation; and particularly for the driving force behind the militant Presbyterian tendency, the London preacher and publicist, John Field.[86] Field was, to say the least, a kindred spirit. His general rather than piecemeal reasons for refusing subscription to the Prayer Book read like an extended version of Knox's letters to Mrs Locke in 1559.[87]

In 1583, Field and the printer Robert Waldegrave, later to serve as king's printer in Scotland, published a little treatise by Knox on the temptations of Christ, 'written for the comfort of certaine private friends, but nowe published in print for the benefit of all that fear God'.[88] This was the private property of Anne Locke, who after marrying and burying the radical and popular preacher Edward Dering was now Mrs Prowse, the wife of the mayor of Exeter.[89] In dedicating the work to Mrs Prowse, Field apologized for 'having kept your papers so long and not returned them'. His excuse was that everything written by such 'an heroicall and bolde spirit' deserved publication. 'It was great pittie that any, the least, of his writings should be lost ... And his Letters being had together, would together set out an whole Historie of the Churches where he lyved.'[90] It is clear from this preface that among the papers Field had borrowed was at least one letter from Knox to Mrs Locke, and likely that Field had in his possession the

---

[86] Patrick Collinson, 'John Field and Elizabethan Puritanism', in his *Godly People*, pp. 335–70, and Collinson, *Elizabethan Puritan Movement, passim*.

[87] John Field, 'A View of Popish Abuses yet remaining in the English Church', in W.H. Frere and C.E. Douglas, *Puritan Manifestoes* (London, 1907, repr. 1954); 'Mr Feilde and Mr Egerton their tolleration' (1584), in Peel, *Seconde Parte of a Register*, I, pp. 284–6; Collinson, 'John Field', pp. 357–9; Collinson, *Elizabethan Puritan Movement*, pp. 251–2.

[88] *A Notable and Comfortable Exposition of M. Iohn Knoxes, upon the Fourth of Matthew, concerning the Tentations of Christ* (STC, no. 15068) (1583), in Knox, *Works*, IV, pp. 85–114.

[89] Collinson, 'The Role of Women', pp. 285–91.

[90] Knox, *Works*, IV, pp. 91–2.

entire Knox–Locke correspondence as it has come down to us via Calderwood.[91]

The documents which were Peter Lorimer's source for *John Knox and the Church of England*, including the letter to Knox from the separatists, were also preserved by Field, for they are to be found among the 'Seconde Parte of a Register' MSS, material which we know Field to have collected[92] and which are now part of the Morrice MSS. And, finally, I think that I have to agree with Martin Simpson, who in a critique of some of my own work[93] suggested that Field must have been involved in the collection and publication of the materials we know as *A Brieff Discours off the Troubles Begonne at Franckford* (which includes the letter from the General Assembly to the English bishops of December 1566).[94] I would still insist (as I did in my very first publication, in 1958) that the major blocks of documentation making up the *Brieff Discours* were put and kept together by the Genevan elder, soldier and Puritan activist, Thomas Wood. But it is impossible to mistake the stamp of Field's notoriously 'bitter' style in the closing pages of the discourse, and in its marginalia.[95]

---

[91] How the letters reached Calderwood we do not know, although David Laing was probably on the right track when he suggested that the letters may have been taken back to Scotland by some of the Scottish ministers who took refuge in England from the Black Acts in 1584; and I would tentatively suggest John Davidson, with whom Field was very friendly. The printer Robert Waldegrave, who left for Scotland after the Martin Marprelate affair, is another but less likely possibility. The extent to which some of the letters have been anglicized may cast a little light on the uses which Field may have intended to make of them.

[92] Peel, *The Seconde Parte of a Register*, I, pp. 1–18.

[93] Martin Simpson, 'Of the Troubles Begun at Frankfurt, A.D. 1554', in Duncan Shaw (ed.), *Reformation and Revolution: Essays Presented to the Very Reverend Principal Emeritus Hugh Watt* (Edinburgh, 1967); Martin Simpson, *John Knox and the Troubles Begun at Frankfurt* (West Linton, 1975); Martin Simpson, *What is Puritanism?* (West Linton, 1981), pp. 93–117. Simpson turned into something of an Aunt Sally; Patrick Collinson, 'The Authorship of *A Brieff Discours off the Troubles Begonne at Franckford*', *JEH*, 9 (1958), 188–208, reprinted in his *Godly People*, pp. 191–211.

[94] Petheram, *A Brieff Discours*, pp. ccxii–ccxv.

[95] An example from the text of the *Brieff Discours*: 'such as are turne coates and can chaunge with al seasons, subscribinge to what so ever, and can cap it can cope it an curry for advantage ... '; and of the marginalia: 'Yff maister Horne [Bishop Robert Horne of Winchester] tooke such deliberation before he would subscribe to that article; what meanethe this that poore ignorant men and wemen must thus subscribe upon the sudden or ells to newgate' – Knox's correspondents of 1567 (Petheram, *Brieff Discours*, pp. cxcv, xcv). Field and his co-author Thomas Wilcox were themselves in Newgate in 1572, following the publication of *An Admonition to the Parliament*, and were interrogated by the chaplain to the Archbishop of Canterbury. Wilcox said, 'I gather by your wordes that you are grieved with the bitterness of the stile,' and blamed Field for that. Field responded, 'I think that thinge speciallie towcheth me, and therfore I answere, as God

But for John Field, my own modest career would never have got off the ground. And but for Field, it would not have been possible to construct this chapter on John Knox and the Church of England and the women of England. Thank you, godly Master Field.

---

hath his Moses, so he hath his Elijah ... It is no tyme to blanch, nor to sewe cushens under mens elbowes, or to flatter them in their synnes.' (Peel, *Second Parte of a Register*, I, p. 89) Was it John Knox who had inspired John Field to become an Elijah?

PART TWO

Political and Theological Thought

CHAPTER FIVE

John Knox and the Early Church Fathers

David F. Wright

The weighty assemblage of papers on *The Reception of the Church Fathers in the West: From the Carolingians to the Maurists*, recently edited by Irena Backus of Geneva, includes no chapter on Scotland and only one reference to a Scottish writer.[1] This almost total silence is not surprising. Very little has been published on the study and use of the Fathers in late medieval and early modern Scotland, in contrast to England in the same period.[2] Nor can the absence of monographs and articles be attributed merely to scholarly neglect. The Fathers were not prominent in Renaissance humanist learning in Scotland, although how significant a minor role they played should become clearer from a growing concentration on this phase of Scottish religious and intellectual history.[3] John Knox never mentions Erasmus. Scottish readers were dependent on England or the Continent for texts or translations of the early Christian writers. Even by 1700, no works of any of the Fathers had issued from a Scottish press.[4]

Questions arise in this context which bear on the heart of the character of the religious Reformation in Scotland – its lateness, its level of learning and commitment to educational renewal, the controversies that were most keenly and extensively agitated within it, its continuity and

---

[1] Irena Backus (ed.), *The Reception of the Church Fathers in the West* (2 vols, Leiden, New York and Cologne, 1997).

[2] For example, the inaugural lecture by my former teacher, Stanley L. Greenslade, *The English Reformers and the Fathers of the Church* (Oxford, 1960); the essay by Mark Vessey, 'English Translations of the Latin Fathers, 1517–1611', in Backus (ed.), *The Reception of the Church Fathers*, II, pp. 775–835, and numerous other studies, not least on Cranmer, Jewel and Hooker. For Scotland, see David F. Wright 'The Fathers in the Scottish Reformation', forthcoming in Markus Wriedt (ed.), *Auctoritas Patrum III* (Mainz, 1999–2000).

[3] Cf. John MacQueen (ed.), *Humanism in Renaissance Scotland* (Edinburgh, 1990); A.A. MacDonald, Michael Lynch and Ian B. Cowan (eds), *The Renaissance in Scotland: Studies in Literature, Religion, History and Culture Offered to John Durkan* (Leiden, 1994).

[4] Cf. Harry G. Aldis, *A List of Books Printed in Scotland before 1700*, revd edn (Edinburgh, 1970).

discontinuity with the pre-Reformation Church, and its dependence on and independence of Reformation movements elsewhere which obviously professed an allegiance to the faith of the first Christian centuries. Unpromising though an investigation of the Fathers' place in the Scottish Reformation must at first blush appear, it must hope to make some contribution to the consideration of these larger questions.

But why begin with John Knox? He is not the single Scottish author named in Backus's collection. Familiarity with Knox's works is likely to have created an assumption that my title is a non-starter. Did not the rigour of his appeal to 'the express Word of God' exclude altogether any scope for the patristic witnesses to influence debate and decision? It is not difficult to come across statements of Knox which evince a minimizing attitude to the Fathers. In 1562 Knox engaged in a public disputation over three days on the Mass with Quintin Kennedy, abbot of the Cluniac house of Crossraguel in Ayrshire, at Maybole in that county. Knox soon perceived a need to set out some of his fundamentals: 'Because I perceave, bothe in your protestation and artickle, that ye dispute not upon these maters as disputable, but as of things alreadie concluded, by the Kirk, General Counselles, and Doctors; I must say somwhat in the beginning how farre I will admit any of the forenamed.' The true Kirk heeds only 'the expres worde' of Jesus Christ or His Apostles. An individual bearing the testimony of God's Scriptures deserves more credit than a General Council's declarations without it:

> And as concerning the authoritie of the Doctors ... , I think my Lorde will bind me no straiter then he hath desyred to be bound him self, that is, that men be not receaved as God; and, therefore, with Augustine I consent, that whatsoever the Doctors propone, and plainly confirme the same by the evident testimonie of the Scriptures, I am hartlie content to receave the same; but els, that it be laughful [lawful] to me with Jerome to say, whatsoever is affirmed without the authoritie of God's Scriptures, with the same facilitie it may be rejected as it is affirmed.[5]

For the purposes of the debate, Kennedy concedes Knox's terms. Knox successfully sees off the Fathers, who are not cited, except twice by Knox. It is worth noting these two instances. Inconstancy, says Knox, ought not to be charged to those who 'retreat there formar error, as in divers heades did that learned Augustine'.[6] The other reference reveals a touch of ironic humour in Knox. In an argument about sacrifice in the

---

[5] Knox, *Works*, VI, p. 194.
[6] Ibid., VI, pp. 195–6. The reference is to Augustine's *Retractationes*, best translated *Revisions* or *Reconsiderations*, in which he reviewed his writings in order and occasionally admitted that he had been wrong.

Mass, Kennedy had challenged him to show why Melchizedek brought forth bread and wine if not to offer them to God (cf. Genesis 14:18):

> As touching the cause wherefore he broght it forth (if place shal be given to conjectors, and that not grounded without great probabilitie, and also with sufrage of some of the ancients, to wit, Josephus and Chrysostom). It may be said that Melchisedec, being an king, broght forth bread and wine to refresh Abraham and his werie souldiors.[7]

Knox's most extended doctrinal treatise was a defence of predestination against the attack of an unnamed English 'Anabaptist' commonly identified as Robert Cooke. It was written probably in 1557 or 1558 while he was resident in Geneva. At one point Knox expresses surprise that his opponent of predestination should 'amongest the ancient Doctors ... seke patrocinie or defense in this mater'. The Anabaptist writer had claimed that 'the ancient Doctors' agreed with his interpretation of God's hardening of the heart of Pharaoh.[8] Knox grants that he does not dissent from the Anabaptists' set practice of deciding everything by the plain text of Scripture: 'If you had produced any Doctor who had confirmed his interpetation by the plaine Worde of God, of reason I oght to have answered, either by the same, or by some other Doctor of equall authoritie, or els to have improved his interpretation by the plaine Scriptures.'[9] The critic's failure to name any theologian leaves the field open to Knox, who proceeds to quote a page of Augustine against Julian,[10] and then to comment more generally:

> Thus far have I alleged unto you the mynd of one Doctor in this our controversie; when ye shall bring forth the mynd of any so well grounded upon Scriptures as he doth his sentence, I promyse to answer, if I can. I am not ignorant that divers of the doctors, (yea, and Augustine himself,) in some places may seme to favour your opinion at the first sight. But if their wordes, in one place, be compared with their plaine mynd, and with the scope of their disputation, in other places, it shall plainely appere, that none that live this day do more plainely speak against your Error then some of them have written.[11]

Knox will never allow himself greater confidence in the Fathers than he evinces here. He has perhaps expressed himself unguardedly in engaging with a writer for whom he knows that the Church teachers of the early centuries count for little.

---

[7] Ibid., VI, p. 202.

[8] Ibid., V, p. 321.

[9] Ibid., V, p. 331.

[10] Ibid., V, p. 332. The margin gives 'Lib. 3. ca. 5', which should be *Contra Julianum* 5.3.13, 5.4.15 (Migne, *Patrologia Latina* 44, cols 790–91, 793).

[11] Knox, *Works*, V, pp. 332–3.

More typical of Knox is the basis for proceeding he lays down in his
Appellation to the Nobility and Estates of Scotland against the ecclesiastical condemnation passed on him in his absence. The *Appellation* too
was written in Geneva, in 1558. He appeals for a public hearing, with
God Himself through His Word as the judge:

> And if they think to have advantage by theyre councils and doctours,
> this I further offer, to admit the one and the other as witnesses in
> all matters debateable; three thinges ... being granted unto me:
> First, That the most auncient Councils nighest to the Primitive
> church, in which the learned and godlie Fathers did examine all
> matters by Goddes Word, may be holden of most auctoritie.
> Secondarely, That no determination of councils nor man be admit-
> ted against the plaine veritie of Goddes Word, nor against the
> determination of those foure chefe Councils, whose auctoritie hath
> bene and is holden by them equal with the auctoritie of the foure
> Evangelistes. And last, That to no Doctour be geven greater
> auctoritie then Augustine requireth to be geven to his writinges: to
> witt, if he plainely prove not his affirmation by God's infallible
> Worde, that then his sentence be rejected, and imputed to the error
> of a man. These thinges graunted and admitted, I shall no more
> refuse the testimonies of Councils and Doctours then shall my
> adversaries.[12]

The marginal note refers the reader to the prologue of Augustine's
Retractationes, where he says something not unlike what Knox assumes.[13] At least here Knox elevates the first four Ecumenical Councils
to the status of a criterion in evaluating other conciliar or human
deliverances. But there is, unless I am mistaken, no place in his corpus
where we observe him operating in accordance with these stipulations.
He must have known when writing the *Appellation* that there was little
enough chance of his plea being accepted and his being granted a public
hearing on these terms.

We come to the two works of Knox in which the Fathers have a more
substantive role. The *Apology for the Protestants who are Holden in
Prison at Paris* is only in part from the pen of Knox, being basically an
English translation of a short French apologia composed in prison itself,
which has survived in the original only in Jean Crespin's *Livre des*

---

[12] Ibid., IV, pp. 518–19. The parallel between the four canonical Gospels and the four
earliest Ecumenical Councils (Nicaea, 325; Constantinople, 381; Ephesus, 431; Chalcedon,
451) goes back to Gregory I, for example, *Registrum Epistularum* I: 24 (*Corpus
Christianorum Series Latina* CXL, p. 32).

[13] Augustine cites I Corinthians 11:31, 'If we judged ourselves, we should not be
judged by the Lord', and Matthew 12:36, 'Of every idle word men speak they shall give
account on the day of judgement'. He comments, 'Hence it remains for me to judge
myself before the sole Teacher whose judgement of my offences I wish to avoid'; Augustine, *Retractationes*, prol. 2.

Martyrs.[14] The translation was done, wholly or in large part, by someone other than Knox,[15] but he added a preface and a handful of additions of varying length, and also exercised 'a greatter libertie than sum men will approve in a translatour or interpretour' in adding much, both words and several sentences, to the last part of the *Apology*.[16] The English *Apology* was a product of Knox's sojourn in Dieppe in late 1557, but was not published, so it seems, until David Laing's edition of the collected works in the mid-nineteenth century.

The interest of the *Apology* for our purposes is that the French original consisted in the main of extended patristic passages, collected by the unknown compilers, 'whairby it sall appeir that sic detestabill crymes in tymes past have bene laid to the charge of the Christianis, to the end that thair purgatioun and wordis may this day serve for oure Defence aganis thois that sclander us'.[17] Tertullian's *Apology* provides over a dozen pages, and extracts of a page and a half or less are drawn from his *Ad Scapulam*, Justin Martyr's *Dialogue with Trypho* and *First Apology*, Cyprian's *Ad Demetrianum*, Hilary's *Against Auxentius*, the

---

[14] See Laing's introduction, Knox, *Works*, IV, pp. 289–95. Laing consulted the Geneva 1619 edition of Crespin's *Histoire des Martyrs*, where the 'Teneur de l'Apologie' is found on ff. 466v–470v. It had appeared first in *Histoire des vrays Tesmoins de la verite de L'Evangile, qui de leur sang l' on signée, depuis Jean Hus vsques au temps present* (Geneva, 1570), ff. 476r–480r. (A photographic reprint, with 'Table complémentaire', was issued by Editions Photographiques Mosa, Profondeville, 1964.) The 1619 text was newly edited by Daniel Benoit in 3 vols at Toulouse in 1887, where the 'Apologie' is found in vol. II, pp. 548–58 (548 n.1 wrongly says that it did not appear in Crespin's martyrology until Simon Goulart's edition of 1582). On Crespin's developing collection, see Jean-François Gilmont, *Bibliographie des éditions de Jean Crespin, 1550–1572* (2 vols, Verviers, 1981), and *Jean Crespin, un éditeur réformé du XVIᵉ siècle* (Geneva, 1981), pp. 165–90, 258. The 'Apologie' was first printed by Antoine de La Roche Chandieu in his *Histoire des Persecutions, & martyrs de l' Eglise de Paris depuis l' An 1557 ...* (Lyons, 1563), whence Crespin took much besides the 'Apologie' (Gilmont, *Jean Crespin*, pp. 180–81). Here the 'Teneur de l'Apologie' occupies pp. 87, 79–108 (pagination irregular).

[15] 'being translatit in the Inglische toung by a faithfull Brother', but the marginal note reads: 'The former and maist part was translatit be anothir, becaus of my othir labouris', Knox, *Works*, IV, p. 301. See also below, with n. 16.

[16] Pierre Janton, *John Knox (ca. 1513–1572). L' homme et l'oeuvre* (Paris, 1967), pp. 433–7, introduces the work and compares part of Knox's translation with the original French. If we exclude Knox's minor but numerous additions to the latter part (presumably *Works*, IV, pp. 337–46; see n. 3 on p. 337; a critical edition alone will determine Knox's contribution), he was responsible for over 20 pages of the 50-page *Apology*, which would have warranted its inclusion in Ian Hazlett's 'A Working Bibliography of Writings by John Knox', in R.V. Schnucker (ed.), *Calviniana. Ideas and Influence of Jean Calvin* (Kirksville, MO, 1988), pp. 185–93, had it been published in the sixteenth century.

[17] Knox, *Works*, IV, p. 306.

letter of the Gallican Churches and Hadrian's rescript to Fundanus, both from Eusebius's *Church History*, and the sufferings of Edessa's Christians under Valens from the *Church History* of Socrates. A longer section of over three pages comes from Minucius Felix, here still identified as Book 8 of Arnobius, having thus been published for the first time at Rome in 1542.[18]

Although Knox appears to have faithfully transmitted the French Protestants' catena, even here he deems it necessary to add comments of his own which imply an attenuated sense of identification with the persecuted early Christians. Not long into his preface he declares:

> For now it is not necessarie that we revolve the bukis of ald and famous wrytteris to understand and learne what was the blind furie and beastlie tirannye of their cruell persecutouris, who schortlie efter Chrystis Ascentioun did trubill his Kirk; nether yit what was the invincibill pacience of sic as than professit him and his doctrine; for presentlie oure eyis may behald and oure earis may heir the ane and the other sa evidentlie.[19]

Nor does the preface convey a corrective note, on the value, nevertheless, of such a catena of testimonies.

In his first extended addition, designed 'For the Better Applycatioun of the Doctouris Wordis to oure Tyme', Knox addresses the obvious difference between Tertullian's age and his own – that then Christians suffered at the hands of idolatrous pagans, but now of Christian authorities: 'The difference standeth onlie in this, that the persecutoris of oure dayis have usurpit the name of the Kirk and of Catholick Christianis, and have imposit upon us the names of Lutherianis, Sismatickis, and Heretikis.'[20] In language that must recall to us the Scots Confession, '[A] name falslie usurpit, (yea, albeit it aperteane to thame be liniall descent, or be successioun, and approbatioun of men,) profitteth nothing whair the workis ar found contrarious to the titillis.'[21] Knox will not dispute the fact of lineal succession, but will deny its validating significance.

His next, and longer, addition picks up the French *Apology*'s somewhat free citation of Tertullian's *Apology* chapter 6. Knox paraphrases: 'He did dampn the Gentiles, becaus thai praisit Antiquitie in word, and yit in lyfe, maneris, and conversatioun, thai wer found insolent'; retaining

---

[18] *Arnobii Disputationum adversus gentes libri octo, nunc primum in lucem editi*, ed. F. Sabaeus (Rome, 1542). Marginal page references in La Roche Chandieu's *Histoire* (1563) and Crespin's *Histoire* (1570) are to the 1546 Basel edition by Sigimund Gelenius, published by Froben and Episcopius (1563, pp. 92–6; 1570, f. 474r–v).

[19] Knox, *Works*, IV, pp. 297–8.

[20] Ibid., IV, p. 310.

[21] Ibid., IV, p. 311. Cf. *Scots Confession*, ed. G.D. Henders... (Edinburgh, 1960), art. 18, p. 71.

and forsaking ancient ways at will.[22] Knox warms to his theme: our adversaries today

> cry in the earis of the ignorant multitude, Antiquitie, antiquitie, antiquitie, Fatheris, fatheris, Consallis, consallis, approve oure Religioun. And we answer, that most gladlie will we that Antiquitie, Consallis, and Fatheris judge in oure cause, provydit, (as Tertulian in the same chapter requyreth,) that that religioun be judgeit maist pure and perfyt whilk salbe proved maist aunccient, and that the Fatheris nor Consallis be not authorised against the manifest testimony of the Halie Gaist.[23]

This amounts to deriving from the Fathers themselves a criterion for not taking them too seriously.

Knox then seeks to demonstrate the hollowness of the alleged antiquity of 'the tuo cheif groundis of thair kingdome', namely, papal supremacy and transubstantiation. The former is no older than Phocas, the Byzantine emperor 602–10, the latter than Lanfranc of Bec in the eleventh century.[24] Knox then unfolds a powerful rhetorical display in which Tertullian is called to pass judgement on the pretensions of a triumphalist papal establishment crying up 'oure halie Mother the Kirk, Fatheris, Consallis, and Antiquitie'. Knox is confident that

> Tertuliane suld pronunce his former sentence, and suld say, 'Theis men of Kirk ar in all poyntis becum lyke to the auncient Gentillis who did first persecut Chryst Jesus in his membris. For thai clame to antiquitie, and do efter a new fassioun, thay leif undone that whilk cheiflie thai aught to do, to wit, to instruct the pepill, and trewlie to preache Chrystis Evangell; and thair do theis thingis whilk thai aught not to do, to reule lyke tirantis, and to persecut the Chrystianis ... And theis simpill men who desyre reformatioun of religioun now decayit ... ar in all poyntis lyke to oure brethren the Chrystianis in my dayis, for whome I wrait my Apologie and Defence ... ' The same [comments Knox] sall everie godlie wrytter and father thrie hundreth yeiris efter him affirme. Whilk thing, God willing, some day I sall mak evident to sic as list tak pane to reid the veritie conteanit in thair wryttingis.[25]

This promise, it appears, Knox never made good. We can but admire the dexterity with which he capitalizes on a martyrological booklet and turns it to controversial dogmatic advantage. Whether his reasoning is wholly consistent is open to scrutiny: on the one hand, Tertullian is invoked to call appeals to antiquity into question, while on the other hand Knox happily endorses the antiquity of the first five centuries.

---

[22] Knox, *Works*, IV, p. 313.
[23] Ibid., IV, pp. 313–14.
[24] Ibid., IV, pp. 314–15.
[25] Ibid., IV, p. 317.

The second work of Knox's in which the Fathers feature prominently is wholly his own, *The First Blast of the Trumpet against the Monstrous Regiment of Women*. Written wholly or largely at Dieppe in late 1557 and published in the spring of 1558, it was directed to the people of England with the removal of Queen Mary Tudor its sole or primary aim.[26] To defend his argument against the aspersion of novelty, he will 'recite the mindes of some auncient writers' to show that his interpretation of Scripture was 'the uniforme consent of the most parte of godlie writers since the time of the Apostles'.[27]

Knox begins with three works of Tertullian, *De habitu muliebri* (i.e. *De cultu feminarum* book 1), *De virginibus velandis* and *Contra Marcionem*.[28] 'Of the same minde is Origen and divers others, yea, even till the dayes of Augustine; whose sentences I omit to avoid prolixitie.'[29] Knox renews the series with extracts from altogether five writings of Augustine, *De ordine, Contra Faustum, De civitate Dei, De Trinitate* and *De continentia*, and a sixth identified in the margin as 'In quaest. Veteris Testamenti, quaest. 43', which turns out to be from Ambrosiaster's *Quaestiones Veteris et Novi Testamenti* 45.[30] Following Augustine come Ambrose's *Hexaemeron* and his (i.e. Ambrosiaster's) expositions of Ephesians 5, 1 Timothy 2, 1 Corinthians 14, and Romans 16.[31] Several homilies of Chrysostom are quoted, not all of them readily identifiable by the marginal indications.[32]

---

[26] See the important article of my colleague Jane E.A. Dawson, 'The Two John Knoxes: England, Scotland and the 1558 Tracts', *JEH*, 42 (1991), pp. 555–76.

[27] Knox, *Works*, IV, p. 381.

[28] Ibid., IV, pp. 381–3. The marginal references in Laing are here and later often inaccurate, but are given in largely corrected form in Roger A. Mason's modernized edition, Knox, *On Rebellion*, pp. 15–16. Mason improves considerably on the poor edition by Marvin Breslow, *The Political Writings of John Knox* (Washington, DC, 1985) [hereafer Breslow], but Mason has followed Breslow's confusion of Justinus, the secular Roman author, possibly of the third century AD, who epitomized the *Historiae Philippicae* of Pompeius Trogus, with Justin Martyr – in fact Ps-Justin's *Discourse to the Greeks* (Breslow, p. 78; Knox, *On Rebellion*, p. 10; cf. Knox, *Works*, IV, p. 375). The source is Justinus, *Historiae*, 2.4. On Knox's reference here to the Amazons, see Simon Shepherd, *Amazons and Warrior Women: Varieties of Feminism in Seventeenth-Century Drama* (Brighton, 1981), pp. 14, 22–4, 203.

[29] Knox, *Works*, IV, p. 383.

[30] Ibid., IV, pp. 383–4, 389–90; Knox, *On Rebellion*, pp. 16–18, 22. Ian Hazlett's review of Breslow, in *SHR*, 66 (1987), pp. 207–9, partly identifies the last reference discussed; Breslow omits it altogether.

[31] Knox, *Works*, IV, pp. 384–6; Knox, *On Rebellion*, pp. 18–19 (but failing to distinguish Pseudo-Ambrose from Ambrose; cf. p. lxi). Breslow, pp. 79 nn. 42–4, apparently aware that Ambrose is now credited with no Pauline commentary but unaware of Ambrosiaster, ingeniously tracks the references to other genuine works of Ambrose.

[32] Knox, *Works*, IV, pp. 386–9, 392–3; Knox, *On Rebellion*, pp. 19–21, 24–5. Breslow, pp. 79 nn. 46–51, 57, seems baffled. See further below.

Finally a summary is given of a sermon of Basil the Great 'upon some places of Scripture', and the briefest mention is made of 'divers other places' where he concludes that woman is not suited to rule nor allowed to teach.[33]

This collection of patristic witnesses in Knox's *First Blast* has been assigned exaggerated significance by writers on the Scottish reformer. In a short but spirited book which argues for Knox a greater regard for early Church tradition than has commonly been recognized, Hugh Watt has him assembling 'a formidable array of citations from the Church Fathers'.[34] Richard Greaves, whose collected essays on *Theology and Revolution in the Scottish Reformation: Studies in the Thought of John Knox* provide with Pierre Janton's study the most solid presentation of Knox's theology yet available, goes further still: Knox 'devoted considerable attention to the patristic fathers [*sic*] with an eye to their views on female sovereigns. The results are impressive'.[35] For the writing of the *First Blast*, Greaves tells us, Knox 'immersed himself in Tertullian, Augustine, Origen, Ambrose, Chrysostom, Basil the Great and others'.[36] This and other writings reveal that the Church Fathers featured among 'a variety of major sources' of Knox's theology.[37] They were even one of the sources of his concept of authority, on which he was nearest to Tertullian. His 'favourite Fathers' were Augustine and Chrysostom, followed by Tertullian and Ambrose. Greaves points out that most of Knox's references to the Fathers appear in writings of the Marian exile years, but he assumes that Knox must have been introduced to the Fathers in his early theological education.[38] This assumption enables Greaves to review the

---

[33] Knox, *Works*, IV, p. 389; Knox, *On Rebellion*, p. 21 n. 15, references unhelpfully only by page in the 1540 Basel edition (and there were two editions of Basil published in 1540 in Basel!), but correctly, to the dubium *Homilia dicta in Lacisis* (*Clavis Patrum Graecorum*, no. 2912), at Migne, *Patrologia Graeca*, 31, col. 1453. Cf. Irena Backus, *Lectures humanistes de Basile de Césarée*, Collection des Etudes Augustiniennes, Série Antiquité, 125 (Paris, 1990), p. 214, no. 472.

[34] Hugh Watt, *John Knox in Controversy* (Edinburgh, 1950), p. 75, and see pp. 40–42.

[35] Richard L. Greaves, *Theology and Revolution in the Scottish Reformation: Studies in the Thought of John Knox* (Grand Rapids, MI, 1980), p. 162.

[36] Ibid., p. 221.

[37] Ibid., p. 223.

[38] Ibid., pp. 12–13. Greaves makes no reference to Beza's record of the effect of Knox's early acquaintance with Jerome and Augustine while a student of John Mair in St Andrews: 'quum iam videretur illo suo praeceptore nihilo inferior Sophista futurus, lucem tamen in tenebris & sibi & aliis accendit. Siquidem Hieronymi & Augustini libros ibi nactus, ex eorum scriptis, non fastidire modo, sed etiam redarguere multa usque adeo libere coepit', *Icones, id est, Verae Imagines Virorum Doctrina simul et Pietate Illustrium* ... (Geneva, 1580), sig. Ee iiir. I read Beza to mean not that Knox criticized much in the works of the two Fathers, but that on the basis of them he began to attack much in

teachings of a handful of Fathers on the duty of active resistance in order to ascertain which might have influenced the stand Knox took as early as 1547 in St Andrews. He rather quaintly concludes that one cannot determine 'precisely how much Knox was influenced by Origen and perhaps Chrysostom on these general issues' – probably less, one reads with relief, than by the medievals and his contemporaries.[39]

Greaves dissents from G.D. Henderson's judgement that on the right of resistance Knox 'shared the view of Ambrose' in particular.[40] Henderson's main argument claims that 'Knox's general view of the Bible' was remarkably close to that of the fourth- and fifth-century Fathers. He endeavours to demonstrate this on a number of topics in their respective doctrines of Scripture – perspicuity, sufficiency, relation of Old Testament to New, verbal inspiration, and so on. In the interest of illustrating 'the amount of the past that survived in [Knox's] attitude, and the extent to which in practice both the subjective method of the Anabaptist and the tradition and authority of the Church forced themselves upon him', Henderson even dares to claim that 'Knox's position is not quite so different from that of the pre-Reformation Church as he would have us suppose'.[41]

Confident judgements on this subject are still premature, for the scholarly groundwork remains to be done. It is regrettably true that we still lack a satisfactory critical edition for any of Knox's writings, except for the jointly authored *First Book of Discipline*, and, with a sizeable reservation for its modernized orthography, Dickinson's version of the *History of the Reformation*. Detailed identification of texts and determination of sources, wherever possible, must precede ambitious verdicts about Knox's predilection for the Fathers in general, or for any Father in particular. The claims of Greaves and Henderson remain at best. unproven, at worst wildly inflated.

Catholic religion. John Spottiswoode, *The History of the Church of Scotland* (London, 1655), p. 264, makes this reading unambiguous: 'By reading the ancients, especially the works of S. *Austen*, he was brought to the knowledge of the truth.' For other early accounts of Knox influenced by Beza, see Peter Hume Brown, *John Knox* (2 vols, London, 1895), I, p. 56. Janton, *John Knox*, seems to interpret Beza differently at p. 57 from p. 225, and most recent writers take no note of Beza. Greaves, *Theology and Revolution*, provides a list, not exhaustive, of references to different Fathers in Knox at p. 227 n. 34 (including 'Firmian'). See also Richard G. Kyle's pedestrian but functional study *The Mind of John Knox* (Lawrence, KA, 1984), pp. 32–3, in the course of his comments on Knox's conception of authority.

[39] Greaves, *Theology and Revolution*, pp. 144–5. Greaves discerns a particular kinship between Origen and Knox, especially on natural law.

[40] Ibid., p. 144; G.D. Henderson, 'John Knox and the Bible', *RSCHS*, 9 (1947), pp. 97–110, at p. 109.

[41] Henderson, 'John Knox and the Bible', pp. 100, 110, *passim*.

When Knox's resort to the Fathers is set alongside that of many another mainstream reformer in the sixteenth century, it appears circumscribed, conventional and derivative. One exception might be the collection of patristic testimonies in *The First Blast of the Trumpet*. It is true that Susan Felch has recently asserted that in this work 'classical texts and Church Fathers are dutifully trotted out' rather than play any fundamental or structural part in Knox's argument. The former Knox himself acknowledges to be a weak element, the latter were necessary to repel allegations of novelty.[42] But no commentator on this much commented treatise has yet identified the source or sources of Knox's patristic citations.[43] Ian Hazlett's review of Marvin Breslow's defective edition proposes that Knox plucked several of his patristic quotations from the section on female subordination in the *Corpus Iuris Canonici*.[44] But a schismatic like Tertullian never made it into the *Corpus*, and a comparison reveals very little common ground between Knox and this supposed source. The only two texts they share are Ambrose, *Hexaemeron* 5.7.18 and Ps-Augustine, *Quaestiones Veteris et Novi Testamenti* 45.3, but Gratian in the *Corpus* lacks the opening phrase of this latter text in Knox ('Howe can woman be the image of God') and does not give it in the form of a question.[45]

Nor is light shed by earlier or contemporary writings on women's role in general or on the gynecocratic issue in particular. It is noteworthy

---

[42] Knox, *Works*, IV, p. 376: 'this parte of nature is not my moste sure foundation'; ibid., IV, p. 381: 'understand this my judgement to be no newe interpretation of Goddes Scriptures, but to be the uniforme consent of the moste parte of godlie writers since the time of the Apostles.' See Susan M. Felch, 'The Rhetoric of Biblical Authority: John Knox and the Question of Women', *Sixteenth Century Journal*, 26 (1995), pp. 805–22, at p. 812. Janton, *John Knox*, p. 225, suggests that Knox could have learnt from Jean Bodin on women's rule, but he appears to have forgotten the chronology. Bodin's *Six livres de la République* was published in 1576.

[43] For example, Amanda Shephard, *Gender and Authority in Sixteenth-Century England: The Knox Debate* (Keele, 1994), in her final chapter loosely surveys the appeal to the Fathers in this and similar works. Paula Louise Scalingi, 'The Scepter or the Distaff: The Question of Female Sovereignty, 1516–1607', *The Historian*, 41 (1978), pp. 59–75, simply notes Knox's use of 'medieval authors' like Chrysostom and Augustine (p. 66). The overstated comments of Richard Greaves in his discussion of 'The Gynecocracy Controversy' in his *Theology and Revolution in the Scottish Reformation: Studies in the Thought of John Knox* (Grand Rapids, MI, 1980), pp. 157 ff., have been touched on above. Note also Francis Lee Utley, *The Crooked Rib: An Analytical Index to the Argument about Women in English and Scottish Literature to the End of the Year 1568* (Columbus, OH, 1944).

[44] In *SHR*, 66 (1987), pp. 208–9.

[45] Knox, *Works*, IV, pp. 383–4 (cf. Knox, *On Rebellion*, pp. 17–18); Gratian, *Decretum* II: causa XXXIII: qn. V: 17–18, in E. Friedberg (ed.), *Corpus Iuris Canonici* (Leipzig 1879), I, cols 1255–6.

that Christopher Goodman, Knox's close associate at Geneva, in his justification of the overthrow of ungodly rulers in *How Superior Powers Oght to be Obeyd*, published in the same place and year as Knox's *First Blast* (Geneva, 1558), advances the case against women's rule with no patristic reinforcement.[46] But then Knox's polemic in effect stands at the fountainhead of the tradition of antigynecocratic literature. Even though this developed out of the wider debate on women's right to exercise authority, the accession of Mary Tudor in 1553 was an essential catalyst.[47]

Nevertheless, the probability must lie with Knox's quarrying from earlier collections of patristic testimonies rather than directly from the texts of the Fathers themselves. This would explain their varying degree of proximity to the original texts, and Knox's occasional misattribution. Several of his citations from the homilies of John Chrysostom are no more than paraphrastic glosses on the passages in the original, that can be identified only with difficulty from the imprecise, incorrect or absent marginal references.[48] Yet the looseness of Knox's citations cannot be granted too much weight in itself, for his biblical quotations were frequently surprisingly imprecise for one who stood so adamantly for 'the express Word of God'.[49] For the present, then, the immediate source or sources of Knox's patristic armoury in the *First Blast* remain undetermined.

The only incontrovertible evidence of Knox's first hand consultation of the Fathers occurs in a letter written to Elizabeth Bowes from Newcastle, probably in 1553. A letter from her had reached him, and Knox writes in reply that, while

> I was sitting at my buke, and in contemplating Mathowis Gospell in this place whairin the Parrable of gud seid is sawin, the enemy also sawing wickit cokill amung the same, I revolved sum maist godlie Expositioun, and amangis the rest Chrisostome, wha nottis upon thir wordis: 'The enemy did this, that we may knaw that

---

[46] Of Scottish responses to the *First Blast*, the one by John Leslie, former Bishop of Ross, *A Defence of the Honour of ... Princesse Marie Quene of Scotlande ... , with a declaration ... that the regimente of women ys conformable to the lawe of God and nature* (London, 1569), uses far more patristic argumentation than David Chambers' *Discours de la legitime succession des femmes aux possessions de leurs parens: & du gouvernement des princesses aux Empires & Royaumes ...* (Paris, 1579).

[47] Cf. James E. Phillips, Jr, 'The Background of Spenser's Attitude toward Women Rulers', *Huntington Library Quarterly*, 5 (1941–42), pp. 5–32, especially pp. 5–8.

[48] See the greater precision provided (but not fully) in Knox, *On Rebellion*, pp. 15–22, 24.

[49] See David F. Wright, 'John Knox's Bible', forthcoming in the papers of the conference on 'The Bible as Book: The Reformation' held under the auspices of The Scriptorium at Hampton Court, Herefordshire in May 1997, to be published by the British Library.

whasaever is belovit of God hes the Divill to his enemy; and thairfoir aucht we maist rejos when we find the Divill maist rage aganis us, for that is an evident signe that we ar not under his bondage, but ar frie servandis to Jesus Chryst; to whome becaus the Devill is enemy, he man also declair him self enemy to us.' In reiding of this his halie judgement, your battell and dolour was befoir my eis.[50]

The verse in question is Matthew 13:28, but Chrysostom's homilies on this Gospel fail to furnish Knox's quotation.[51] The ultimate source is instead the *Opus Imperfectum in Matthaeum*, composed by an unidentified sixth-century Arian bishop but long attributed to Chrysostom and included as such in the early sixteenth-century editions of his works.[52] But Ps-Chrysostom provides only the first sentence of Knox's quotation: *Et non intelligis, quod a Deo diligitur, hoc a diabolo expugnatur* ('And you do not understand, what is loved by God, this is assaulted by the Devil').[53] Yet Knox clearly intended the whole of what Laing printed in quotation marks to be understood as Chrysostom's – 'this his halie judgement'. Perhaps he was reading a commentary on Matthew's Gospel (or a harmony of the Synoptic Gospels) constructed in the form of a catena from the Fathers, or more broadly from approved expositors, such as Robert Estienne (Stephanus) and Augustin Marlorat compiled for Bible students of the reformed community. The continuation of Knox's quotation, identifying us as 'frie servandis to Jesus Chryst', has a Lutheran ring to it.

It is not the purpose of this essay to catalogue all the references to the Fathers in Knox's writings. Some additional illustrations will nevertheless fill out the picture already outlined. In his *Letter to the Commonalty of Scotland* of July 1558, which accompanied his *Appellation* to the nobles and estates of the realm, Knox enunciated what should by now be a recognizable theme tune:

---

[50] Knox, *Works*, III, pp. 350–51. Cf. Peter Lorimer, *John Knox and the Church of England* (London, 1875), p. 165: 'In another interesting letter … we see the great preacher "sitting at his book", with a folio of Chrysostom lying open on his study table beside his English Bible.'

[51] The marginal reference to one of Chrysostom's homilies on Matthew in *The First Blast of the Trumpet* (Knox, *Works*, IV, p. 387; Knox, *On Rebellion*, p. 20, n. 12) is in reality to Ps-Chrysostom, *Opus Imperfectum in Matthaeum Homilia*, 44 (Migne, *Patrologia Graeca*, 56, col. 880), on Matthew 23:14. On this work, see the following note.

[52] See J.H.A. van Banning, 'The *Opus Imperfectum in Matthaeum*: Its Provenance, Theology and Influence' (unpublished University of Oxford D.Phil. thesis), 1983); *Clavis Patrum Graecorum*, no. 4569; *Clavis Patrum Latinorum* (3rd edn, 1995), no. 707 – which strangely omits van Banning's *Praefatio* towards a new edition, in *Corpus Christianorum Series Latina* LXXXVII B (Turnhout, 1988).

[53] *Homilia*, 31; Migne, *Patrologia Graeca*, 56, col. 794. The text continues with no point of contact with Knox's letters.

[N]either is the long processe of tyme, neither yet the multitude of men, a sufficient approbation which God will allow for our religion. For as some of the most auncient writers do witnesse, neither can long processe of tyme justifie an errour, neither can the multitude of such as follow it chaunge the nature of the same ... For if antiquitie or multitude of men could justifie any religion, then was the idolatrie of the Gentiles, and now is the abomination of the Turkes, good religion.[54]

The margin identifies Knox's 'most auncient writers' as 'Lactantius. Firmian. Tertulian. Cyprian'. Breslow's attempt to elucidate provides Cyprian, *Ad Demetrianum*, Lactantius, *Divine Institutes* 2 and Tertullian, *Apology* – with no more detailed specification. 'Firmian.' is conspicuously absent.[55] Mason recognizes the impossibility of being 'precise about which works of these authors Knox had in mind', but suggests Lactantius, *Divine Institutes* 2.7, 5.20, Tertullian, *Apology, passim* and Cyprian, *The Vanity of Idols, passim*.[56] On 'Firmianus' (his completion of the name) he says nothing; he is surely Firmilian of Caesarea in Cappadocia, whose letter to Cyprian in Latin translation is preserved among the latter's collection.[57] More pertinent, surely, is the question where Knox might have picked up this grouping of 'most auncient writers'. It is far from obvious that we should assume that Knox knew them well enough to have had a particular work of each in mind.

An assessment of the use Knox made of the early Fathers must not lose sight of the mobility of his life – and hence of the question of the availability of their works at his different staging-posts. Geneva and Frankfurt must have offered richer collections than Dieppe or Berwick, and England in general than Scotland, although Edinburgh in the 1560s and 1570s cannot have been too poorly off for editions of the Fathers. Further research will be needed before more confident estimates can be advanced.[58] One may assume with safety that Knox did not transport a patristic library of any size around with him from place to place. Nor must reports of the destruction of volumes of the Fathers in the turmoil of the Reformation in Scotland be altogether ignored.

Nor again did the ready availability of the patristic texts mean that Knox eagerly consulted them. References to the Fathers in Knox's longest theological treatise, the defence of predestination written at Geneva,

---

[54] Knox, *Works*, IV, pp. 524–5.

[55] Breslow, p. 158, n. 1.

[56] Knox, *On Rebellion*, p. 116 with n. 2.

[57] *Clavis Patrum Graecorum*, no. 1760. Firmilian supported Cyprian in his dispute over schismatic baptism with Bishop Stephen of Rome. Each side charged the other with innovation.

[58] See the comments in the forthcoming paper referred to in n. 2 above.

are derived very largely if not entirely from different works of Calvin.[59] Early-Church historical exempla, such as the emperor Julian the Apostate, come readily enough to his pen,[60] and occasionally he appears as a more fulsome champion of patristic antiquity, as in the Preface to the *Forme of Prayers*, where Pliny's letter to Trajan is cited in support of singing verses or psalms to God: 'Seing therfore God's Woorde dothe approve it, antiquitie beareth witenes therof, and best reformed Churches have receyved the same, no man can reprove it, except he will contemne God's Worde, despice Antiquitie, and utterly condemne the godlie reformed Churches.'[61] More characteristically, the patristic card is played by Knox not in invoking the relatively pure Church of the age of the Fathers, but in driving the criterion of antiquity back to the very earliest times. As he wrote to Mary of Guise in 1558: 'But as touching antiquitie, I am content with Tertullian to say, "Let that be the most pure and perfect religion, which shall be proved most auncient."'[62] And so, in controversy with the Jesuit James Tyrie, in what became Knox's last published treatise, the reformer assumed an uncompromising position on apostolic succession: '[W]e are able to shaw the succession of our Kirk directly and laughfully to have flowed from the Apostles. And our reason is, becaus that in our kirkis we nether admit doctrine, ryte, nor ceremonie, which be their wrytingis, we find not authorised.'[63] Tyrie's claim to a 'continuall succession of doctrine ... in all ages; as it is manifest till ony man that hes red all ancient wryteris afoir our tymes' was to Knox 'a moste impudente lie'. Neither papacy nor Mass was known of in the age of the Apostles, or of the immediately following Fathers:[64]

> We are not bound to credite whatsoever the Fathers have spoken: but our faith ... is buylded upon the sure Rock, Jesus Christ, and upon the fundatioun of the Apostles and Prophetes. So far as any Fathers aggre therewith, we reverently do imbrase it; but if the Fathers have affirmed anything without the warrand of the written

---

[59] See Knox, *Works*, V, pp. 32, 38, 39, etc. The exceptions are not significant. The passage in Augustine's *De dono perseverantiae* that is probably alluded to by Knox (p. 62) was not quoted by Calvin (7.14; Migne, *Patrologia Latina*, 45, col. 1001), nor the citations from Augustine's *Contra Iulianum* 5.3.13, 5.4.15 (*Patrologia Latina*, 44, cols 791, 793), at Knox, *Works*, V, p. 332. These two works by Augustine had been heavily quarried by Calvin and others before Knox.

[60] For Julian, see Knox, *Works*, IV, p. 401 (*First Blast*), V, pp. 258, 357 (*Predestination*).

[61] Ibid., IV, p. 165.

[62] Ibid., IV, p. 446.

[63] *Ibid.*, VI, p. 498. On Tyrie, see briefly John Durkan in N.M. de S. Cameron (ed.), *Dictionary of Scottish Church History and Theology* (Edinburgh, 1993), p. 833.

[64] Knox, *Works*, VI, pp. 500, 501.

word of the Eternall our God ... it is as laughfull to us to reject that which proceedeth from man and not from God, as it is easie to them to affirme it.[65]

At root, asserts Knox, is an ecclesiological divide. Tyrie's argument is postulated on 'a visible succession'. '[W]here universally befor we use to say, *Credo sanctam Ecclesiam*, etc., he must say *Video sanctam Ecclesiam*':

Maister Tyrie will acknowledge no Kirk except that which hes bene, and is visible. We, in the contrare, acknowledge and reverence the spous of Christ Jesus, somtymes exyled from the world, receaving sometymes the wynges of an egle that she may fle to the wyldernes, whereof God, and not of man, she hath her place prepared.[66]

The only Scot to rate a mention in the impressive collection on the reception of the Fathers put together by Irena Backus is Ninian Winzet, for his translation of the *Commonitorium* of Vincent of Lerins.[67] Winzet had been a schoolmaster at Linlithgow who later graduated at Douai and became abbot of the Schottenklöster at Ratisbon in 1577. He was perhaps the most devoted Scottish student of the Fathers in the sixteenth century. Although his patristic competence remains to be fully investigated, at first sight it scores more highly on quantity than quality. His *Buke of the Four Scoir Thre Questions* addressed to Scotland's Protestant preachers (published at Antwerp in 1563) begins by challenging readers to choose between the martyrs and other ancient Doctors of the primitive Kirk and John Calvin and his accomplices in the present day. The list of primitive Fathers begins, in chronological order, with Dionysius, Clement, Martialis, Ignatius.[68] Winzet is not only unaware, or dismissive, of widespread doubts as to the authenticity of Dionysius the Areopagite but has even fallen for the utterly implausible Martialis, the shadowy third-century bishop of Limoges who in the ninth century was enrolled among the 72 disciples of Jesus and in the twelfth century even ranked as an Apostle.[69]

---

[65] Ibid., VI, p. 501.

[66] Ibid., VI, pp. 501, 502.

[67] Mark Vessey, 'English Translations of the Latin Fathers, 1517–1611', in Backus (ed.), *The Reception of the Church Fathers*, II, pp. 775–835, at pp. 815, 828.

[68] Ninian Winzet, *Certain Tractates together with the Book of Four Score Three Questions and a Translation of Vincentius Lirinensis*, ed. J.K. Hewison (2 vols, STS, Edinburgh, 1888–90), I, p. 60. On Winzet and the Fathers, see further the paper mentioned in n. 2 above.

[69] See David F. Wright's forthcoming study of the sixteenth-century reception of Ps-Martial's two letters.

Knox intended to publish a reply to Winzet's *Four Scoir Thre Questions*, but apparently never did so.[70] Perhaps he would have dealt solely with three questions that impugned his own vocation,[71] but a more comprehensive response would have enabled Knox to fulfil his undertaking, given a few years earlier in the English version of the Parisian Protestants' *Apology*, to set forth his evaluation of the patrimony of the Doctors of the early centuries. Hugh Watt has speculated on Knox's failure to produce his promised reply to Winzet, emphasizing the difficulty of making a serious rejoinder to a controversialist whose patristic authorities were so miscellaneous.[72]

Other possible reasons bear on the character of Knox as a reformer who was not a bookish, text-focused scholar. In both Greek and Hebrew he was an opsimath, unlike Latin, in which he was obviously at home, and in which most of the available works of the Greek Fathers appeared in translation. Knox's writings reflect more a biblicist cast of mind, inclined to a short-circuit resort to the Scriptures alone and not overly concerned to rest much on the Fathers, markedly different from the humanist Catholic-evangelical culture of Calvin, Bucer, Beza, Melanchthon and Cranmer and other English reformers. Knox professes a familiarity with the early Church which he rarely gets round to demonstrating, as in this defiant protestation in his letter to Mary of Guise:

> And as for their Counsels, when the mater shall come to triall, it shall be easelie seen for whom the most godlie and most auncient Counsels shall most plainlie speake. I will prove by a counsel, that of more authoritie is the sentence of one man, founded upon the simple truth of God, then is the determination of the hole Counsel without the assurance of Goddes Worde. But that all their determinations which we impugne are not onlie maintained without any assurance of Scriptures, but also are established against the truth of the same, yea, and for the most part against the decrees of the former Counsels, I offer my selfe evidentlie to prove.[73]

The authentic Knoxian notes can all be heard here: the early Councils testify in favour of reformed doctrine; one individual with God's Word is a higher authority than a whole Council without it – and a Council itself affirms this position; the papists' teachings run counter to the Councils' decrees – a claim which Knox was ready to vindicate. He never did so.

---

[70] Knox, *Works*, VI, p. 193 with n. 2.

[71] Questions 33–5, in Winzet, *Certain Tractates*, I, pp. 98–100. Cf. Knox, *Works*, VI, pp. 152–3; Winzet, *Certain Tractates*, I, pp. xxxvi–xxxviii.

[72] Watt, *John Knox in Controversy*, pp. 44–7.

[73] Knox, *Works*, IV, pp. 446–7.

It is not easy to pinpoint any doctrine or debate or document in the Scottish Reformation in which the testimony of the Fathers counted decisively. The same could well be said of John Knox in particular. In part the lateness of the reform movement in Scotland determined this. The Fathers had already been ransacked high and low in Germany and Switzerland and England, and the Scots could exploit the booty without repeating the exercise. In part also the critical issues fought out in Scotland were not ones which invited patristic determination. When Winzet challenged 'the Calviniane precheouris' what they had written against the Anabaptist rejection of infant baptism, as the Lutherans had done by appealing, like Origen and Augustine, to 'the Apostolik traditioun, and universal observatioun of the haly Catholik Kirk', Knox's rejoinder was ready to hand.[74] Silence did not betoken default, for paedobaptism was not a bone of contention in sixteenth-century Scotland.

Antiquity was an important criterion for Knox. He repeatedly indicted the Mass, transubstantiation and the papacy as latter-day novelties. Yet he displayed little consistency in his chronology of the fall of the Church into such calamitous errors, identifying now Gregory the Great's devising of a new litany, now Lanfranc of Bec (d. 1089) or Nicolas II (pope 1058–61) as the one by whom the Devil hatched the bird of transubstantiation, now the Emperor Phocas as the architect of papal supremacy, now the ingenuity of pope after pope in securing their exemption from civil authority and law.[75] But antiquity itself, without the all-decisive witness of God's express Word, was a broken reed:

> And if antiquitie of time shall be considered in such cases, then shall not onlie the idolatrie of the Gentiles, but also the false religion of Mahomet, be preferred to the Papistrie: for both one and the other is more auncient then is the Papisticall religion: yea, Mahomet had established his Alcoram before any Pope in Rome was crowned with a triple crowne.[76]

Thus speaks Knox *ipsissimus*: the rhetorical controversialist, not the student of Christian antiquity.

---

[74] Winzet, *Certain Tractates*, I, p. 117.

[75] Knox, *Works*, III, pp. 38–40, IV, pp. 314–15 (and III, pp. 278–9, with a correction to n. 5), 511–12, 508.

[76] Ibid., IV, p. 446.

CHAPTER SIX

Knox:
Scholastic and Canonistic Echoes

J.H. Burns

James Kirk, in Chapter One of this collection, reminds us of the antitheses that are seemingly inseparable from the attempt to understand and evaluate the achievement and historical significance of John Knox. One such antithesis is relevant to the subject of this chapter. Biographers have differed sharply in the interpretation of Knox's relationship to the scholastic tradition in which (we may safely assume) he had been trained. Peter Hume Brown seems to have been entirely persuaded that Knox not only began within that tradition but continued to adhere to its methods, however much, in his substantive doctrine, he may have diverged from his scholastic mentors. Indeed, we are told bluntly that

> it was impossible that Knox could really break with the mental habit and modes of thought that distinguished the schoolmen. Though he frequently speaks of them with contempt, the truth is that alike by the themes he handled and his manner of handling them Knox is essentially a schoolman himself.[1]

This may be contrasted with the view taken by Jasper Ridley, when considering the suggestion by Beza and by David Buchanan that Knox positively outdid John Mair in the dialectical niceties of scholastic reasoning. For Ridley

> it is difficult to believe that Knox could ever have rivalled Major as a schoolman, for in most of his writings in later life his approach was very different from that of the schoolmen. He was intelligent enough to understand the subtleties of scholastic theology, but temperamentally had no inclination to do so.[2]

The theme is obviously important in the context of Knox's theological doctrine at large. It is, however, a theme of some specific significance under the rubric of 'political ideas'; and that is where the 'echoes' with which this essay is concerned are to be heard – or not heard, as the case may be. With this in mind, it is useful to consider a third biographer – still,

---

[1] Peter Hume Brown, *John Knox: A Biography* (2 vols, London, 1895), I, pp. 27–8.
[2] Jasper Ridley, *John Knox* (London, 1968), p. 17.

in many respects, the most notable of them all. Thomas McCrie's *Life of John Knox* is indeed a remarkable book. One remarkable thing about it is the care McCrie took to go back to the writings of John Mair – not to the familiar *Historia* but to the then neglected and largely forgotten theological works – in order to see something of what the youthful Knox may have heard from Mair's lips. It is of little consequence that McCrie, like Hume Brown many decades later, assumed that Knox had 'sat under' Mair in Glasgow. In fact, or at least according to what seems now to be the probable hypothesis, it was in St Andrews that Knox had whatever university education he received. The interesting point is that it was from Mair's ecclesiology and political theory that McCrie heard echoes in the works of John Knox.

What McCrie said, and this was for a long time to enjoy the status of received wisdom, was that there was an 'affinity' between, on the one hand, Mair's 'opinions respecting civil government' and his 'analogous' views 'as to ecclesiastical polity' and, on the other, 'the political principles afterwards avowed by Knox, and' – for good measure – 'defended by the classic pen of Buchanan'. This affinity was indeed 'too striking to require illustration'. The principles in question were

> that the authority of kings and princes was originally derived from the people; that the former are not superior to the people, collectively considered: that if rulers become tyrannical, or employ their power for the destruction of their subjects, they may lawfully be controlled by them, and proving incorrigible, may be deposed by the community as the superior power; and that tyrants may be judicially proceeded against, even to capital punishment.[3]

And McCrie cites, with specific textual references, Mair's commentaries on Book III of the *Sentences* and on St Matthew's Gospel.[4] He has indeed given a pretty fair account of essential elements in Mair's theory of monarchy – though tyrannicide as distinct from deposition was for Mair at best a problematic concept.

Having argued at length for almost half a century over the precise nature of the relationship between the political ideas of Mair, Knox and Buchanan, I do not propose to labour the theme here. In terms of the title of this chapter, it may suffice to say that, while there are certainly 'echoes' in Knox's writings on rebellion of Mair's complex and nuanced scholastic analysis, there is, at the very least, some distortion in the reverberations. To this extent at least, and in this connection, there may

---

[3] Thomas McCrie, *Life of John Knox* (6th edn, Edinburgh and London, 1846), pp. 5–6.

[4] Ibid., pp. 384–5 (Note D). McCrie's second quotation, from the 1517 *Super Tertium*, makes it clear that Mair was prepared to justify judicial execution, not assassination.

be more to be said for Ridley's view than for Hume Brown's. Whatever Knox was doing in his pamphlets of the 1550s he was not discussing issues *more scholastico*. To quote words written as long ago as 1952, 'a real and fundamental difference of character and intellect ... must have greatly complicated and modified any influence [Mair] may have had upon [Knox]'.[5]

Leaving these broader considerations aside, it is time to turn from the scholastic to the canonistic aspect of the problem. In respect of method, of course, that is not so much a specific distinction as a distinction between genus and species. For present purposes, however, 'scholastic' echoes come from the works of theologians and philosophers. The 'canonistic' notes are, obviously, those sounded by canon lawyers.

It is certainly worth bearing in mind that the only professional formation which we can be sure that Knox received was his training as a notary. Ridley observes that '[f]or at least three years Knox was a small country lawyer'. That may strike us as an unexpectedly Balzacian description of the 'trumpeter of God'; but we may do well to recollect that, as Ridley also remarks, such lawyers have, historically, 'provided ... many successful politicians and revolutionary leaders in every part of the world since Knox's time'.[6] Moreover, it may well have been the case that the *petit notaire* had readier access than the *curé de campagne* to the lairds who were to be so significant a factor in the later politico-religious revolution. To pursue that argument would, however, be to stray too far from the proper concerns of this chapter.

To refer to Knox's notarial training is to turn to a subject of which (it may be said) just enough is known to be frustrating. We do know, to be sure, that, a decade or so before Knox's birth, the subject was of sufficient concern to attract parliamentary attention and legislation. The statute of 1504 seems to reflect uneasiness as to the quality of service then being provided by the notaries who had become an increasingly numerous class in Scotland over the preceding three-quarters of a century or more.[7] A similar concern at much the same time is reflected, it has been argued, in William Elphinstone's plans for the faculty of canon law in the new University of Aberdeen.[8] In principle, it seems, a would-be notary should have served a five-year apprenticeship, under the authority, formally (in the case of notaries apostolic, of whom Knox

---

[5] J.H. Burns, 'The Theory of Limited Monarchy in Sixteenth Century Scotland' (unpublished PhD thesis, University of Aberdeen, 1952), p. 384.

[6] Ridley, *Knox*, p. 20.

[7] *APS*, II, p. 250, c. 8.

[8] L.J. Macfarlane, *William Elphinstone and the Kingdom of Scotland 1431–1514* (2nd edn, Aberdeen, 1995), pp. 301–4.

was to be one), of the diocesan bishop. More substantive responsibility for the matter belonged to the official of the diocese.[9] We need not, nor can we, assume that the system was rigorously or uniformly enforced; but we may reasonably suppose that Knox served his time – or at least some significant time – in pupillage of this kind.

On that basis it may be worth while to pause and ask under whose auspices Knox was trained. There is, to be sure, little prospect of our ever knowing who his notarial master was. We can, however, say something about the man who probably had the effective supervisory responsibility for Knox's training. John Weddell is someone of whom, although we know a fair amount, it would be useful to know more. A St Andrews determinant of the mid-1490s, he was subsequently – though we do not know where – licensed to teach both canon and civil law. Subdean of Moray in 1508, he was appointed as official of St Andrews and also as commissary in 1516. Soon afterwards he returned to the arts faculty of his *alma mater*, being received *ad gremium Facultatis* on 2 March 1517. Two years later, still a canon of Moray (he subsequently became rector of Flisk) as well as official of the archdiocese, he was appointed for the first of several terms of office as rector of St Andrews University. Weddell continued as official until 1523 or 1524; but it seems that his career from then until the early 1530s was mainly academic. Whether he taught law as well as arts is uncertain; but, given what Annie Dunlop described as the 'popularity' of canon-law studies, it seems likely enough that Weddell's expertise would have been put to work in that faculty. In any case, he would certainly have been a notable figure in the university when – on what is now the generally accepted view – Knox was a student there. In 1528 John Mair (having returned to Paris from St Andrews two years or so before) dedicated the last of his published works in logic to Weddell – *bonarum artium doctori*. In 1530 Weddell began a second term – this time for three years – as official of St Andrews; and from 1533 until 1540 he was official of Lothian, where Knox was to spend the notarial phase of his career. Thereafter, until at least 1548, Weddell was one of the senators of the College of Justice.[10]

---

[9] Ibid., pp. 64–5, 302.

[10] Weddell's career is summarized by Simon Ollivant, *The Court of the Official in Pre-Reformation Scotland* (Stair Society, Edinburgh, 1982), Appendix II, p. 173; and cf. (as index in each case) J.M. Anderson (ed.), *Early Records of the University of St Andrews* (SHS, Edinburgh, 1926); A.I. Dunlop (ed.), *Acta Facultatis Artium Universitatis Sancti Andree 1413–1588* (SHS, Edinburgh, 1964); D.E.R. Watt, *Fasti Ecclesiae Scoticanae Medii Aevi ad annum 1638*, Second Draft (St Andrews, 1969). For Mair's 1528 dedication, see A. Constable (ed.), *A History of Greater Britain … by John Major* (SHS, Edinburgh, 1892), p. 442.

John Weddell thus combined academic and practical legal experience in a career of some distinction. That the notarial training for the supervision of which, as official, he was responsible was essentially practical must certainly be conceded. The functions a notary like Knox discharged in the early 1540s were no doubt petty enough, even if one may prefer to avoid the pejorative term 'pettifogging'. Those functions had doubtless little enough to do with the great theoretical and doctrinal issues of canonistic (or civilian) jurisprudence. Yet it will do no harm to bear in mind that case-law, recorded in the *consilia* of the jurists, was arguably the principal way in which, especially in its later phases, medieval canon law had been developed. To be trained in that law – however basic and practice-directed the training may have been – was certainly to have some degree of contact with one of the great monuments of scholastic learning.

The nature and the extent of that contact is (it must be admitted) frustratingly hard to determine. A trained notary would have known something, at second-hand if not directly, of the voluminous contents of what has been called 'the standard textbook on procedure in the later Middle Ages and the early modern period': the *Speculum iuris*, or *Speculum judiciale*, of Guillaume Durand – the Speculator of so many later references.[11] Some points, indeed, bearing directly upon his future professional concerns, might reach him – by way of his master's instruction if not his own reading – from Rolandino Passaggeri's *Summa artis notariae*. This was a key text, upon which Durand, Rolandino's thirteenth-century contemporary, drew extensively in compiling his *Speculum*. 'Some [Scottish] notaries,' we are assured, 'must have had' Passaggeri's manual on their shelves.[12] And certainly, if we could allow ourselves to suppose that Knox heard canon-law lectures by John Weddell as well as theology lectures by John Mair, we should have identified a potential source of some significance for his later thinking. It is now indeed time to ask what echoes, if any, of canonistic texts do, in fact, resound in the Knox we know from his writings and recorded utterances.

The answer may begin with what will seem – and no doubt is – a distant echo, but still a striking one. It comes from one of the great set

---

[11] Kenneth Pennington, *The Prince and the Law 1200–1600: Sovereignty and Rights in the Western Legal Tradition* (Berkeley, Los Angeles and Oxford, 1993), p. 164.

[12] John Durkan, 'The Early Scottish Notary', in Ian B. Cowan and Duncan Shaw (eds), *The Renaissance and Reformation in Scotland: Essays in Honour of Gordon Donaldson* (Edinburgh, 1983), pp. 28–9.

pieces of Knox's *History of the Reformation* – the account of his first interview with the Queen of Scots at Holyrood, a fortnight after her return from France. Towards the end of that confrontation, Mary declared: 'I will defend the kirk of Rome, for I think it is the true kirk of God.' Knox's reply was, 'Your will, Madam, is no reason'; and many of his readers must have felt that the retort was both characteristically Scots and quintessentially Knoxian.[13] What I, for one, failed for a long time to recognize is the resounding negation and rejection of an absolutist maxim with its origins far back in medieval canon law. It was, so far as we can tell, Laurentius Hispanus, writing (it is intriguing to note) in or about the same year as that of the English Magna Carta, who borrowed and adapted from Juvenal the phrase *est pro ratione voluntas*. Will, on this view, takes the place of reason when the will is that of a prince.[14] The prince of whose absolute power Laurentius was writing was, of course, the Pope; and the maxim passed rapidly into the common currency of juristic discourse. Specifically, we may note, it was reproduced by Durand in his *Speculum*.[15] Of Laurentius, Knox had probably never heard; of Durand he probably knew at least a little; but we can in any case be certain that he knew of the Juvenalian maxim, knew of its application to papal authority, and knew that the fullness of power it implied was being claimed by temporal sovereigns as well as by the head of 'the kirk of Rome'.

To validate these claims I move from the late summer of 1561 to the early summer of 1558 and from Edinburgh to Geneva. In a notable passage of *The Appellation of John Knox*, the appellant turns his fire against 'such exemption and privilege as papists do this day claim' – the alleged immunity of the clergy from civil authority and temporal jurisdiction. The source of this lies, Knox argues, in the original usurpation of temporal power in Italy by 'the bishops of Rome, the very Antichrists', as 'is evident in their own law and histories'. The law, of course, is canon law; and Knox proceeds to specific citations in support of his case. He begins with three basic texts from Gratian, all asserting the absolute superiority of the see of Rome to any authority that might presume to judge it.[16] Then, in a still more striking passage, Knox turns to '[t]he author of the gloss upon their canon', who

---

[13] Knox, *History*, II, p. 17.

[14] See Pennington, *The Prince and the Law*, pp. 46–7 and n. 39.

[15] Durand, *Speculum iuris* (Frankfurt, 1668), I.i.6: p. 48 col. 1. It is perhaps worth noting that this part of Durand's text is concerned in general with legatine powers – a topic of some interest in Scotland during the 1530s and 1540s.

[16] Knox, *On Rebellion*, pp. 107–8. The citations from the *Decretum* (C.9 q.3 c.13; C.9 q.3 c.14; D.19 c.2) were all standard *loci* for the discussion of papal authority.

affirmeth that if all the world should pronounce sentence against the pope, yet should his sentence prevail. For saith he: 'The pope hath a heavenly will and therefore he may change the nature of things; he may apply the substance of one thing to another, and of nothing he may make somewhat; and that sentence which was nothing (that is, by his mind false and injust), he may make somewhat that is true and just.' 'For (saith he) in all things that please him his will is for reason. Neither is there any man that may ask him why doest thou so. For he may dispense above the law, and of injustice he may make justice. For he hath the fullness of all power.'[17]

For this classic account of the papal *plenitudo potestatis* Knox gives a marginal reference to the decretals of Gregory IX, to which he no doubt had ready enough access in Geneva.[18] If, however, as a student or apprentice notary in Scotland he had had the opportunity of turning the pages of Durand's *Speculum*, he need not have turned very many before encountering the same formulations. Or if he had heard any lectures – by John Weddell or anyone else – based upon that 'standard textbook on procedure', his attention could well have been arrested by those resounding assertions.[19] Nor should such hypotheses be dismissed out of hand on the ground that such high matters were beyond the sphere of the 'small country lawyer' Knox was then training to be. The language of the canonists in such matters was indeed highly charged and big with ideological implications. Yet at the same time it was in its way thoroughly practical. The validity of a papal dispensation might and often did affect and even determine the outcome of the kind of case in which notaries were concerned. The question whether the Pope could 'change the nature of things' or 'make somewhat out of nothing' may seem metaphysical – may appear even to verge upon the realm of Metternich's 'sublime mysticism and nonsense'.[20] And yet the issue to which such language was applied might be a humdrum practical question affecting the legal status – clerical or marital or the like – of an

---

[17] Knox, *On Rebellion*, p. 108.

[18] Knox is quoting from the Ordinary Gloss by Bernard of Parma (d. 1266) on the *Decretals* of Gregory IX (X. 1.7.3 – not 'c.2' as Mason has it in Knox, *On Rebellion*, p. 108, n. 10). An edition of these was published in Lyons in the same year as Knox's *Appellation*, though it is unlikely that he saw this. He could, however, have found the passage in, for example, *Decretales d[omi]ni pape Gregorii noni* (Paris, 1512), fo. 72 vo. B. In any case, the gloss was followed by Durand in his *Speculum iuris*.

[19] See n. 15 above.

[20] Kenneth Pennington, *Pope and Bishops: The Papal Monarchy in the Twelfth and Thirteenth Centuries* (Philadelphia, 1984), pp. 19, 24, suggests that Laurentius Hispanus 'inaugurated a tradition of high-flown and exaggerated language which became a characteristic of later canonistic discussions of the papal office', but also that 'Laurentius' contribution to the history of political thought was to clothe sovereignty in language that preserved decorum but attracted notice'.

individual engaged in litigation. Knox in the 1550s might – he plainly did – see such language as the 'blasphemous sentences' of 'that pestilential generation (I mean the vermin of the papistical order)'.[21] Knox in the 1530s, however, may have heard it with less sensitive ears or read it with the less censorious eyes of an apprentice concerned to master the rules of his trade.

We know, however, that, by the time Knox faced the challenge of preaching his first sermon in St Andrews, he had what were now for him the enormities of canonistic arrogance before his eyes – and in his sights. It is surely a striking fact, and one perhaps meriting more attention than it has received, that the theme of that sermon was primarily ecclesiological. However far Knox had by then travelled from the point in St John's Gospel where (he later said) he 'first cast anchor' towards his final theological haven, the great issues of grace and justification, prominent though they were in that first sermon, were there deployed instrumentally in a discourse concerned centrally with authority in the Christian community and with the nature of the Church. And the notary turned preacher's handling of those issues was bold and, in our current phrase, confrontational. True, the issues had not been raised by Knox and his new associates, but by their opponents. John Annand, the founding father and principal of St Leonard's College, in the course of a disputation of which it would be fascinating to know more than Knox tells us in his *History*, had appealed to the authority of the Church as his ultimate defence against the heresy being preached by the Dominican and former St Leonard's student, John Rough, backed up in writing by Knox. The reply to this argument was naturally a demand that the true nature and 'notes' of the Church be first established. Knox, by his own account, used language he was to repeat almost word for word in the *Appellation* of 1558:

> as for your Roman Kirk, as it is now corrupted, and the authority thereof ... I offer myself, by word or writ, to prove the Roman Church this day further degenerate from the purity which was in the days of the Apostles, than was the Church of the Jews from the ordinance given by Moses when they consented to the innocent death of Jesus Christ.[22]

This was the offer Knox endeavoured to make good in his first public sermon.

Richard Greaves has argued that Knox, by joining the Castilians in St Andrews, was inaugurating his ideological commitment to the justification

---

[21] Knox, *On Rebellion*, pp. 108, 109.
[22] Knox, *History*, I, p. 84.

of temporal rebellion or civil disobedience.[23] This is debatable; but certainly Knox's challenge to the sovereign authority of the Catholic Church is of great significance for his 'political thought' in a wider sense. And that significance is closely connected with Knox's attitude to canon law. A central point in his 1547 sermon was that 'the papistical laws repugned to the law of the Evangel'. Recalling his text (Daniel 7:24–5, echoed in Revelation 13:5) – 'There shall one arise unlike to the other, having a mouth speaking great things and blasphemous' – he turned for exemplification to the canon law:

> 'the Successor of Peter', 'the Vicar of Christ', 'the Head of the Kirk', 'most holy', 'most blessed', 'that cannot err', that 'may make right of wrong, and wrong of right', that 'of nothing, may make somewhat', and that 'hath all verity in the shrine of his breast', yea 'that has power of all, and none power of him', nay, 'not to say that he does wrong, although he draw ten thousand million of souls with himself to hell'; if these ... and many other, able to be shown in his own Canon Law, be not great and blasphemous words, and such as mortal man never spoke before, let the world judge.[24]

Whatever Knox the notary apostolic knew and thought of the canon law he was in some small way engaged in administering, Knox the emerging Protestant preacher of 1547 plainly saw it as a supreme embodiment of an unscriptural and usurped spiritual tyranny. If there were echoes of canonistic learning here, they now rang in Knox's ears like demonic shrieks: he did, in fact, invoke St Paul's reference to 'the doctrine of devils' to support his condemnation of 'the corruptions of the Papistry'.[25] Yet the echoes are there, and they allow us to regard canon law as a factor that did indeed influence Knox's thinking.

The argument must not be pushed too far. It is not to be supposed, nor is it being suggested, that the lore of the canonists was a major element in the furnishing of Knox's mind. Yet it is surely a point of some importance that this was the direction in which his mind turned when considering the difference between true and false conceptions of the Church. Priority in such matters, after all, could be claimed – and was being vigorously claimed in the early sixteenth century – by the theologians. Divided and opposed though they might be in some of their crucial ecclesiological conclusions, John Mair and Cardinal Cajetan

---

[23] Richard L. Greaves, *Theology and Revolution in the Scottish Reformation: Studies in the Thought of John Knox* (Grand Rapids, MI., 1980), pp. 127, 134.

[24] Knox, *History*, I, pp. 85–6.

[25] Ibid., I, p. 85; cf. 1 Timothy 4:1.

were at one in that claim – in their insistence that questions as to the nature and authority of the Church were questions first and foremost for theologians and only secondarily for canon lawyers. More generally, it has been said that '[n]obody had been more critical of the excessive place given to canon law to the detriment of theology than John Mair and John Annand'.[26] That remark was made, interestingly, in the context of another St Andrews occasion when the primacy of God's revealed law over 'men's traditions' was pressed beyond the limits of the orthodoxy the two college heads both upheld. This was in the 1536 Lenten sermons of Alexander Seton, a Dominican like Knox's later associate, John Rough. If Seton went too far for Mair, however, the latter (according to Knox) had approved beforehand the preaching, two years or so earlier, of another friar, William Arth, in which one of the targets was the abuse of excommunication – and thus of the ultimate sanction of canon-law jurisdiction.[27]

Yet there were inescapable paradoxes in asserting the prior claim of theologians to be the front-line defenders of the Church and its authority. Ecclesiology as a specific sub-discipline, so to speak, had developed relatively late in the history of Catholic theology. It was only at the start of the fourteenth century that James of Viterbo wrote what has been called *[l]e plus ancien traité de l'Eglise*; and Juan de Torquemada's *Summa de Ecclesia* – the first comprehensive treatise on the subject – was a product of the mid-fifteenth century.[28] By then, moreover, the subject was deeply and sharply controversial. The confrontation between papalist and conciliarist views as to the location of supremacy within the Church had been superimposed, we might say, upon the older conflict between the spiritual and temporal power in Christendom – itself, by the sixteenth century, a conflict ever more appropriately characterized as a contention between Church and State. The paradoxes to which I have referred arose because the theologians who strove to vindicate their authority over such issues found, again and again, that

---

[26] John Durkan, 'The Cultural Background in Sixteenth-Century Scotland', in David McRoberts (ed.), *Essays on the Scottish Reformation 1513–1625* (Glasgow, 1962), p. 307, n. 189.

[27] Knox, *History*, I, pp. 15–17 for Arth; I, pp. 19–21 for Seton; and see also II, pp. 230–32 (Appendix II) for Seton's letter to James V. Cf. Durkan, 'Cultural Background', pp. 306–7. The date of Arth's preaching is uncertain. Ian B. Cowan, *The Scottish Reformation: Church and Society in Sixteenth-Century Scotland* (London, 1982), pp. 94–5, places it in 1528; but this cannot be correct if Knox's reference to the part played by Mair (who was in Paris throughout that year) is accurate.

[28] H.-X. Arquilliere, *Le plus ancien traité de l'Église: Jacques de Viterbe, De regimine christiano (1301–1302)* (Paris, 1926; English translation, ed. R.W. Dyson, Woodbridge, Suffolk, 1995). Torquemada's *Summa*, completed in 1449, was not printed until 1561.

the canonists had been there before them. Thus Brian Tierney finds the foundations of later conciliarism and some at least of the origins of papal infallibility in the canonists.[29] If we look at Cajetan's two tracts against the purported Council of Pisa and Milan in 1511–12 – the work of a man who, at the very outset, makes a strenuous point of asserting the primacy of theology – we find almost 200 canon-law references compared with a combined figure of less than 100 citations from his theological masters Aquinas and Torquemada.[30]

Coming nearer home in the present discussion, we may consider the case of John Mair himself. When Hugh Trevor-Roper inadvertently described Mair as a canonist,[31] the slip was not entirely without excuse. Canon-law citations are both frequent and crucial for Mair's account of ecclesiastical authority in his 1518 commentary on Matthew. The section of the text dealing with the subject is by no means lengthy. It takes up no more than 27 pages out of over 300 in the relevant volume in the series *Cambridge Texts in the History of Political Thought*, yet it contains 20 canon-law references.[32] It was, quite simply, impossible to analyse and debate such issues in that period without engaging in canonistic discourse.

In this sense and to this extent the dichotomy assumed here between scholastic and canonistic discourse is false. Knox could have caught echoes of canon-law doctrine from theological – certainly from ecclesiological – sources. He might, specifically, have done so by hearing Mair's lectures or by reading Mair's works. And yet this does not, on closer inspection, seem to be a very plausible derivation of the canon-law precepts or maxims we find Knox actually quoting, considering and condemning. So far as I know, he makes no identifiable reference to any scholastic theologian in whose pages he would have been likely

---

[29] Brian Tierney, *Foundations of the Conciliar Theory: The Contribution of the Medieval Canonists from Gratian to the Great Schism* (Cambridge, 1955); Brian Tierney, *Origins of Papal Infallibility 1150–1350: A Study on the Concepts of Infallibility, Sovereignty and Tradition in the Middle Ages* (Leiden, 1972).

[30] See V.M.J. Pollet, O.P. (ed.), *Thomas de Vio Cardinalis Caietanus: Scripta Theologica*, vol. 1 [no more published] (Rome, 1936). At the same time it is worth bearing in mind that Torquemada himself was arguably as much a jurist as a theologian: Walter Ullmann, *Law and Politics in the Middle Ages* (Cambridge, 1975), pp. 187–8, 301, referred to his 'combining theology and jurisprudence' and having applied a 'fine juristic mind' in 'a highly intelligent adjustment of Thomist themes to contemporary ecclesiological problems'.

[31] H.R. Trevor-Roper, 'George Buchanan and the Ancient Scottish Constitution', *EHR*, supplement 3, 1966, p. 9: 'Buchanan ... had studied in the "Gallican" university of Paris under the "conciliar" canonist John Mair'.

[32] J.H. Burns and T.M. Izbicki (eds), *Conciliarism and Papalism* (Cambridge, 1997), pp. 285–311.

to find those phrases. Mair, of course, does refer to Cajetan's arguments for papal supremacy in order to refute them; but we do not find in Mair's pages the battery of extreme papalist texts Knox excoriated in the 1540s and 1550s. It still seems to be necessary to postulate another, a more direct – in fact a canonistic – source for Knox's knowledge of what he sought to reject.

The theme of rejection provides a cue for the concluding part of this chapter. The scholastic ecclesiology Knox could have encountered in Mair would obviously have differed widely from the position he was eventually to adopt. He would doubtless have found Mair's conciliarism less distasteful than the papalism of a Torquemada or a Cajetan, if only on account of the rebuttal of the extravagant claims for papal power and the insistence both on the fallibility of Popes and on the enforceable limits set to their authority. Yet if that authority was, for Mair and other conciliarists, essentially ministerial and ultimately subordinate to the collective authority of the Church, it was still, within its sphere, supreme; and for that supremacy a scriptural warrant was claimed which to Knox was radically unconvincing. The more fundamental point, however, is that Knox had little if any interest in this kind of debate. His ecclesiological concerns were real enough; but they were of a different order. That the Church was one, holy, catholic and apostolic Knox would of course have accepted. That 'it was the pillar of verity and ... could not err' he had declared explicitly in his first sermon, when he 'defined the true Kirk [and] showed the true notes of it'. The true Church thus defined, however, was an invisible spiritual society, guided by 'the voice of its true pastor, Jesus Christ'.[33] The visible institutional Churches which sought to manifest Christ's truth on earth were conceived by Knox in forms to which late medieval ecclesiology had little to contribute.

Indirectly, perhaps, that ecclesiology in its conciliarist version may have had some share in shaping, not Knox's notions of spiritual authority, but his attitudes to a defaulting or oppressive civil power. This is the old story mentioned at the outset and illustrated from McCrie's *Life*. How much credence it should receive remains a difficult point to resolve. It is certainly the case that Knox *could* have derived from Mair – and from Mair in the *Historia* with no imperative need to refer to his theological doctrine – such 'communitarian' elements as may be found in the pamphlets of the 1550s, echoed at certain points in the *History of the Reformation*. Whether he did derive these ideas from that source may in the end be an unanswerable question; what is clear is that he

---

[33] Knox, *History*, I, p. 85.

need not have so derived them. And when all is said and done, the use to which Knox put any political principles he brought with him from his scholastic point of departure was determined by polemical circumstances so far removed from those surrounding Mair's academic discourse as to ensure their effectual transformation into doctrine of a very different kind.

So we return finally to those canonistic formulae which seem to have burnt themselves into Knox's mind far more deeply than anything he retained from scholastic theology or philosophy. If that was the case, I think it was for one probable – indeed virtually certain – reason, and perhaps for a second related reason which has a more direct bearing on Knox's 'political thought'. The obvious reason is that the extreme claims made by canon lawyers for papal power fostered and sustained Knox's apocalyptic view – his vision, one could say – of the Catholic Church as the quintessential Antichrist. The secondary or subordinate reason for the hold such language evidently had on Knox's memory and imagination is that it crystallized or encapsulated a concept of absolute power vested in a human ruler which he was determined to reject. Was that rejection, however, total – as absolute, indeed, as the power claimed for the Pope by the canonists? That question may be more problematic. That Mary Stewart's will was no reason might be clear enough; and her attempt to invoke the authority of her conscience met the blunt reply, 'Conscience, Madam ... requires knowledge; and I fear that right knowledge ye have none'.[34] Suppose, however, a case in which the sovereign does have 'right knowledge' and a will guided by an informed conscience: what then? 'Calvinism,' it was shrewdly observed many years ago, 'needed a converted king and it never found him; nor did it ever find any alternative.'[35] Had such a king been found, would Knox still have rejected, in regard to this godly prince, the 'absolutist' formulae of the canonists? The answer to that question – if it can indeed be answered – lies far beyond the scope of this chapter; but it is surely a question worth asking.

---

[34] Ibid., II, p. 18.

[35] Douglas Nobbs, *England and Scotland 1560–1707* (London, 1952), p. 38. He goes on: 'Scottish Calvinism remained tied to monarchy ... The dilemma of the church was cruel. It could not consistently press for limitations on political authority without making its ideal society impossible; but neither could it strengthen political authority without endangering its own freedom and authority ... '.

€ vi.   F ij.

No Queene in her kingdome can oz ought
to lye falt,
Jf Knokes oz Goodmans boo kes blowe
any true blalt.

7.1   Woodcut of Goodman and Knox

CHAPTER SEVEN

Trumpeting Resistance: Christopher Goodman and John Knox

Jane E.A. Dawson[*]

On 14 December 1565, Peter Frarin of Antwerp presided over a special disputation in the Arts Faculty at Louvain University. The matter under consideration was the well-worn Roman Catholic argument that 'under pretence to refourme religion' Protestants were prepared to subvert all civil order and authority. Among his many targets for attack Frarin had selected Christopher Goodman and John Knox because of their resistance tracts written during Mary Tudor's reign. The disputation was turned into a book which was translated into English by John Fowler and published in Antwerp in May 1566.[1] Its marvellous pictorial index provided a series of woodcuts depicting the book's main Protestant targets together with a short verse encapsulating the charge against each of them. The picture of Goodman and Knox showed them facing two Queens on their thrones with each man blowing a trumpet (Figure 7.1). The verse read:

> No Queene in her kingdome can or ought to syt fast
> If Knokes or Goodmans bookes blowe any true blast.

In the woodcut Goodman had raised his trumpet and was giving a loud blast at the Queen who was lifting her hand in admonishment, or possibly to cover her ears against the noise. By contrast Knox was depicted as rather more tentative; he was still in the process of bringing his trumpet level before sounding forth. Knox was also weighed down with a large volume, presumably the Bible, tucked under his other arm. Whether deliberately or not, this illustration offered a very accurate image of the resistance theories of Goodman and Knox: both playing

[*] I am most grateful to J.H. Burns and Roger Mason for their helpful comments upon an earlier draft of this chapter.

[1] *STC*, no. 11333, Peter Frarin, *An Oration against the Unlawfull Insurrection of the Protestantes of our time* (Antwerp, 1566).The index is described as 'The Table of this Booke set out not by order of Alphabete or numbre but by expresse figure, to the eye and sight of the Christian Reader, and of him also that cannot reade'. Also see S.R. Maitland, *Essays on subjects connected with the Reformation in England* (London, 1899), pp. 109–10.

the same tune but Goodman's uncompromising radicalism sounding out whilst Knox was taking his time to reach the main theme.

It was no accident that Goodman and Knox were portrayed standing almost back to back in mutual support and defence. The two men were the best of friends and Goodman was probably the closest male companion Knox ever had.[2] They first came into contact in Edwardian England when they were both on the radical wing of the Edwardian Church and shared a number of friends. Their first recorded meeting was during the famous Frankfurt controversy when Christopher Goodman found himself supporting John Knox and opposing Richard Cox, his old Dean at Christ Church.

When Knox was forced to leave Frankfurt and go to Geneva, Goodman emerged as one of the leaders of the 'Knoxian party' alongside Anthony Gilby and Goodman's childhood friend, William Whittingham.[3] Having failed to find a tolerable settlement to the 'troubles', the 'Knoxian party' departed *en masse* arriving in Geneva on 13 October 1555. Knox had left the Swiss city around the end of August on the trip which was to culminate in his preaching tour of Scotland of 1555–56, but he had helped to prepare for the planned arrival of the English exiles. They were able to 'erect' their Church in Geneva on 1 November 1555 when they elected as their ministers Christopher Goodman and John Knox, and Anthony Gilby to cover during the latter's absence. Goodman and Knox remained as joint ministers in Geneva until the congregation disbanded and returned to England after the death of Queen Mary Tudor. They worked together extremely well as colleagues even though Knox was absent from Geneva for considerable periods of time on his tours of Scotland and France.[4]

The English congregation in Geneva managed to escape the usual contentious consequences of being an exile Church. Goodman wrote to

---

[2] For the importance of Knox's female friends, see Chapter 4 by Patrick Collinson in this volume.

[3] See Euan Cameron, in Chapter 3 of this volume. For Goodman's intervention, see J. Petheram (ed.), *A Brieff Discourse of the Troubles begun at Frankfort [1575]* (London, 1846), p. xlvii, and see Jane E.A. Dawson, 'The Early Career of Christopher Goodman and his Place in the Development of English Protestant Thought' (unpublished University of Durham PhD thesis, 1978), pp. 150–58.

[4] Having left Geneva at the end of August 1555 Knox did not return until September 1556. He left again in September 1557 returning around March 1558. His final departure was 28 January 1559. Jasper Ridley *John Knox* (Oxford, 1968), pp. 224, 237, 249, 264, 307. Gilby only acted as Knox's replacement for the first of these absences, at other times Goodman was left on his own.

his friend Peter Martyr 'of that happy agreement and solid peace which by the great blessing of God we enjoy in this place'.[5] In his autobiography, Thomas Hancock, a member of the congregation, fondly recalled his stay in Geneva: 'In the which citie, I prayse God, I dyd se my lord God most pewrly and trewly honored, and syn moste straytly punnisshed; soo hytt, may be well called a holy citie, a citie of God'.[6] The probable secret of their tranquillity was the employment of the congregation's energies in several major projects rather than channelling them into internal strife. As a secure foundation, the Church organized itself efficiently holding annual elections of ministers, elders and deacons, and recording its memberships and all christenings, marriages and burials in its book, later called the *Livre des Anglois*.[7] Apparently without any controversy, the congregation agreed upon a complete service book, The Forme of Prayers, which was printed on 10 February 1556 and which, after 1560, would become The Book of Common Order of the Scottish Kirk.[8] An even more substantial achievement was the work of biblical translation which culminated in the Geneva Bible published in 1560.[9]

The most notorious products of the English exile congregation at Geneva were the resistance tracts of 1558 and especially those by Goodman and Knox. It was this horrifying association with resistance which remained uppermost in Queen Elizabeth's mind whenever she thought of Geneva and throughout her reign fuelled her misdirected hostility towards the city and towards Calvin and Beza. Her predictable antagonism to Knox's and Goodman's condemnation of female rule ensured that neither of them were welcomed back to England in 1559. Having waited in vain at Dieppe for a passport to travel through England, Knox sailed directly to Leith in May of that year. Goodman did manage to slip back into England and remained in hiding protected by the members of the Genevan congregation. Because Knox was most anxious that Goodman join him in Scotland, he sent urgent messages to his main English contact, Mrs Anne Locke. On 23 June 1559 he wrote

---

[5] 20 August 1558, Zürich Staatsarchiv, EII 368 fo. 258v, printed in H. Robinson (ed.), *Original Letters relative to the Reformation* (2 vols, Parker Society, Cambridge, 1846–47), II, p. 769.

[6] Autobiography of Thomas Hancock in J.G. Nichols (ed.), *Narratives of the Reformation* (Camden Society, London, 1859), p. 84.

[7] Reprinted in C. Martin, *Les protestants anglais refugiés à Genève* (Geneva, 1915), pp. 331–8.

[8] W.D. Maxwell, *The Liturgical Portions of the Genevan Service Book* (Edinburgh, 1965). For the authorship and importance of the Form in relation to the Genevan congregation, see Dawson, 'Early Career', pp. 162–76, 369–70.

[9] Introduction by Lloyd Berry to *Geneva Bible* (facsimile of 1560 edn, Madison, WI, 1969).

to her concerning 'my deir brother, Mr Gudman, whose presence I more thrist, than she that is my own fleshe',[10] providing a series of instructions to get his friend safely into Scotland. After one abortive attempt to cross the border, Goodman did arrive in Scotland in the late summer of 1559 and went as minister to the burgh of Ayr, the great stronghold of Protestantism in the south-west. There he was warmly welcomed and provided with all his needs by an attentive burgh council who decided that their minister should be furnished with very generous travelling expenses, rent and furnishings along with clothes worth £9 11s, which included black silk buttons for his coat![11]

After the triumph of the Lords of the Congregation, there was a general reassessment of the scant ministerial resources available for the infant Kirk. In that reorganization, Goodman was appointed on 20 July 1560 as minister to the burgh of St Andrews. He was very happy at St Andrews and enjoyed helping Knox to establish a reformed Kirk in Scotland. John Calvin, who knew both men well from their stay in Geneva, was aware of how important Goodman's support was for Knox and wrote in the spring of 1561 urging him to remain in Scotland.[12] Although he had no desire to move,[13] the unstable political situation finally forced Goodman to leave St Andrews in the autumn of 1565. As one of the closest associates of Lord James Stewart, Earl of Moray, he was implicated in the rising against the Darnley marriage which ended in the fiasco of the Chaseabout Raid. By early December 1565 Goodman was with Moray and the other Scottish rebels in Newcastle and the earl was trying to secure a licence for him to preach.[14] Throughout the remainder of his long life, Goodman stayed in close contact with his friends from Ayr and St Andrews, but was never able to fulfil his wish to return to Scotland.[15]

---

[10] Knox, *Works*, VI, p. 27.

[11] G.S. Pryde (ed.), *Ayr Burgh Accounts, 1534–1624* (SHS, Edinburgh, 1937), pp. 30, 132. Margaret Sanderson, *Ayrshire and the Reformation: People and Change, 1490–1600* (East Linton, 1997), pp. 97–8.

[12] Calvin to Goodman, 23 April 1561, Knox, *Works*, VI, p. 125.

[13] In 1562, Goodman had turned down the request from Ambrose Dudley, Earl of Warwick to act as chaplain to the English expedition to France: Warwick to Robert Dudley, Earl of Leicester, 16 December 1562; Warwick to Cecil, 28 December 1562, *Calendar of State Papers, Foreign, Elizabeth*, ed. J. Stevenson et al. (23 vols, London, 1863–1950), V (1562), nos 1269 and 1363.

[14] Thomas Randolph to Francis Russell, Earl of Bedford, 9 November 1565, *CSP Scot.*, II, no. 301; James Stewart, Earl of Moray to William Cecil, 7 December 1565, *CSP Scot.*, II, no. 316; James Stewart, Earl of Moray to Robert Dudley, Earl of Leicester, 7 December 1565, BL, Egerton MS 1818 fo. 39.

[15] Goodman to Knox on Regent Moray's assassination *c*. 15 March 1570: Knox, *Works*, VI, p. 573; Robert Campbell of Kinzeancleuch still in touch, 16 April 1574:

For Knox, who had relied heavily upon his close friend and colleague, Goodman's departure from Scotland was a bitter blow. When news came via John Wood, Moray's secretary, that Goodman was involved in the difficult task of evangelization in Ireland, Knox wrote sadly, 'God grant Mr Goodman a prosperous and happie successe in the acceptation of his charge ... and so I will the more patientlie beare his absence, weaning myself from all comfort that I looked to have receaved be his presence and familiaritie'.[16] The depth of Knox's personal loss was revealed in his last letter to Goodman a few months before his own death:

> Beloved Brother ... That we sall meit in this life, there is no hope; for to my bodie, it is impossible to be caried from countrie to countrie, and of your comfortable presence where I am, I have small, yea, no esperance. The name of God be praised, who of his mercie hath left me so great comfort of you in this life, that ye may understand, that my heart is pierced with the present troubles.[17]

This last quotation underlines the fact that Goodman was Knox's close confidant and that they were in the habit of discussing all the problems which they faced as colleagues and friends. From the start of their relationship they could agree on their fundamental approach to such problems because they shared a common method of interpreting the Bible. Each was deeply conscious of his vocation as a preacher and, especially for Knox, his calling to be a prophet. They drew inspiration for their ecclesiastical and political ideals directly from Scripture and deliberately chose to express their ideas in biblical language. Goodman and Knox were most confident and certain of their message when they were preaching and the sermon became their preferred form of expression.

This homiletical style lent itself to the presentation of their rigorist hermeneutic which developed from the premise that the Will of God was clearly and directly revealed in the Bible in the form of mandatory precedents. The Will of God was reduced to a series of divine commandments which needed to be understood and followed in both their positive and negative aspects. A positive command or warrant located in Scripture was required to justify all godly actions, especially those

---

Calderwood, *History*, VIII, pp. 200–201; Thomas Randolph to Earl of Leicester, 21 November 1580, R. Lemon (ed.), *Calendar of State Papers, Domestic 1547–80* (London, 1865), p. 688; Edward Bulkeley to George Buchanan, 28 November 1580, G. Buchanan, *Opera Omnia* (2 vols, Leiden, 1725), II, pp. 762–3.

[16] Knox to John Wood, 14 Feb 1568, Knox, *Works*, VI, p. 558.

[17] Knox to Goodman, July 1572, ibid., VI, p. 618.

concerned directly with divine worship.[18] Following God's Will equally
required understanding the meaning of His negative commands. It was
not enough to abstain from what was forbidden, the hidden positive
implication of a command must also be obeyed. Full and active obedience to God's Will was achieved by performing the very opposite of
what had been forbidden, over and above the passive avoidance of the
forbidden deed itself: 'doing the contrary', as Goodman phrased it. For
example, as well as refraining from committing murder, the commandment 'Thou shalt not kill' required action to help one's neighbour to
live as full a life as possible.[19]

Goodman and Knox were convinced of the necessity of this positive
alignment with the Will of God through a rigid adherence to biblical
tenets drawn from positive and negative divine commands. This approach provided both of them with the same uncompromising vision,
and the dynamism to achieve it. In whichever country they found themselves, Goodman and Knox laboured to explicate in theory and create
in practice their ideal of a fully reformed Church and a godly society.
Although many of its basic premises were common to the whole of the
reformed tradition, the rigorist double interpretation of scriptural commandments was the key feature of the 'puritan mentality' which
characterized the Scottish Kirk and Puritanism throughout the English-
speaking world.[20]

However, the agreement of Knox and Goodman on this fundamental
approach did not mean that their ideas were identical. A close examination of their writings reveals several significant divergences in presentation,
and even in content, which can be seen most sharply in their resistance
theories. Comparing the ideas of the two men is complicated by the fact
that Goodman only wrote one resistance tract whilst the evolution of
Knox's thought on resistance can be traced over a long period and
through many of his writings. This chapter does not attempt a comprehensive comparison between the two men, but rather tests the extent of
their radicalism against the wider context of sixteenth-century Protestant

---

[18] Richard Kyle, 'John Knox's Methods of Biblical Interpretation: An Important Source
of his Intellectual Radicalness', *Journal of Religious Studies*, 12 (1986), pp. 57–70; J.C.
Spalding, 'Restitution as a Normative factor for Puritan Dissent', *Journal of the American Academy of Religion*, 44 (1976), pp. 47–63. For Knox's attitude towards 'ceremonies'
and the Book of Common Prayer, see Euan Cameron in Chapter 3 of this volume.

[19] Jane E.A. Dawson, 'Resistance and Revolution in Sixteenth-Century Thought: The
Case of Christopher Goodman', in J. Van Den Berg and P. Hoftijzer (eds), *The Church,
Change and Revolution* (Leiden, 1991), p. 71.

[20] J.S. Coolidge, *The Pauline Renaissance in England* (Oxford, 1970), pp. 1–22; T.F.
Torrance, *Scottish Theology from John Knox to John McLeod* (Edinburgh, 1996), pp. 1–
47.

theories of resistance. Quentin Skinner has established three yardsticks by which the political thought of the Marian exiles can be judged in relation to their European counterparts: obedience as a Christian duty, particularly when it rested upon the maxims of Romans 13; the concept of the biblical covenant; and the identification of those permitted to resist. In each of these three areas the Marian exiles were willing to advocate more extreme positions than other European Protestant theorists.[21]

Knox has acquired a reputation for extreme radicalism which he probably does not merit. One reason was the undoubted vehemence of his language and rhetorical style.[22] While Knox employed violent and sometimes abusive prose in his resistance tracts, the theories themselves were not as extreme as his linguistic fervour made them appear. When his resistance theories are examined in relation to Skinner's three yardsticks, Knox emerges as moving much more slowly and tentatively than Goodman to radical positions.

The gradual development of Knox's thinking can be seen most clearly when his views on obedience as a Christian duty are charted. The distance between his initial pronouncement and his mature position was considerable. Knox's final and most complete statement upon the nature of Christian obedience was given in the sermon upon Romans 13:1–4 which he preached at the opening of the General Assembly on 25 June 1564, and defended in the following day's debate.[23] Ever since Luther had returned them to the very centre of political thought, these verses had provided for Protestants the fundamental text on obedience.[24] All the magisterial reformers used these injunctions to justify

---

[21] Quentin Skinner, *The Foundations of Modern Political Thought* (2 vols, Cambridge, 1978), II, chaps 7–9 (pp. 227–38 for three measures).

[22] For a general discussion of Knox's style, see David Murison, 'Knox the Writer', in Duncan Shaw (ed.), *John Knox: A Quatercentenary Reappraisal* (Edinburgh, 1975), pp. 33–50.

[23] 'Let everie soule be subiect unto the higher powers: for there is no power but of God: and the powers that be are ordeined of God. Whosoever therfore resisteth ye power, resisteth the ordinance of God: and they that resist, shall receive to them selves iudgement. For princes are not to be feared for good workes, but for evil. Wilt you then be without fear of the power? do wel: so shalt thou have praise of the same. For he is the minister of God for thy wealth: but if thou do evil, feare: for he beareth not the sworde for noght: for he is the minister of God to take vengeance on him that doeth evil' (Romans 13:1–4, Geneva Bible translation).

[24] Harro Höpfl (ed.), *Luther and Calvin on Secular Authority* (Cambridge, 1991), pp. xv–xvi; W.D.J. Cargill-Thompson, *The Political Thought of Martin Luther* (Brighton, 1984), pp. 7–8, 93, 173; Francis Oakley, 'Christian Obedience and Authority', in J.H. Burns (ed.), *The Cambridge History of Political Thought, 1450–1700* (Cambridge, 1991), pp. 159–92.

political obedience as a Christian duty. From the first verse they deduced that all holders of political power held their authority from God and were ordained by Him. The very possession of power was itself proof of divine approbation, whether the ruler was godly or not. The second verse was used to assert that in no circumstances was resistance permissible, since to resist a ruler was to resist God Himself. This was not a doctrine of absolute obedience for it contained a conscience clause to cover those occasions when a subject was instructed to perform an ungodly act.[25] In such an instance the subject must refuse to obey any order which directly contravened the commandments of God. However, the refusal was to be entirely passive and never accompanied by active resistance to a ruler. These were the essential components of the doctrine of non-resistance which was so loudly proclaimed in the first half of the sixteenth century by Protestants in Scotland, England and on the Continent.[26] It was a major obstacle in the path of any Protestant wishing to advocate resistance.

In the early part of his career Knox's exposition of the key verses from Romans 13 followed these conventional Protestant lines. The emphasis lay upon the strict duty of obedience to which Knox alluded in his summary of the twelfth chapter of Balnaves's *Treatise on Justification* of 1548. 'Politicke justice is, an obedience which the inferiour estate giveth to their superiour; which should be keept, because it is the command of God that Princes be obeyed.'[27] By 1554 when he consulted Bullinger and Calvin, Knox was thinking around the problem of obedience, but he still did not want to attack the basic interpretation of Romans 13.[28]

Rather than a frontal assault on the Pauline maxims, in his incitement to political obedience Knox adopted the Lutheran emphasis upon the Apostle's use of the plural, 'powers'. That plural underpinned the theory that in an empire or kingdom a range of people held their political authority directly from God. Such 'inferior magistrates' were as divinely ordained as their superiors. The duties of inferior magistrates, especially that of upholding true religion, were juxtaposed with the general obligation of political obedience. Such a line of reasoning became one of the central arguments in Knox's *Appellation* of 1558 which was directly addressed to 'the Nobility and Estates of Scotland', whom he regarded as Scotland's inferior magistrates. Knox grounded his description of the

---

[25] Usually linked to the text from Acts 5:29: 'We ought to obey God rather than men.'
[26] Skinner, *Foundations*, II, chaps 1–3.
[27] Knox, *Works*, III, pp. 18, 25–6, and 27.
[28] Ibid., III, pp. 221–6; J.H. Burns, *The True Law of Kingship: Concepts of Monarchy in Early Modern Scotland* (Oxford, 1996), pp. 132–4.

nobles' duties firmly upon Romans 13. After rehearsing the first four verses he commented:

> As the Apostle in these wordes moste straytly commaundeth obedience to be geven to lawfull powers, pronouncing God's wrathe and vengance against such as shall resist the ordonaunce of God; so dothe he assigne to the powers theyre offices ... Now, if you [the Scottish nobility] be powers ordeined by God (and that I hope all men will graunte), then, by the plaine wordes of the Apostle, is the sworde geven unto you by God, for maintenance of the innocent, and for punyshement of malefactors.[29]

By applying the Lutheran assertion that the Pauline maxim included inferior as well as superior magistrates, Knox sidestepped any challenge to the doctrine of obedience as a Christian duty owed to all those who held political authority. This point – that there were no exemptions to the universal obligation of obedience – was underlined later in the *Appellation* when Knox again cited the opening verse of Romans 13 in order to prove that clerical immunity did not exist.[30] Knox had also hinted in this treatise that the person and the office of the ruler could be separated. This theme became far more significant within his resistance theories after 1558 and changed the tone of his interpretation of Romans 13.[31]

The final shift in his interpretation of the Pauline maxims was revealed in Knox's 1564 sermon. During the ensuing debate on the nature and extent of political obedience, William Maitland of Lethington made a report upon the sermon which emphasized Knox's distinction between the person and the office of the magistrate and his conclusion that resistance was permissible. Knox agreed that he had declared that 'the ordinance of God, and the power giffin unto man, is one thing, and the persone clad with the power or with the authoritie, is ane uther ... that the Prince may be resistit, and yit the ordinance of God nocht violatit, it is evident'.[32]

---

[29] Knox, *Works*, IV, p. 482; Knox, *On Rebellion*, pp. 84–5.

[30] Knox, *Works*, IV, pp. 500–501; Knox, *On Rebellion*, p. 107. For a discussion of the reference alleged to be from Chrysostom, see David Wright in Chapter 5 of this volume.

[31] Knox, *On Rebellion*, p. 154; Knox, *History*, I, p. 168. By 22 May 1559 when the Lords of the Congregation sent an open letter to the nobility of Scotland, which was probably penned by Knox, a sharp distinction was drawn between the ruler's person and his office and the implications were consciously threatening: 'All authority which God hath established is good and perfect, and is to be obeyed of all men, yea, under the pain of damnation. But do ye not understand that there is a great difference betwixt the authority which is God's ordinance and the persons of those which are placed in authority? The authority and God's ordinance can never do wrong ... But the corrupt person placed in this authority may offend.'

[32] Knox had 'maid difference betwix the ordinance of God and the persounis that wer placeit in authoritie; and ye affirmed, that men mycht refuise the persounis, and yit nocht

Knox's sharp separation between the ruler and his office finally broke the link between God's ordinance and the mere possession of political power. Divine approval became instead a selective and conditional process. Only those who used their authority properly could be regarded as ordained by God and so worthy of obedience. In his discussion of the second verse of his text Knox clarified his new position:

> The power in that place is nocht to be understande of the unjuste commandiment of men, but of the just power whairwith God hes armit his Magistratis and Lieutenentis to punische syn, and mentene vertew ... But so it is nocht, gif that men in the feir of God oppone thame selfis to the furie and blynd rage of Princes; for so thai resist nocht God, but the Devill.[33]

The act of resistance no longer automatically implied opposition to divine authority. On the contrary, resisting a wicked superior had not only become lawful, it took on the nature of a Christian duty. In his characteristic desire to present all choices in simple black and white terms, Knox could now describe the duty to resist as part of the apocalyptic struggle against the Devil. By finally abandoning the conventional interpretation of Romans 13, Knox could offer a more consistent theory of resistance and join Goodman in a new understanding of that text.[34]

The second yardstick of radicalism, the notion of the biblical covenant, ran like a silver thread throughout the writings of John Knox.[35] For Knox's Scottish readers, the tradition of making bonds of manrent ensured that both the language and the practice of contractual relationships were deeply familiar and could readily be fused with the concept of a biblical covenant. Knox turned to the Old Testament for his picture of the covenant relationship which God had made with His people. He began with the premise that the covenant was not restricted to the Jews but was equally available for Christian societies. In the *Appellation* he told his readers that 'The Gentiles, (I mean everie citie, realme,

---

to offend againis Godis ordinance ... Subjectis wer nocht bound to obey thair Princes gif thai commandit unlauchfull thingis; but that thai mycht resist thair Princes, and wer nocht ever bound to suffer.' Knox, *Works*, II, pp. 435–6; Knox, *On Rebellion*, p. 191.

[33] Knox, *Works*, II, pp. 437–8; Knox, *On Rebellion*, p. 192.

[34] Compare with Goodman's formulation: *How Superior Powers Oght to Be Obeyd of their subjects: and Wherin They May Lawfully by God's Worde Be Disobeyed and Resisted* (Geneva, 1558) [hereafter *HSP*], p. 110 and below at note 53.

[35] Only those aspects which help to provide a comparison with Goodman's views on the covenant will be discussed in this chapter. For a full discussion of Knox's views on the covenant, see Burns, *True Law*, chaps 4 and 5; Richard L. Greaves, *Theology and Revolution in the Scottish Reformation* (Grand Rapids, MI, 1980), chap. 6; Roger A. Mason, 'Covenant and Commonweal: The Language of Politics in Reformation Scotland', in Norman Macdougall (ed.), *Church, Politics and Society: Scotland 1408–1929* (Edinburgh, 1983), pp. 97–126.

province, or nation amongest the Gentiles, embrasing Christ Jesus and his true religion) be bound to the same leage and covenant that God made with his people Israel'.[36]

The essential sign of the existence of a covenant relationship was the public acceptance of true religion by the whole of a political community. His discussion of the operation of the covenant was drawn from a broad biblical base and, although he referred to the Mosaic covenant, Knox ranged widely through the history of Israel to make his points. He selected most of his covenant examples from the historical and prophetic books of the Old Testament, particularly those describing the kings and queens of Israel and Judah. These stories had the added advantage of allowing Knox to exploit the parallels between his own vocation and that of the Old Testament prophets, especially Jeremiah and Ezekiel. It was a prophet's duty, which Knox applied to himself, to act as a watchman for Israel and to warn the people of God when they were straying from the path of true religion and endangering their covenant relationship with God.

In Knox's exposition the main emphasis fell upon the theme of remaining faithful to the covenant, rather than establishing it in the first place. The greatest threat to the covenant, in the Old Testament and the present, was the practice of idolatry. The covenant's essential requirement was the rejection of all forms of idolatry and the punishment of idolaters. As he had pointed out in 1554 to his English congregations, the practice of idolatry placed the whole covenant relationship in jeopardy: 'In making whilk league, solemnedlie we sweir never to haif fellowschip with ony religioun, except with that whilk God hath confirmit be his manifest Word ... ye will admit it to be necessarie that ydolatrie be avoydit, yf the league betuix God and us stand inviolatit.'[37]

A clear and comprehensive definition of idolatry flowed from the rigorous hermeneutical principle which Knox had adopted at the start of his career. By asserting the necessity for a positive scriptural command to justify all aspects of what he deemed to be 'true religion', Knox created a massive catch-all category of potentially idolatrous practices. He had removed all middle ground and denied the existence of any group of 'things indifferent'. In 1550, he had argued that the sacrifice of the Mass was idolatry and had employed a syllogism which stated: 'All worshipping, honoring, or service inventit by the braine of man in the religion of God, without his own express commandment, is Idolatrie.'[38]

---

[36] Knox, *Works*, IV, p. 505; Knox, *On Rebellion*, p. 103.

[37] *A Godly Letter of Warning*, Knox, *Works*, III, p. 191.

[38] *A Vindication of the Doctrine that the Sacrifice of the Mass is Idolatry*, 4 April 1550 in Knox, *Works*, III, p. 34. Richard G. Kyle, 'John Knox and the Purification of

For the rest of his life Knox never wavered from the stark presentation of true religion or idolatry as the only options. In practice this inclusive definition of idolatry was not applied as strictly as Knox's formulation implied.

Such a black and white duality was applied to the promise made by the people of God which was placed within a rigorist interpretation of divine commandments. The covenant promise comprised both the positive duty of upholding true religion and the negative one of removing any trace of idolatry. When faced with the terrible prospect of England's apostasy and the reintroduction of the Mass during Mary Tudor's reign, Knox and his fellow Protestants declared a Nicodemite compromise to be impossible. The message was plain: in the letters of advice written to his former congregations within England, attendance at the idolatrous Mass was forbidden, even if this brought martyrdom. The reintroduction of Catholic worship furnished a personal test of faith for individual believers. It held even greater significance for the welfare of the whole nation. Protestant polemicists warned the English that God would punish their apostasy by sending disasters to afflict the Queen and her people. Idolatry would bring ruin for the realm in its wake, exactly as it had to ancient Israel.

The public and national consequences of England's apostasy and idolatry, which were drawn from the parallel with the Old Testament, gave Knox and his fellow exiles a unique dilemma. They could not employ the same analysis and advice given to their persecuted co-religionists in other parts of Europe. As Knox demonstrated in his *Apology* of 1557 for the French Protestants, the situation which the Huguenots faced was analogous to the sufferings of the early Christian martyrs. The French, like their fellow Protestants in England, had to avoid any contact with the idolatrous Mass, but the national consequences were different. Because France had not accepted true religion, it was not a covenanted nation and the existence of idolatry did not break a covenant promise. The same reassurance held good for Scotland before 1559 and was reflected in Knox's tracts written for his native country before his final return.[39] However, for England the presence of idolatry in the kingdom was a denial of its covenant. That relationship could only be restored by a complete reversal of religious policy and a 'cleansing' of idolatry from the realm. Such a covenant-based analysis of the English situation raised for Knox the problem of deciding who

---

Religion: The Intellectual Aspects of his Crusade against Idolatry', *Archiv für Reformationsgeschichte*, 77 (1986), pp. 265–80.

[39] Jane E.A. Dawson, 'Revolutionary Conclusions: The Case of the Marian Exiles', *History of Political Thought*, 11 (1990), pp. 257–72.

had the authority to punish idolaters. In his efforts to pinpoint who had the right to punish, Knox developed his ideas of lawful resistance.

The identification of those permitted to resist, which provides the third yardstick of radicalism, was the most sensitive issue for those who advocated any form of resistance. From the very beginning of the Reformation, Roman Catholics had accused Protestants of undermining all forms of order and asserted that the rejection of the Church's authority would inevitably lead to a challenge to the social and political order. As has been seen, in 1566 Peter Frarin still found this a lively propaganda theme. The magisterial reformers countered these charges by loudly asserting their doctrine of non-resistance and their political loyalty in an attempt to lay the terrible ghost of the Anabaptist rising in Münster in 1534 which haunted them for the remainder of the century. The justifications for resistance which had been formulated by the Lutherans had gone to extravagant lengths to restrict the right to resist. One of the many attractions of the varied 'inferior magistrate' theories was that they gave a precise answer to the question who may lawfully resist. The category of 'inferior magistrates' was greatly expanded by later thinkers from its original and highly specific definition based on the Imperial constitution, but they still guarded against any suggestion that the right to resist included those without political office. The idea that the 'common people' possessed such a right was shocking and conjured up visions of anarchy and revolution in most sixteenth-century minds. In contrast, Marian exiles such as Goodman and Ponet[40] were prepared to proclaim that resistance was a right given to all people. Such overt radicalism was partly the consequence of the unique situation English Protestants faced when they contemplated the re-Catholicization or apostasy of their country.[41]

Knox was also radicalized by the English situation, as his notorious *First Blast* demonstrated,[42] but on the thorny matter of who should resist his ideas developed more tentatively. His belief in the absolute necessity of punishment for idolaters was one of the main pressures which pushed him into an increasingly radical stance. Writing from Dieppe in January 1554 Knox's *Godly Letter of Warning* faced the issue directly. He posed

---

[40] John Ponet advocated resistance in his tract *Shorte Treatise of Politike Power* (Strasbourg, 1556); G. Bowler, 'Marian Protestants and the Violent Resistance to Tyranny', in Peter Lake and Maria Dowling (eds), *Protestantism and the National Church in England* (London, 1987), pp. 124–43; Donald R. Kelley, 'Ideas of Resistance before Elizabeth', in H. Dubrow and R. Strier (eds), *The Historical Renaissance* (Chicago, 1988), pp. 48–76.

[41] Dawson, 'Revolutionary Conclusions', pp. 260–69.

[42] Burns, *True Law*, pp. 145–8; Jane E.A. Dawson, 'The Two John Knoxes: England, Scotland and the 1558 Tracts', *JEH*, 43 (1991), pp. 555–76.

and answered the question: 'Sall we go and slay all ydolateris? That were the office, deir Brethrene, of everie Civill Magistrate within his realme. But of yow is requyreit onlie to avoyd participatioun and company of thair abominationis ... the slaying of ydolateris appertenis not to everie particular man.'[43] This was a plain denial of the right of the common people or of individuals to punish idolatry; their duty was accomplished by remaining free of idolatry themselves. Equally, Knox was not endorsing the right of the inferior magistrates to act; as J.H. Burns has demonstrated, the phrase 'everie Civill Magistrate within his realme' referred to the ruler and not to the inferior magistrates.[44]

The experience of exile and the onset of the burnings of English Protestants in 1555 sharpened Knox's thinking. His description of England's fate altered focus from a concentration upon the just punishment for the lack of godly zeal under Edward VI to warnings of the divine vengeance which would be poured down upon Queen Mary and her subjects. Although it did not imply a major change of view, Knox's fervent prayer in the *Faithfull Admonition* of 1554 that God send a deliverer, like another Jehu, to take bloody revenge upon the idolatrous Queen and so pacify the wrath of God, indicated a hardening of attitude.[45] It was the use of such extreme language and the unflattering identification of Europe's rulers with specific biblical characters which brought Knox his dismissal from Frankfurt.[46]

A different set of issues concerning idolatry confronted Knox after his Scottish visit in 1555–56. Scotland, like France, was not a covenanted nation and idolatry was viewed within a New rather than an Old Testament perspective. Knox had expounded at length during his visit and in his subsequent letters upon the basic requirement that participation in Roman Catholic worship must be avoided.[47] This hard line raised the issue of how 'privy kirks' could be protected and true worship could be provided. When he discussed idolatry in the Scottish context, Knox's main target for attack was the Catholic clergy, who received the full force of his colourful invective. His calls for disobedience and forms of resistance were directed against the Church and its hierarchy and not against the civil authority.

Knox also turned his attention to the Scottish nobility as potential supporters and protectors of the cause of 'true religion'. Knox used the

---

[43] Knox, *Works*, III, p. 194.

[44] Burns, *True Law*, p. 131.

[45] Knox, *Works*, III, p. 309.

[46] Specifically the identification of Emperor Charles V with Nero, see Euan Cameron in Chapter 3 of this volume.

[47] Knox's *History*, I, pp. 120–21, 132–6.

plurality of 'powers' mentioned in Romans 13 to enlarge upon the nature of the religious duty of the nobility, whom he identified as inferior magistrates within the kingdom of Scotland. In his *Appellation* Knox urged the nobility to act to restrain the Catholic clergy and to reform religion. He also returned to his preoccupation with the punishment of idolatry. Here he shifted his argument and affirmed that the whole people were involved in the punishment of idolatry, but immediately drew back and instead demanded action from the nobility.[48]

Knox's hesitations were removed by the events of 1559–60 which brought the formal acceptance of true religion in Scotland and signalled the nation's entry into a full covenant relationship with God. The question of who might punish idolatry could now receive a straightforward answer from Knox. He expanded the right to punish idolatry into a more general duty to enforce all of God's laws directly against the ruler. The covenant promise became the foundation for a communal right of resistance. In his debate with Maitland of Lethington in June 1564 Knox asserted:

> subjectis may nocht onlie lauchfullie oppone tham selfis to thair kingis, whensoevir thay do onie thing that expressedlie repugnes to Goddis commandiment, but also that they may execute jugement upoun thame according to Goddis law; so that if the king be ane murtherar, adulterar, or idolater, he soulde suffer according to Godis law, nocht as ane king, but as ane offender, and that the peopill may put Godis lawes in executioune.[49]

In his 1564 pronouncements Knox came closest to the radical position adopted six years earlier by Goodman. He had abandoned the conventional interpretation of Romans 13 and had clarified his

---

[48] Knox, *Works*, IV, p. 504; Knox, *On Rebellion*, p. 102; Burns, *True Law*, pp. 149–51. 'The punishment of idolatrie doth not appertaine to kinges only, but also to the whole people, yea, to everie membre of the same, according to his possibilitie ... Yf this be required of the whole people, and of everie man in his vocation, what shall be required of you, my Lordes [the Scottish nobility] ... whose handes he [God] hath armed with the sword of his justice?' For a fuller discussion of these points and of Knox's *Letter to the Commonalty* (Knox, *Works*, IV, pp. 523–38; Knox, *On Rebellion*, pp. 115–27), see Roger A. Mason, *Kingship and the Commonweal: Political Thought in Renaissance and Reformation Scotland* (East Linton, 1998), chap. 5. I am most grateful to Dr Mason for allowing me to consult his work prior to publication.

[49] Knox, *Works*, II, p. 452; Knox, *On Rebellion*, p. 203. At the end of the debate Knox concluded his summation, 'And last, That Godis pepill hes executit Godis law aganis thair King, having no farther regaird to him in that behalf, than gif he had bene the moist simpill subject within this Realme. And thairfoir ... I am assureit that nocht onlie Goddis pepill may, but also, that thai ar bounde to do the same whair the lyke crymes ar committit, and when he gevis unto thame the lyke power'. Knox, *Works*, II, p. 453; Knox, *On Rebellion*, p. 204.

thinking about the covenant. He had taken the right to punish idolatry and slowly turned it into a justification for resistance by the common people. Although they were not developed, there were also hints that he had adopted Goodman's private-law arguments for resistance.[50] Knox's radicalism had taken a decade to reach fruition but, despite the assertiveness of his language, he never achieved the devastating directness of argument produced by Goodman.

Christopher Goodman's radicalism was starkly displayed in his tract *How Superior Powers oght to be obeyd of their subiects: and wherin they may lawfully by Gods worde be disobeyd and resisted*, which was published on 1 January 1558 by the Genevan printer Jean Crespin. Characteristically, the ideas in the tract had begun life as a sermon preached before the English exile congregation sometime during the previous year when he had taken as his text Acts 4:19, where the Apostles Peter and John defied the Sanhedrin with the words, 'Whether it be right in the sight of God to obey you rather then God, iudge you'.[51] This verse was the proof text of the conscience clause for non-resistance and it was the most vulnerable part of the doctrine. Goodman changed it from a justification for passive disobedience, and consequent suffering, into a call for active resistance. To achieve this transformation he employed his idea of 'the contrary', which was a specific application of the rigorous hermeneutic he shared with Knox. He took the idea of the hidden positive implication embedded in a negative divine command and employed it to justify active opposition to idolatry and direct resistance to those who introduced idolatrous practices.[52]

Having demolished non-resistance and removed passive disobedience as an option, Goodman turned his attention to the main text of Romans 13, the first yardstick of radicalism. Here he simply cut the Gordian knot which had bound earlier Protestant theorists. In an extremely direct manner he reinterpreted the first verse of the text:

> For thogh the Apostle saith: There is no power but of God: yet doth he not here meane anie other powers, but such as are orderly and lawfullie institute of God ... For he never ordeyned anie lawes to approve, but to reprove and punishe tyrantes, idolaters, papistes and oppressors. Then when they are suche, they are not Gods

---

[50] For example in the phrases 'nocht as ane king, but as ane offender' and 'the moist simpill subject'. For Goodman's theories, see below at note 66 f.

[51] *HSP*, p. 15.

[52] Dawson, 'Resistance and Revolution', pp. 70–72.

ordinaunce. And in disobeying and resisting such, we do not resiste Gods ordinaunce, but Satan.[53]

This refuted the assumption that all holders of political power were sanctioned by God and enabled Goodman to make divine approbation dependent upon a ruler's perfomance. If a ruler acted in a manner which was manifestly tyrannical or ungodly, it proved that he lacked divine approval. This opened the door to resistance because opposing tyranny and ungodliness would be resisting the Devil and not God.

By dealing with these two key New Testament texts, Goodman completely redefined the doctrine of obedience as a Christian duty. The ruler's qualifications and actions became the criteria by which lawful authority should be judged and the Pauline maxim became a conditional rather than an absolute duty. Obedience was owed only to those rulers who were 'orderly and lawfullie institute of God'; others could be resisted with impunity. By denying an automatic association between obedience and the possession of political power, Goodman moved the whole debate into new territory. Although arriving from a different direction, Goodman had brought the resistance debate back to arguments made by medieval political theorists on how to distinguish just from unjust rulers and how to deal with tyranny.[54]

In his own discussion of obedience and resistance Goodman was anxious to leave New Testament texts and concentrate instead upon the Old Testament covenant, the second yardstick of radicalism. He was convinced that God had provided a clear model for Christian political life within the Old Testament, which paralleled the New Testament model for ecclesiastical life. Like Knox, Goodman believed that the covenant relationship between God and His people extended beyond the Jews and was a pattern which God had given to all Christian nations. But Goodman was much more precise in his understanding of the covenant, restricting it to the eternal model located in the Pentateuch. God had directly revealed the nature of the covenant relationship and encapsulated it within the Mosaic Law. It was freely available in the books of Deuteronomy and Exodus for use by any kingdom which sought to become God's people. Goodman stressed that the example of the Mosaic covenant 'ought never to departe from the eyes of all such as are, or woulde be Gods people. Wherin as in a most clere glasse it

---

[53] *HSP*, p. 110. Compare Knox above at note 33.

[54] J.H. Burns, *Lordship, Kingship and Empire: The Idea of Monarchy, 1400–1525* (Oxford, 1992); J.H. Burns, 'Scholasticism: Survival and Revival', in J.H. Burns (ed.), *The Cambridge History of Political Thought, 1450–1700* (Cambridge, 1991), pp. 135–55.

dothe appeare how they are bownd to God, what God requireth of them, and what they have promised to him'.[55]

Both Knox and Goodman assumed that the whole people entered into the covenant when they openly adopted 'true religion', as had been the case in Edward VI's England. Although rather vague about the mechanisms by which entry was achieved, Goodman was in no doubt about the covenant's duties and obligations which were listed in the Mosaic Law.[56] Having rehearsed an elaborate series of parallels between Moses and Christ, Goodman concluded that Christian communities possessed one major advantage over the Israelites. The clearer revelation of the Will of God brought by Christ liberated the people of God on two levels, first by abrogating the ceremonial parts of the Mosaic Law and second by freeing the Law for its new purpose of providing a pattern for a Christian commonwealth.[57] The Law brought a form of political freedom by guaranteeing the rights of the people in relation to their rulers. Goodman was at pains to emphasize that, while the obedience owed to God in the covenant was absolute, the political obedience due to the rulers of a Christian kingdom was always conditional.[58]

Goodman's concentration upon Mosaic Law entailed a rejection of the generalized model of the covenant in operation employed by Knox and other Protestant thinkers. A second, distinctive feature of his covenant thinking was the emphasis upon the dual nature of assent to the promise, both by the whole people communally, and by each person individually. The link between baptism and entry into a covenant with Christ had been a common Protestant theme. The crucial difference found in Goodman's ideas was that he transferred the identification between the covenant and baptismal promises from its ecclesiological setting into the arena of political life. He could then argue that at baptism each individual had entered into a covenant relationship with God and promised to uphold the Laws of God. 'God hath charged thee beinge one of his people, with the same Lawes (the Ceremonies except) wherwithe he charged his people Israel before, and willith thee no less to knowe his preceptes, and to obeye them, then he willed the Israelites.'[59]

---

[55] *HSP*, pp. 164–5.

[56] Ibid., pp. 162–5.

[57] Ibid., pp. 168–9, 55, 97. By treating Mosaic Law as the pattern for political behaviour, Goodman removed it from any conflict between law and grace in the soteriological debate.

[58] Ibid., pp. 44, 116–17.

[59] Ibid., p. 168.

The parallels drawn between the Israelites and contemporary Christians, together with the tight focus upon the Mosaic covenant, enabled Goodman to reduce the covenant promise to the formula of upholding the Laws of God. This obligation rested upon the people collectively and upon each of its members. When he spelt out the implications of the individual obligation Goodman explicitly stated that it remained intact even if the communal obligation were neglected:

> If the Magistrates would whollye despice and betraye the iustice and Lawes of God, you which are subiectes with them shall be condemned except you mayntayne and defend the same Lawes agaynst them ... for this hath God required of you, and this have you promised unto him not under condition (if the Rulers will) but without all exceptions to do what so ever your Lorde and God shall commande you.[60]

The combination of a communal and an individual responsibility to uphold the covenant was essential to Goodman's ideas. It allowed him to answer the question of who was permitted to resist a ruler in an extremely radical fashion. In this third measure of radicalism Goodman was the least afraid of all the Marian exiles of trumpeting his belief that the common people possessed both a right and a duty of resistance. In the first place he justified resistance on the grounds of the dual obligation within the covenant which bound the people communally and individually to uphold the laws of God. This was interpreted as ensuring that those who broke the law were punished. In a more comprehensive and inclusive manner than Knox, Goodman transposed the right to punish into the right to resist. The tradition of discussing the right to punish in terms of the metaphor of the sword of justice and employing the same image to symbolize the essence of political authority, facilitated the elision of the two concepts.[61] Goodman adopted the language of the sword with its complex iconography and spoke of the people wielding the sword of justice and punishing those who had broken God's commandments. In ringing tones he declared that the people did not need an 'inferior magistrate' to lead the resistance but had divine authorization to act directly themselves:

> And thoghe you had no man of power upon your parte: yet, it is sufficient assurance for you, to have the warrant of Godds worde upon your side, and God him self to be your Capitayne who

---

[60] Ibid., pp. 180–81. Goodman expected the inferior magistrates to resist and employed a series of arguments to justify their actions. I hope to discuss Goodman's thought at greater length in the future.

[61] J.H. Burns, 'Jus gladii and jurisdictio: Jacques Almain and John Locke', *Historical Journal*, 26 (1983), pp. 369–74.

> willeth not onely the Magistrates and officers to roote out evil
> from amongest them, be it, idolatrie, blasphemie or open iniurie,
> but the whole multitude are therwith charged also, to whom a
> portion of the sworde of iustice is committed, to execute the
> iudgementes which the Magistrates lawfully commande.[62]

The suggestion that the common people could enforce the law upon
their superiors provoked an intensely hostile reaction among many of
Goodman's contemporaries.[63] The very language which Goodman employed, that of Christ as a military captain, directly recalled, and so
gave substance to, the spectre of Anabaptist uprisings.[64] Even Goodman
recognized how shocking his ideas would be, but he refused to compromise and reiterated his call for resistance by the people:

> And thoghe it appeare at the firste sight a great disordre, that the
> people shulde take unto them the punishment of transgression, yet,
> when the Magistrates and other officers cease to do their duetie,
> they are as it were, without officers, yea, worse then if they had
> none at all, and then God geveth the sworde in to the peoples
> hande, and he him self is become immediatly their head. (Yf they
> will seeke the accomplishment of his Lawes).[65]

Knox and Goodman shared the justification of resistance by the
common people based upon the covenant, although it had taken Knox
longer to transform the right to punish into a clear mandate to resist.
Even in Knox's mature position of 1564, only hints can be found of
Goodman's other principal justification which was derived from
Lutheran private-law arguments. Goodman was again prepared to push
arguments in a much more radical direction that his predecessors. He
relished adopting the most extreme position which the logic of the
argument could be made to support. In its original Lutheran form the
private-law theory combined the Roman-law tenet of self-defence, that
it was permissible to repel unjust force, with the canon law maxim, that
an unjust judge could be resisted when he acted unlawfully.[66] This
rather convoluted appeal to legal formulae produced the argument that
when a 'public person', that is one with political authority, acted in a
manner which broke the bounds of his office, he automatically forfeited
his 'public' status and became a 'private' person who could then be
resisted on grounds of self-defence.

---

[62] *HSP*, p. 180.

[63] Dawson, 'Revolutionary Conclusions', p. 257.

[64] In a masterly understatement Mr Morley, who had been given his copy of *How
Superior Powers* by the author, jotted down in the margin of page 187 'an open way to
rebellion' (copy of *HSP* in Durham University Library).

[65] *HSP*, p. 185.

[66] Skinner, *Foundations*, II, pp. 194–206.

When applied to political authority in an empire or kingdom, the theory offered a sharp distinction between the office and the person of the ruler or 'superior magistrate'. Criteria were laid down determining which of a ruler's actions entailed the loss of his public status. These private-law arguments had served to justify the actions of the Protestant princes and cities who had formed the Schmalkaldic League. They possessed one major difficulty in that they implicitly challenged part of the fundamental doctrine of non-resistance, that all rulers were ordained by God. The Lutherans had found this problem insoluble and had been obliged to ignore it. On most of the occasions when Knox had employed the important distinction between the office and the person of the magistrate he had done so within the framework of an inferior magistrate theory.

Goodman did not face the acute Lutheran dilemma because he had reinterpreted Romans 13 and dispensed with the assumption that every holder of political authority was automatically approved by God. He was able to adopt the more coherent position that wicked rulers were not divinely authorized; God's approval was linked directly to the actions of the ruler in the performance of his office, not to his person nor to the actual possession of power. This allowed Goodman to concentrate upon the requirements of the magistrate's office which was, in its traditional formulation, to defend good and to punish evil.[67]

By focusing attention upon the fulfilment of the office, Goodman could describe the situation when a ruler failed so badly in his duty that he automatically ceased to be a magistrate.

> But where as the kinges or Rulers are become altogether blasphemers of God, and oppressors and murtherers of their subiectes, then oght they to be accompted no more for kinges or lawfull Magistrats, but as private men, and to be examined, accused, condemned and punished by the Lawe of God, wherunto they are and oght to be subiect.[68]

Unlike the care taken by the Lutheran theorists, Goodman wasted little time over the categorization of offences which entailed the loss of public status. He made the basic distinction between private wickedness and public acts of injustice and tyranny, explaining that

> so longe as their wikednesse brasteth not out manifestly agaynst God, and his Lawes, but outwardly will see them observed and kept of others, punishing the transgressors, and defending the innocent: so longe are we bounde to render unto such, obedience, as to evill and roughe Maisters ... if without feare they transgresse

---

[67] *HSP*, p. 111.
[68] Ibid., pp. 139–40.

> Gods Lawes them selves, and commande others to the like, then
> have they lost that honor and obedience which otherwise their
> subiectes did owe unto them: and oght no more to be taken for
> Magistrates: but punished as private transgressors.[69]

Here, as throughout his tract, Goodman was quick to move from the
identification of the offence against the law straight to its punishment.
The private-law arguments were employed to make that transition
smoother and to allow resistance to be discussed almost exclusively as
the right to punish. Goodman was thus able to subsume the idea of self-
defence, which was central to the original theory, within the concept of
self-preservation. This permitted the essentially reactive and defensive
stance of repelling unjust force to be transmuted into an aggressive and
active right to self-preservation.

Goodman was impatient with potential objections to his massive
expansion of the private-law theories. He brushed aside the distinction
between acceptable actions undertaken by the common people when
they had no ruler and resistance to a wicked magistrate. To him the
people should take the same action in both cases and the private-law
theory was utilized to ensure that the two situations appeared identical.
He boldly asserted that

> it is all one to be without a Ruler, and to have such as will not rule
> in Gods feare. Yea it is much better to be destitut altogether, then
> to have a tyrant and a murtherer. For then are they nomore publik
> persons, contemning their publik auctoritie in usinge it agaynst the
> Lawes, but are to be taken of all men, as private persones, and so
> examyned and punished.[70]

Throughout his discussions of the private-law ideas Goodman retained
and even emphasized the role of the individual which other exponents
had been so anxious to remove. He explicitly uncoupled the right to
resist from the inferior magistrates theory and stated quite plainly that,
although the common people might authorize their inferior magistrates
to resist on their behalf, they never surrendered the right to resist
themselves.[71] Whichever justification Goodman employed for the common people's right to resist, he made it more radical.

---

[69] Ibid., pp. 118–19.

[70] Ibid., pp. 187–8.

[71] Many later theorists employed the fact of delegation to the inferior magistrates to
remove the direct involvement of the people in resistance: Robert Kingdon, 'Calvinism
and Resistance Theory, 1550–1580' in J.H. Burns, *The Cambridge History of Political
Thought, 1450–1700* (Cambridge, 1991), pp. 194–218; Skinner, *Foundations*, II, chaps
8–9.

By all three measures of radicalism, Christopher Goodman was a more extreme thinker than John Knox. In his conclusions, if not always in language or delivery, Goodman sounded the clearer trumpet call for resistance. But, by 1564 at the latest, both men were playing from the same score. They had abandoned the traditional interpretation of Romans 13 and promulgated a new doctrine of Christian obedience. They had transformed the right to punish idolaters into a justification for resistance by the whole people. Finally, and as a more positive legacy, they had set out their vision of a covenanted nation as the sole pattern for Christian politics. Knox and Goodman ensured that the twin themes of covenant and resistance would resonate within Scottish political and ecclesiastical thought.[72] With less of a fanfare these themes entered into Anglo-Scottish Protestant culture and so became part of the heritage of the British Reformations and the culture of the whole English-speaking world.[73]

---

[72] Roger A. Mason, 'Usable Pasts: History and Identity in Reformation Scotland', *SHR*, 76 (1997), pp. 54–68; Roger A. Mason (ed.), *Scots and Britons: Scottish Political Thought and the Union of 1603* (Cambridge, 1994); Jenny Wormald, 'Resistance and Regicide in Sixteenth-Century Scotland: The Execution of Mary, Queen of Scots', *Majestas*, 1 (1993), pp. 67–87.

[73] Jane E.A. Dawson, 'Anglo-Scottish Protestant Culture and the Integration of Sixteenth-Century Britain', in Steven Ellis and Sarah Barber (eds), *Conquest and Union: Forging a Multi-National British State* (London, 1995), pp. 87–114; Donald R. Kelley, 'Elizabethan Political Thought', in J.G.A. Pocock (ed.), *The Varieties of British Political Thought* (Cambridge, 1993); Nicholas Phillipson and Quentin Skinner (eds), *Political Discourse in Early Modern Britain* (Cambridge, 1993).

CHAPTER EIGHT

Knox, Resistance
and the Royal Supremacy

Roger A. Mason

On 7 July 1568, the General Assembly of the Kirk of Scotland, meeting in Edinburgh with John Willock as moderator, commanded the printer, Thomas Bassenden (or Bassandyne), to recall all copies of a book which he had recently published entitled *The Fall of the Romane Kirk*.[1] The decree appears to have been effective as no copy of the offending tract is known to have survived. It may be tentatively identified, however, as a reprint of an anonymous little work, first published in England in 1547, and reissued there in 1548 and 1550 as well as in Dutch translation in 1553 and 1570, whose full title runs: *Here begynneth a boke, called the faule of the Romyshe churche, with all the abhominations, wherby euery man may know and perceyue the dyuersitie of it, betwene the primatiue churche, of the whiche our souerayne Lorde and Kynge is the supreme head and the malignant churche a sunder*.[2] The General Assembly's objections to the work were evidently based less on its contents – an unexceptional attack on the idolatry of the Roman Catholic Mass – than on hostility to this extended title and to the inference that the young King James VI was 'supreame head of the primitive kirk' in Scotland: hostility, that is, to the doctrine of the royal supremacy.[3]

The royal supremacy was, of course, fundamental to the course and character of the Reformation in England. In the 1534 Act of Supremacy, it was declared 'by authority of this present Parliament' that:

> the king our sovereign lord, his heirs and successors kings of this realm, shall be taken, accepted and reputed the only supreme head in earth of the Church of England called the *Anglicana Ecclesia*, and shall have and enjoy annexed and united to the imperial crown of this realm as well the title and style thereof, as all honours, dignities, preeminences, jurisdictions, privileges, authorities,

---

[1] *BUK*, I, pp. 125–6; Calderwood, *History*, II, p. 423.

[2] See *STC*, nos 21305–21307.5, for details of these editions.

[3] *BUK*, I, p. 125: 'It waas delatit and found that Thomas Bassandine, printer in Edinburgh, imprintit ane buke, intitulat the Fall of the Romane Kirk, nameing our king and sovereigne supreame head of the primitive kirk'.

immunities, profits and commodities, to the said dignity of the same Church belonging and appertaining.[4]

Characteristically articulated in the language of empire, most resoundingly in the celebrated preamble to the 1533 Act in Restraint of Appeals to Rome,[5] the royal supremacy vested in the English Crown the same caesaropapal powers which were believed to have been exercised by the Christian emperors of Rome, notably the allegedly British-born Constantine who had presided over the Council of Nicaea and who was seen as exemplifying the supreme authority in matters ecclesiastical as well as civil which Henry VIII had recovered for the English Crown when he repudiated the usurped authority of Rome.[6] If Elizabeth was later to modify the title of 'supreme head ' to 'supreme governor' of the Church in England, this hardly altered the fact that England's magisterial Reformation found its focus and control in the imperial ideology elaborated to sustain the doctrine of the royal supremacy. As emperors in their own kingdom, Tudor monarchs were believed to be jurisdictionally self-sufficient, wielding an authority in matters spiritual as well as temporal which was, in the words of the Act of Appeals, 'plenary, whole and entire'.[7] At the very least, therefore, the imperial English Crown was 'absolute' in the restricted sixteenth-century sense that it was subject to no higher power but God alone.

Needless to say, Scotland's Reformation was of a very different nature from its English counterpart. There the Reformation was neither controlled nor contained by the Crown's authority, but was initiated and secured in defiance of it: a Reformation 'from below' rather than a Reformation 'from above'. Almost 40 years after the Reformation Parliament of 1560 James VI reflected in wistful but apposite terms that 'the reformation of religion in Scotland' was 'extraordinarily wrought

---

[4] 26 Henry VIII, c. 1, quoted from G.R. Elton, *The Tudor Constitution: Documents and Commentary* (Cambridge, 1965), p. 355.

[5] 24 Henry VIII, c. 12; Elton, *Tudor Constitution*, p. 344.

[6] On the development of this imperial ideology, see J.A. Guy, 'Thomas Cromwell and the Intellectual Origins of the Henrician Revolution', in J.A. Guy and A. Fox, *Reassessing the Henrician Age: Humanism, Politics and Reform 1500–1550* (Oxford, 1986), pp. 151–78; Walter Ullmann, 'This Realm of England is an Empire', *JEH*, 30 (1979), pp. 173–203; Graham Nicholson, 'The Act of Appeals and the English Reformation', in Claire Cross, David Loades and J.J. Scarisbrick (eds), *Law and Government under the Tudors* (Cambridge, 1988), pp. 19–30; and Dale Hoak, 'The Iconography of the Crown Imperial', in Dale Hoak (ed.), *Tudor Political Culture* (Cambridge, 1995), pp. 54–103.

[7] Elton, *Tudor Constitution*, p. 344. On interpretations of the royal supremacy, see J.A. Guy, 'The Henrician Age', in J.G.A. Pocock (ed.), *The Varieties of British Political Thought, 1500–1800* (Cambridge, 1933), pp. 13–46, esp. pp. 35–46; see also Claire Cross (ed.), *The Royal Supremacy in the Elizabethan Church* (London, 1969), for documents and commentary.

by God, wherein many things were inordinatly done by a popular
tumult & rebellion'; manifestly, he lamented, it did not proceed 'from
the Princes ordour, as it did in our neighbour country of England, as
likewise in Denmark, and sundry parts of Germany'.[8] Nor, following
the successful Protestant settlement of 1560, did the return of the
Catholic Mary Stewart to her kingdom do anything to create conditions
in which a magisterial Reformation might proceed on English lines.
Only with the deposition of Mary in 1567, and the accession to the
Scottish throne of her year-old son, James VI, was it possible to envis-
age a godly Scottish commonwealth presided over by a godly Scottish
king. Under the circumstances, Bassenden may well have considered it
appropriate, within a year of James VI's coronation in July 1567, and
within months of his mother's defeat at Langside and flight to England
in May 1568, to celebrate the accession to the Scottish throne of a
godly magistrate in whom supreme authority over both civil and ecclesiastical affairs might at last be vested.

Evidently the General Assembly disagreed. Why so? Why was the
Scottish Kirk apparently so reluctant to follow England's lead and
concede to the Crown the title of 'supreme head' – or even, one may
surmise, 'supreme governor' – of the Church in Scotland? To frame the
question in this way is to take one immediately to the very heart of an
ongoing historiographical debate – or, perhaps more accurately, an
ongoing struggle for the soul of the Scottish Kirk – which has been
waged virtually since the Reformation itself, but which finds its most
redoubtable modern protagonists in James Kirk and the late Gordon
Donaldson. Put crudely, it was Donaldson's belief that the watchword
of the Scottish Reformation was from the outset 'conformity with England'. It was his firm conviction that the idea of the Church's
independence of State or Crown control – the idea, that is, of the 'two
kingdoms' – was wholly foreign to the first generation of Scottish
Protestant reformers. Instead, he saw them as consistently inspired by a
vision of a godly commonwealth presided over by a godly prince mod-
elled in all essentials on the 'Erastian' principles embodied in the English
royal supremacy.[9] James Kirk, on the other hand, has adduced a great
deal of evidence to suggest to the contrary that this same generation of
Scottish reformers was from the outset determined to establish and
maintain the Kirk's autonomy. They certainly envisaged the establishment

---

[8] James Craigie (ed.), *The Basilikon Doron of King James VI* (2 vols, STS, Edinburgh,
1944–50), I, p. 75.

[9] See in particular Gordon Donaldson, *The Scottish Reformation* (Cambridge, 1960),
esp. pp. 130–35; see also Gordon Donaldson, 'The Scottish Church 1567–1625', in
A.G.R. Smith (ed.), *The Reign of James VI and I* (London, 1973), pp. 40–56.

of a godly commonwealth presided over by a godly Protestant prince, but in this case the king would openly recognize and support the Kirk's freedom from Crown control and its right to exercise ecclesiastical jurisdiction independently of the civil magistrate. The theory of the two kingdoms is thus not for Kirk, as it was for Donaldson, an exotic foreign import foisted on the Scots by the Geneva-trained Andrew Melville; rather it was an idea, wholly incompatible with the imperial pretensions of an English-style royal supremacy, which lay from the beginning at the very heart of Scottish reformed ecclesiology.[10]

As will become clear, Kirk's interpretation of the available evidence is, in my view, a good deal more convincing than that of Donaldson. However, it is not the purpose of this chapter to review the debate between them in detail. Rather my intention here is to focus more narrowly on John Knox himself and to examine the development of his view of the role of the civil magistrate in a reformed commonwealth. Curiously, this is an aspect of Knox's thought which has not received much in the way of detailed attention from historians. Many commentators have sought to trace the development of Knox's radical political ideas in the 1550s and beyond, but an emphasis on what a godly people may or may not do in the face of an ungodly ruler has tended to ensure that the 'higher powers' feature predominantly as the object of Knox's frustration and anger rather than as the focus of a more positive appraisal of their role as godly magistrates. Seldom does Knox's understanding of the powers of a godly prince – or his view of the royal supremacy – feature more than incidentally in such analyses.[11] It seemed worth while, therefore, to look more closely at Knox's understanding of the scope and nature of the authority wielded by the civil magistrate and to throw into sharper relief his view of the relationship between Church and State, the spiritual and temporal realms.

That said, it is as well to begin with two preliminary caveats. First, quite apart from its relations with the State, Knox's conception of the Church itself is a complex enough issue. As Richard Kyle has put it: 'The church of John Knox displayed many faces. Alternately and even simultaneously, as historical circumstances dictated, Knox's church was invisible and visible, universal and local, a small flock and a national

---

[10] Most fully argued in James Kirk, *Patterns of Reform: Continuity and Change in the Reformation Kirk* (Edinburgh, 1989), pp. 232–79; see also the lengthy introduction to James Kirk (ed.), *The Second Book of Discipline* (Edinburgh, 1980), esp. pp. 57–65.

[11] See for example the most recent and fullest analysis of the development of Knox's views on resistance in J.H. Burns, *The True Law of Kingship: Concepts of Monarchy in Early Modern Scotland* (Oxford, 1996), chaps 4–5. Knox's resistance theory is considered in more detail by Jane E.A. Dawson in chapter 7 in this volume.

organisation, suffering and triumphant, elected and covenanting, a true church and an anti-church'.[12] For the purposes of this analysis, the 'small flock' – a godly (often persecuted) remnant without legal recognition in an ungodly commonwealth – will figure occasionally; but it is with the visible Church in a national context, an established Church seen as coterminous with a Christian commonwealth, that what follows is principally concerned. Put briefly, my aim is to explore whether Knox saw the godly prince exercising 'imperial' or unitary authority over both Church and State within the territorial bounds of his kingdom or whether he conceived of the visible Church as a separate entity, coextensive with the temporal realm, but not subject to the authority of the civil magistrate.

Second, it is worth highlighting at the outset that, never the most systematic of thinkers, Knox's views on these issues are by no means as straightforward or clear-cut as one would like. For example, as we shall see, he could and did refer to England's 'imperial crown', but not in ways which give a very clear indication that he saw the monarch as possessing the kind of caesaropapal powers which Henry VIII arrogated to himself. Likewise, while there are a number of passages in his writings in which the powers of a godly prince are described in remarkably elevated terms, the extent and nature of that prince's authority in relation to the Church is generally somewhat less than crystal clear. In fact, it will be argued here that, at least by 1559, Knox had come to believe in the necessity of the Church's independence of the civil authorities and that it was this view of the matter which he urged on the new Elizabethan Church and helped to impose on the reformed Scottish Kirk. However, if we turn first of all to the extent to which the idea of the two kingdoms informed his political thought before that date, such evidence as there is suggests a much more confused and contradictory situation.

With that in mind, it is heartening to be able to begin with a statement which, at least on the face of it, is wholly unambiguous. In 1547, in the disputation with Prior John Winram which followed hard on the heels of his first sermon, Knox was accused of teaching nine 'articles' which the Catholic authorities considered 'heretical and schismatical'. The first of these articles was summed up in the blunt statement: 'No mortal man can be the head of the Church.'[13] While this was quite clearly

---

[12] Richard G. Kyle, 'Church–State Patterns in the Thought of John Knox', *Journal of Church and State*, 30 (1988), pp. 71–87, at p. 72.

[13] Knox, *History*, I, p. 87; Knox, *Works*, I, pp. 193–4.

aimed at the usurped authority of an Antichristian papacy, it is hard to believe that Knox would have been at all comfortable with the Henrician solution of simply substituting royal for papal headship of the Church. To be sure, there was in Scotland an established tradition which viewed the Scottish Crown in the kind of imperial terms more usually associated with England.[14] Moreover, in the latter years of James V's reign, there were undoubtedly lay evangelicals at the Scottish court who were attracted by the Henrician approach to ecclesiastical reform and who might well have been prepared to invest in the Scottish Crown the same caesaropapal powers signified by the imperial Crown of England.[15] Regrettably, however, Knox himself offers no further gloss on his 'heretical' statement and, while it would appear to be wholly incompatible with the idea of the royal supremacy, his views on the nature and extent of political authority at the time when he embarked on his Protestant ministry remain elusive.

In fact, the closest we come to an elucidation of his early thinking is in his endorsement of the essentially Lutheran doctrines propounded in 1548 by his fellow Castilian, Henry Balnaves of Halhill. On the fall of St Andrews Castle to the French, Balnaves was imprisoned in Rouen rather than enslaved like Knox on the galleys and, during his captivity, he was not only able to write a treatise on justification by faith alone, but also somehow to convey it to Knox for revision and endorsement.[16] Knox, indeed, prepared a *Briefe Sommarie* of the treatise, and both it and Balnaves's original work were sent back to Scotland, presumably in the hope that this 'Confession of our Faith' would be published.[17] There we find it stated, in conventional enough terms, that temporal power is ordained by God and that, as Knox put it in his *Sommarie*, subjects owe unstinting obedience to their rulers 'in all things not repugning to the command of God'.[18] While this offers little comfort to those in search of Knox's radical resistance theory, there is some evidence in the treatise that Balnaves understood the powers of the princely office to be

---

[14] See Roger A. Mason, '*Regnum et Imperium*: Humanism and the Political Culture of Early Renaissance Scotland', in Roger A. Mason, *Kingship and the Commonweal: Political Thought in Renaissance and Reformation Scotland* (East Linton, 1998), chap. 4.

[15] See Carol Edington, *Court and Culture in Renaissance Scotland: Sir David Lindsay of the Mount* (Amherst, MA, 1994), esp. pp. 48–57.

[16] Balnaves's treatise in printed in Knox, *Works*, III, pp. 431–542, together with a brief biographical sketch of its author, pp. 405–30.

[17] For the *Briefe Sommarie*, together with a prefatory epistle to the congregation of the castle of St Andrews, see Knox, *Works*, III, pp. 1–28. Both this and the original treatise were finally published in Edinburgh in 1584 as *The Confession of Faith, conteining how the troubled man should seeke refuge in his God*.

[18] Knox, *Works*, III, p. 26.

restricted to temporal affairs. Certainly, he believed that the prince possessed the *ius reformandi*, the authority (and duty) to reform a corrupt Church and restore 'the true, pure, and syncere Christian religion'.[19] Yet he also tells us that those 'called to the office, estate, or dignitie of a King, Prince or any supreme power' hold 'jurisdiction of people in the civil ordinance'.[20] As Kirk has argued, this would seem to imply a clear distinction in Balnaves's thinking between the civil and ecclesiastical spheres, and to confine the magistrate's jurisdiction under normal circumstances to the temporal kingdom. Yet as Kirk is forced to admit, Balnaves 'gave little thought to the visible or institutional church', and his treatise sheds no real light on the nature of its relationship with the civil authorities.[21]

While such evidence is at best exiguous, it is not inconceivable that at this early stage in his career Knox shared with Balnaves a basically Lutheran conception of the two kingdoms and that he saw the prince's role essentially in terms of restoring and preserving the 'true religion' rather than actively regulating the affairs of an established Protestant Church. The distinction is an important one for in his later writings Knox makes frequent reference to the duties of temporal magistrates in terms which echo the affirmation in the *Scots Confession* of 1560 that it is 'to Kings, Princes, Rulers and Magistrates ... that chieflie and most principallie the conservation and purgation of the Religioun apperteinis; so that not onlie they are appointed for Civill policie, bot also for maintenance of the Religioun, and for suppressing of Idolatrie and Superstition whatsoever'.[22] For Donaldson such an assertion was tantamount to an affirmation of the royal supremacy; for Kirk, not surprisingly, it is nothing of the kind.[23] This is obviously a crucial difference in interpretation to which we must return. It is worth bearing it in mind, however, as we trace the development of Knox's views on princely power in the more propitious circumstances of Edwardian England and, much more fully, during the ensuing years of the Marian exile.

In fact, Knox's years in the England of Edward VI, from February 1549 to January 1554, yield very little of interest to the historian of his political ideas.[24] Even if he did harbour misgivings about the royal

---

[19] Ibid., III, p. 528.

[20] Ibid., III, pp. 526–7.

[21] Kirk, *Patterns of Reform*, pp. 233–5.

[22] G.D. Henderson (ed.), *The Scots Confession, 1560* (Edinburgh, 1937), p. 95 (article 24); Knox, *Works*, II, p. 118.

[23] Donaldson, *Scottish Reformation*, pp. 134–5; Kirk, *Patterns of Reform*, pp. 253–4.

[24] In his *History*, Knox himself says astonishingly little about his years in England, reducing his experience to a single sentence: 'The said Johne was first appointed preachar

supremacy, he kept them to himself. He had more important things to do: the uprooting of idolatry and the spread of the true Word of God in the darkest corners of the land. England might have officially embraced the 'true religion', might be ruled by a potentially godly prince, but it was hardly as yet a godly commonwealth. Under these circumstances, Knox came into his own as, for the very first time, he was able to fulfil to the full his vocation as a preacher, denouncing the idolatry of the Mass with unsparing zeal and ministering to the needs of his congregations at Berwick and Newcastle with unflagging commitment. It was perhaps inevitable, however, that Knox's hardline evangelical Protestantism should eventually bring him into conflict with the political authorities. After all, he was as much a servant of the Crown as he was of the fledgling Church. Licensed to preach by the Privy Council, and latterly dependent on the patronage of the Duke of Northumberland, he pursued his ministerial labours within an ecclesiastical system subject to the will of the civil authorities.[25]

It is perfectly possible that, like many contemporary reformers, Knox took the view during the early years of his Edwardian sojourn that there was little to be gained from rocking the political boat too much. So long as the work of Reformation was proceeding, so long as the godly Edward VI remained receptive to the Word of God, some compromise with the political authorities might have seemed a tolerable price to pay. Certainly, as we shall see in a moment, he was in retrospect to articulate in remarkably powerful terms his sense of identity with the Church and people of his adopted English homeland. Nevertheless, at the time Knox became increasingly impatient of the brake on a more thorough-going, Scripture-based Reformation which the restraining hand of the civil authorities imposed. His celebrated run-in with Archbishop Cranmer over the 1552 Prayer Book, and his dust-up with Northumberland over his refusal to accept the bishopric of Rochester, may well mark the point at which, as it were, the iron entered Knox's soul: thereafter he was to be increasingly suspicious of the interference of the civil authorities in ecclesiastical affairs. Bruising though such brushes with political realities must have been, however, in late 1552, in the wake of his

---

to Berwik, then to Newcastell; last he was called to London, and to the sowth partes of England, whare he remained to the death of King Edwart the Sext' (Knox, *Works*, I, p. 231). For a fuller account, see Jasper Ridley, *John Knox* (Oxford, 1968), chaps 6–7.

[25] The point was presumably brought home to Knox as early as April 1550 when he was summoned before the Council of the North, albeit by Bishop Cuthbert Tunstall, to defend his attacks on the Roman Catholic Mass. He used the occasion to deliver *A Vindication of the Doctrine that the Sacrifice of the Mass is Idolatry*, in Knox, *Works*, III, pp. 29–70. On his relations with Northumberland, see David Loades, *John Dudley Duke of Northumberland 1504–1553* (Oxford, 1996), pp. 196 ff.

effective defeat at Cranmer's hands, Knox was still preaching Christian obedience to the 'higher powers' in a letter which he sent to his former congregation at Berwick.[26] Perhaps Diarmaid MacCulloch is correct to speculate that, had Edward VI been succeeded by a Protestant monarch, a thoroughly Englished and steadily mellowing Knox would not only have conformed to the liturgical conservatism of the Anglican Church but eventually accepted an appointment as Bishop of Newcastle, 'benevolently taking no notice of the advanced congregation's in his diocese who received communion sitting'.[27]

Perhaps. Edward VI, however, was not succeeded by a Protestant and, within months of the accession of the Catholic Mary Tudor, Knox had taken refuge on the Continent. It was the experience of exile which, above all else, was to radicalize Knox's political thought. Yet it did so only gradually; moreover, the end result was a good deal less revolutionary than the often corruscating biblical rhetoric in which it is couched might lead one to believe.[28] It is now well established, for example, that for all their prophetic fury, the series of admonitory epistles which Knox dispatched to his former congregations in England in the course of 1554 go no further than to advocate a policy of passive disobedience rather than active resistance in the face of persecuting Catholic authorities.[29] While these letters are certainly disappointing in terms of the development of any radical theory of resistance, they do nevertheless reveal a great deal – and for the first time – about Knox's conception of a godly commonwealth and the role of a godly prince within it.

Not surprisingly, it is a conception which is not so much shaped by as saturated in the Bible in general and the Old Testament in particular. Thus, in *A Godly Letter*, written (or at least begun) in England and published almost immediately on his arrival in Dieppe early in 1554, Knox embarked on an extended identification of England's recent history with the history of biblical Judah.[30] Himself playing Jeremiah to Edward

---

[26] This letter is not included in Laing's edition of Knox, *Works*, but see Peter Lorimer, *John Knox and the Church of England* (London, 1875), pp. 251–66, esp. p. 259; cf. Burns, *True Law*, pp. 129–30. That the inclusion of the 'black rubric' in the 1552 Prayer Book was a victory for Cranmer rather than Knox is persuasively argued in Diarmaid MacCulloch, *Thomas Cranmer: A Life* (New Haven and London, 1996), pp. 525–33.

[27] MacCulloch, *Cranmer*, p. 618.

[28] See Roger A. Mason, 'Knox on Rebellion', in Mason, *Kingship and the Commonweal*, chap. 5, for a fuller account of the development of his resistance theory.

[29] See Burns, *True Law*, pp. 130–36; and Jane E.A. Dawson in Chapter 7 in this volume.

[30] *A Godly Letter of Warning or Admonition to the faithful in London, Newcastle and Berwick* (1554), in Knox, *Works*, III, pp. 157–216. Thus he writes (p. 187): 'Hitherto haif I recytit the estate of Juda befoir the distructioun of Jerusalem and subversioun of

VI's Josiah, he argued that the people of England were now being punished for breaking the 'league and covenant' with God which they had
entered into when they had publicly and corporately renounced idolatry
and embraced the 'true religion'.[31] If the reintroduction of idolatrous
practices to the kingdom continued, if there was no evidence of true
repentance, then England must surely suffer the same terrible fate as had
befallen Judah at the hands of Nebuchadnezzar. Under Josiah's successors, Jerusalem, and Judah with it, had been utterly destroyed. So, asked
Knox, 'gif England be worse than Juda was, sall we think that the Lordis
vengeance sall sleip, mannis iniquitie being so rype?'[32]

It was perhaps logical enough, given Knox's intense biblicism, that he
should find in the covenant a compelling means of conceptualizing both
a godly commonwealth and godly kingship.[33] Just as a godly commonwealth was one which adhered to its obligations under the covenant, so
a godly prince was one who, like a latter-day Josiah, reformed religion,
uprooted idolatry and renewed his own personal as well as his people's
corporate covenant with God. In a covenanted nation, Church and
people were co-extensive. At least in retrospect, the Christian commonwealth of Edwardian England had become for Knox a latter-day Judah
or Israel, a covenanted community ruled by a godly prince in accordance with the law of God. Indeed, although the covenant does not
always figure as explicitly in Knox's writings as it does in A Godly
Letter, its presence can be detected beneath the surface of almost all his
writings in exile. Certainly, as we shall see, it underwrote the radicalism
of the 1558 tracts and helped to determine the different agendas which
he set out therein for a covenanted England and an uncovenanted
Scotland. Before examining the 1558 writings in more detail, however,
it is worth briefly touching on the second major letter of 1554 which
Knox addressed from Dieppe to his former congregations in England.
For some six months after he penned A Godly Letter, Knox wrote A
Faithful Admonition unto the Professors of God's Truth in England in
which there emerges a rather different and largely neglected dimension
of his conception of the Christian polity of England.[34]

---

that commonwelth. Now, I appele to the conscience of any indifferent man, in what ane
poynt differis the maneris, estait and regiment of England this day from the abuse and
estait rehersit of Juda in theis dayis ... '

[31] On the covenant, see especially ibid., III, pp. 190–97.

[32] Ibid., III, p. 188.

[33] For fuller analyses of Knox's understanding of the covenant, see Richard G. Kyle,
The Mind of John Knox (Lawrence, KS, 1984), pp. 153–7, and Richard L. Greaves,
Theology and Revolution in the Scottish Reformation: Studies in the Thought of John
Knox (Grand Rapids, MI, 1980), pp. 114–25.

[34] For the full text of A Faithful Admonition, see Knox, Works, III, pp. 251–330.

In *A Faithful Admonition*, Knox took as one of his texts the New Testament story of Christ stilling the tempest and embarked on an elaborate comparison of 'the afflicted Churche of God within the Realme of Englande' with a boat storm-tossed on a raging sea.[35] At times this reads as if Knox had retreated from a national vision of a covenanted Church and people to a narrower vision of an exclusive 'small flock' of the elect. But as it proceeds, and it proceeds at some length, the tract in fact takes an increasingly inclusive as well as secular turn. Thus not only are England's laws and liberties repeatedly invoked, but England itself – 'O Englande, Englande!' – is repeatedly apostrophized.[36] It is, moreover, in this tract, and this tract alone, that Knox ever referred with any frequency to England as an empire. Manifestly, however, this had less to do with any commitment to the royal supremacy than with fear that the impending Spanish marriage of Mary Tudor – 'an open traitoresse to the Imperiall Crown of England' – would lead not just to 'the overthrowe of Christianitie and Goddes true religion', but to 'the utter subversion of the whole publicke estate and common wealthe of Englande'.[37] Thus when Knox denounced Stephen Gardiner, Bishop of Winchester, as a 'dissemblyng hypocrite and double faced wretch' for having abandoned the anti-papal principles set out in his *De vera obedientia* (1535), he was evidently much less concerned with the significance of Gardiner's work as a highly accomplished defence of the royal supremacy than he was with the bishop's role in betraying 'thy native country' to Catholic Spain: 'O wretched caytive!', he asked, will you 'be the cause that England shal not be England?'[38]

An Faithful Admonition marks a distinct high point in the Englishing of Knox: nowhere else is his identification with England's secular as well as ecclesiastical structures more powerfully expressed. At the same time, it is also the point at which his distrust of the temporizing world of the politicians (lay and clerical) first becomes fully manifest. The two are

---

[35] Ibid., III, pp. 272 ff. (quotation from p. 275). A marginal note indicates that the biblical text is in Matthew 8 (verses 23–7), but it is clearly Matthew 14:22–33 with which Knox is principally concerned.

[36] See in particular ibid., III, pp. 307–9, where Knox claims to be quoting from a sermon he had preached at Amersham 'after the death of that innocent and moste godlye kynge, Edwarde the Sixte, whyle that great tumulte was in Englande for the establyshyng of that most unhappye and wycked Womanes authoritie (I mean of her that nowe raigneth in Goddes wrath)', Mary Tudor. On the place of such apostrophizing in subsequent English pulpit oratory, see Patrick Collinson, 'Biblical Rhetoric: The English Nation and National Sentiment in the Prophetic Mode', in Claire McEachern and Debora Shuger (eds), *Religion and Culture in Renaissance England* (Cambridge, 1997), pp. 15–45.

[37] Knox, *Works*, III, p. 295.

[38] Ibid., III, p. 298.

probably not unconnected. For fuelling both Knox's prophetic fury and
his vicious *ad hominem* attacks on 'wyly Wynchester, dreaming Duresme,
and bloudy Bonner, with the rest of their bloudy butcherly broode' was
his own acute sense of personal responsibility for England's apostasy.[39]
After all, had he not himself been deeply implicated in the compromising
and compromised political world of 'that wretched (alas!) and miserable
Northumberlande'?[40] Had he not, in effect, tarried for the magistrate
when God's Word and his own conscience dictated otherwise? 'Yf that
we the preachers within the Realme of England,' he lamented, 'were
appointed by God to be the salt of the earth (as his other messengers were
before us), alasse! why helde we backe the salt, where manifest corrupcion
dyd appere? (I accuse none but my selfe)'.[41] Knox's impassioned defence
of England's laws and liberties, and even of England's imperial Crown,
rested on a profound sense of guilt at having betrayed an adopted homeland to which he had developed a powerful emotional attachment. In
January 1554, almost immediately after his flight from England, he addressed to his future mother-in-law, Mrs Bowes, *An Exposition upon the
Sixth Psalm of David* in which his sense of loss is expressed in a manner
all the more effective for being far less declamatory:

> Somtyme I had thought that impossible it had bene, so to have
> removed my affection from the Realme of Scotland, that eny Realm
> or nation could have bene equal deare unto me. But God I take to
> recorde in my conscience, that the troubles present (and appearing
> to be) in the Realme of England, are double more dolorous unto
> my hert, then ever were the troubles of Scotland.[42]

If in 1554 Knox was presenting himself as more English than Scots,
over the next two years he was to rediscover his Scottish roots with
implications as interesting for his ecclesiology as they were for his
resistance theory. Paradoxically perhaps, one might almost have expected the clandestine mission which he undertook to Scotland in
1555–56 to have led him to develop (and clarify) the English imperial
thinking which first surfaces in *An Faithful Admonition*. For had not
Protector Somerset's military assault on Scotland in 1547–48 been accompanied by a barrage of unionist propaganda in which England's
imperial crown was redefined in explicitly British (or Anglo-British)
terms?[43] Had not the proposed marriage of Mary Stewart and Edward

---

[39] Ibid., III, p. 285.

[40] Ibid., III, p. 277.

[41] Ibid., III, p. 270.

[42] Ibid., III, p. 133.

[43] For this and what follows, see Roger A. Mason, 'The Scottish Reformation and the
Origins of Anglo-British Imperialism', in Roger A. Mason (ed.), *Scots and Britons:*

Tudor been hailed – by a Scotsman, James Henrisoun, no less – as a providential opportunity to re-create the British kingdom of Constantine the Great, a kingdom as emphatically Protestant as it was historically imperial? For all his undoubted unionism, however, Knox never employs the British imperial rhetoric so characteristic of Somerset's propaganda campaign.[44] His mission to Scotland may well have reminded him of the lost opportunities of the 1540s, but it did not lead him to ponder the historicity – or future destiny – of an imperial British Crown. Rather, it led him to set the particular experience of both Scotland and England within a broader international framework – a framework defined more explicitly than ever before by the universal laws of nature and of God.

There seems little doubt that, shuttling between Geneva, France and Scotland, freed of the claustrophobic and apparently rather introverted world of the English congregation at Frankfurt, Knox's awareness of a Protestant international began to take precedence over and to dilute his adopted English identity. His rediscovery in 1555–56 of Scotland – and perhaps his own Scottishness – may well have reinforced this process, leading him to re-evaluate the particularities and peculiarities of England's recent past in a broader framework capable of accommodating – and making meaningful – the very different experience of his native country. As a result, when in 1558 his frustration finally got the better of him and he vented his pent-up anger in the often lurid pages of the First Blast, he rested his case against female rule on the universality of divine and natural law.[45] While addressed to 'the Isle of Great Brittany', however, there is implicit in Knox's ill-tempered and ill-timed tract a clear distinction between Scotland and England. The universal laws of nature and of God were not in fact equally applicable in both countries. On the contrary, it was the English alone who were enjoined to ensure that that monstrous Jezebel, Mary Tudor, should 'die the death'.[46]

What lay behind the apparent inconsistency in Knox's application of natural and divine law was to become much clearer a little later in 1558 when he published his Appellation to the Nobility and Estates of

---

Scottish Political Thought and the Union of 1603 (Cambridge, 1994), pp. 161–86, reprinted in Mason, Kingship and the Commonweal, chap. 9.

[44] For more on Knox's unionism, see Stephen Alford's Chapter 10 in this volume.

[45] For the text of the First Blast, see Knox, Works, IV, pp. 349–422; Knox, On Rebellion, pp. 3–47.

[46] This and the argument that follows owes a great deal to Jane E.A. Dawson, 'The Two John Knoxes: England, Scotland and the 1558 Tracts', JEH, 42 (1991), pp. 555–76; see also Mason, 'Knox on Rebellion'.

Scotland.[47] For there, he differentiated very clearly between England as
a covenanted nation and Scotland as an uncovenanted one. Picking up
and universalizing the idea of the covenant first adumbrated in 1554 in
A Godly Letter, Knox declared in the *Appellation*: 'I fear not to affirm,
that the Gentiles (I mean everie citie, realme, province or nation amongst
the Gentiles, embrasing Christ Jesus and his true religion) be bound to
the same leage and covenant that God made with his people Israel.'[48] In
the case of England under Edward VI, Knox was clearly of the view
that magistrates and people had publicly and corporately entered into
precisely such a covenantal relationship. Consequently, they were duty
bound to carry out God's ordinance and 'punish to the death such as
labour to subvert the true Religion' – including 'Marie, that Jesabel
whome they call their Queen'.[49] Scotland, in contrast, had never publicly or corporately embraced Protestantism and was not therefore bound
under the covenant in the same way as England. Thus Knox demanded
of the Scottish nobility only (and by comparison rather lamely) that
they punish 'obstinate and malepert idolaters (such as all your bishops
be)'[50] – a plea no doubt made all the more heartfelt by the fact that in
1556 the bishops had condemned Knox as a heretic and had had him
publicly burned in effigy.

If it was exactly that judgement against him which had occasioned
the *Appellation*, the point to note here is that the experience of exile
had effectively internationalized Knox's perceptions and led him to
differentiate between the experience of Scotland and England within the
universal framework of divine law. It was a divine law, moreover,
increasingly driven by providentialist and apocalyptic assumptions.[51]
For it was only in terms of an ongoing and universal struggle between
the forces of Christ and Antichrist, God and the Devil, that Knox could
make sense of either the otherwise unfathomable will of God or the
specificities of current Scottish and English experience. If anything, as
regards England, such apocalyptic ruminations served to heighten still

---

[47] For the full text, see Knox, *Works*, IV, pp. 461–520; Knox, *On Rebellion*, pp. 72–
114.

[48] Knox, *Works*, IV, p. 505; Knox, *On Rebellion*, p. 103.

[49] Knox, *Works*, IV, p. 507; Knox, *On Rebellion*, p. 104.

[50] Knox, *Works*, IV, pp. 507–8; Knox, *On Rebellion*, pp. 104–5.

[51] On Knox's apocalyptic thinking, see Kyle, *Mind of Knox*, pp. 215–39, and Katharine
R. Firth, *The Apocalyptic Tradition in Reformation Britain* (Oxford, 1979), pp. 111–31.
There is also much to be learned from Arthur H. Williamson, *Scottish National Con-
sciousness in the Age of James VI: The Apocalypse, the Union and the Shaping of
Scotland's Public Culture* (Edinburgh, 1979), esp. chap. 1; though cf. Roger A. Mason
'Usable Pasts: History and Identity in Reformation Scotland', in Mason, *Kingship and
the Commonweal*, chap. 6.

further Knox's guilt and anguish over the lost opportunities which the Edwardian experiments in reform had come to represent for him. Why had things gone so horribly wrong? Why was England being punished with bloody persecution while Scotland under Mary of Guise was not? Seen through Knox's universalist and apocalyptic eyes, the answer was becoming ever more painfully clear. England had not honoured her obligations under the covenant, had not seized the opportunity in Edward VI's reign to pursue reform more rigorously, to uproot idolatry and establish a *truly* godly commonwealth. The English had failed their God, had allowed politics to take precedence over the work of the Lord, and were reaping the inevitable whirlwind.

Many years ago J.H. Burns drew attention to the possible significance of Knox's fear of 'political contamination' in shaping the development of his theory of resistance.[52] There is every reason to believe that the same consideration affected his ecclesiology in general and his view of the royal supremacy in particular. Yet, Knox being Knox, it is not quite so straightforward as one might hope. Throughout his exilic writings, for example, he makes constant reference to that great triumvirate of Old Testament kings: Josiah, Hezekiah and Jehoshaphat. It is these kings, above all others, who are held up as models of godly kingship and who indubitably possess the *ius reformandi*, the duty to cleanse Church and people alike of idolatry and superstition.[53] What is much less clear, however, is what authority these paragons were thought to wield over a Church once reformed and established. Did they possess for Knox the caesaropapal powers embodied in the English royal supremacy? In so far as the royal supremacy had acted under Henry VIII and Edward VI as a constraint on (and danger to) the process of reform, one might expect Knox to impose severe limits on the Crown's authority over the visible Church as a means of protecting it from the taint and corruption of the temporal authorities. Yet he never says anything quite so clear-cut as that. Indeed, in the *Appellation*, he appears to imply quite the opposite. For there, in one of his most explicit

---

[52] J.H. Burns, 'The Political Ideas of the Scottish Reformation', *Aberdeen University Review*, 36 (1955–56), pp. 251–68, at p. 258; cf. Burns, *True Law*, pp. 132–3, 143.

[53] Thus he informed Mary of Guise in *The Letter to the Regent* that 'vayn it is to crave reformation in manners where the religion is corruptit' and went on to cite those 'moste godly princes Josias, Ezechias and Josaphat' who, seeking God's favour for themselves and their peoples, 'before all things began to reforme the religion'; Knox, *Works*, IV, pp. 81–2; Knox, *On Rebellion*, p. 61. For further examples, see *The First Blast* in Knox, *Works*, IV, p. 398, and Knox, *On Rebellion*, p. 29; and *The Appellation* in Knox, *Works*, IV, pp. 486 ff., and Knox, *On Rebellion*, pp. 87 ff. The same triumvirate also of course features in article 24 on the civil magistrate in the *Scots Confession* of 1560 (ed. Henderson, p. 95; Knox, *Works*, II, pp. 118–19).

pronouncements on the subject, he firmly subordinates the priestly
authority of Aaron to the civil authority of Moses.[54] Was this simply a
rhetorical strategy? Was it an argument thrown in to the *Appellation* to
encourage the civil magistrates to whom it was addressed – the nobility
and estates of Scotland – to punish the unreformed Scottish clergy? Or
was this a more settled statement of Knox's understanding of the relationship between the civil and ecclesiastical authorities?

A full answer to these questions only emerges in a rather roundabout
and convoluted way. The *Appellation*, as is well known, was published
in Geneva along with Knox's famous *Letter to the Commonalty* as well
as a brief summary of the proposed contents of his *Second Blast of the
Trumpet*. While we shall return to the *Letter to the Commonalty* in a
moment, it is worth highlighting at this point that there was a further
tract bound together in the same volume. This was *An Admonition to
England and Scotland to Call them to Repentance*, written by Knox's
colleague in Geneva and fellow Marian exile, the Englishman, Anthony
Gilby.[55] Gilby evidently shared the same basic mindset as Knox and his
pamphlet takes the same sort of apocalyptic view of the lost opportunities of the Edwardian years, including the failure to exploit the
providential opportunity to effect a 'godlie conjunction' between Scotland and England.[56] Gilby, however, goes much further than that. For in
lamenting England's apostasy, he launches into a ferocious attack on
Henry VIII and the royal supremacy. There was, he writes, 'no reformation, but a deformation, in the tyme of that tyrant and lecherous
monster'.[57] Henry VIII was nothing more (or less) than a 'monstrous
bore [pig]' who

> must nedes be called the Head of the Churche in paine of treason,
> displacing Christ, our onlie Head, who oght alone to have this
> title. Wherefore in this point, O England, ye were no better then
> the Romishe Antichrist, who by the same title maketh hymselfe a
> God, sitteth in mennes consciences, bannysheth the Worde of God,
> as did your King Henrie, whome ye so magnifie. For in his best

---

54 Knox, *Works*, IV, pp. 486–7; Knox, *On Rebellion*, pp. 87–8.

55 Printed in full in Knox, *Works*, IV, pp. 541–71.

56 Ibid., IV, p. 560, where with reference to the proposed marriage of Mary Stewart
with Edward Tudor, Gilby blamed the Catholic clergy of Scotland for pursuing a dynastic alliance with France 'mindinge by that meanes to cutt for ever the knot of the
frendship that might have ensued betwixt England and Scotland by that godlie conjunction'. Earlier he had blamed Satan whose 'old fostred malice, and Antichrist his sonne,
could not abyde that Christ should grow so strong by joynynge that Ile togither in
perfect religion, whome God hath so many waies coupled and strengthened by his worke
in nature'; ibid., IV, p. 558.

57 Ibid., IV, p. 563.

time, nothing was hard but the Kinges booke, and the Kinges
procedings; the Kinges Homelies in the Churches, where Goddes
word should onely have bene preached. So made you your King a
god, beleving nothing but that he allowed.[58]

To be sure, for Gilby, things had improved under Edward VI. But they
had not improved either fast enough or far enough. England was suffering the plagues and punishments of God for a covenant that was broken
and a Reformation that was never more than half-hearted, incomplete
and deformed.

Did Knox share Gilby's view of Henry VIII, the royal supremacy and
the English 'deformation'? He certainly shared many of the broader
assumptions which underlay Gilby's Jeremiad, but nowhere in Knox's
surviving writings is there anything quite comparable to Gilby's vitriolic
condemnation of either Henry VIII or the royal supremacy. Nevertheless, it may well be that, close colleagues as they were in Geneva,
Gilby's view of the baleful role played by the Crown in England's
Reformation did have some influence on Knox. For the following year,
1559, in the wake of Elizabeth's accession to the English throne and in
the fond hope that he might himself yet return to his English congregations, Knox issued A Briefe Exhortation to England for the Spedie
Imbrasing of Christ's Gospel, in which he echoed the phraseology as
well as the substance of Gilby's earlier attack on the 'king's proceedings'.[59]

In A Briefe Exhortation, Knox was evidently concerned that England,
having been given an unexpected and undeserved second chance, should
not repeat the heinous mistakes of Edward's reign. He therefore urged
that, in renewing their covenant with God, they should avoid any
compromises with the civil authorities and recreate a godly commonwealth in strict accordance with the law of God. In terms reminiscent of
Gilby, he thundered:

> Let not the King and his proceadinges (whatsoever they be), not
> agreable to his Worde, be a snare to thy conscience. O cursed were
> the hartes that first devised that phrase [the king's proceedings] in
> matters of religion, wherby the simple people were broght to one
> of these two inconveniences: to wit, That either they dyd esteme
> everie religion good and acceptable unto God, which the King and
> Parliament dyd approve and commande; or els, that God's religion,
> honor, and service, was nothinge els but devises of men. O Eng-
> land, England! let this blasphemie be first of all others removed.
> For how horrible is it to remember, that the religion and honoring
> of the Eternal God shalbe subject to the appetites of folishe and

---

[58] Ibid., IV, p. 564.
[59] For the full text of A Briefe Exhortation, see ibid., V, pp. 495–522.

inconstant men! Let God's Worde alone be the rule and line to measure his religion. What it commandethe, let that be obeyde; what it commandeth not, let that be execrable, because it hathe not the sanctification of his Worde under what name or title soever it be published.[60]

Such views are hardly compatible with the doctrine of the royal supremacy. Indeed, they are tantamount to condemning the caesaropapal powers vested in the English Crown as blasphemous. But Knox went still further. For 'as touching the execution of Discipline', he pronounced that 'yf the King himself wolde usurpe any other autoritie in God's religion, then becometh a membre of Christ's body', he should first of all be 'admonished according to God's Worde; and after, yf he continue the same, be subject to the yoke of discipline'.[61] In other words, just as a king (or queen) was no more than a member of the Church, so like every other member of that Church, he (or she) must be subject to its discipline.

Thus far the issue of discipline has featured much less prominently in this chapter than it should have done. Knox's experience of it in Geneva, for example, that 'maist perfyt schoole of Chryst', needs much fuller consideration than it is possible to give it here.[62] Suffice it to say that, during his time in Geneva, discipline assumed such importance in Knox's thinking that it attained along with preaching and the right administration of the sacraments the status of a 'note' or 'mark' of a truly reformed Church.[63] In the Geneva Form of Prayers of 1556, prepared by Knox and others for the English congregation at Geneva and formally adopted in Scotland in 1565, discipline is described as the 'synewes in the bodie which knit and joyne the membres together with decent order and comelynes' and as 'an ordre left by God unto his Churche, wherby men learne to frame their wills and doings accordinge to the law of Gode'.[64] Crucially, the power to enforce such discipline – up to and including the power of excommunication, 'the greatest and last punishement belonginge to the spirituall Ministerie' – was vested in the Church itself and it was clearly intended that it should be exercised

---

[60] Ibid., V, pp. 515–16.

[61] Ibid., V, pp. 519–20.

[62] Though see Chapter 13 by Michael F. Graham in this volume. Knox's oft-quoted remark about Geneva – 'the maist perfyt schoole of Chryst that ever was in the erth since the dayis of the Apostillis' – occurs in a letter to Mrs Locke of December 1556; see Knox, *Works*, IV, pp. 239–41.

[63] See Kirk, *Patterns of Reform*, pp. 270 ff. Although Calvin himself never formally designated discipline a 'mark' of the Church, it clearly loomed as significantly in his thought as it did in that of Knox.

[64] Knox, *Works*, IV, p. 203.

independently of the civil authorities.[65] To be sure, the Form of Prayers acknowledged that, 'besides this Ecclesiastical censure', there also belonged to the Church 'a politicall Magistrate, who ministreth to every man justice, defending the good and punishinge the evell; to whom we must rendre honor and obedience in all thinges, which are not contrarie to the Word of God'.[66] But implicit in such phraseology was the assumption that the political magistrate was also a member of the Church and thus subject to a spiritual jurisdiction which derived its authority immediately from God rather than mediately from the civil authorities.

Some further light may be shed on Knox's understanding of discipline by glancing briefly at that much misunderstood missive published along with the *Appellation* in 1558: that is, his *Letter to the Commonalty of Scotland*.[67] For the *Letter* is assuredly not simply the populist and revolutionary call to arms which it is too often construed as being. To be sure, in it Knox meditates, often quite movingly, on the spiritual equality of all men before God, but he neither translates spiritual parity into social equality nor does he proceed from there to advocate untrammelled popular rebellion. Leaving the latter point aside, however, there were undoubtedly significant ecclesiological conclusions to be drawn from the belief expressed in the *Letter* that, while God 'hath put and ordeined distinction and difference betwixt the King and his subjects, betwixt the Rulers and commune people in the regiment and administration of Civile policies, yet in the hope of the life to come he hath made all equal'.[68] For if all men were equal in the sight of God, they were surely all also equal in the eyes of His Church. Thus it followed, as we have seen Knox state in the clearest possible terms in *A Briefe Exhortation*, that in a godly commonwealth, highest and lowest alike are mere members of the Church and must be subject to its discipline. Arguably, for Knox, this view of the visible Church as co-extensive with the nation, but wielding authority independently of the civil magistrate, who was no more than an ordinary member of it, was firmly set by 1559.

It was this understanding of the relationship between the temporal and spiritual powers which Knox not only urged unsuccessfully upon the new Protestant establishment in England, but which he also sought

---

[65] Ibid., IV, pp. 203–6 (for excommunication, see p. 205).

[66] Ibid., IV, pp. 172–3.

[67] For the full text, see Knox, *Works*, IV, pp. 521–38; Knox, *On Rebellion*, pp. 115–29. For the interpretation of the *Letter* that follows, see Mason 'Knox on Rebellion'.

[68] Knox, *Works*, IV, p. 527; Knox, *On Rebellion*, p. 118.

to impose with rather more effect on the Scottish Church and nation in the wake of the successful Reformation-Rebellion of 1559–60. At least in some quarters he was evidently pushing at an open door. For in May 1559, at the very outset of the rebellion, in a letter usually attributed to John Erskine of Dun, Mary of Guise was informed that the government of the Church belonged only to Christ – 'ffor he is the heid thairoff, all wther ar her memberis vnder him' – and was warned to 'tak na authoritie wpone you abwe the kirk of Christ, for than seik ye to be equall with him quha can hef na merrowis'.[69] It has been argued that this represents a view of the two kingdoms diametrically opposed to Knox's vision of an imperial Scottish monarchy wielding supreme authority in both temporal and spiritual affairs.[70] Yet it is, on the contrary, wholly consistent with the views he had expressed in *A Briefe Exhortation*.

Likewise, it is wholly consistent with the thinking of *The First Book of Discipline* where it was stated that the Church was empowered 'to draw the sword which of God she hath received' and to discipline its members – and ultimately to excommunicate them – without reference to the civil magistrate.[71] Indeed, in an unambiguous echo of Knox's *Briefe Exhortation*, the *Book of Discipline* asserted: 'To Discipline must all Estaitis within this Realme be subject, as well the Rulers as they that are ruled'.[72] It is surely in this light that article 24 of the *Scots Confession* of 1560 ought to be read. Certainly the *Confession* affirmed in the strongest possible terms the duty of Christian obedience to 'the supreme power, doing that thing quhilk appertains to his charge'. It even acknowledged 'that sik persouns as are placed in authoritie ar to be loved, honoured, feared, and halden in most reverent estimatioun; because that they are the Lieu-tennents of God, in whose Sessiouns God himself does sit and judge'. Yet its further, and crucial, affirmation that political authority was established by God 'chieflie and most principallie [for] the conservatioun and purgatioun of the Religioun', while indubitably vesting a godly prince with the *ius reformandi*, stopped some way short of arrogating to the Scottish Crown the caesaropapal powers associated

---

[69] For the full text, see J. Stuart (ed.), *Spalding Club Miscellany IV* (Spalding Club, Aberdeen, 1849), pp. 88–92 (quotations from p. 89). It is discussed more fully in Kirk, *Patterns of Reform*, pp. 235–40, and Frank Bardgett, 'John Erskine of Dun: A Theological Reassessment', *Scottish Journal of Theology*, 43 (1990), pp. 59–85.

[70] Williamson, *Scottish National Consciousness*, pp. 16–17.

[71] *The First Book of Discipline*, ed. J.K. Cameron (Edinburgh, 1972), pp. 167 ff.; see also *The Ordoure of Excommunicatioun and of Publict Repentance used in the Church of Scotland* (1569), in Knox, *Works*, VI, pp. 447–70.

[72] Cameron (ed.), *First Book of Discipline*, p. 173.

with the English royal supremacy.[73] In stark contrast to the circumspect wording of the *Scots Confession*, for example, the Elizabethan Act of Supremacy of 1559, in restoring the English Crown's imperial authority, had recognized Elizabeth simply as supreme governor of the realm 'in all spiritual or ecclesiastical things or causes as temporal'.[74]

As Kirk has argued, the Scottish reformers' continuing hostility to the royal supremacy is evident not only in the swift and decisive action taken in 1568 against the printer, Thomas Bassenden, but also in the fact that in 1572, when a Scottish Oath of Supremacy was drawn up on the basis of its English equivalent, the key phrase from the Act of Supremacy quoted above was carefully replaced by the formula first devised for the *Scots Confession*. It was thus acknowledged, not that James VI was supreme governor 'in all spiritual or ecclesiastical things or causes as temporal', but rather that he was 'the onlie supreme governor of this realme, als weill in things temporall as in the conservatioun and purgatioun of religioun'. Moreover, in an alteration none the less telling for being consistently overlooked, the English oath's reference to 'the *imperial* crown of this realm' was modified in favour of the less overtly caesaropapal '*royall* crown'.[75] In fact, it was only in the so-called Black Acts of 1584 that the phrase 'conservation and purgation of religion' was finally dropped and the Crown vested simply with 'royall power and auctoritie over all statis asweill spirituall as temporall within this realme'.[76] Unlike the General Assembly of 1568, James VI would have had no problem at all with Bassenden's desire to attribute to the Scottish Crown the supreme headship of the primitive Kirk in Scotland.

As for Knox, in the years following his return from exile in 1559, he could only contemplate with rising distaste and foreboding a situation

---

[73] *Confession of Faith*, ed. Henderson, pp. 93–7. The most complete analysis is W. Ian P. Hazlett, 'The Scots Confession 1560: Context, Complexion and Critique', *Archiv für Reformationsgeschichte*, 78 (1987), pp. 287–320, though Hazlett does not comment specifically on the significance of the phrase 'conservation and purgation of the Religioun'.

[74] 1 Eliz. I, c. 1; Elton, *Tudor Constitution*, pp. 363–8.

[75] The two oaths are printed on facing pages of W.C. Dickinson, Gordon Donaldson and Isobel A. Milne (eds), *A Source Book of Scottish History* (3 vols, London and Edinburgh, 1952–54), III, pp. 12–13. For the interpretation followed here, see Kirk, *Patterns of Reform*, pp. 251–5.

[76] *APS*, III, pp. 292–3. It is worth noting that, while the Black Acts themselves make no reference to James VI possessing imperial authority, the omission was fully repaired by Archbishop Patrick Adamson in a brief defence of the statutes, published in Edinburgh in 1584, entitled *A Declaratioun of the Kingis Maiesties Intentioun and Meaning toward the Lait Actis of Parliament*. See my 'George Buchanan, James VI and the Presbyterians', in R.A. Mason, *Scots and Britons*, pp. 112–37, esp. pp. 129–31.

where in England the monarch lorded (or ladied) it over an ill-reformed Church, while in Scotland she remained outside it altogether. For in so far as Scotland and England were both now covenanted nations, their incomplete and compromised Reformations were courting the wrath of a vengeful God. As early as October 1559, Knox wrote bitterly to Mrs Locke of the 'bastard religion' with its 'mingle mangle' of ceremonies which still prevailed in the Church in England: 'Alas! Sister, I fear a plague shortlie to follow this cold beginning, after so manifest a defectioun'.[77] It was a fear, fed by his experience in Edwardian England, which never subsequently left him. Indeed, it was immeasurably increased by the religious compromise which accompanied Mary Stewart's return to her native kingdom in 1561. Knox's sense of betrayal at the hands of those politique courtiers who sought to accommodate the Queen's Mass not only ran deep but may even have led him to contemplate the abandonment of his vision of a national covenanted Church in favour of a more committed 'small flock' of the elect.[78] Whatever faith he had once had in a latter-day Josiah reigning supreme over both the spiritual and temporal realms had long since vanished. In the dark days of May 1566, from the refuge of his internal exile in Ayrshire, Knox found an explanation for the 'miserable dispersioun of goddis people within this Realme' which was no less heartfelt for being utterly predictable: it was because 'suddandlic the most parte of us declyned from the puritie of Goddis word, and began to follow the warld; and so agane to schaik handis with the Devill'.[79] There is perhaps a sense in which, for Knox, it was political magistracy itself which had become the Devil whose hand, first shaken under Northumberland, would never again be grasped with confidence.

---

[77] Knox, *Works*, VI, pp. 83–5; cf. VI, pp. 11–15.

[78] See Ian Hazlett's analysis of the crisis of 1566 in Chapter 9 of this volume.

[79] Knox, *Works*, II, p. 265; Knox, *History*, II, p. 4 (the preface to Book IV of the *History*).

CHAPTER NINE

Playing God's Card:
Knox and Fasting, 1565–66

W. Ian P. Hazlett

> The Monkis of Melros maid gude kaill [broth]
> On Frydayis quhen thay fastit ... [1]

Tackling the sixteenth century conditioned with post-Enlightenment and modernist notions of aesthetics, epistemology and acceptable religion can unnecessarily generate perplexity, disbelief, and even disdain. Fasting, especially of the collective public kind, is so alien to modern western culture and religion, so anachronistic and exotic, that it barely appears on the agenda of Reformation or early modern historians. As regards Scotland, this historiographical neglect is even more surprising. For it can be argued that the mechanism of the general public fast, articulated by John Knox in 1566, became a unique occasional instrument of lawful public protest against government policy or other ominous developments. While it developed as a form of resistance and opposition, however, fasting was also indissolubly tied to repentance and intercession with the Deity. Between 1566 and 1601 there were about a dozen general fasts proclaimed by the General Assembly, though there may have been more.[2] Issues provoking the fasts included *inter alia* the Counter Reformation, social injustice, economic recession, epidemics, moral and religious decline, crime waves, royal ecclesiastical policy, religious wars abroad, church ministerial incompetence and rural educational mediocrity. The focus of this essay, however, is the original public general fast of 1566, its context, rationale, objectives and implementation.

In Reformation studies, fasting has not been an object of inquiry, its image being implausible and esoteric. It has been widely perceived as

---

[1] *The Gude and Godly Ballatis*, ed. A.F. Mitchell (STS, Edinburgh, 1897), p. 206.

[2] See Calderwood, *History*, II, pp. 317, 324, 486; III, p. 384; IV, pp. 304–5, 676, 682–3; V, pp. 179, 278, 737; VI, pp. 113–16. The 1569 General Assembly also empowered provincial superintendents and commissioners to order a general fast without prior Assembly authorization. See ibid., II, p. 486. I am informed by Dr Alan MacDonald that the Privy Council also exercised such a right.

one of those tedious and oppressive Catholic observances which the Protestant Reformation hastily disposed of.[3] It is true that the received ecclesiastical tradition of fasting was subject to Reformation critique. But the baby was not thrown out with the bath water. What was attacked was not fasting *per se* but its canonical prescription on regular fixed days or periods, as in Gratian's Decree, incorporated in canon law. The objection was that while such mandatory fasting was part of the law of Moses (and the Pope), it was not part of the law of Christ. Consequently, obligatory fasting was seen as unscriptural, even if Christ and the Apostles themselves had actually fasted. No Christian conscience could be bound by such a work, due to evangelical freedom.

The Catholic Luther had adumbrated such ideas in 1513–16 in his lectures on Romans and the Psalms, and then more forcibly in 1521– 22.[4] The *Augsburg Confession* developed the line in Article 26: Christianity required addiction to faith and love, and not to holy days and other ecclesiastical festival ordinances. These, by virtue of false security and confidence in routine human rituals, only induced superstitious notions of sanctity among the people. Fasting, like all good works, has nothing to do with satisfaction or atonement of sins, since the work of Christ achieved that. Christians were then free in the matter, which belonged to the realm of things indifferent, or optional. Fasting was only to be undertaken by those who wanted to participate and were able to do so.[5]

It is well known that one of the catalysts of the Zurich Reformation was the Lenten fast. But in his tract of 1522, *On Freedom in the Choice of Food*, Zwingli did not call for the abandonment of fasting as such.

---

[3] Volume 5 of the *Real-Encyclopädie für protestantische Theologie und Kirche*, ed. Albert Hauck (24 vols, Leipzig, 1896–1913) does have a ten-page article on fasting, but the Protestant tradition of it is ignored! The *Oxford Encyclopedia of the Reformation*, ed. Hans Hillerbrand (4 vols, New York and Oxford, 1996), does not devote an article to it; there are some passing references in vol. I, p. 479, the chief purport of which is that the reformers delivered fasting a 'deathblow'. Less unhappily, the *Theologische Realenzyklopädie*, ed. Gerhard Müller (Berlin and New York, 1976–) devotes a section to Reformation thinking on the subject, in which the Scottish fast of 1566 is highlighted, vol. XI, pp. 55–7.

[4] On Romans, see *D. Martin Luthers Werke* (Weimar, 1883–), LVI, p. 394, 27; on Psalms, see ibid., IV, pp. 245–6 (English: *Luther's Works*, eds Jaroslav Pelikan and Helmut T. Lehmann [Philadelphia, 1955–], XI, pp. 381–2); and for his later position, see *Luthers Werke*, VII, pp. 808–13; X³, pp. 36–40 (English: *Luther's Works*, XI, pp. 61–6, 86–8).

[5] *Die Bekenntnisschriften der evangelisch-lutherischen Kirche* (8th edn, Göttingen, 1979), pp. 100–107 (English: *The Augsburg Confession*, eds Theodore G. Tappert and Theodore Gerhardt [Philadelphia, 1980], art. 26; and Leif Grane, *The Augsburg Confession: A Commentary*, trans. by John H. Rasmussen [Minneapolis, 1987], art. 26).

Rather his attitude was comparable to that of Luther – within Christian liberty there is neither injunction nor prohibition in respect of such secondary practices: 'If you want to fast, do so. If you do not want to eat meat, don't eat it. But allow Christians a free choice.'[6] And in his *Sixty-Seven Articles* of 1523, he formulated the same principle in Article 24: 'God has not decreed it, therefore one may eat any food at all times.'[7] The issue then was not whether there should be fasting or not, but rather the difference between false (compulsory) and true (spontaneous) fasting. In his *Commentary on True and False Religion* of 1525, Zwingli dwelt momentarily on the difference:

> We [traditionally] fast ... either that our frugality may be displayed, or that our thin pale faces may indicate sanctity, or that dainties and delicacies may be served up to us [i.e. alternatives to meat], or that we may reduce the size of our fat bellies to enable us to fit in to our old clothes, or to save a penny [like the worst misers], or to perform a good work. Instead, it ought to be done simply to call us away from [fleshly preoccupations], to hear better the word and bidding of the Spirit. [In ways like that], I say, we measure all things with reference to ourselves, and not to Him.[8]

Fasting's true function, according to Zwingli, is to revive faith's alertness to sin. The exercise externalizes prior alienation, despair, spiritual morbidity, uncertain faith and absence of communion with Christ.

Both Bucer and Calvin thought similarly. In the *Tetrapolitan Confession* (1530), Bucer holds that although fasting is a lesser virtue, it should enable a better conversation between the soul and God. It ought to be occasional rather than regular. Characteristically, he observes that it is only profitable when the benefit of others rather than self is advanced.[9] Considering fasting as 'highly recommended', but 'not necessary for salvation', Bucer pleads for the notion of collective public fasting in *On the Kingdom of Christ* (1550): 'It is necessary for those who wish to see the Kingdom of Christ solidly restored to retrieve the discipline of fasting ... especially if some calamity befalls the Church ...

---

[6] *CR, Werke Zwinglis* (Berlin, 1905–), LXXXVIII, p. 106, 15–17 (English: *Ulrich Zwingli Early Writings*, ed. Samuel Macauley Jackson [New York, 1912; repr. Durham, NC, 1987], p. 87).

[7] *CR*, LXXXVIII, p. 461 (English: *Ulrich Zwingli (1484–1531). Selected Works*, ed. Samuel Macauley Jackson [Philadelphia, 1901], p. 113, and *Reformed Confessions of the Sixteenth Century*, ed. Arthur Cochrane [London, 1966], p. 39).

[8] *CR*, XC, p. 679, 39–680, 5 (English [modified]: *Commentary on True and False Religion*, in *Zwingli*, eds Samuel Macauley Jackson and Clarence Nevin Heller [Philadelphia, 1929; repr. Durham, NC, 1981], p. 104).

[9] *Martin Bucers Deutsche Schriften*, ed. Robert Stupperich (Gütersloh and Paris, 1960–), III, articles 7–10, pp. 69–83 (English: Cochrane, *Reformed Confessions*, pp. 61–6).

the people should gather in holy assembly ... to repent for sins and pour forth prayers.'[10] Calvin addresses fasting and related matters in his *Institutes*. There he deals with it under the rubric of discipline, but not as part of the discipline subject to the power of the keys. Fasting should only be occasional and extraordinary, and not a normative feature of Church life. Guided chiefly by Jewish biblical precedents, apparently exercised by the Apostles too, Calvin's chief interest lies in collective public fasting 'if either pestilence, or famine, or war begins to rage ... in order that by supplication the Lord's wrath may be averted'.[11] As in Bucer, true and collective fasting is joined with self-humiliation, repentance, and prayer – it is not just abstinence alone. Nor is it meritorious or worship of God, but rather a preliminary to special dialogue with the Deity. The one logion of Christ cited in support is at Matthew 9:14–15.

In the specific Lutheran and Zwinglian traditions, fasting was confined essentially to the individual and private sphere. However, within the Strasbourg–Geneva axis not only private, but also general public fasting is strongly recommended (though there does not seem to be much evidence that it was practised). The idea was relatively innovative. And when we come to look at Knox, it is plain that the orientation of his more radical thought on the matter is initially derived from that Bucer-Calvin nexus.

In Reformation Scotland, fasting as an issue did not make its initial (recorded) appearance with Knox, but rather with George Wishart. In the account of his trial in 1546, he responded to the charge that he denounced fasting thus: 'I find that Fasting is commended in the Scripture: therefore I were a slanderer of the Gospel, if I condemned fasting ... But God knoweth only who fasteth the true fast.'[12] The last remark is significant. Is there a dearth of studies on fasting in connection with Protestant Reformation piety and spirituality because it was a dead letter, or because in the nature of the thing it is not easily verifiable? By the definition of 'true' fasting, evidence for a secret or closet practice can be hard to find – especially if exercised along the lines the reformers inculcated in accordance with Christ's counsel on discreet fasting in Matthew 6:16–18.

---

[10] *De regno Christi*, ed. François Wendel, in *Martini Buceri opera latina* (Paris and Gütersloh, 1955), XV, p. 85 (English: ed. Wilhelm Pauck, Library of Christian Classics, XIX [Philadelphia, 1969], p. 254). See also *Consilium theologicum privatim conscriptum*, ed. Pierre Fraenkel, in Bucer, *Opera latina*, IV, p. 74, no. 321.

[11] Calvin, *Institutes of the Christian Religion*, Book IV, ch. 12, 14–21. CR, *Opera Calvini* (Braunschweig, 1863–), XXX, cols 914–18 (English: eds John T. McNeill and Ford Lewis Battles, Library of Christian Classics, XXI [Philadelphia, 1960], pp. 1241–8, quotation from p. 1243). Best text: *Institution de la religion chrestienne*, ed. Jean-Daniel Benoit (5 vols, Paris, 1957–63), IV, pp. 250–57.

[12] Knox, *History*, II, p. 243.

Fasting theory and practice seems to have been one of the matters of contention between Knox and the Catholic controversialist, Ninian Winzet, in 1560–61. Question 79 of Winzet's *Buke of Four Scoir Thre Questions* sent to Knox in 1561 as a manuscript, and then in 1562 in published form, deals with the matter.[13] While conceding that in received ecclesiastical practice there is an element of travesty, Winzet resorts to biblical and early Church authority for its usage. His understanding is that Knox and his followers are 'against' fasting. Presumably then, Knox's tract of 1566 would have come as a surprise to Winzet. In December 1563, the Council of Trent, on the last day of its last session, confined itself to an affirmation of the principle of regulation without actually disputing the reformers' voluntary concept; a general exhortation to adhere to Church laws was enunciated, but no special recommendations were made.[14] Nor in Knox's tract is there any special polemic against Rome on the topic; yet he does intimate at the end that he will presently return to the subject, particularly the Lenten fast, about which he had been taunted by Winzet.[15]

Most biographies of Knox, most histories of the Scottish Reformation, and all histories of Scottish reformed worship do at least mention the fact that in December 1565 the General Assembly commissioned the publication of a little book in preparation for a public fast to be held some months later.[16] It was entitled *The Ordour and Doctrine of the Generall Faste, appointed be the Generall Assemblie of the Kirkes of Scotland*,[17] and from 1587 it was incorporated into the *Book of Common Order*.[18] Very little attention has been paid to the book or indeed

---

[13] In *Certain Tractates*, ed. James King Hewison (2 vols, STS, Edinburgh, 1888–90), I, pp. 126–7. Also in Robert Keith, *History of the Affairs of Church and State in Scotland, from the Beginning of the Reformation to the Year 1568*, eds J.P. Lawson and C.J. Lyon (3 vols, Edinburgh, 1844–50), III, pp. 439–507 (question 79: pp. 496–7).

[14] *Decrees of the Ecumenical Councils/Conciliorum oecumenicorum decreta*, ed. Norman P. Tanner (2 vols, London and Georgetown, 1990), II, p. 797.

[15] Knox, *Works*, VI, p. 416.

[16] *BUK*, I, p. 76; Calderwood, *History*, II, p. 304.

[17] W. Ian P. Hazlett, 'A Working Bibliography of Knox's Writings', in Robert V. Schnucker (ed.), *Calviniana: Ideas and Influence of Jean Calvin* (Kirksville, MO, 1988), p. 191, no. 23. Full text in Knox, *Works*, VI, pp. 391–426. Also (anglicized) in George W. Sprott and Thomas Leishman (eds), *The Book of Common Order of the Church of Scotland, commonly known as John Knox's Liturgy* (Edinburgh and London, 1868), pp. 150–91.

[18] William McMillan, *The Worship of the Scottish Reformed Church* (London, 1931), pp. 330 ff. Only from early this century, with the edition by George W. Sprott, *The Book of Common Order of the Church of Scotland, Commonly Known as John Knox's*

to the subsequent fasts. In older works, like those of Patrick Fraser Tytler, Robert Keith, David Hay Fleming and Peter Hume Brown, the chief point of interest was the precise date of the first fast.[19] This arose out of the suggestion that the fast had been devised and postponed for a week as psychological preparation for the beleaguered Reformation party in advance of the holy killing of David Riccio, the Queen's Chief Secretary, when Parliament (postponed to 7 March 1566) was sitting. This occasioned acute controversy, to which we shall return. A handful of modern writers do pause over Knox's book and the fast. Jasper Ridley's account is essentially reportage, though he makes some pertinent observations; Pierre Janton and Richard Greaves briefly consider the significance of certain aspects of the fast text, Janton in connection with Knox's 'little flock' ecclesiology, and Greaves in relation to Knox's social awareness and thinking.[20] Oddly, however, even in more recent specialist studies of the specific situation to which the fast was a response, it is either just acknowledged in passing or ignored.[21] In view of the likelihood that there was actually more fasting (including abstinence as a civil requirement) in Scotland after the Reformation than before it, it is also surprising that writers advocating elements of continuity in the Scottish Reformation have not made more of it.

Historians of worship are naturally concerned primarily (if somewhat cursorily) with the order of service section at the end of the tract.[22] Only William McMillan considers other aspects of fasting and abstinence in Scottish life and society, such as the continuing practice of

---

Liturgy (Edinburgh and London, 1901), has the overwhelmingly larger part of the booklet, the 'doctrine', been omitted from the *Book of Common Order*. The last edition to retain the whole text was that of Sprott and Leishman, see previous note.

[19] Patrick Fraser Tytler, *History of Scotland* (10 vols, Edinburgh, 1892), VII, pp. 21–3, 26, 33–4, 427–38; Keith, *History*, II, pp. 407–11; David Hay Fleming, *Mary Queen of Scots from her Birth to her Flight into England: A Brief Biography* (London, 1897), pp. 396–8, 495–6; and Peter Hume Brown, *John Knox: A Biography* (2 vols, London, 1895), II, pp. 228–9, 305 n. 1.

[20] Jasper Ridley, *John Knox* (Oxford 1968), pp. 443–6; Pierre Janton, *Concept et sentiment de l'Eglise chez John Knox le réformateur écossais* (Paris, 1972), pp. 75–9; Richard L. Greaves, *Theology and Revolution in the Scottish Reformation: Studies in the Thought of John Knox* (Grand Rapids, MI, 1980), pp. 188–9.

[21] Michael Lynch, *Edinburgh and the Reformation* (Edinburgh, 1981), p. 115; Ian B. Cowan, 'The Roman Connection', and Julian Goodare, 'Queen Mary's Catholic Interlude', both in Michael Lynch (ed.), *Mary Stewart: Queen in Three Kingdoms* (Oxford, 1988), pp. 105–22, 154–70.

[22] Charles G. McCrie, *The Public Worship of Presbyterian Scotland historically treated* (Edinburgh, 1892), pp. 122–5. William D. Maxwell, *A History of Worship in the Church of Scotland* (London, 1951), pp. 108–9. George W. Sprott, *The Worship and Offices of the Church of Scotland* (Edinburgh and London, 1882), pp. 175–80. See also Sprott, *Book of Common Order* (1901 edn.) pp. l–li.

pre-Communion fasting, and the civil prohibition of meat-eating in Lent and on Fridays for market economic and animal husbandry reasons.[23] Other more recent contributions on the history of Scottish reformed worship either devote a paragraph to the topic[24] or disregard it.[25] The *Dictionary of Scottish Church History and Theology* has no entry on fasting, and even in those articles where one would expect some attention to the subject, only passing references occur.[26]

Why has the matter been passed over, or indeed bowdlerized in this way? Various factors seem to have militated against serious focus on it. First, as already suggested, it reflects the lack of interest in the fasting issue in Reformation studies generally. In the settled Reformations at large, (private) fasting was perhaps too marginal, private, and non-contentious to arouse much attention. But Scotland was surely the exception. What with continuing *de facto* abstinence on Wednesdays, Fridays, and during the Lenten season, pre-Communion fasting, and intermittent general public fasts as well as special local ones, Scotland was ironically in the vanguard of the fasting tradition until the eighteenth century and beyond. Furthermore, this was (in performance) popular, not just presbyterial fasting. Yet its historiographical profile is very modest.

Secondly, apart from Zwingli's initial tract, no reformer published a monograph on the subject. As a result, it seems like a stray salvo inaugurating hostilities over greater matters. But throughout the 1520s and 1530s, fasting regularly appears in the tracts or documents of controversial theology, if always in conjunction with other topics like celibacy, invocation of saints, images, and so on.[27] In general historiography, however, it is perceived as something of a non-issue

---

[23] McMillan, *Worship*, pp. 151, 197, 226–7, 324–6, 330–33.

[24] Gordon Donaldson, 'Reformation to Covenant', in Duncan Forrester and Douglas Murray (eds), *Studies in the History of Worship in Scotland* (2nd edn, Edinburgh, 1994), p. 45.

[25] John M. Ross, *Four Centuries of Scottish Worship* (Edinburgh, 1972); Ian B. Cowan, *The Scottish Reformation: Church and Society in Sixteenth Century Scotland* (London, 1982), pp. 139–58.

[26] Ed. Nigel M. de S. Cameron (Edinburgh, 1993). Of two small anthologies, fasting is ignored in Ian B. Cowan, *Blast and Counterblast: Contemporary Writings on the Scottish Reformation* (Edinburgh, 1960), but does figure in Henry R. Sefton, *John Knox: An Account of the Development of His Spirituality* (Edinburgh, 1993), pp. 114–15.

[27] E.g. *Enchiridion locorum communium adversus Lutherum et alios hostes ecclesiae (1525–1543)*, ed. Pierre Fraenkel (Münster Westfalen, 1979), Corpus Catholicorum, XXXIV, pp. 162–7 (English: *Enchiridion of Commonplaces of John Eck*, ed. Ford L. Battles [Duquesne University, 1976], pp. 100–103). *Augsburg Confession*, art. 26. *Tetrapolitan Confession*, arts. 7–10. Martin Bucer, *Defensio contra axioma catholicum … episcopi Abrincensis* (Strasbourg, 1534), fos F6v–7v.

after Zwingli, though it did continue to be on the agenda up to *c.* 1541. The effect of this has been that Knox's relatively sensational tract of 1566 has languished in oblivion. The cursory treatment of the issue to which historians of liturgy usually confine themselves is all the more remarkable since the Scottish Reformed Church was the only Reformation Church anywhere to prescribe a liturgical fasting Order. It is true that the English *Book of Common Prayer* sets out days for fasting and abstinence, such as Lent and Ascension; but no Order is provided.[28] Anyway, fasting in the Scottish public sense was hardly what its authors had in mind.

Thirdly, in modern Scottish religio-historical consciousness, post-Reformation fasting is associated more with the sacramental fasting practised in the covenanting era.[29] The religious fanaticism which tainted that era induced repugnance to many of the phenomena associated with it. Historians of the subsequent establishments, whether Episcopalian, Humian agnostic, Moderate, Evangelical or Liberal were hardly likely to be attracted to a subject not only associated historically with Knoxian Protestant excess and covenanting zeal, but now also perceived as a 'relic of Popish superstition'.[30] Fasting was, all in all, an embarrassing anachronism in the Scottish post-Reformation religious tradition.

Finally, one must raise the question of the subliminal impact of the four major documents of the Scottish Reformation, the *Scots Confession* (1560), the *First Book of Discipline* (1560–61), the *Second Book of Discipline*, and Knox's *History*. None of the first three mentions fasting as such, though fasting, properly understood, was condoned. The promotion of public fasts from 1566 onwards as well as the continuing practice of pre-Communion fasting[31] testify to this – as does the General Assembly's endorsement of the *Second Helvetic Confession* in 1566, which included specific approval of proper private and public fasting.[32] That apart, the silence of the three core documents, plus the scant mention of the 1566 fasting episode in Knox's *History*,[33] may well have helped to determine the location of the subject on the remote periphery of historiography.

---

[28] *The Book of Common Prayer*, ed. Archibald J. Stephens (3 vols, London, 1849), I, p. 294.

[29] George B. Burnet, *The Holy Communion of the Reformed Church of Scotland 1560–1960* (Edinburgh and London, 1960), pp. 130–31.

[30] Thomas McCrie, *Life of Mr Robert Blair* (Edinburgh, 1848), p. 7.

[31] Burnet, *Holy Communion*, pp. 51–2.

[32] *Die Bekenntnisschriften der reformierten Kirche*, ed. E.F. Karl Müller (Leipzig, 1903), pp. 215–16 (English: Cochrane, *Reformed Confessions*, pp. 292–3).

[33] Knox, *History*, II, pp. 176, 178, 180, 182.

The general and particular context giving rise to the General Assembly's commissioning, late in December 1565, of a public fast is well known, if not uniformly understood, in so far as such an imbroglio is comprehensible at all.[34] In domestic as well as external terms, Scotland in the 1560s was highly unstable. But at least the personal reign of Mary provided an orthodox focus of authority and sovereignty, even if it generated jealousies and rivalries about the exercise of power in a society which had not known a conventional power-wielding monarch for nearly 20 years.

Mary's religious policy can best be described as an attempt to accommodate the largely aristocratic and bourgeois supporters of the Reformation, while retaining a perfectly natural but discreet Catholic bias, which only latterly became more explicit.[35] Her attitude was hardly bullish, nor was she was a persecutor, and so no Mary Tudor (despite papal encouragements[36]). Her policies were more akin to those of Mary of Guise and Catherine de' Medici, confined largely to what was realistically possible, aimed (successfully) at avoiding religious war (with its high risk of foreign intervention) such as was happening in France. Yet there were conflicting signs and messages: Protestant doctrine was sanctioned by Parliament and the reformed Church was officially permitted, if not yet established; but at the same time Catholicism (both popular and court, though uncoordinated) was renascent in the Edinburgh region,[37] though combined with leaderless and stagnant Catholicism in the country areas.[38]

This is not the place to analyse Mary's religious policy in depth. But significantly it did divide the Protestants, at least until 1566, since many

---

[34] Knox, *History*, II, pp. 157–87; Calderwood, *History*, II, pp. 291–321; Keith, *History*, II, pp. 344–432; Hay Fleming, *Mary*, pp. 105–34; Gordon Donaldson, *All the Queen's Men: Power and Politics in Mary Stewart's Scotland* (London, 1983), pp. 70–80; M. Lynch (ed.), *Mary Stewart: Queen in Three Kingdoms* (Oxford, 1988).

[35] See *RPC*, I, pp. 208–9, 267, 356, 338–43.

[36] A letter to Mary from Pius V of 23 January 1566 urged her to be diligent in weeding out 'the thorns and tares of heretical pravity'; *Papal Negotiations with Mary Queen of Scots during her Reign in Scotland, 1561–1567*, ed. John H. Pollen (SHS, Edinburgh, 1901), p. 237. His predecessor, Pius IV, in a Consistory speech on 12 October 1565 had pleaded that Mary not spare what he saw as the religious rising of some of the nobles at that time, and that she should see the heretics' demands on the Mass as a 'casus belli', ibid., pp. 227–9.

[37] Lynch, 'Introduction', *Mary Stewart*, pp. 14–20.

[38] Cowan, 'Roman Connection', in ibid., pp. 108–113. The general views of Lynch and Cowan of the religious balance are essentially corroborated by a realistic report in July 1567 of the Spanish Ambassador in London, Guzman de Silva, to Philip II, following an interview with Dr Roche Mamerot, Mary's confessor in Edinburgh: 'Nearly all the nobles are heretics … the greater part of the common people are Catholic; they would be lost little by little'; Pollen, *Papal Negotiations*, p. 520.

of the more politic among them were able to live, if not indefinitely, with the provisional nature of the religious situation, and tolerate the Queen's private Mass in Holyrood Palace. Mary's attitude to the religious question was expressed in a letter to the English diplomat, Nicholas Throckmorton: 'I am none of those that will change my religion every year; I mean to constrain none of my subjects, but would wish that they were all as I am.'[39] The conceptual card that she repeatedly played was 'liberty of conscience' and 'freedom of worship',[40] ideas circulating in contemporary France, but no more acceptable to militant Protestants than to militant Catholics.[41] However, for reasonably informed (possibly vaguely Erasmian) lay Protestants, aware that the Reformation was instigated originally over a 'conscience' issue, but perhaps not particularly *au fait* with the much less porous concept of 'Christian conscience' as propounded by Reformation theologians, such a slogan may have been persuasive (assuming that their interests were not solely materialist). They may even have been inheritors of an early *laissez-faire* Lutheran tradition surviving in Scotland.[42] However, for more uncompromising Protestants like Knox, what he saw as the majority[43] in the Protestant political nation was being duped by Mary. Their compliance was betraying the Reformation, and so God, with its 'perfida defectio a Christo'.[44]

The period from the summer of 1565 to the spring of 1566 was one of several *anni horribiles* for Knox and his supporters, coming as it did

---

[39] William Forbes-Leith (ed.), *Narratives of Scottish Catholics under Mary Stuart and James VI* (Edinburgh, 1885), p. 56.

[40] Calderwood, *History*, II, pp. 295–6. See also A. Labanoff, *Lettres et mémoires de Marie, reine d'Ecosse* (7 vols, London, 1844), I, pp. 289–90.

[41] See Keith, *History*, II, p. 269. Goodare, 'Mary's Catholic Interlude', p. 161.

[42] See one of Luther's famous 'Wittenberg Sermons' of 1522: 'To hold a Mass in such a manner is sinful, and yet no one should be dragged away from it by the hair; for it should be left to God, and his Word should be allowed to work alone, without our work or interference ... this forcing and commanding results in mere mockery, an external show, a fool's play, man-made ordinances, sham-saints, and hypocrites ... I do say: abandon the Mass, it is not right, you are sinning when you do it; I cannot refrain from telling you this. But I would not make it an ordinance for them, nor urge legislation'. *Luthers Werke*, X³, pp. 14, 35–16, 2 (*Luther's Works*, LI, p. 76). Luther's principle was that preachers have the *ius verbi*, but not its *executio* (claimed by Knox).

[43] As he acknowledged in his despairing and begging letter to Calvin in October 1561, complaining that with Mary's coming, the 'idolum missalicum' was put in place 'again', and that since even the majority of confessing Protestants were not willing to act against this, Catholicism had re-entered Scotland unchallenged through the front door. See CR, XLVII, cols 73–5; Knox, *Works*, VI, pp. 133–5; Alexandre Teulet, *Relations politiques de la France et de l'Espagne avec l'Ecosse au XVIᵉ siècle* (5 vols, Paris, 1862), II, pp. 172–3. Cf. Knox, *History*, II, pp. 23–4, 133–4.

[44] In the same letter to Calvin, Knox, *Works*, VI, p. 134.

after a series of disappointments and reversals, as well as at a time when the general outlook for the Reformation in western Europe was gloomy. It began with the General Assembly of June 1565 petitioning the Queen to have the Mass definitively terminated in Scotland, especially in her palace, and complaining (among other things) about the misappropriation of funds from the thirds of benefices which had been promised for the support of the ministry.[45] This was followed in July by Mary's controversial marriage to Henry Lord Darnley, precipitating a revolt led by high-profile Protestant sections of the nobility, but which failed to command widespread Protestant support. On the revolt's failure, the rebels were threatened with forfeiture and the charge of treason. The revolt had not been ostensibly over religion, but religion was interwoven with a range of other issues, even if allegedly only as 'a cloak to cover their ungodly designs'.[46] As a result of the revolt, which saw the Protestant interest deprived of the more committed section of its political leadership, the religious dangers were clearly perceived.[47] Also, the apparent freezing of funds for the ministry was provoking a staffing crisis in the reformed Church, since ministers were suffering hardship and some were abandoning the ministry.[48] There was talk of a crusade by international Catholicism to extirpate the Reformation, orchestrated by that failed moderate, the Cardinal of Lorraine, to which Mary was reputed (wrongly) to be party.[49] Due to bad winters and harvests, there were food shortages, epidemics and news of plagues elsewhere.[50] The Queen told the General Assembly that she would not abandon the Mass.[51] It was also apparent that in the Parliament summoned to meet in March 1566, Scottish Catholicism was to be set on a more viable footing, even if this only took the form of legal toleration of the Mass

---

[45] Calderwood, *History*, II, pp. 287–9.

[46] Proclamation of Mary and Henry, Knox, *History*, II, p. 166; *RPC*, I, p. 370. For Knox and doubtless others, however, the royal marriage did entail an implicit religious threat, *RPC*, I, pp. lxi–ii.

[47] Knox, *History*, II, p. 172

[48] Knox, *Works*, VI, pp. 431–6.

[49] George Buchanan, *History of Scotland*, ed. John Watkins (London, 1843), p. 433; Sir James Melville of Halhill, *Memoirs of his own Life, mdxlix-mdxciii* (Edinburgh, 1836), p. 147; Pollen, *Papal Negotiations*, p. 233; Keith, *History*, II, pp. 391–2; Hay Fleming, *Mary*, pp. 124, 379–80; Conyers Read, *Mr Secretary Cecil and Queen Elizabeth* (London, 1955), p. 305; Malcolm R. Thorp, 'Catholic Conspiracy in Early Elizabethan Foreign Policy', *Sixteenth Century Journal*, 15 (1984), pp. 431–48, at pp. 432, 435; Goodare, 'Catholic Interlude', pp. 164–5.

[50] See Ridley, *Knox*, p. 424 and n. 1 for some sources; also *RPC*, I, p. 402; Samuel G.E. Lythe, *The Economy of Scotland in its European Setting 1550–1625* (Edinburgh and London, 1960), p. 17.

[51] Calderwood, *History*, II, p. 295.

and the ungagging of the rump hierarchy. This ominous period ended with the assassination of David Riccio for a variety of reasons, including religion, followed by Knox's voluntary (or was it?) internal exile and, paradoxically, by the restitution of rights to the rebel Lords of the Congregation.

Such was the backdrop to the General Assembly meeting, in an atmosphere of urgency, on Christmas Day 1565. The Assembly's agenda was a climax to the 'widespread anxiety, felt by Knox, as much as by [James Stewart, Earl of] Moray',[52]Mary's half-brother, and leader of the nobles' abortive rebellion. Pessimism pervades Knox's own writings around this time, not least his sermon preached on 19 August 1565 and published the following month. In referring in a spirit of resignation to the 'dolorous storme of [God's] present displeasure',[53] he alluded to a theme that was to feature prominently in his forthcoming fasting tract. Likewise in the preface to Book IV of his *History*, written in 1566, there are echoes of the core of the analysis in his fasting tract: the Reformation has degenerated since the heady days of 1559–61; the majority of confessing Protestants have opted for worldly pragmatism as against the Word of God; the policy of accommodation to the Queen's Catholicism by the Protestant politiques is apostasy and the source of current miseries; and Catholic restoration is being planned as divine punishment, along with natural and social afflictions.[54] Knox had no illusions about the impasse the Reformation movement in Scotland had been in since 1561. His last stand, public and religio-political, was his fasting tract, a prophetic manifesto announcing the final chance for true believers to repent, to follow not only the right belief, but also the right life, in the face of a God about to wreak vengeance. In short, in Knox's view, doom was imminent in the face of licensed idolatry and social injustice – a characteristic Knoxian theme and register.[55]

It would be ill-advised to assess the proceedings of the December 1565 General Assembly as primarily Knox driven. In the absence of a godly princess, the Assembly, not having any official constitutional status, had been compelled to operate informal working arrangements with the godly magistrates, the Privy Council. This had a pro-Reformation majority,

---

[52] Lynch, 'Introduction', *Mary Stewart*, p. 17.

[53] Knox, *Works*, VI, p. 272.

[54] Knox, *History*, II, pp. 3–6.

[55] See W. Ian P. Hazlett, '"Jihad" against Female Infidels and Satan: John Knox's *First Blast of the Trumpet*', in Willem van 't Spijker (ed.), *Calvin: Erbe und Auftrag. Festschrift für Wilhelm H. Neuser* (Kampen, 1991), p. 285.

whether confessional or politique. The relationship therefore was ambiguous, and the enthusiasm was not quite mutual in the absence of direct Crown involvement. The turning-point was the royal marriage. Sceptical about Mary's reassurances on religion, Protestant nobles began to see a more positive role for the Assembly as a counterweight to royal policies. Some unnamed lords attended the June 1565 Assembly. At the December Assembly, when Mary was riding the crest of a wave, not only were the Justice Clerk and the Clerk Register present, but so too were lords like Lindsay, Morton and Mar, as well as Maitland of Lethington: 'The tide had turned in favour of the Assembly.'[56]

However, the substance of the new relationship was immediate self-interest. Knox was readopted as a mouthpiece to restart and complete the revolution begun in 1559, but which in the meantime had ground to a halt. For the first time since 1558–60, Knox's prophetic mission and the collective interests of the Protestant nobility largely coincided, interests which it would be rash to characterize as singularly secular or political. Moreover, while it may be more orthodox to read this situation as the nobles using Knox, there is no reason to exclude his use of them; mutual interest does not bar mutual exploitation. The fasting tract and the subsequent exercises, invoking the impending judgement of God on current affairs, were the outcome.

On the first day of the Assembly, the commissioners received and responded to the Queen's answer to the Assembly's petition of the previous June, concerning chiefly the Mass and the misappropriation of the Church's share of the thirds of the benefices.[57] The minister of Perth, John Row, drafted the response.[58] The gist of it was, first, that if the Queen was not yet convinced of the truth of the reformed faith, then she should allow a disputation with the court theologians; secondly, the Mass was denounced again; thirdly, alliance with the King of Kings was declared preferable to alliance with any earthly king (France); and fourthly, and more expansively, claim to the patrimony of the Kirk was reaffirmed and the wish expressed that the Queen should make good her declared general intention to provide for the maintenance of the ministry. The General Assembly was edging towards confrontation.

In addition, deliberations on the state of the ministry accentuated the seriousness of the crisis arising from lack of funds – namely,

---

[56] Duncan Shaw, *The General Assemblies of the Church of Scotland 1560–1600* (Edinburgh, 1964), p. 44. See also pp. 39–43.

[57] *BUK*, I, pp. 59–60, 67–9; Calderwood, *History*, II, pp. 287–9, 295–6; Knox, *History*, II, pp. 148–50, 151–3.

[58] *BUK*, I, pp. 69–71; Calderwood, *History*, II, pp. 297–9; Knox, *History*, II, pp. 176–7 (garbled summary).

resignations.[59] The principle was enunciated that whereas ministers in poverty, or in situations of hostility, might seek charges elsewhere, they should on no account abandon their vocation, since their calling was apostolic with no guarantee of a comfortable life. Knox was commissioned to compose a pastoral letter to this effect, which was published as an appendix to the fast tract.[60]

That the general situation called for extraordinary measures is reflected in the decision on 27 December to have a public fast proclaimed and an explanatory text published by Robert Lekprevik.[61] That neither the analysis nor the remedy derived solely from paranoia in Knox is suggested by the fact that the sources show little or no hint of scepticism, even from Privy Councillors at the Assembly like Maitland. Also, the inextricable link between the spiritual function of a fast and its ulterior socio-political goals is evident in one of the few other contemporary sources, the *Diurnal of Occurrents* (though the author's use of 'appeirandlie' does perhaps suggest an element of incredulity in one respect):

> to pray to the eternall God that he wald fastene and pacifie his angerie wraith quhilk appeirandlie is to come upoun us for our synnis, and speciallie that God wald inform, mollifie and mak fast the hartis of our souveranis towardis our nobilitie quhilkis ar now banist in Ingland, at the parliament present quhairintill thai ar summond to compeir ... to heir and sie the doom of foirfaltour ... for the crymes of lesmajestie.[62]

That Knox wrote the tract is an assumption in need of some qualification. Being an authorized Church booklet, it bore no author's name. Among the early publications of the reformed Kirk, it is by far the most disputatious. But if Knox's is the chief recognizable spirit informing the contents (consisting of two parts, the 'doctrine', and the 'form' or 'order'), the evidence makes it clear that it was in part a collective effort. Accounts of the proceedings in Calderwood and in the *Booke of the Universall Kirk* show that that there was a division of labour. A research team of eight people was asked to 'collect the heads and causes of a public fast'.[63] This meant establishing the layout and contents of the document, such as biblical sources and warrants as well as specific earthly reasons justifying such an undertaking. The team included John

---

[59] Calderwood, *History*, II, p. 301.

[60] Calderwood, *History*, I, pp. 306–10; Knox, *Works*, II, pp. 423–6.

[61] Calderwood, *History*, II, pp. 303–4.

[62] *A Diurnal of Remarkable Occurrents that have passed within the Country of Scotland ... till the Year M.D.LXXV* (Edinburgh, 1833), p. 88.

[63] Calderwood, *History*, II, p. 304; *BUK*, I, p. 76

Craig, minister of the Canongate, and John Douglas, Rector of St Andrews University (both former schoolmen), but not Knox. Also in the group was the minister of Leith, David Lindsay, related to the earls of Crawford, and like Knox, with a Genevan background. Following their preliminary report the next day, the Assembly asked Craig and Knox to draw up the form or manner of the exercise; this version of the procedure is supported by Knox's Continuator in the *History*, except that he makes Knox the sole author of the form of action and Church service.[64] But it does seem that Knox took charge of the final draft of the entire text, despite the initial collective effort.[65]

The formal presentation of the 'doctrine' or *apologia* is remarkably clear and systematic. Rhetorically, it is a striking combination of the deliberative (persuade to action), expository, and prophetic styles. It displays the basic classical rhetorical features of the *inventio* and *dispositio* and *partitio* (initial indications about amassing material, its arrangement and subdivision in the subsequent text), the *commiseratio* (lamentation), and so on.[66] There is also discreet evidence of scholastic method as well; for example, in the intermittent *quaestiones*, *propositiones*, and *probationes* (proofs, corroboration) along with the various *responsiones* and *objectiones*. There are also some *hypotheses* considered, reminiscent of the scholastic *quodlibeta*, that is, points brought up for the sake of argument. While scholastic traits are evident in other of Knox's writings, their prominence here might reflect the input of the university men, Douglas, possible ex-Sorbonnist, and Craig, the ex-Dominican.

The original tract was in small octavo consisting of 54 pages. In Laing's edition, the 'doctrine' section amounts to 22 pages, and the 'order' to seven pages. The biblical quotations are derived from the Genevan English Bible. After an announcement of the public fast and an *exordium* (preparation for what is to follow), including remarks dissociating this fasting from Catholic usage, the first main section defines and

---

[64] Knox, *History*, II, p. 176.

[65] At the end of the text, Knox states that he would have liked to have dealt with the issue of Lent (probably in response to Winzet's *Book of Four scoir and thre Questions*), 'but these we are compelled for this present to pretermit, be reason that the tyme [from the last Sunday in February] appoynted to this present exercise of Fasting approacheth so nye'. Knox, *Works*, VI, p. 416.

[66] See Lee A. Sonnino, *A Handbook to Sixteenth-Century Rhetoric* (London, 1968). This may reflect Knox's legal training as discussed by J.H. Burns in Chapter 6 above, and compare James K. Cameron, 'John Knox', in *Theologische Realenzyklopädie*, ed. G. Müller (Berlin and New York, 1976–), XIX, p. 286.

illustrates true fasting, private and public.[67] The keynotes of 'troubles', humiliation, repentance, confession and supplication are introduced. Substantial illustration from biblical precedents in their historical context (idolatry, backsliding, cultural assimilation and dilution, withdrawal of God or His punitive threats, tyrants, foreign threats, resistance of the faithful few) are laid out in detail. These are found chiefly in the books of Samuel, Chronicles, Judges, Joshua, Jonah, Kings, Ezra, Esther, Daniel, and from the New Testament, Matthew (6:16–18) and Acts (13:1–3).

Two initial observations can be made. Firstly, although the author availed himself of Calvin's brief treatment of the matter in the *Institutes* for basic guidelines, only some of these biblical references are cited by Calvin. Knox's list is more comprehensive. Either he or someone else had recourse to what in reality was Calvin's own source, namely Martin Bucer's *Commentary on the Gospels*. For in Bucer's excursus at Matthew 6:16 – 'Quid ieiunium in Scripturis significet' – the catena of biblical precedents laid out by him corresponds on the whole to that in Knox's tract.[68] If this is the case, it is one of the few pieces of evidence indicating direct use of Bucer by Scottish reformers – normally very difficult to establish.[69]

Secondly, this section along with the next two illuminates Knox's fundamental *Weltanschauung*, informed by a biblicism more radical than that of the mainline reformers:[70] sixteenth-century Scotland is a kind of northern Israel, where everything basic to Israel is applied typologically and literally to Scotland, just as previously Knox had applied it to England. The difference between the Old and New Testaments almost evaporates. The fast text presupposes that Scotland is equally bound by God's covenant with Israel, with the corollary that anything undermining the covenant, internally or externally, such as pagan idolatry (i.e. the Roman Mass), social injustice, or religion without heart (i.e. soft Protestantism) must be eradicated if God is not to abandon the nation to disaster.[71] Knox was inflexible, not because he

---

[67] Knox, *Works*, VI, pp. 393–9.

[68] *In sacra quatuor Evangelia, Enarrationes perpetuae*, Strasbourg, 1530; Basle, 1536 (Geneva, 1553), fo. 65r–v.

[69] See David F. Wright, 'Martin Bucer and England – and Scotland', in Christian Krieger and Marc Lienhard (eds), *Martin Bucer and Sixteenth Century Europe: Actes du colloque de Strasbourg, 28–31 août 1991* (2 vols, Leiden, 1993), II, pp. 530–32.

[70] See Wilhelm Neuser, 'John Knox und die Scottische Reformation', in Carl Andresen (ed.), *Handbuch der Dogmen- und Theologiegeschichte* (Göttingen, 1988), II, pp. 298–9; Hazlett, 'Jihad', p. 285.

[71] Elsewhere, he formulates the doctrine thus: 'And therefore I fear not to affirm, that the Gentiles (I mean everie citie, realme, province, or nation amongst the Gentiles, embrasing Christ Jesus and his true religion) be bound to the same league and covenant

was a bigot, but because he was addicted to a very demanding and unmitigated theology.

The second section of the tract illustrates the benefits of true fasting, chiefly that when done genuinely, God will stay His anger and turn matters to a godly people's favour; trust in the merciful divine promises can yield results 'beyond man's expectations'.[72]

The third section, a long one, highlights the relevance of the project for contemporary Scotland.[73] Various reasons ('causes') are examined within an effective question–answer–objection–hypothesis–conclusion format. The section is illuminating for the image it deliberately presents of the fragility and vulnerability of the Reformation in Scotland after a tenuous existence of six years. The sort of question dealt with is: why the need for this fast now, and not in 1558–60? The answer is that, initially, there was sincere conviction and zeal, but now there is accommodation, compromise and the supremacy of 'carnall wisdom' among many Protestant nobles, so that the idol of the Mass has been granted a pied-à-terre and safe haven. Thereby God's wrath has been provoked. At the start, a small and laughably inexperienced Protestant militia, with the support of God and foreigners (the English), so frightened the establishment 'that the expertest soldiers feared the poor plowmen'. Now all hope of the Queen's conversion has dissipated, so that not only does she have a Mass, but she is sponsoring some preaching friars in Edinburgh. Moreover, even if Scotland were a new Jerusalem (which she assuredly is not), what hope is there of resisting the reputed plans for an international Catholic crusade to annihilate the Reformation in Europe? Thousands of Protestants have already been slaughtered in the religious war in France.

Responding to the objection that such an analysis is too pessimistic and alarmist, Knox replies with exemplary warnings from the Old Testament, such as King Hezekiah's refusal to accept the intelligence that the Babylonian, Sennacherib, and his superior army were no longer a mortal threat, since God had 'put a bridle in their nosethirles' (see Isaiah 37:29). The pious Hezekiah refused to be taken in by such assurances, and by relying on spiritual weapons, he was in the event able to rout the Babylonians. Accordingly, the Catholic armies of Europe should not be underestimated, and so divine aid should be invoked,

---

that God made with his people Israel'; *The Appellation*, in Knox, *Works*, IV, p. 505. Accordingly, 'For the idolatry of a small number is God's wrath kindled against the multitude not punishing the offenders', ibid., IV, p. 503. Hence Knox's wrath against Mary, not because she was spearheading any public Catholic counter-offensive, but because she shielded the idolatrous Mass in the palace.

[72] Knox, *Works*, VI, pp. 399–400.
[73] Ibid., VI, pp. 400–406.

but in an appropriate manner. Further, the relative political stability of the previous six years should not be allowed to induce a false sense of security – let rumours of plagues elsewhere, religious wars in France and wars in Scandinavia serve as a warning. Nor should political calm be allowed to conceal other dark shames in Scotland. Apart from religious ambiguities, there is public and personal depravity: the unscrupulous are praised and rewarded for their skill at exploiting ordinary people; the legal system is corrupt and discredited – 'slaughter and murder is esteemed small sin, if any man have friends in the Court'; the hedonistic life styles of the rich are a waste of resources; contempt for ministers is linked to contempt for the poor. This raises the question: if we are so bad, what hope is there of being spared at all? Turning to God with repentance is the answer; self-humiliation before God generates true righteousness, that is, pursuit of justice, equity, temperance, and care of the poor, which is what the holy life is about.

The fourth section anticipates resistance within the so-called reformed community to the idea of a general fast.[74] In reality such sceptics are pseudo-Christians and atheists,[75] of whom there are more in Scotland than committed Catholics. 'Let not the godly be offended by the brocardes [lampoons] and lardons [gibes] of such godless people.' Isaiah (22:12–13) encountered the same derision, complaining: 'When the Lord calleth to sackcloth and ashes ... they said "Let us eat and drink, the morow we shall dye".' Such rebellion will be costly, provoking national chastisement by God, as the disasters which befell Israel show. The minority of true believers must declare themselves and stand against the tide, for God does not require the majority to be godly before He will show indulgence.

Here it should be noted that the call to fast is not addressed to the nation as such. Rather it is directed to the committed core of authentic believers, the 'saints', the 'elect', the 'little flock', on whom responsibility for the ultimate welfare of the alienated nation depends, with their true witness. The fast at this stage is not a device for a national, a state, or a people's Church; rather it is a means for the genuine remnant to identify themselves, and exercise public judgement on a degenerate political leadership and the dissolute multitude. Notions of a 'popular Reformation' have no place in this bleak scenario, as the Scottish reformers at this time knew only too well.

---

[74] Ibid., VI, pp. 406–7.

[75] Not in the modern sense of unbelievers, but rather nominal believers living without or apart from God. See Zwingli, *Commentary on True and False Religion*, eds S.M. Jackson and C.N. Heller (Philadelphia, 1929; repr. Durham, NC, 1981), p. 154.

The fifth section takes up the question of the authority for public fasting.[76] It is neither a Church nor a human ordinance. Its mandate is solely divine and absolute, communicated through prophets who, like Ezekiel, call the people to self-humiliation in the face of portents. Knox, the watchman of Scotland, liked to identify himself with Ezekiel, the Watchman of Israel.[77] Spiritual guard is best exercised by a general fast to stimulate faith in the mercy and promises of God. Yet Knox, showing that in fact he is not totally an Old Testament literalist, does admit that, through Christ, regulated and fixed Jewish ceremonies, like the Day of Atonement fast, are abolished. But God's judgement is neither mutable nor cancelled, so that there is still place for *ad hoc* fasting exercises in crisis situations, as both Testaments amply testify.

The seventh, last and longest section deals with the proper understanding of fasting in both the theological and practical senses: what it is not, and what it should be in terms of its consequences here and now.[78] On the theological plane, the Catholic argument that the Protestant fast is reintroducing the notion of merit is rebutted. Joel (2:12–13) provides the guidelines (he is quoted on the title-page): 'Return to me with all your heart, with fasting and weeping, and with mourning; and rend your hearts and not your garments.' Fasting is not a work of merit, it is only a preparatory exercise; the external performance is not decisive, but rather the inward disposition. It is a special expression of faith in God's mercy, and outwardly joined to humiliation, mourning, confession, and repentance. Any successful outcome then is based not on the merit of the faster, but on divine mercy only.

On the practical level of 'outcome', or 'fruits of repentance', the powerful critique of hypocritical fasting by Isaiah (58:3 ff.) provides the keynote. The dethronement of idolatry is forgotten about; instead the focus is on social injustice in contemporary Scotland. This is not just the social theology of Isaiah and other prophets at work, it reflects strongly the Christian social–ethical concerns of the south German and Swiss Reformations with their stress on individual and collective sanctification accompanying justification. But in Knox, this takes a much less circumspect and more abrasive form – he was never after all a court or magisterial theologian. The target of the critique is not just positive exploiters, abusers and malefactors in society, whether they be earls, barons, burgesses, merchants, judges, craftsmen or artisans, but also the avarice-based jungle economy with its penury, landlessness and

---

[76] Knox, *Works*, VI, pp. 407–8.

[77] See Zwingli, *Commentary*, p. 154. A prominent mirror-image in the *First Blast of the Trumpet* too, see Hazlett, 'Jihad', p. 285.

[78] Knox, *Works*, VI, pp. 408–15.

unemployment; exposed also is civil righteousness, that is, external rectitude motivated by self-interest. All of these things offend God. The Sermon on the Mount and the Golden Rule are cited. In connection with oppressive land rent practices, Knox asks how landowners would like it if they had been born agricultural labourers or humble tenants?[79]

The limitations of Knox's prescriptions, as with those of most theologians or prophets, are not to be denied: society's ills were identified and deplored, but no serious solution other than spiritual and moral amendment was offered – an appeal, as here, to 'conscience'. Knox, however, does deal in the tract with the objection that he has an impossible dream of a perfect world. Interestingly, he retorts that the fast appeal is not universal. The call is rather for true believers to witness, at least in their own lives, to the will of God by displaying mercy. And his relative realism leads him to admit that the heroic self-sacrifices of the biblical saints can hardly be emulated – though, ironically, the accompanying circular to lapsing ministers demanded just that!

By way of conclusion, it is worth drawing attention to a number of problems and anomalies thrown up by Knox's fast tract. First, conspicuous by its absence is another 'cause' Knox might have adduced as necessitating a fast to assuage divine ire. This is that Scotland was suffering a female monarch. It could have been that he wanted to cite this, but that the suggestion was vetoed.

Second, explicit castigation of the affluent upper and middle classes might tempt some to argue that this was the Scottish reformers angling for support from the peasantry and 'poor labourers of the ground'. But the latter are not seen as noble innocents either.[80] Political strategy did not determine such a critique, but rather (as Knox himself says) the strong social justice themes of biblical prophecy and the Sermon on the Mount.

Thirdly, it is worth noting that the Old Testament prophetic theology underlying the crisis-fast phenomenon has been appropriated by Knox with impressive accuracy. A recent study of biblical fasting as collective lamentation over the withdrawn and damning God bears this out.[81] Associated ideas, extrapolated by Knox, were the stress on human responsibility for the situation of affliction, present and impending, so

---

[79] Cf. Margaret H.B. Sanderson, *Scottish Rural Society in the Sixteenth Century* (Edinburgh, 1982), pp. 28–9.

[80] Knox, *Works*, VI, p. 414.

[81] Thomas Podella, *Som-Fasten: kollektive Trauer um den verborgenen Gott im Alten Testament* (Neukirchen-Vluyn, 1989).

that the alienated God is not to blame, but rather man. The escape is self-abasement and the willingness to reappropriate God's promises and fulfil His expectations. Here, Knox points the finger chiefly at the false friends of 1558–60.

Fourthly, in connection with the spectre of an international Catholic crusade against the Reformation, characterized by Knox as one of the imminent 'plagues', a puzzle in the text is what may be provisionally called 'Knox's false Tridentine decree'. From 1559, general apprehensiveness in Reformation circles was heightened by what seemed like the emergence of an irresistible coalition of the papacy, Spain, the Council of Trent, the Jesuits, and possibly a wholly re-Catholicized France. Wild rumours in Protestant Europe flowed from the secret (but abortive) conference at Bayonne in 1565 between Catherine di' Medici, the Cardinal of Lorraine, the Duke of Alba and Philip of Spain's wife, Elizabeth;[82] already in England and Scotland, there were rumours of an offensive Catholic League – 'a band latelie devised', allegedly involving Mary.[83] All this engendered a shadow world of conspiracy, plots and final solutions. Knox claims to substantiate all this by inserting a decree of the Council of Trent to this effect.[84] There was no such decree, of course, as the published Council decrees available in Edinburgh since 1564 could verify.[85] Was this a scare stunt by Knox? Or was he the victim of a dark hoax? The source of Knox's 'decree' remains a mystery, though it does broadly correspond to recorded papal aspirations.[86]

---

[82] See F. Combes, *L'entrevue de Bayonne de 1565 et la question de la Saint-Barthélmy* (Paris, 1882); Martin Philippson, *Westeuropa im Zeitalter von Philipp II, Elisabeth I und Heinrich IV* (Berlin, 1882), pp. 120–22; H. Forneron, *Histoire de Philippe II* (2 vols, 3rd edn, Paris, 1887), I, pp. 315–22; Erich Marcks, *Die Zusammenkunft von Bayonne* (Strasbourg, 1889); Ludwig von Pastor, *The History of the Popes* (40 vols, London, 1928), XVI, pp. 184, 202, 287–9; Nicola M. Sutherland, *Princes, Politics and Religion 1547–1589* (London, 1984), pp. 39–41, 163–4; Robert M. Kingdon, *Geneva and the Consolidation of the French Protestant Movement 1564–1572* (Geneva, 1967), pp. 162–3; Thorp, 'Catholic Conspiracy', pp. 435 ff.

[83] Melville, *Memoirs*, pp. 146–7; Tytler, *History*, VII, pp. 20–21; Keith, *History*, II, pp. 391–2.

[84] Knox, *Works*, VI, pp. 402–3: 'Those Fathers of the last Counsall of Trent ... in one of their last sessions have thus concluded: "All Lutheriens, Calvinistes, and such as are of the new Religion, shall be utterlie exterminate. The beginning shalbe in France ... France and Germanie (say they) being by these measures so chastised, abased, and conducted to the obedience of the holie Romaine Church, the Fathers dout not but tyme shall provide counsal and commoditie, that the rest of the realmes about may be reduced to one flok".' The orthography of 'Lutheriens' and 'Calvinistes' suggests a French or Genevan source.

[85] John Durkan, 'Mary's Library', in Lynch, *Mary Stewart*, p. 87.

[86] As articulated in the report of Pius IV's Consistory speech on 12 October 1565: 'Hortatusque est protectores principum qui aderant ut principes suos, imperatorem,

Finally, the date the fast actually took place has been a problem. The Assembly had specified the eight days between 23 February and 3 March 1566. Most of the near-contemporary sources declare that it was held a week later, coinciding with the postponed Parliament.[87] This view was orthodox for many generations, and helped fuel the notion in a genre of somewhat anti-Knox literature[88] that the whole exercise was an outrageously self-justifying preliminary to the Protestant assassination of Riccio (even though he seems occasionally to have received the reformed eucharist![89]). This whole construction received a setback when Hay Fleming published the entry in the minute book of the Canongate kirk session, showing that the fast took place as originally planned, the week before Parliament met.[90] However, this is not to deny the role of religious motives in Riccio's death – something a modern writer does to the extent that references to the religious factor in that affair in the contemporary sources are edited out in order to justify the assertion, that Riccio was 'sacrificed on the altar of politics [only], not religion'.[91]

To sum up, in the fasting programme, Knox recycles the ancient tradition[92] of fasting and prophecy along radically biblical lines – in this

regem christianissimum, regem catholicum admonerent, hoc ad eorum officium pertinere, ut Catholicos omni ope atque auxilio tueantur', Pollen, *Papal Negotiations*, p. 229. See also von Pastor, *Popes*, XVI, pp. 288–9.

[87] Knox, *Works*, II, pp. 178, 180 (Continuator); *Diurnal of Remarkable Occurrents*, p. 89; Calderwood, *History*, II, p. 317 (wrongly printed as 'May').

[88] For example: Walter Goodall, *An Examination of the Letters, said to be written by Mary Queen of Scots, to James Earl of Bothwell* (2 vols, Edinburgh, 1754), I, pp. 247–51, 257–8, 272–3; Keith, *History*, II, pp. 407–11; John Hosack, *Mary Queen of Scots and Her Accusers* (Edinburgh and London, 1879), p. 135; Tytler, *History*, VII, pp. 7, 21 ff., 26, 33–4; John Skelton, *Mary Stuart* (London, 1893), p. 79; Ridley, *Knox*, pp. 435–52.

[89] *The Buik of the Kirk of the Canagait*, ed. Alma B. Calderwood (Edinburgh, 1961), p. 109.

[90] Ibid., pp. 39–40; Hay Fleming, *Mary*, pp. 397–8. See also Hume Brown, *Knox*, II, pp. 304–10.

[91] Goodare, 'Mary's Catholic Interlude', p. 166. Moreover, it is there stated that 'even Knox and Buchanan portray the conspirators as angered *solely* by a hastily devised forfeiture campaign'. But see the actual Knox: [The conspiring Lords] 'made a bond to stand to the religion and liberties of the country, and to free themselves of the slavery of the villain David Riccio', *History*, II, p. 179; and the actual Buchanan: 'The heads were: "For the establishing [of] religion, as it was provided for at the queen's return to Scotland, to restore the persons lately banished ... and to destroy Rizzio"', *History*, p. 438.

[92] Compare Rudolph Arbesmann, 'Fasting and Prophecy in Pagan and Christian Antiquity', *Traditio*, 7 (1949–51), pp. 1–71.

respect he is ultra-conservative. He hopes thereby to furnish a potent occasional instrument of reform, amendment, and protest in Church and society. Corporate public fasting is to be an aid to religious sanitization (the elimination of Roman Catholicism), ecclesiastical security, social justice, and public and private morality. Furthermore, the document provides an illustrative cameo of Knox's mindset, his national and international perceptions, and his understanding of his prophetic vocation. On these grounds, it is surprising that this swan-song text has hitherto escaped serious attention.

PART THREE
The Scottish Reformation

CHAPTER TEN

Knox, Cecil and the British Dimension of the Scottish Reformation

Stephen Alford

John Knox was an extremely busy man in the spring and summer of 1559. In April he wrote to Elizabeth I's Principal Secretary, William Cecil, in an effort to build up English support for the Scottish Reformation. Knox reminded Cecil of his 'common iniquitye' and 'horrible defection from the trueth' during the reign of Mary Tudor, and set out to defend *The First Blast of the Trumpet*; then, typically, he asked for Cecil's support and encouragement. In July Knox began to act as clerk to the Protestant Lords of the Congregation. But perhaps most striking of all for historians of Britain in the sixteenth century, Knox called for English solidarity with Scotland. 'My eie hath long looked to a perpetual concord betuix these two Realmes,' he told Cecil in early July, 'the occasion wharof is now most present, yf God shall move your hartes unfeanedlie to speak the saim for humilitie of Christ Jesus crucified.' Events in Scotland were 'somwhat violent, becaus the adversareis be stubburn'. This was a Reformation which echoed the Edwardian stripping of the altars in England, reinforced by an expression of 'the amytie and league betwene you and us contracted and begun in Christ Jesus'.[1]

In 1559 Knox was not, of course, a new player on the political and religious scene. Jane Dawson has drawn a distinction between an English Knox writing for an English audience in 1558 and a Scottish Knox; and there were also British and European dimensions to his work and personality which stretched back into the 1540s and 1550s.[2] He knew the English ecclesiastical scene in the 1550s; he knew the north of England and ministered to congregations in Berwick and Newcastle. And this was during a period when men like Protector Somerset, the

---

[1] For Knox's early letters to Cecil, see Knox, *Works*, VI, pp. 15–21 (10 April 1559), 31–2 (28 June 1559), 45–7 (19 July 1559); for the originals, see PRO SP 52/1.

[2] Jane E.A. Dawson, 'The Two John Knoxes: England, Scotland and the 1558 Tracts', *JEH*, 42 (1991), pp. 555–76, especially p. 556, n. 3.

Duke of Northumberland, Cecil, William Patten and John Hooper were beginning to make strong connections between England's traditional claim to power over Scotland and a distinctive form of British Protestantism. Knox himself, in July 1559, wrote to Cecil of 'materis' in which he had 'laubored ever sence the death of King Edward': links between England and Scotland, common religion, and united dynasties.[3]

So there were, to a degree, shared aims. The main subject of this chapter is the Scottish Reformation and union or friendship between Scotland and England: what this meant, the languages or vocabularies that were used, ecclesiastical concerns, and political dimensions. It will compare and contrast the British creeds of Knox and Cecil: not to argue that one was better or more advanced than the other but to demonstrate that they were different and complementary. In the eyes of Knox a sixteenth-century courtier or councillor could become a politique, a term which has bedevilled later Tudor political history. Northumberland fumed in 1552, Cecil patiently endorsed Knox's uncomfortably challenging letters of 1559, and William Maitland of Lethington heard the charge levelled against him in the General Assembly in 1564.[4] These men shared the same faith and were part of the same political and religious tradition, but for Knox it was the preacher, and not the politician, who was one step nearer to becoming a prophet.

England's relationship with Scotland in the 1560s could be defined or conceptualized in two ways. First, there was a claim to English feudal superiority which could be traced back through medieval histories and chronicles to the myth of Brutus. The basic argument was that the English monarch was a superior monarch because medieval Scottish kings had paid homage to their southern counterparts and – as a second line of attack – because the Archbishop of York had traditionally exercised archepiscopal jurisdiction over Scotland. These were keynotes of Henry VIII's propaganda campaign in the 1540s, explored, explained, and restated in *A Declaration, Conteynyng the Just Causes and Consyderations, of this Present Warre with the Scottis*, printed by Thomas Berthelet in 1542.[5] But the traditional account of Brutus's division

---

[3] Knox to Cecil, 12 July 1559, PRO SP 52/1, fo. 111r; Knox, *Works*, VI, p. 46.

[4] Northumberland to Cecil, 7 December 1552, SP 10/15, fo. 137r, printed in Patrick Fraser Tytler (ed.), *England under the Reigns of Edward VI and Mary ...* (2 vols, London, 1839), II, p. 148; Knox, *On Rebellion*, pp. 182–209.

[5] *STC*, no. 9179; cf. Marcus Merriman, 'War and Propaganda during the "Rough Wooing"', *Scottish Tradition*, 9–10 (1979–80), pp. 20–30.

of his kingdom between his three sons – when the eldest, Locrine, received England and his two younger brothers received Scotland and Wales – was significant enough even in 1569 to grace the title-page of Richard Grafton's *A Chronicle at Large and Meere History of the Affayres of Englande*, a book dedicated to William Cecil. Among Grafton's main sources were Caxton, Geoffrey of Monmouth, and Ranulph Higden's *Polychronicon*.[6]

The second way of defining England's relationship with Scotland was, on the face of it, more enlightened and positive. Henry VIII's campaigns against Scotland in the early 1540s were fought on the grounds of dominant superiority; but although Protector Somerset's invasion was just as aggressive, English propaganda changed to suit the religious priorities of the new regime. William Patten was a member of Somerset's expedition into Scotland in 1547 and wrote as an enthusiastic Edwardian unionist. England and Scotland were 'seperate by seas from all oother nacions, in customes and condicions littell differinge, in shape and langage nothyng at all'. Significantly, Patten used William Cecil's diary to reconstruct the details of the campaign.[7] But there are more personal connections. John Hooper, the Edwardian Bishop of Gloucester, a close and sympathetic correspondent of Cecil's in the early 1550s, and (like Knox) a Marian exile, published *A Declaracion of Christe and of His Offyce* in 1547. Hooper's sections on Anglo-Scottish unity relied, in part, on increasingly stereotypical statements of friendship, but his vocabulary is still important. He wanted 'thold Amite and frendshippe restoryd that God by the creacion of the worold appoyntyd to be in that one Realme and Ilond devydyd from all the worold by imparkyng of the sea'. There was a 'naturall discent of parentayge and blud' and a unity of language and 'maner and condicion of lyvyng'.[8] Hooper blurred some serious distinctions between Scotland and England but his themes and arguments became commonplaces. *An Epistle or Exhortacion, to Unitie & Peace*, attributed to Somerset and printed by Richard Grafton in 1548, emphasized the 'one bloude, one lignage and parentage' of the 'twoo brethren of one Islande of greate Britayn'. There was a common language. Grafton also extended the main political opportunity for Anglo-Scottish union – the marriage of Queen Mary Stewart and Prince Edward Tudor – to the two kingdoms, 'but that it

---

[6] *STC*, no. 12147; cf. Roger A. Mason, 'Scotching the Brut: Politics, History and National Myth in Sixteenth-Century Britain', in Roger A. Mason (ed.), *Scotland and England 1286–1815* (Edinburgh, 1987), pp. 60–84.

[7] William Patten, *The Expedicion into Scotlande of the most woorthely fortunate Prince Edward, Duke of Soomerset ...* (*STC*, no. 19479; London, 1548), sig. B2r.

[8] (*STC*, no. 13745; London, 1547), sig. A3r.

was Gods pleasure it should bee so, that these twoo realmes should joyne in mariage, and by a godly Sacrament, make a Godly, perpetuall, and moste frendly unitie and concord'.[9]

Some Scots also pressed the merits of the union and tackled the issue politically or felt the urge to go into print. Knox was tutor to the sons of John Cockburn of Ormiston, an 'assured Scot' who collaborated with the English in the 1540s. Alexander Whitelaw of New Grange converted fellow Scots 'to the fayth and opinioun of Ingland', carried instructions to English commanders, and travelled to London between 1547 and 1548.[10] It was Whitelaw who visited Knox in Edinburgh in July 1559, on a day when Knox also received a servant travelling between Sir Henry Percy and William Kirkcaldy of Grange; Percy was Cecil's main contact with the Lords of the Congregation.[11] One of Whitelaw's and Knox's Edwardian contemporaries, the Edinburgh merchant James Henrisoun, published *An Exhortacion to the Scottes to Conforme themselves to the Honourable, Expedient & Godly Union betweene the Realmes of England & Scotland* in 1547. Some of its main themes are a common racial identity, providence, Protestantism and union through the marriage of Mary and Edward.[12]

But there was no clear dividing line between the arguments for English superiority and the call for Protestant solidarity. Protector Somerset wanted the abolition of the jurisdiction of Rome, the preservation of law in Scotland, and unity 'in ane name by the name of Britounis'.[13] As part of the Edwardian campaign of persuasion – and in the same year that he published *An Epistle or Exhortacion* – Richard Grafton printed *An Epitome of the Title that the Kynges Majestie of Englande, hathe to Sovereigntie of Scotlande*; in it he discussed the 'whole Empire & name of greate Briteigne' – 'I mean this realme now called Englande the onely supreme seat of the empire of greate Briteigne' – and referred to the evidence of homages and archepiscopal

---

[9] (STC¹, no. 9181; STC², no. 22268; London, 1548), sig. A4v–A5r; A6r–v; B7v.

[10] M.H. Merriman, 'The Assured Scots: Scottish Collaborators with England during the Rough Wooing', *SHR*, 47 (1968), pp. 23–4.

[11] Knox to Cecil, 19 July 1559, Knox, *Works*, VI, p. 46.

[12] Roger A. Mason, 'The Scottish Reformation and the Origins of Anglo-British Imperialism', in Roger A. Mason (ed.), *Scots and Britons: Scottish Political Thought and the Union of 1603* (Cambridge, 1994), pp. 161–86, at pp. 171–5; Jane E.A. Dawson, 'William Cecil and the British Dimension of Early Elizabethan Foreign Policy', *History*, 74 (1989), pp. 196–216; Merriman, 'Assured Scots', pp. 22–3; Marcus Merriman, 'James Henrisoun and "Great Britain": British Union and the Scottish Commonweal', in Mason (ed.), *Scotland and England*, pp. 85–112 .

[13] *The Warrender Papers*, eds Annie I. Cameron and Robert S. Rait (2 vols, SHS, Edinburgh, 1931–32), I, p. 17.

jurisdiction over Scotland.[14] John Hooper called for Anglo-Scottish Protestant brotherhood; he also talked about Scotland's traditional 'disobedience unto here Naturall and Laufull prince and superiour powre the Kynges majestie of Englond'.[15] There were two competing but, at the same time, oddly complementary traditions: the call for Protestant unity backed up by the argument that England had a historically valid claim to superiority over the other British kingdoms. By the 1550s there was a comprehensive and developed argument for an Anglo-British Protestant imperialism connected to the concept of union through dynastic marriage.[16] Both Knox and Cecil understood and, in some ways, had helped to form this rather schizophrenic political tradition. If there were differences between the two men, there was at least also some sense of shared and common ground.

The death of Mary Tudor in 1558 and the religious and political rebellion against Mary of Guise by the Lords of the Congregation in 1559 were massive political opportunities. Knox, notoriously, fatally timed his *First Blast of the Trumpet*, although in his letters to Elizabeth and Cecil in 1559 he seemed hardly embarrassed by its message. Nevertheless, Knox's *First Blast* did not help the English councillors who supported financial or military support for the Congregation. The Elizabethan regime had to ask itself some serious practical questions over the summer, autumn, and early winter of 1559. Could England support subjects in opposition to their monarch? What form should aid take: purely financial or a military expedition? Was it strategically necessary to pre-empt a French attack against England by entering Scotland? But the core issue – and the one which Protestant councillors found it so difficult to broach with such an instinctively conservative Queen – was one of identity and solidarity. The English Privy Council knew that it was dealing with support for a Protestant revolution and by the beginning of July 1559 it had the names of the main members of the Congregation, men 'in band with them who hathe not yet declarit them selfis', and others who would 'subscrybe with them to keip owt the frenche men'.[17]

---

[14] (*STC*, no. 3196; London, 1548), sig. A3v, A5v; E2r–E4v (homages); C1r (jurisdiction).

[15] John Hooper, *A Declaracion of Christe and His Offyce* (London, 1547), sig. A3r–v.

[16] Mason, 'Anglo-British Imperialism', in Mason (ed.), *Scots and Britons*, pp. 161–86; Jane E.A. Dawson, 'Anglo-Scottish Protestant Culture and Integration in Sixteenth-Century Britain', in Steven G. Ellis and Sarah Barber (eds), *Conquest and Union: Fashioning a British State, 1485–1725* (London and New York, 1995), pp. 87–114.

[17] Kirkcaldy of Grange to Percy, 1 July 1559, PRO SP 52/1, fo. 94r.

But could the Scots be supported as fellow Protestants or was it better to argue for the preservation of an oppressed ancient nobility? The Congregation itself was extremely conscious of these two agendas and identities.[18] So what Cecil had to do in 1559 and 1560 – and indeed throughout the rest of the decade – was balance the practical against the openly ideological. Godly amity and British Protestant unity *did* underpin Cecil's concept of the relationship between England and Scotland; but he was equally prepared to argue for the preservation of an ancient nobility and the strategic benefits of forcing the French out of Scotland. Even this argument did absolutely nothing to convince Elizabeth. In perhaps the first main debate on British and European policy of the reign – and the only one in the 1560s in which final individual judgements are listed – 14 out of 16 councillors argued for financial aid for the Scots and the defence of England; five out of 16 'stode dowtfull towchyng any exploict into scotland'; and only one, the Earl of Arundel, argued against military intervention 'and ageynst any oppen, or costly ayding of the scottes'. The main issue was not ideology; it was a difference of strategic opinion.[19]

In 1559 Knox could speak the language of Anglo-Scottish Protestant solidarity, using a vocabulary which had been moulded by the Edwardian experience. Two key terms were 'league' and 'amity'. It is true that William Lamb, whose *Ane Resonyng of ane Scottis and Inglis Merchand betuix Rowand and Lionis* was written as a reply to English claims of superiority over Scotland, used both words to refer to treaties between monarchs and marriage; it is equally true that both Elizabeth and Mary Stewart used league and amity as terms to describe the relationship between cousins and queens.[20] But, at the same time, the propaganda campaign of the late 1540s gave the words a potentially Protestant edge. *An Epistle or Exhortacion*, in 1548, made a connection between 'the Gospell of Christ' and the call of the English to the Scots 'to libertie, to amitie, to equalitie with us'. This was the great opportunity 'to joyne in mariage from high to low, bothe the realmes, to make of one Isle one realme, in love, amitie, concorde, peace, and Charitie'. More significantly, this was not a call for mutual toleration but 'a godly purpose, of uniting the realmes'.[21] And these were some of the main

---

[18] Roger A. Mason, 'Covenant and Commonweal: The Language of Politics in Reformation Scotland', in Norman Macdougall (ed.), *Church, Politics and Society: Scotland 1408–1929* (Edinburgh, 1983), pp. 97–126.

[19] 27 December 1559, PRO SP 12/7, fo. 190v.

[20] William Lamb, *Ane Resonyng of ane Scottis and Inglis Merchand betuix Rowand and Lionis*, ed. Roderick J. Lyall (Aberdeen, 1985), pp. 23, 31.

[21] *An Epistle or Exhortacion*, sig. A3v, A7v, A8r, B8r; cf. Dawson, 'Anglo-Scottish Protestant Culture', in Ellis and Barber (eds), *Conquest and Union*, pp. 99–103.

themes of Knox's correspondence with Cecil, of his drafts for the Congregation to Elizabeth and Cecil, and of the Congregation's instructions to Knox in June and July 1559. They figured, moreover, in Anthony Gilby's *Admonition to England and Scotland* added as an appendix to *The Appellation of John Knoxe* in 1558. 'O England and Scotland,' Gilby wrote, 'both makinge one Iland most happie, if you could know your own happines.' The depressing reality of 1558 was that the opportunity for a 'godlie conjunction' between the two kingdoms, the attempt by 'faithfull' Scots and the 'earnest travail of our English nation' to introduce Scotland into 'the Lords vineyard in the tyme of king Edward' had failed.[22]

But 1559 was different. The unionist Whitelaw was in Edinburgh in July, with Knox at Berwick in August, and carrying messages for the Congregation in the same month.[23] In a letter to Cecil in July Knox called for a 'perpetuall accord' between England and Scotland. A 'perpetuall amytie', 'joyfull connection' and an 'amytie and league betwene you and us contracted and begun in Christ Jesus' were some of the striking phrases of Knox's draft of a text from the Congregation to Cecil.[24] And these key words kept reappearing and were always expressions of the advancement of 'true religion' in England and Scotland. In July 1559 the Congregation gave Knox 'commission to speak and propose' a number of 'Heades'. The first maintained that the 'league' between Scotland and England was a new one, 'other then heirtofoir hath bein contracted or commoned upon betuix the two Realmes'. The Congregation felt that the league it wanted had two causes:

> formar, That the glory of God, the trew preaching of Christ Jesus, with the rycht ministratioun of his Sacramentis, may be universallie and openlie manteaned in this Yle, and that the tyrannye and superstition of that Romane Antichrist may be uterlie suppressed and abolissed in the same. Secondarlie, That the liberties, lawes, and priviledges of both these Realmes may remane inviolated by any straunge or foren power ... .[25]

Perhaps the most interesting point is that Cecil could speak exactly the same language. In early July 1559 he wrote a letter to Sir Henry Percy, the contents of which he expected Percy to pass on to Kirkcaldy of Grange. Cecil wanted to know 'what manner an amytye might ensue

---

[22] Anthony Gilby, *An Admonition to England and Scotland to Call them to Repentance*, in *The Appellation of John Knoxe* ... (STC, no. 15063; Geneva, 1558), pp. 59v, 64v–65r, 66v, reprinted in Knox, *Works*, IV, pp. 553–71.

[23] Knox, *Works*, VI, pp. 46, 61, 65.

[24] Ibid., VI, pp. 31, 41–2.

[25] Ibid., VI, pp. 56–7.

betwixt theis ij realmes, and how the same might be hoped to be perpetuall'. He wanted 'the perpetuite of a brotherly and nationall frendshipp betwixt the ij realmes'; but, like the Congregation, he associated the amity with protection against the 'aunciént libertyes' of the nobility of Scotland and the maintenance of 'the truth of Christian relligion ageynst impycte'.[26] A couple of weeks later, he wrote to the senior members of the Congregation and wished that the abandonment of idolatry in England could be extended to Scotland, 'and therby this terrestryall kyngdom of Christ may be dilated thrugh this noble Ile, and so the old Great ennemyes of the trew Chirch of God, may be kept owt, and putt to confusion'.[27] Cecil had already corrected a letter from the Privy Council to 'the Lords of Scotland'. There is a sense in which the four men who signed it – the Marquess of Northampton, the Earls of Bedford and Pembroke, and Lord William Howard of Effingham – had almost dusted down their copies of Grafton and Hooper. The draft maintained that they would 'not neglect such Godly and honorable enterprisees, uppon hope that therby this famose Ile, maye be conjoyned at the last in hartes as it is in Contynent with one sea, and in one uniformyte of language, manners and Conditions'.[28] After the negotiation of the Treaty of Berwick, Cecil promised the Earl of Huntly that he would for his

> part assure yow that what soever it shall please God to offer to the concord of theis ij realmes being at the Creation knitt in one Ile and with one language, and one sort of people having no difference but name, I will employe my indevor to the performance therin of Godes favor and good will.[29]

In *Scottish National Consciousness in the Age of James VI*, Arthur Williamson argued that Knox understood the implications of the revolution of 1559 because 'reformation also implied union'.[30] And godly union, in 1559 and 1560, meant dynastic union. But there were no obvious or serious candidates, a thought which crossed the mind of one of Lord Robert Dudley's correspondents. 'Me thinkethe it were to be wisshed of all wyse men,' he wrote, 'and her Majesties good subjectes, that the one of these two Quenes of the Ile of Bryttaine were transfformed

---

[26] 4 July 1559, PRO SP 52/1, fo. 101r–v.
[27] 28 July 1559, PRO SP 52/1, fo. 147r.
[28] 27 July 1559, PRO SP 52/1, fo. 146r.
[29] 18 March 1560, Hatfield House Library, Hertfordshire, Cecil Papers 152, fo. 68r.
[30] Arthur H. Williamson, *Scottish National Consciousness in the Age of James VI: The Apocalypse, the Union and the Shaping of Scotland's Public Culture* (Edinburgh, 1979), p. 15.

into the shape of a man, to make so happie a mariage, as therby ther might be an unitie of the holl Ile, and their appendances.' If the Queen's subjects had read their histories, they would understand that 'estates hathe by no on[e] thing growen so greate, and Lastyd in their greatnes, as by mariages, whiche have unytid contreyres, that do confyne together'.[31] Dynastic union had been the key to the Anglo-Scottish promise of the early 1540s. Even as late as 1558 Anthony Gilby told Scots how the crucial opportunity had been lost when Sir Ralph Sadler went into Scotland 'to perfurm the mariage contracted betwixt king Edward and your yonge quene' but 'finally by the pride of the papistes was that leage broken'.[32] Perhaps the only dynastic option in 1559 and 1560 was a marriage between Elizabeth and James Hamilton, Earl of Arran. This was enthusiastically proposed by Protestant Scots but like other marriage possibilities for the Queen – with Eric XIV of Sweden and Robert Dudley – the plan fizzled out.

Cecil's sense of the relationship between England and Scotland was different. He was profoundly aware of the need to bind the two kingdoms (and Ireland if possible) into a defensive, Protestant alliance for the preservation of the regime and the ecclesiastical settlement in England. But the key was not dynasty: it was a political and constitutional settlement based, in its most embryonic form in 1559, on Councils and Parliaments and, at its most developed in 1568, secured by a tripartite treaty between Elizabeth, Mary, and James VI, underwritten by the imperial (and thus superior) power of the English monarch. In 1559 and 1568 Cecil used the forbidden language of Edward I's Great Cause – very probably in private, possibly for consumption by Elizabeth, and definitely in an attempt to work out 'Whither it be mete that England shuld helpe the Nobilite, and Protestantes of Scotland to expell the french or no'. This was one element of Anglo-British Protestant imperialism in its purest form. England had 'a just and unfeyned title, of longer continuance, than the frendshipp, betwixt scotland and fraunce, unto the superioryte of Scotland' and there were 'good auncient and habundant storyes' to prove it: homages, Scottish 'accesses to the Perlementes of england', 'the Episcopall Jurisdiction of the sea of york over scotland', and so on. The principle was simple: Mary Stewart owed homage to Elizabeth, the English monarch was bound to defend Scotland 'no less than the emperor ought to defend the state of Millane',

---

[31] BL Harley MS 6990, fo. 5r, printed in Joseph Stevenson (ed.), *Selections from Unpublished Manuscripts in the College of Arms and the British Museum illustrating the Reign of Mary Queen of Scotland 1543–1568* (Maitland Club, Glasgow, 1837), p. 84.

[32] *The Appellation of John Knoxe* (STC, no. 15063; Geneva, 1558), p. 66r; Knox, *Works*, IV, p. 560.

and the issue was not one of helping subjects to rebel against their monarch 'but betwixt a superior kyng and a realme of the one parte, and an inferior kyng alone joyning with straungers on the other part'.[33] This was not abstruse historical research. Cecil used the same sort of evidence nine years later to argue that Elizabeth could act as the 'umpere and principal arbitrer' of a proposed settlement which would have endorsed the complete supervision of the Queen of Scots by Council and Parliament, the protection of Regent Moray's regime, security for Scotland's religion, and the ability of the Queen of England acting with supervisory institutions north of the border to remove Mary's Crown if she broke the terms of the treaty.[34]

Knox must have been profoundly unconvinced by English claims of imperial superiority. He may well have found them threatening: statements of archepiscopal jurisdiction over Scotland, reinforced by an English model of royal supremacy over the Church, and backed up by military action could have wrecked the pattern of the Scottish Reformation.[35] In fact, the reality was certainly less disturbing – debate, discussion and the interchange of ideas between Protestant Anglo-Scots. Soon after its publication, Elizabeth's representative in Edinburgh, Thomas Randolph, presented Lord James Stewart with an edition of John Jewel's *Apologia Ecclesiae Anglicanae*.[36] As early as July 1559 Cecil asked Argyll, Glencairn, James Stewart, Boyd and Ochiltree to consider the Danish Reformation. He knew of 'no better example in any reformed state than I have hard to be in Dennmark'. 'I lyke no spoyle,' he told the Congregation,

> but I allow to have good thynges putt to good uses: as to the enrichyng of the Crowne, to the help of the yowth of the nobilite, to the mayntenance of ministery in the Chirch, of lerning in scooles,

---

[33] BL Cotton MS Caligula B. 10, fos 33r–34r, 86v; cf. Arthur Clifford (ed.), *The State Papers and Letters of Sir Ralph Sadler* (2 vols, Edinburgh, 1809), I, pp. 378–9.

[34] BL Cotton MS Caligula C. 1, fo. 230v; Stephen Alford, 'William Cecil and the British Succession Crisis of the 1560s' (unpublished University of St Andrews PhD thesis, 1996), pp. 199–204.

[35] There is no evidence that this was ever a serious possibility, but cf. some of the early Stuart proposals for Anglo-Scottish ecclesiastical union, discussed in Bruce R. Galloway and Brian P. Levack (eds), *The Jacobean Union: Six Tracts of 1604* (SHS, Edinburgh, 1985), pp. xxxix–xl; and John Morrill, 'A British Patriarchy? Ecclesiastical Imperialism under the Early Stuarts', in Anthony Fletcher and Peter Roberts (eds), *Religion, Culture and Society in Early Modern Britain* (Cambridge, 1994), pp. 209–37. Knox's attitude to an English-style royal supremacy is discussed further by Roger Mason in Chapter 8 of this volume.

[36] For a facsimile of Randolph's dedication on the flyleaf of the *Apologia*, see Gordon Donaldson, *Scottish Church History* (Edinburgh, 1985), p. 121 facing.

and to releve the poore membres of Christ being in body and lymmes impotent.

Neither in Cecil's letter nor in the Danish *Ordinatio Ecclesiastica* (1537) is there a bishop in sight; in fact, there are real similarities between the *Ordinatio* – with its provisions for schools, ministers and the poor, superintendents, doctrine, sacraments, and rites and ceremonies – and the rejected Scottish *Book of Discipline* drafted by Knox and others in 1560.[37] In 'A memoriall of certain pointes meete for restoring the Realme of Scotland to the Auncient Weale', written in August 1559, Cecil called for Scotland's freedom from idolatry; and in 1568, in a paper which set down the principles for a negotiated treaty between the Queen of Scots, her subjects, and Elizabeth, he argued for the preservation of 'The relligion allredy stablished in scotland', and 'no other to be used except the same, and the formular of england'.[38] In the context of the union tracts of 1604, it was probably Robert Pont who was the nearest to Cecil's position when he pointed out that the English and Scottish Churches 'agree in doctrine, and their difference in some matters of discipline empeacheth not so their religion but that their may be a sweet harmony in their kingedomes and unity in their churches'. Cecil wanted solidarity and close co-operation; he did not look for – or even think that England and Scotland needed – complete ecclesiastical uniformity.[39]

But effective and protected religion also meant British political security and this, in turn, involved defensive alliances against organized European Catholic conspiracy. From the earliest days of Elizabeth's reign – and perhaps more coherently after England's loss of Calais at the Treaty of Cateau-Cambrésis in spring 1559 – Cecil established the vocabulary of anti-Catholicism so familiar to historians of the Elizabethan crises of the 1580s. As Principal Secretary he collected, collated and synthesized intelligence from the Continent, from Ireland and Scotland, and from England; he often presented his analyses to the Council. Cecil was convinced that there was a strong relationship between the conspiracies of the Guise, the King of Spain, the Pope, dissaffected Englishmen and Mary Stewart's claim to the English throne. Every

---

[37] 28 July 1559, SP 52/1, fos 147v–148r; Gordon Donaldson, '"The example of Denmark" in the Scottish Reformation', in Donaldson, *Scottish Church History*, p. 67.

[38] Alford, 'Cecil', pp. 282, 298.

[39] Galloway and Levack, *Jacobean Union*, p. 7; Dawson, 'Anglo-Scottish Protestant Culture', pp. 99–100; cf. Jenny Wormald, 'The Creation of Britain: Multiple Kingdoms or Core and Colonies?', *Transactions of the Royal Historical Society*, sixth series, 2 (1992), pp. 175–94, at p. 177.

single piece of evidence which developed or explained this model in the
ten years immediately after the Scottish and English Reformations –
French activity in Scotland in 1559, panic over potentially disloyal
justices of the peace in 1564, the Queen of Scots' marriage to Darnley
in 1565 – was absorbed and rationalized. In 1569 he explored a metaphor: the kings of France and Spain and the Pope were using Mary
Stewart as an 'instrument' to operate on their 'pacient', Elizabeth.[40]
Cecil was, like Knox, strongly committed to the overthrow of Antichrist; he was also in an important political position and able to do
something about it at a national and an international level. A move to
the east was one possibility: alliance with Protestant German princes
was mentioned in 1559, 1562, 1568 and 1569.[41] But for 'inward peace'
in Scotland and the security of England there had to be 'a perpetuall
good amyty betwixt these ij realmes'. In May 1569 Cecil argued that
'the gretest felicite that can be devised for scotland is to have a perpetuall
peace and love stablished betwixt it and England'.[42] A month later, it
was equally clear for England 'that ther is no contrey with which it may
be more profittably knitt than with scotland, and next to it with some
leage of the princes Protestantes of the Emperor'.[43] But Cecil had already made his definitive statement. In 1568 he maintained that England
and Scotland 'being frendly and peacibly Joyned with Irland quieted,
may savely preserve them selves with good government, from the malice
of france, and the rest of Christendom'.[44]

In May 1568 John Wood, a graduate of St Andrews and servant to the
Earl of Moray, complained to Sir Nicholas Throckmorton about the
changing nature of politics. He had seen 'these latte mutationis chancit
to us whome to novvelteis are no novelteis sa wele ar we accustumytt
with changis'.[45] Strangely enough, one of the most serious changes in

---

[40] Hatfield House Library, Hertfordshire, Cecil Papers 157, fo. 2r, printed in Samuel
Haynes (ed.), *Collection of State Papers … left by William Cecil, Lord Burghley* (London, 1740), p. 579.

[41] Cecil to Throckmorton, 24 March 1562, BL Additional MS 35831, fo. 22r–v; E.I.
Kouri, *England and the Attempts to Form a Protestant Alliance in the late 1560s: A Case
Study in European Diplomacy* (Helsinki, 1981); E.I. Kouri, 'For True Faith or National
Interest? Queen Elizabeth I and the Protestant Powers', in E.I. Kouri and Tom Scott
(eds), *Politics and Society in Reformation Europe* (Basingstoke and London, 1987),
pp. 411–36.

[42] 'Consideration of the matters betwixt the Quene of Scottes and hir sonne and
subjectes', 1 May 1569, BL Cotton MS Caligula C. 1, fos 413r, 414r.

[43] 7 June 1569, PRO SP 12/51, fo. 10v.

[44] May 1568, BL Cotton MS Caligula C. 1, fo. 98r.

[45] 14 May 1568, Magdalene College, Cambridge, PL 2502, fo. 795.

the relationship between England and Scotland occurred in 1561 and not in the crisis years of 1559–60 and 1567–69. Mary Stewart seemed fairly easy to deal with when she was in France and, in spite of the intricacies and dangers of trying a sovereign monarch, the period after May 1568 and her confinement in England gave councillors like Cecil the opportunity to sort out the political state of Britain once and for all. But between August 1561 – when the Queen of Scots returned to Scotland – and 1567 – the outbreak of civil war in Scotland – the English Privy Council found itself apparently robbed of one of its most valuable assets: sympathetic Scots like Maitland of Lethington and Moray. Politically, this was extremely disconcerting. But Knox found the change in attitude equally disturbing and it frustrated and insulted him when some of the major players in the revolution apparently turned their backs on the godly. John Wood was exactly one of those men. In Book IV of his *History*, written before the end of 1566, Knox recorded how in December 1561 Wood, 'who before had shown himself very fervent in the cause of God ... plainly refused ever to assist the [General] Assembly again'. This was part of a 'Division between the Lords and the Ministers'. And lurking in the background were Knox's enemies after 1561, the 'courtiers'.[46]

Two years later, in 1568, Knox was on better terms with Wood. But Knox's position was clear: he was 'a painfull Preacher' of God's 'blessed Evangell'. When he shared with Wood his fears of 'domesticall enemies' in Scotland and the malice of the Pope and the Guise, they occupied common ground.[47] But Knox found it impossible to adapt to the politics and the religion of Mary's return to Scotland. He found it galling that James Stewart protected the Queen of Scots' Mass and that the principle 'that the subjects might not lawfully take her Mass from her' was turned into the issue of 'the obedience dew unto princes'. John Row, George Hay, Robert Hamilton and Knox argued against some of the shining (and perhaps even radical) lights of the Scottish Reformation – the Earl of Morton, Lord James Stewart, William Maitland of Lethington and George Buchanan's fellow commissioner in the Moray camp at York in 1568, the shadowy Clerk Register James McGill of Nether Rankeillor.[48] There were 'courtiers' opposing true religion from the beginning. In 1561; in June 1564, during Maitland of Lethington's 'harangue' at the General Assembly; and in 1565, when Knox 'in these most corrupt dayes' preached a sermon to 'rancke papistes, dissembled

---

[46] Knox, *History*, II, p. 25; Knox, *Works*, II, p. 295.

[47] Knox, *Works*, VI, pp. 558–9 (14 February 1568), 560–61 (10 September 1568).

[48] Knox, *History*, II, p. 23; Knox, *Works*, II, pp. 291–2; J.H. Burns, *The True Law of Kingship: Concepts of Monarchy in Early-Modern Scotland* (Oxford, 1996), p. 174.

Hipocrites, & no small number of covetous clawbaks [sycophants, flatterers] of the new court'. His text was taken from Isaiah: 'For loe the Lorde commeth out of his place to visite the iniquitie of the inhabitants of the earth upon them: and the earth shall disclose her bloude, and shall no more hide her slayne.'[49]

To Knox these changes were distressing. 'To speak plane,' he wrote to Cecil two months after the Queen of Scots' return, 'those that alwaies have had the favor and estimation of the most godlie, begyn to cum in contempt, becaus thei oppon not themselves mor stoutlie against impietie.' The position of the Earl of Moray and William Maitland of Lethington was a particular cause for concern. 'Ye know my Lord James and Ledingthon, whome yf God do not otherwiese conduct, thei ar liek to lose that which, not without travall, hath heirtofore bien conquest.'[50] Two years later, he told the Earl of Leicester that 'zeall, joyned with knowledg, ones appeared in a great part of our nobilitie' but it was 'now judged to be waxen cold'. 'Yea, I am eschamed and confounded within myself, when I considder so great mutacion within so schort a space.'[51] But there were wider implications. The realities of Anglo-Scottish politics post-1561 altered the relationship between the British Protestant élites. Contact and correspondence did not stop but its focus changed.[52] From campaigning for English help in 1559 and 1560, for example, Maitland of Lethington began to press the Queen of Scots' claim to Elizabeth's throne. He even tackled the uncomfortable issue of the authenticity of Henry VIII's will.[53]

The pattern of Anglo-Scottish diplomacy changed once again in the middle of the 1560s and it was really only following the disintegration of political life in Scotland after 1566 that Cecil could again refer to 'our frendes ther' with any solid meaning.[54] So was there any truth in Knox's consistent charge that senior members of Scotland's Protestant nobility were no more than courtiers and flatterers after 1561? And was Knox involved in the resurrection of the relationship between the English and Scottish Protestant élites? Probably not. 'Men deliting to swym

---

[49] Knox, *On Rebellion*, pp. 182–209; *A Sermon Preached by John Knox ... upon Sonday, the 19 of August 1565 ...* (STC, no. 15075; n.p., 1566), sig. A2v, A4v, B2v; Isaiah 26:20; Knox, *Works*, VI, pp. 221–73.

[50] 7 October 1561, Knox, *Works*, VI p. 132.

[51] 6 October 1563, ibid., VI, p. 531.

[52] Simon Adams, 'The Lauderdale Papers 1561–1570: The Maitland of Lethington State Papers and the Leicester Correspondence', *SHR*, 67 (1988), pp. 51–4.

[53] Maitland of Lethington to Cecil, 4 January 1567, BL Harley MS 444, fos 21r–27r.

[54] Cecil to Sir Henry Sidney, 24 June 1566, PRO SP 63/18, fo. 62r.

betwix two watters, have often compleaned upon my severitie' was Knox's defence of his own inflexible position.[55] The Duke of Northumberland provided the model reply when Knox wrote to him in 1552 and wondered whether he was a 'dissembler in religion or not'. 'I have for xx yere stand [stood] to oon[e] kynd of religion in the same which I doo nowe profes, and have I thanke the lorde past no smalle daungers for yt.'[56] But there are two related issues. The first is the concept of service to the monarch which, even in the middle part of the sixteenth century, was still extremely personal. Men like Moray and Maitland of Lethington were radicalized by the end of the 1560s but they owed natural allegiance to Mary on her return to Scotland in 1561.[57] The second is outward conformity balanced against the personal religion of a monarch – anathema to a purist like Knox but a fairly natural response even to Calvinists like Cecil. Like Knox, historians have often found it difficult to reconcile the fact that major political players could be truly religious *and* serve monarchs like Mary Tudor or the Queen of Scots. There was a serious European debate about conformity in the 1540s and 1550s and its significance is only just being worked into accounts of the period.[58] It is too easy and probably wrong to dismiss senior members of the Scottish nobility as godless politiques.

The Earl of Moray, Maitland of Lethington and John Wood were major characters in the reconstruction of effective Anglo-Scottish Protestant politics. Diplomatic dispatches between 1561 and 1566 were based on personal expressions of love and friendship between two Queens in a language which was seriously challenged by some of the crises of the first five years of Mary's personal rule. After 1567 – when the extremely agile Sir Nicholas Throckmorton had to restrain some Scottish noblemen from arguing for the trial and execution of Mary and 'bothe the moost parte of the Counsellours, and a great number of others' were pressing for her prosecution, condemnation and imprisonment, and the coronation of Prince James – the relationship between the Protestant élites of England and Scotland changed.[59] At this crucial point in the history of British political thought (in the year when George Buchanan probably drafted his *De Jure Regni apud Scotos*), it was Moray, Maitland of Lethington, Cecil, Leicester, and the English Privy

---

[55] Knox to Cecil, 7 October 1561, Knox, *Works*, VI, p. 131.

[56] PRO SP 10/15, fo. 137r; Tytler, *Edward VI and Mary*, II, p. 148.

[57] Cf. John Guy, 'Tudor Monarchy and its Critiques', in John Guy (ed.), *The Tudor Monarchy* (London, 1997), pp. 78–109.

[58] Andrew Pettegree, 'Nicodemism and the English Reformation', in A. Pettegree *Marian Protestantism: Six Studies* (Aldershot, 1996), pp. 86–117.

[59] Throckmorton to Elizabeth, 19 July 1567, BL Cotton MS Caligula C. 1, fos 28r–31v.

Council who were working through some of the practical alternatives to personal rule by the Queen of Scots.

The main positive alternative was a Protestant regency for Scotland. In July 1567 the Earl of Bedford reported that Mary seemed 'contente' to 'renounce her title, and committ the Governement of the Prince to the lordes, and she heer selfe to go abrode into a fforayne Realme'.[60] By August settlement was a step nearer. Cecil told Sir Henry Sidney that he thought Moray 'will be by perswasion induced to take the Government of scotland'.[61] Moray himself eventually accepted what he thought of as 'this present wechtye charge that Is layd upon my shulderis', 'compellit and conwict in conscience to yeild to the manyfald preassinges of Many noble mony godly and best men heirabout'. He wanted to do at least two things: encourage 'the Quyetyng and perpetuall weall of this puir Realme with the commodite of the haill body thairof', and engage the help of other peers 'in planting of the treu religion, Justice, and polycye within this meserable cuntrye'.[62] Sir Walter Mildmay teased out some of the English and British implications. 'If the governement rest onely in the Erle of Murray,' he wrote to Cecil, 'it wilbe well as I thinke for stablishing of Religion, and contynuaunce of amytie here.' 'I pray god that twoo thinges may stand: first Religion, and the Amitie of thes twoo countries. And I never looke for the latter to hold long, except the first be surelie stablisshed.'[63]

How Knox would have rationalized or explained this radical change in his *History* is uncertain. He was clearly on the periphery of events. Only John Lesley, Bishop of Ross, wrote an account of the proceedings against Mary and incorporated some of the narrative into books and pamphlets at the end of the decade. He also acted as one of her representatives in England.[64] James McGill and Maitland of Lethington reappeared to liaise with a core group of the English Privy Council, the members of which had consistently demonstrated their commitment to Anglo-Scottish amity: Cecil, the Earl of Leicester, Lord Admiral Edward Clinton and Lord Chamberlain William Howard of Effingham, with the

---

[60] Bedford to the Earl of Shrewsbury, 22 July 1567, Lambeth Palace Library, MS 3196, fo. 213, printed in Edmund Lodge (ed.), *Illustrations of British History, Biography, and Manners* ... (3 vols, London, 1791), I, p. 363.

[61] 20 August 1567, PRO SP 63/21, fo. 183r.

[62] Moray to Lord Herries, *c.* 24 August 1567, Darnaway Castle, Forres, TD 94/56, no. 58.

[63] Mildmay to Cecil, 4 August 1567, PRO SP 12/43, fo. 89r; Mildmay to Cecil, 15 August 1567, PRO SP 12/43, fo. 117r.

[64] BL Lansdowne MS 231, fos 244r–322v; [Lesley,] *A Defence of the Honour of the Right Highe, Mightye and Noble Princesse Marie Quene of Scotlande* ... (*STC*, no. 15503; [Paris,] 1569).

slightly more conservative additions of the Lord Steward, the Earl of Arundel and Chancellor of the Duchy of Lancaster, Sir Ralph Sadler. The result was a covert deal 'secretly to be imparted to the sayd Erle of Murray'. If the Queen of Scots could be found guilty then England would openly support the regency and Mary could be held in England or Scotland.[65]

That was in October 1568. Seven months later, in May 1569, a 'wrytyng' was delivered to John Wood, who had been acting as messenger between Regent Moray and the English Privy Council since at least March, 'in charge to do sum service convenient' for his master.[66] It was an English proposal, endorsed by Cecil, and based on the principles of a British settlement he had consistently worked for after 1567. There were 'Three degrees' which had been 'collected uppon spechees projected by such as hawe communed and dewysed of the Quene of Scottes cause'. The first was Mary's acknowledgement of 'the estat' of James VI, according to the proceedings of the Scottish Parliament during the Queen of Scots' imprisonment in Lochleven. If this failed, the second was a joint reign with her son, 'And the governement to Remayn during hir sonnes minoritie in the order of ane regent an a Counsal of the land'. If the Queen of Scots refused these two degrees – which was pretty likely – the 'wrytyng' restated the main elements of a settlement: a full and universal recognition of Scotland's religion 'as it Is now professed by the Regent and the subjectis Joyned with hym', with an option for Mary 'in her awyn personne' to conform to 'the Mannere of the Relligion used in England'; a Moray regency and government by council; and a 'perpetuall league' between England and Scotland. The treaty would be 'accorded trypartitly' between Mary, Elizabeth, and James and 'stablisshed by parlyament in scotland'. If the Queen of Scots broke any part of the treaty, then Elizabeth, Moray, and 'more part of the Counsal' could transfer the Crown to James without a coronation.[67]

John Knox and William Cecil had radical instincts. They shared a cultural outlook and a common language. Both men could, and did, challenge the dark forces of European Catholicism and its principal

---

[65] 9 October 1568, Hatfield House Library, Hertfordshire, Cecil Papers 155, fo. 130r; 30 October 1568, BL Cotton MS Caligula B. 9, fo. 359r–v.

[66] Moray to Valentine Brown, 23 March 1569, Darnaway Castle, Forres, TD 94/56, no. 81.

[67] PRO SP 52/16, fo. 45r–v; Hatfield House Library, Hertfordshire, Cecil Papers 156, fo. 31r–v, printed in Haynes, *State Papers*, p. 516; BL Cotton MS Caligula B. 5, fo. 327r–v.

agents. In 1562 Cecil thought that when the Guise had succeeded in promoting their niece to the English Crown, when Ireland had fallen under Spanish influence, when the 'Generall counsell' had condemned all Protestants, and when Catholics in England were ready to 'assayle this realme or Irland', 'than will it be to late to seke to withstand it; for than the matter shall be lyke a great rock of stone that is fallyng downe from the topp of a mountayn, which whan it is comming no force can stey'.[68] In other words, we are *not* dealing with two characters who had radically different interpretations of how political life in Europe worked in the sixteenth century. It was how they approached the problem of England's and Scotland's apparent isolation, their priorities, and their solutions which were distinct and distinctive. This was, in some ways, an issue of self-perception. Knox marketed himself as the 'painfull Preacher' of the 'blessed Evangell', the minister and prophet who told – or *had* to tell – people unpalatable truths about their religion, the consistency of their beliefs or, if they were in Elizabeth's position, their monstrous rebellion against order and nature. He bore down on weakness; on any sign of outward conformity or defection or change. Cecil, on the other hand, was more flexible. In 1564 he described his position as 'a secretory of estate', 'an artificer of practisees and Cou[n]suls'.[69] He was committed to a Protestant model of Britain but more able to adapt to political change. These differences seriously affected the way in which Cecil and Knox perceived and dealt with the issues raised by the British Reformations of the late 1550s and 1560s.

There were some crucial common denominators. Both men believed that the establishment of 'true religion' was the central aim of the English and Scottish settlements. They understood that close co-operation between England and the Lords of the Congregation was the main way to ensure success. Knox's duties as clerk to the Congregation in 1559 allowed him to deploy the language of 'perpetual league' and 'amity'; Cecil and the English Privy Council happily replied in kind. Perhaps the main difference between the two men was the nature of the long-term guarantee of Anglo-Scottish union. Knox believed that union meant dynastic marriage, but in this he was not alone. Even committed Protestant Anglo-Scots like the Earls of Leicester and Moray, Maitland of Lethington, and Sir Nicholas Throckmorton, conscious of the regimes'

---

[68] 20 July 1562, PRO SP 70/39, fo. 106r–v; cf. Malcolm R. Thorp, 'Catholic Conspiracy in Early Elizabethan Foreign Policy', *Sixteenth Century Journal*, 15 (1984), pp. 431–48; and M.R. Thorp, 'William Cecil and the Antichrist: A Study in Anti-Catholic Ideology', in Malcolm R. Thorp and Arthur J. Slavin (eds), *Politics, Religion, and Diplomacy in Early Modern Europe* (Missouri, 1994), pp. 289–304.

[69] Cecil to Sir Thomas Smith, 11 January 1564, BL Lansdowne MS 102, fo. 56r.

failure to deal effectively with the Queen of Scots in 1568, thought that Mary's marriage to Thomas Howard, fourth Duke of Norfolk could unite England and Scotland. After all, Elizabeth's councillors *did* think that Mary could and would conform to the English Church settlement.

Cecil's priorities were quite different. He wanted a Britain bound into a defensive league organized against the power of the aggressively Catholic continental kingdoms. Cecil did not want this union held together by marriage but by a political treaty signed by the principal parties in England and Scotland, policed by Council, Parliament and (after 1567) regency in Scotland, and underwritten by the superior power of the English Crown. He did not want to extend the English royal supremacy to Scotland or force the Scots to adopt an English ecclesiastical model. Nevertheless, use of the English Prayer Book was a voluntary option; and he certainly wanted Scotland at least to abandon 'idolatry' and abolish the jurisdiction of Rome in the same way that England had done in its 'first Reformation' in the 1530s. Cecil's reading of British and European politics in the 1560s gave the terms 'amity' and 'league' a far sharper edge even than they had had in the late 1540s. They stood for religious and political solidarity and a strong common relationship between members of the Anglo-Scottish Protestant élite. Unity also meant, on occasions, apparent concessions – principally, perhaps, Cecil's strategic use of the old arguments for English superiority over Scotland. Knox did not like concessions: but, after all, Knox would not have been Knox if he had been content to let his contemporaries live in peace.[70]

---

[70] For a more complete discussion of Cecil's British politics in the 1560s, see Stephen Alford, *The Early Elizabethan Polity: William Cecil and the British Succession Crisis 1558–1569* (Cambridge, 1998).

CHAPTER ELEVEN

Godly Reformer, Godless Monarch: John Knox and Mary Queen of Scots

*Jenny Wormald**

Poor John Knox. My text is taken from the first three words of the opening sentence of Jane Dawson's fascinating article, 'The Scottish Reformation and the Theatre of Martyrdom'.[1] Her sympathy was directed to the sense of inferiority Knox felt when he wrote his Scottish martyrology, the first book of the *History of the Reformation in Scotland*; for, unlike his more fortunate English friend John Foxe (if 'fortunate' is the word), whose *Book of Martyrs* was stuffed with examples of those who died for their faith, Knox was somewhat strapped for lack of martyrs, even if he did succeed in discovering rather more than he had at first thought. And indeed, given the vigour and passion of Knox's prose style, and his burning desire to present a picture of a suffering and oppressed Scotland delivered from bondage by God, one may well sympathize with him; for undoubtedly his abhorred Scottish Regent, Mary of Guise, and her daughter whom he characterized as the Scottish Jezebel, let him down very badly by an infuriating tolerance which allowed Scottish Protestants to live their lives singularly free from that persecution visited on their English counterparts by the English Jezebel Mary Tudor, and so necessary to his vision of the heroic struggle of God's chosen people. Already, therefore, the stakes look a little lower than Knox claimed. His problem in depicting the 1550s, when Mary Queen of Scots was in France and her mother was in control, was that the Regent, while giving the Scottish Protestants little chance to advance their cause, had equally given them no chance to be martyrs. But the replacement of the Catholic Mary Tudor in 1558 with

---

* I would like to thank Sally Mapstone for her many instant responses to requests for advice, and Roger Mason whose patience and helpfulness as an editor has, fortunately for me, remained unchanged since the last time I wrote an article for him.

[1] Jane E.A. Dawson, 'The Scottish Reformation and the Theatre of Martyrdom', in D. Wood (ed.), *Martyrs and Martyrologies*, Studies in Church History, 30 (Oxford, 1994), pp. 259–70.

her sister Elizabeth, the death of the Regent in June 1560, and English intervention in Scotland which saw the withdrawal of her French troops, gave Scottish Protestants their chance at last; and it was seized with enthusiasm in the Reformation Parliament of August 1560, which abolished the authority of the Pope and the saying of Mass, and issued one of the most moving Confessions of Faith of the sixteenth century.[2]

Only a year later, in August 1561, did Mary Queen of Scots get round to returning to her kingdom, having failed to find a European replacement for her dead husband Francis II of France who would enable her to continue to lead a life of continental luxury, and irresponsibility. This Catholic Queen was now coming back to rule her newly Protestant kingdom. The fact that, remarkably, she had allowed the Scottish Protestants, who from her point of view had rebelled against her in the summer of 1560, to spend a year digging in, and her obsession with being named as Elizabeth's successor, which made it politic for her to identify with these Scottish Protestants, did not mean that there were no grounds for fear. No one could be sure that she might not be used by the great Catholic powers of Europe, France and Spain, now united in an effort to extirpate heresy after their fruitless 60-year struggle with one another in the Italian peninsula, to aid the Catholic cause in Scotland and, by extension, England. And, even if this seemed unlikely, the very fact that she insisted on her right to her private Mass in her Palace of Holyrood by definition threatened the Protestant Church, given the agreement at Augsburg in 1555 that the religion of the prince should be the religion of his realm.

In such circumstances, it is not in the least surprising that Catholic ruler and Protestant reformer should clash. That clash is described in relentless detail by Knox in his *History*, in his account of the four famous interviews between them, an account which leaves an abiding impression of weeping ruler and ranting reformer.[3] Because both Mary and Knox are famous figures in Scottish history, these interviews have taken on great significance. They have all the artistic and dramatic rightness which was so lacking in Mary's relations with Elizabeth that later writers had to invent similar interviews between the two Queens. Great protagonists must meet. And Knox and Mary duly did meet.

Were these meetings, however, really of great significance? Do they help to explain the early years of the reformed Kirk and its aspirations? At one level, they do tell us about an attitude of the godly ministers of the new Kirk, from which both Mary and her two successors James VI

---

[2] *APS*, II, pp. 525–35.
[3] Knox, *History*, II, pp. 13–20, 43–6, 71–4, 81–4.

and Charles I suffered; Scottish ministers certainly felt it their right and their duty to hector and bully their monarchs. But immediately that in itself reduces the importance of the interviews between Knox and Mary, which begin to look rather less dramatic, and certainly not unique, when compared to Mary's son's regular exchanges with Knox's ministerial successors. His astonishing rudeness to his sovereign, which he recounts with apparent pride, can after all be readily paralleled in these later exchanges. Even the best known example, that much-quoted phrase from the first interview of 4 September 1561, in which he declared that 'if the realm finds no inconvenience from the regiment of a woman [I] shall be as well content to live under your Grace as Paul was to live under Nero', has its later echoes; in 1585, James Gibson compared his persecuting King, James VI, to Jeroboam, and threatened him with being the end of his race.[4] There is no real difference between Knox and the Jacobean ministers. But the difference between Mary and James becomes immediately clear. For in Knox's *History*, Mary consistently played into his hands by trying to argue with him politely, even on occasion with womanly modesty, acknowledging her inferiority; thus in the same interview, when they had moved on to the question of the true faith, Knox was predictably aggressive, Mary almost questioning:

> My conscience (said she) is not so. Conscience, madam (said he) requires knowledge; and I fear that right knowlege ye have none. But (said she), I have both heard and read. So (said he), Madam, did the Jews that crucified Christ Jesus ... Ye interpret the Scriptures (said she) in one manner, and they [Pope and Cardinals] interpret in another. Whom shall I believe? And who shall be judge?

This was an obvious tactical error, because of course Knox told her at length, leaving her to say, weakly, 'Ye are oure sair [too hard] for me ... but and if they were here that I have heard, they would answer you'. And so the interview ground down to its conclusion, when Knox, perhaps inevitably, grabbed the last word, if a rather unexpected one, praying God 'that ye may be as blessed within the Commonwealth of Scotland, if it be the pleasure of God, as ever Deborah was in the Commonwealth of Israel'.[5]

It was a distinctly lengthy exchange, although Knox tells us that he described only a part. How very differently did James VI respond to his hectoring minister in 1585. There was no modest appeal; rather, 'I will not give a turd for thy preaching', and off Gibson went, to ward in Edinburgh Castle. There were, of course, many occasions when James

---

[4] Ibid., II, p. 15; Calderwood, *History*, IV, pp. 486–7.
[5] Knox, *History*, II, pp. 18–20.

did allow lengthy exchanges; but that most skilled debater and highly educated theologian-king was never out-argued, never displayed his mother's doubts about her own competence to argue. Godly the ministers – Knox, Gibson, John Davidson, Andrew and James Melville – might be; thugs and bullies they undoubtedly were, to their own Protestant opponents just as much as to a Catholic Queen. Scottish godly invective was hard-hitting in the extreme. Phrases like 'vyld filthie bellie-god beast ... Let that perjured apostat's filthie memorie stink, rot, perish' seemed to flow from their lips as readily as did their sermons; thus did the godly minister John Row respond to the death of George Gledstanes, Archbishop of St Andrews.[6] These were indeed men of utter commitment to Christ Jesus, and it may simply be an anachronistic modern reaction to think that some leavening of Christian charity would not have come amiss. Much more to the point, King James succeeded where Queen Mary failed simply because he was not overawed by it.

It is, of course, entirely understandable that Mary was overawed. That first interview took place a mere two days after her ceremonial entry into Edinburgh, where the show put on by the burgh had a pointedly Protestant dimension to it.[7] The Queen, nurtured in the adulatory court of France, petted and flattered since the age of five, was having her first dramatic experience of the cold reality of the political–religious world which she was expected to control, and a brutal experience it was. Her son, though spared the memory of a John Knox sermon at his coronation because it took place when he was a year-old infant, had survived in childhood the brutality of his tutor, the European humanist of distinction but ferocious teacher George Buchanan, and was therefore rather better trained in the art of dealing with bullying and invective. But miserable as Mary's experience was, in her first and later interviews with Knox, and try as Knox might, on the occasions themselves and in his description of them, to paint the picture of a man of God doing his ordained duty in haranguing his godless monarch, there is rather more to the exchanges between Mary and Knox than merely establishing a pattern of clashes between monarch and ministers which were to assail the first three post-Reformation Stewart rulers, Mary, James and Charles I. For in that very first interview, there was one very surprising moment, and an equally surprising postscript.

---

[6] John Row, *The History of the Kirk of Scotland* (Wodrow Society, Edinburgh, 1842), p. 303.

[7] A.A. MacDonald, 'Mary Stewart's Entry into Edinburgh: An Ambiguous Triumph', *Innes Review*, 42 (1991), pp. 101–10; A.R. MacDonald, 'The Triumph of Protestantism: The Burgh Council of Edinburgh and the Entry of Mary Queen of Scots, 2 September 1561', *Inner Review*, 48 (1997), pp. 73–82.

The surprising moment came when Mary, once again playing to her enemy, asked, 'Think ye that subjects having power may resist their princes?' To which the answer was of course a resounding, if distinctly protracted, yes. This silenced Mary, who 'stood as it were amazed, more than a quarter of an hour'. No doubt that pleased Knox. But what is very curious is that her bastard half-brother, the leading Protestant noble Lord James Stewart, 'began to entreat her, and to demand, "What has offended you, Madam?"' Surely it was obvious enough. Lord James, like Mary, had just listened to a speech which had invoked the example of children restraining a frenzied father by binding and imprisoning him as proof that such could be done to 'princes that would murder the children of God that are subject unto them', and that such action 'is no disobedience against princes, but just obedience, because that agreeth with the will of God'. Naturally Mary was offended. So why did Lord James ask what, on the face of it, looks like a very silly question? Mary's answer was, after all, logical and, from the point of view of those placed in authority, shocking enough: 'Well, then, I perceive that my subjects shall obey you, and not me; and shall do what they list, and not what I command: and so must I be subject to them, and not they to me.'[8] Knox had stated an extreme form of resistance theory. Mary's reply was certainly à propos. And it is inconceivable that Lord James failed to see the point. So why did he ask his question? In the fractured world of the Reformation, any resistance theory had its potential danger. Yet in part the answer may lie in the fact that in 1561 those in authority had as yet been faced only with the comparatively impotent resistance theories of the Marian exiles; it was not until the next decade that the more worrying theories of the Huguenots and George Buchanan would raise the stakes, bringing the debate on to a European level which would provoke a backlash, most famously from Bodin and James VI. Perhaps even more to the point, no one knew better than Lord James about the difference between the theory and practice of resistance; it had not been the thunderings of Knox but the actions of the secular Protestant leaders which had determined the sensational events of 1559–60, culminating in the Reformation Parliament of August 1560. And no one knew better than Lord James the profound difference between the ruler the Protestants had then faced, Mary of Guise, and the ruler with whom they now had to deal, Mary Queen of Scots.

Thus it was not stupidity but lack of real concern which produced Lord James's question. And this surely suggests that Knox, having demonstrated a myriad of mistakes on Mary's part, now made his own

---

[8] Knox, *History*, II, pp. 16–17.

one mistake; in his confident recounting of an exchange in which he was the easy winner, he let slip the fact that the most powerful Protestant noble in Scotland was not quite taking his resistance theory seriously. The great reformer, author in the 1550s of *The First Blast of the Trumpet against the Monstrous Regiment of Women* and other highly polemical resistance tracts, was utterly wedded to his theory;[9] God gave the godly the right and the duty to resist, and Knox in his own account of his own dealings with Mary was fulfilling that duty to the full. Yet Lord James was unimpressed. And this means that, within a month of Mary's return to Scotland, the self-appointed custodian of God's truth was being shown up as a man whose outspoken theory did not command the support of his secular co-religionists.[10] Perhaps, then, Knox's *History of the Reformation* is not quite the authoritative account it has been taken to be?

This underpins the surprising postscript: 'John Knox's own judgement being by some of his familiars demanded, What he thought of the Queen? "If there be not in her (said he) a proud mind, a crafty wit, and an indurate heart against God and his truth, my judgement faileth me".' And Knox reiterated the point in a letter to William Cecil a month later.[11] But on Knox's own evidence, Mary had shown anything but a proud mind and a crafty wit, whatever the state of her heart. It begins to be possible to reconstruct the interview. Knox had hectored, and at least one member of his audience had not been overawed. Whatever points he had scored with the Queen, he had not had the same effect on the Queen's brother, his most important Protestant ally. We know, of course, that later Knox was to turn on Moray for his lack of zeal; the last sentence of Book IV, the Book which contains the account of the critical years 1561–64, is an almost forced anticlimax: 'In all that time the Earl of Moray was so formed ['fremmed': alien] to John Knox that neither by word or write was there any communication between them.'[12]

---

[9] For these tracts, see Knox, *On Rebellion*, and Chapters 7 and 8 by Roger Mason and Jane Dawson, in this volume; see also Jane E.A. Dawson, 'Revolutionary Conclusions: The Case of the Marian Exiles', *History of Political Thought*, 2 (1990), pp. 257–72, and 'The Apocalyptic Thinking of the Marian Exiles', in M. Wilks (ed.), *Prophecy and Eschatology*, Studies in Church History, Subsidia 10 (Oxford, 1994), pp. 75–91. See also note 34 below.

[10] Knox himself was already becoming all too aware of the lack of zeal of his co-religionists, who had refused when Mary returned to Scotland to oppose her private Mass. He witheringly referred to 'the subtle persuasions of her supposts (we mean even of such as sometimes were judged most fervent with us) ... blinded all men': Knox, *History*, II, p. 12 and note 2, where W. Croft Dickinson suggests that by the 'judged most fervent', Knox meant in particular Lord James and Lethington.

[11] Knox, *History*, II, p. 20; Knox, *Works*, VI, pp. 131–2.

[12] Knox, *History*, II, p. 134.

Thus, on that bitter and utterly personal note, did Knox end his great account of his history of God's design for Scotland. He himself dated the beginning of the coldness to 1563.[13] But it does look as though Moray, crucial figure in the success of the Reformation, set less value on the Knox of the 1561 exchange with the new Queen than did Knox himself. And if that was so, then Knox had to upgrade Mary, precisely because she was the sovereign, even if he could not give her a sufficiently starring role in the interview itself. For in the interview, what mattered was his superiority as the minister of God over the person who failed, was indeed an obscenity, on two counts: as woman ruler and Catholic ruler. Thereafter, the position was rather different. To justify his theory, he had to persuade his fellow Protestants, already causing him deep anxiety, that she was utterly terrifying, the agent of the destruction of God's cause in Scotland. She had, therefore, to be the opponent worthy of his steel, worthy of legitimate resistance. Hence the 'proud mind', the 'crafty wit', that craft, as he told Cecil, 'as I have not found in such age'.

Poor John Knox. Poor Mary Queen of Scots. The one lacking the authority, the influence, which he so passionately believed, as God's agent on earth, was rightly his, the other turned into the monstrous and satanic opponent, a role for which by intellect and inclination she was utterly unfitted. And there was a further reason for Knox's need to cast Mary as the satanic opponent. For it now had to be the Scottish earth on which God's agent operated. Knox, that great hero of Scottish history, had in his earlier career been remarkably indifferent to the Scottish earth, preferring the English. He had been a minister in England under Edward VI, making enough of an impact to be appointed royal chaplain. He had fled from England with the English Marian exiles. And he had shown some reluctance to return from Geneva to advance the Protestant cause in Scotland. But he had had the sheer bad luck to lapse into a stupendous piece of mistiming; for he produced his *First Blast of the Trumpet* in 1558, and 1558 was the year of Elizabeth's accession. That, of course, finished Knox in England, not least because the real target of the book was neither of the Scottish Maries, but the English Mary Tudor; and since Knox based his argument not only on the particular case, but on the general principle of the unacceptability of female rule, with the exception of Deborah, his assertions to Elizabeth

---

[13] Ibid., II, pp. 78–9. At the beginning of Mary's personal rule, Knox already had misgivings (see note 10), but still regarded Moray as his best hope; writing to Calvin on 24 October 1561, he told him that 'James, the Queen's eldest brother, who alone among those that frequent the Court, opposes himself to ungodliness, salutes you': Knox, *Works*, VI, p. 135.

that he had not intended his strictures for her hardly convinced her, particularly as Knox remained Knox. His way of justifying himself was to write the new Protestant Queen of England a singularly blunt letter in July 1559, telling that most flattery-demanding of monarchs that 'if I should flatter your Grace I were no friend, but a deceivable traitor', and ending with another invocation of his Deborah image:

> If thus, in God's presence, ye humble yourself, as in my heart I glorify God for that rest granted to his afflicted flock within England, under you a weak instrument, so will I with tongue and pen justify your authority and regiment as the Holy Ghost hath justified the same in Deborah, that blessed Mother in Israel.

And it was this remarkable outpouring which was designed to persuade Elizabeth that his book 'touched not your Grace's person' and that 'nothing in my book contained, is, nor can be prejudicial to your Grace's just regiment, provided that ye be not found ingrate unto God'.[14]

There is a striking difference between Knox's relations with non-royal women, so long as they were godly, and his treatment of royal ones; an unexpectedly human side to Knox appears, for example, in the patience with which he dealt with his mother-in-law's endless fears for her salvation.[15] But Knox's virtually unmitigated horror at female rule made it virtually impossible for any female ruler to meet the standards of the one exception to his principle; and of course a Catholic female ruler had no hope at all.[16] But how Catholic was Mary? From Knox's point of view, not nearly Catholic enough, visibly different from Mary Tudor, certainly not a persecutor and not even – to the profound dismay of Catholics at home and abroad – a Queen determined to impose her religious faith on her kingdom. Reality, therefore, created an intolerable quandary. For Knox, the struggle between good and evil had to be on a titanic scale; and if the real Mary obstinately refused to play the part which he assigned to her in that struggle, his only way out was to create a mythical one who would. In their first encounter, he got a tiny snippet of help from Mary herself, goaded beyond endurance into telling him that 'ye are not the Kirk that I will nourish. I will defend the Kirk of Rome, for I think it is the true Kirk of God'.[17] That was not in fact the

---

[14] Ibid., I, pp. 291–4.

[15] See Patrick Collinson's Chapter 4 in this volume.

[16] There is a wealth of literature on the problem of female rule in early modern Europe. I am very grateful for the chance to read in advance of publication a significant Scottish contribution to the discussion, David Parkinson, '"A Lamentable Storie": Mary Queen of Scots and the inescapable *Querelle des Femmes*', in L.A.J.R. Houwen, A.A. MacDonald and Sally Mapstone (eds), *A Palace in the Wild: Scottish Culture in the Late Middle Ages and the Renaissance* (Groningen, forthcoming, 1999).

[17] Knox, *History*, II, p. 17.

policy she followed. But Knox, now committed utterly to God's cause in Scotland, desperately needed a Scottish Mary Tudor. Hence the transference of his language. It was now Mary Queen of Scots who could never be a Deborah, who was the Jezebel that had once been Mary Tudor. Indeed, if Book IV of the *History* was written as the last part of 'an extended sermon on the duty of Scottish Christians to rely solely, obediently and unflinchingly on God', and it was Mary's very success up until 1566 which goaded Knox, then in hiding in Kyle, to write that Book as a commentary on the backsliding of a people so recently liberated by God from their idolatry, then it seems that God's second miracle, Mary's downfall in 1567, mitigated Knox's relentless personal hatred for her not one jot. For it was in his revision of Book I, clearly after February 1567 and probably after Carberry in June of that year, that he wrote in the phrase 'Harry [Darnley], umquhile [late] husband to our Jezebel Mistress'.[18]

But if that was Knox's agenda, it was certainly not the agenda of the leading Protestant politicians with whom he had shared the triumph of the summer of 1560. Lord James could indeed respond to Knox's assertion of legitimate resistance by, in effect, asking his sister why she was bothered by it, precisely because he knew all too well that she was no Mary Tudor. Knox, an embarrassment to Scottish and English Protestants alike because of Elizabeth's reaction to his book, was an equal embarrassment to Scottish Protestants because of his insistence that Mary play the part he was writing for her. In October 1561, William Cecil's postbag contained not only Knox's letter with its violent strictures on Mary, but one from William Maitland of Lethington, close associate of Moray and Mary's great secretary, giving a rather different and much more convincing reaction to their first encounter:

> You know the vehemence of Mr Knox spriet, which cannot be brydled; and that doth sometymes uter soche sentences as can not easaly be dygested by a weake stomach. I wolde wish he sholde deal with her more gently, being a yong princess onpersuaded, for this am I accompted to be politik, but suerly in her comporting with him she doth declare a wisdome far exceeding her age. God grant her the assistance of his Spriet. Suerly I see in her a good towardnes, and think that the Quene your Soverayne shalbe able to do moche with her in religion, if they ever enter in a good familiarity.[19]

Maitland's Mary was, of course, an entirely different being from Knox's; and Maitland, like Knox, was adapting her to his own agenda.

---

[18] Robert M. Healey, 'John Knox's "History": A "Compleat" Sermon on Christian Duty', *Church History*, 61 (1992), pp. 319–33; Knox, *History*, I, p. 59.

[19] Knox, *Works*, VI, pp. 136–7.

For Maitland, as for Moray, maintenance of the Protestant religion in Scotland and amity with England were the cornerstones of their policy; it was, therefore, in Maitland's interests to depict a compliant Mary. Yet his picture of her as young and inexperienced, reiterated in a conversation with the English diplomat Thomas Randolph in January 1562, strikes a personal note which brings us into the presence of the real Mary, as opposed to Knox's monstrous creation.[20] And Maitland is credible where Knox is not, precisely because Mary was behaving exactly as he described. In the first year of her personal rule, she was showing a willingness to maintain the Protestant Church in Scotland; and she was far less concerned with the rantings of John Knox when she met him than with her passionate desire to arrange a meeting with Queen Elizabeth.

This was not, of course, the first time that Knox had so embarrassed the Protestant nobility, and been rebuffed by them. On 3 December 1557, a group of them – five signatories, though apparently there were 'many others' – had taken the brave step of trying to break through the limbo created by Mary of Guise's tolerant attitude to them, and subscribed to the First Band of the Lords of the Congregation of Christ, thus moving the traditional and habitual practice of secular bonding on to the plane of religious commitment and action.[21] Yet the earlier months of that year had witnessed a curious exchange of letters between the Protestant nobles and Knox. On 10 March 1557, four of the five signatories of the First Band had written to Knox in Geneva, exhorting him to come back to Scotland. That greatest champion of Scottish Protestantism proceeded to dither through the spring and summer, until in September he was virtually thrown out of Geneva by Calvin, who told him to do his duty and sent him off to Scotland. Arriving in Dieppe in October, however, he found letters telling him to stay where he was. He was, as he said in a lengthy and blistering response to the nobility, 'partly confounded' and 'partly pierced with anguish and sorrow', a response no doubt all the more keen because he had not wanted to come in the first place. The aftermath looks like a prolonged sulk; it was in these circumstances that he turned his attention back to England and settled down to write the *First Blast*. Later, in his *History*, he did his best, predictably enough, to rewrite the past, asserting that it was his letter which inspired the Scottish nobles to 'new consultation' and renewed commitment, which led to the making of the First Band.[22] It is infinitely more likely that in Scotland in 1557, the Protestants who were

---

[20] *CSP Scot.*, I, p. 591: Randolph to Cecil, 15 January 1562.
[21] Knox, *Works*, I, pp. 273–4.
[22] Knox, *History*, I, pp. 131–6.

gearing themselves up to make their first great public statement felt that Knox's fire would be an ill-timed political embarrassment.

That is understandable. What may initially appear more puzzling, in the same way that Lord James's question at the first interview appears initially puzzling, is the reaction to Knox's preaching at the time of that high point of Protestant success, the Reformation Parliament of August 1560. After a year of slogging between the troops of the Queen Regent and those of the Lords of the Congregation, events suddenly moved very fast in the summer of 1560. The death of the Regent, the throne in practice vacant, the expulsion of the French with English help and then the withdrawal of the English themselves, combined to give the Scottish Protestants their glorious moment of opportunity, and how that moment was seized. But the fact that their Parliament, held in defiance of the Crown, looked like the culmination of a year's resistance to authority made it all too easy to assume that hand-in-hand with religious reformation went secular rebellion, even revolution. It was not an idea which most leaders of the Protestant movement, secular and religious, wanted to engender. Knox, however, steeped in his theories of resistance, predictably tried to bring the two together, having a wonderful time preaching on the writing of the prophet Haggai, who in two short chapters offered a superb source of justification:

> Thus speaketh the Lord of hosts, saying, This people say, the time is not come, the time that the Lord's house should be built ... [But] according to the word that I covenanted with you when ye came out of Egypt, so my spirit remaineth among you; fear ye not. For ... it is a little while, and I will shake the heavens and the earth, and the sea, and the dry land. And I will shake all nations, and the desire of the nations shall come: and I will fill this house with glory, saith the Lord of hosts ... And I will overthrow the throne of kingdoms, and I will destroy the strength of the kingdoms of the heathen ... (Haggai 1:2; 2:5–7, 22).

'The doctrine,' said Knox, 'was proper for the time.' Indeed, he would think that. Here was the moment for which he had called, in his appeals of 1558 to the nobility and to the commonalty of Scotland. Here was the moment for the Lord's work. Here, therefore, was the moment for John Knox. He tells us that in his teaching 'he was so special and so vehement', and we may well believe him. But what was the response? 'Some, (having greater respect to the world than to God's glory), feeling themselves pricked, said in mockage, "We must now forget ourselves, and bear the barrow to build the houses of God".' The speaker appears to have been Maitland of Lethington.[23]

---

[23] Ibid., I, p. 335. Knox does not tell us who said this, contenting himself with 'God be merciful to the speaker'. Calderwood, *History*, II, p.12, names him as Lethington.

Knox's own account therefore tells us that in 1560 Maitland, and in 1561 both Maitland and Moray, were by no means as enchanted by Knox's message as Knox undoubtedly felt that they should have been. Neither was a rebel nor a revolutionary; neither responded to the call for resistance. And in the end, in 1567, when Mary did bring down disaster upon herself, she would do so without the slightest help from that would-be and willing accomplice in her overthrow, John Knox; and, be it added, she had to work very hard indeed to persuade her leading Protestant subjects to collaborate in that disaster. And in terms of Knox's dealings with Mary, the supreme irony is that it was that downfall, which he had so ardently desired but in which he had no part, which at last opened the way for his emergence as the great reformer of the early years of the Reformation.

And this surely is the tragedy for all resistance theorists *cum* religious reformers. For all the wealth of writing, by the Marian exiles in the 1550s, Buchanan, Beza and the Huguenots in the 1570s, there was no occasion on which men took action as a direct result of resistance theory. Perhaps Buchanan came closest to success; but even he was justifying resistance after the event, when he was wheeled out to produce an explanation of Mary's overthrow for the benefit of Elizabeth.[24] The sad fact was that resistance theory was always the last cry of despair by men whose cause seemed to have failed, whether it was the reversal of the English Protestant cause with the accession of Mary Tudor in 1553 or that of the French Huguenots with the Massacre of St Bartholomew's Day in 1572. It is indeed a measure of that despair that the theorists of the 1570s worked so hard to create an aura of legitimacy which was notably absent from the writings of the 1550s, based on ancient constitutions, contractual kingship and lesser magistracies, all designed to give resistance a sort of veneer of constitutional respectability.

Knox's own spectacular mistiming in 1560 and 1561, however, had a quite different dimension. For Knox was insisting on resistance when there was absolutely nothing to resist. In 1560, Mary Queen of Scots' convenient willingness to remain in France left her Scottish Protestant subjects an absolutely clear field. In 1561, Knox was threatening resistance to a Catholic Queen who had already assured her brother earlier

---

[24] Jenny Wormald, 'Resistance and Regicide in Sixteenth Century Scotland: The Execution of Mary Queen of Scots', *Majestas*, 1 (1993), pp. 67–87. On Buchanan and his Scottish context, see J.H. Burns, *The True Law of Kingship: Concepts of Monarchy in Early Modern Scotland* (Oxford, 1996), chap. 6. For a useful survey of the wider European debate, see Robert M. Kingdon, 'Calvinism and Resistance Theory', in J.H. Burns (ed.), *The Cambridge History of Political Thought 1450–1700* (Cambridge, 1991), pp. 193–218.

in the year that she would not attempt to alter the present state of religion in Scotland, provided that she herself could keep her Mass. It was a promise which she kept, despite the counter-offers of John Lesley, Bishop of Ross, and George Gordon, Earl of Huntly, to aid her in Catholic restoration, reinforcing it within a week of her arrival in Scotland on 19 August 1561 with a proclamation on 25 August forbidding any 'alteration or innovation of the state of religion... which her majesty found public and universally standing at her majesty's arrival in this her realm'.[25] It was issued the day after her first experience of what 'public and universally standing' could mean for at least some of her Protestant subjects, for the previous day, Sunday, had witnessed the rumpus at her first private Mass, when Lord James had to honour his assurance to her by guarding the door of her chapel in Holyrood. And she kept that promise for the rest of her reign, even during her brief five-week 'Catholic interlude' in February–early March 1566, when for the first and only time in her reign she gave some political prominence to leading Scottish Catholics.[26] Political priorities, at the top of which stood the English succession, and personal inclination – the refusal 'to press the conscience of any man'[27] – combined to dictate her course, anathema though that was to John Knox. In these circumstances, the irritating fact that she would not ratify the acts of the Reformation Parliament until in desperate straits in 1567 turned out to be, in practice, a mere bagatelle. In these circumstances, what need for resistance – in theory or in practice?

In calling for the advancing of God's cause in the localities, it was Knox's misfortune that no secular leader, noble or laird, could afford the luxury of his single-mindedness, caught up, as they inevitably were, by considerations wider than, and sometimes conflicting with, that advance.[28] The same was true at the 'centre'. Time and again, in 1561–62, we find Knox snarling impotently from the sidelines. Knox himself, in his letter to Cecil of 7 October 1561, showed growing concern about Maitland and Lord James, in describing an early defeat:

---

[25] *RPC*, I, pp. 266–7.

[26] Julian Goodare, 'Queen Mary's Catholic Interlude', in Michael Lynch (ed.), *Mary Stewart: Queen in Three Kingdoms* (Oxford, 1988), pp. 154–70.

[27] Knox, *History*, II, p. 152. Mary had asserted before she came to Scotland that this would be her policy, in her discussion with Nicholas Throckmorton on 18 June 1561, when she told him that in matters of religion 'I mean to constrain none of my subjects': ibid., I, p. 368. It was a policy she stuck to; and naturally she expected the same from her subjects.

[28] Jenny Wormald, '"Princes" and the Regions in the Scottish Reformation', in Norman Macdougall (ed.), *Church, Politics and Society: Scotland 1408–1929* (Edinburgh, 1983), pp. 65–84.

> Ye know my Lord James and Ledingthon, whome yf God do not
> otherwiese conduct, thei ar liek to lose that which, not without
> travall, hath heirtofore blen conquest. Att this verrey instant ar the
> Provost of Edinburgh and Balleis thairof command to ward in
> there Tolboght, be reason of thare Proclamation against papists
> and hoormongars. The hole blame lyeht upon the necks of the two
> fornamed, be reasson of thare bearing. God deliver us from the
> plage which manifestlie appeareht ...

He was referring to Mary's impending dismissal of the Protestant provost, Archibald Douglas of Kilspindie, and four of the bailies, which
happened on 8 October, because after their recent election they had
reissued ordinances of June 1560 and March 1561 against priests,
whoremongers, adulterers and fornicators (that litany which would
become so familiar in the annals of the Kirk). Knox claimed that the
reissue was no more than standard practice by an incoming council. But
this was a much exaggerated claim, and one which concealed Protestant
sharp practice within Edinburgh, probably aimed against Mary.[29]

In the event, he failed to carry his point. And over the succeeding
months, Randolph's letters to Cecil provide further graphic instances of
his failure to convince. In January 1562 he referred to Knox and other
ministers as, 'to be playne with your Honour, as wylfull as lerned,
which hartelye I lamente'. In February, he described a sermon in which
Knox 'gave the crosse and the candle such a wype, that as wyse and
lerned as him self wysshed hym to have hylde his peace'. In August, he
recounted a letter from Knox warning him of mischief-makers in the
west borders, drily commenting that 'it is trewe that Mr Knox hathe
manie tymes geven me warning of practisers, but thys is the fyrste that
ether he or anye man else culde assure me of, and yet dothe he wryte no
more then your Honour may fynde in this lettre'. And on 16 December
he gave Cecil a lengthy account of an impassioned and vitriolic outburst
by Knox against Mary:

> He is so full of mystrust in all her doynges, words and sayengs, as
> thoughe he wer eyther of Godes privie consell, that knowe howe he
> had determined of her from the begynynge, or that he knew the
> secretes of her harte so well, that nether she dyd nor culde have for
> ever one good thought of God or of his trewe religion ...

Randolph emphatically did not agree. He had more hope of Mary,
certainly in terms of the amity with England, and even in religion. And
although on 30 December he told Cecil of what looked like a triumph
for Knox at last, writing that 'Mr Knox is so harde unto us that we

---

[29] Knox, *Works*, VI, p. 132; Knox, *History*, II, pp. 21–3; Michael Lynch, *Edinburgh
and the Reformation* (Edinburgh, 1981), pp. 97–8, and Chapter 12 in this volume.

have layde asyde myche of our dansinge', he promptly went back on it, saying that 'I dowte yt more for heavines of harte, that thynges procede not well in France then for feare of hym'.[30]

We have then a compelling picture of Knox's burning frustration, leading to the violence of his outburst to Randolph in December 1562. And nowhere is this better illustrated than in his exchanges with his critic of 1560–61, Maitland of Lethington, exchanges which were much less dramatic than his confrontations with Mary, but politically much more telling. For Knox, who had to invent a royal opponent who could measure up to him, seems to have regarded Maitland, even more than Moray, as the man of intellectual calibre with whom he could match. And if Mary, in Knox's treatment of her, was turned into the cardboard cut-out of the Catholic limb of Satan, Maitland was for him the genuine article of horror, the backsliding Protestant. In the first year of Mary's rule, it was Knox and Maitland who clashed, time and again. It is worth noting that, unlike his record of his exchanges with Mary, when he told his readers explicitly that it was he, John Knox, who had the courage to face up to and lecture his Queen, in his account of his early exchanges with Lethington he tended to keep himself rather anonymous. In the first clash, over the subject of the Queen's right to her Mass – 'the subjects might not lawfully take her Mass from her' – Knox did give names to the adversaries, including 'secretary Lethington' among the supporters, and the mere 'John Knox' as the last name on the list of the principal ministers who backed the contrary judgement, 'Mr John Row, Master George Hay, Master Robert Hamilton and John Knox'.[31] But in the General Assembly of December 1561, over the question of holding the assemblies of the Kirk, Knox not only made the remarkable and wholly inaccurate comment that 'gladly would the Queen and her Secret Council have had all assemblies of the godly discharged', which, given the heavily Protestant composition of Mary's Council, makes no sense at all except in terms of the image he so desperately sought to create, but also referred to himself in his argument with Lethington simply as 'the other'.[32] Then there was the row over the thirds of benefices, the first and very ramshackle scheme to finance the new Church by taking one-third of the revenues of existing benefice holders and giving it to the Crown who would pay the ministers. Knox duly tells us of his speech claiming that:

---

[30] CSP Scot., I, pp. 597 (30 January), 603 (12 February), 650 (31 August), 672–3 (16 December), 674–5 (30 December); Knox, Works, VI, pp. 138–9, 144, 146–8. The date of the letter of 16 December is given in the Works but not in CSP Scot.

[31] Knox, History, II, p. 23.

[32] Ibid., II, pp. 25–7.

the Spirit of God is not the author of it; for, first, I see two parts freely given to the Devil, and the third must be divided betwix God and the Devil. Well, bear witness to me that this day I say it, ere it be long the Devil shall have three parts of the Third; and judge you then what God's portion shall be.

To which Lethington replied that 'the ministers being sustained, the Queen will not get at the year's end to buy her a pair of shoes'. But when Lethington subsequently launched an attack on the ministers who 'have this much paid unto them by year, and who yet ever bade the Queen "grandmercies" for it?', it was Knox concealed under the guise of 'one' who smiled and answered that there had been nothing received *gratis* from the Queen.[33] Knox did not wholly disguise his role in arguments with Lethington but, in contrast to the arguments with Mary, he certainly played it down. Perhaps because Mary was wholly a lost cause, while Lethington was not, he was a little more circumspect in displaying himself as God's spokesman. Certainly in the succeeding years there were further dramatic exchanges with Mary; but it was Lethington with whom Knox really wanted to debate, Lethington by whom he seemed especially provoked and goaded.

The great irony of all this is that the Knox who comes through to us from the vivid writing of the *History*, and much else besides, was consistently damaging his own cause. Lethington, and with him Moray, were to be abhorred precisely because they saw, as Knox refused to see, that Mary was not a threat to the new Kirk. Indeed, she was supporting it by proclamation, and she was helping to finance it. It may have been a curious role for a Catholic monarch to adopt, but that is not the issue here. For as long as Mary threw in her lot with Lethington and Moray, the future of the Kirk was reasonably assured, as was a tolerable level of friendship with England. And that was precisely what Knox actually wanted. But he could not go along with it. The great reformer's response to Lethington's taunt that the ministers had shown no gratitude to Mary over the thirds was in fact shabby. It was also self-revealing. It seems that, having created his Scottish Mary Tudor, he came to believe in her with ever-increasing obsession. From his viewpoint, co-operation with her, no matter how expedient, no matter how beneficial, was in the eyes of his Calvinist God utterly and irrevocably wrong. Godly Protestants were absolutely bound under their covenant with God to depose their Catholic Queen; that would be the evidence of their godliness.[34] And so he created division within the ranks of the faithful.

---

[33] Ibid., II, pp. 29–31.

[34] The subtlety of Knox's covenanting theology is beautifully analysed in Jane E.A. Dawson, 'The Two John Knoxes: England, Scotland and the 1558 Tracts', *JEH*, **42**

That division was maintained through the period up to 1564 covered by the last Book of his *History*, Book IV. Knox continued to rail at Mary, to insist on expounding his resistance theory. There were three more personal meetings with the Queen. On 15 December 1562, they clashed over a sermon in which Knox, provoked by her excessive dancing which he claimed was in celebration of the success of her uncles in France, preached on the subject of the vanity and lack of virtue of princes. Summoned to her presence, he promptly gave her a *précis* of the sermon, pointing out to her that 'if there be into you any sparkle of the Spirit of God, yea, of honesty or wisdom, ye could not justly have been offended with anything that I spake'. Once again, Mary tried the soft approach; she could not, she told Knox, blame him for having no good opinion of her powerful uncles, the French and Catholic Duc and Cardinal de Guise. 'But,' she went on, 'if ye hear any thing of myself that mislikes you, come to myself and tell me, and I shall hear you.' This moderate response merely produced a ferocious insult to Mary's uncles, and a refusal 'to whisper my mind in your Grace's ear' in private. In his account, he had the high moral ground, and ended the victor. But Randolph, describing the meeting, suggests that it concluded with a very effective comment by Mary on the subject of conscience and answerability to God – for them both.[35]

Their third meeting happened four months later, in April 1563, when the ministers, outraged by the Masses said publicly at Kirkoswald and Maybole by Archbishop Hamilton at Easter, were demanding that the Queen should punish them. Initially she argued against it with Knox, asking him to use his influence to prevent men from being punished for using the religion which pleased them. Once again, however, Mary was conciliatory, warning Knox against the appointment of Alexander, Bishop of Galloway as superintendent; Knox defended him, but subsequently came to discover that Mary's doubts of this 'dangerous man' were right, and even admitted as much. They then had what, by their standards,

---

(1991), pp. 555–76; and in Mason's introduction to Knox, *On Rebellion*, pp. viii–xxiv. See also Chapters 7 and 8 in this volume.

[35] Knox, *History*, II, pp. 42–6; Knox gets the chronology wrong here, putting this meeting in May 1562 when in fact it happened on 15 December. Randolph to Cecil, 16 December 1562: Knox, *Works*, VI, p.147; *CSP Scot.*, I, p. 673. The two versions curiously differ: *Works*: 'she neyther [suffered] hym to speake hys conscience, as he wolde answer before God, and as she wolde also in her doings.' *CSP Scot.* (modernized text): 'she willed him to speak his conscience, as he would answer before God, as she would also in her doings'. The first version is, of course, by far the more dismissive of Knox. But both give Mary a highly effective last word. And it should be noted that this comes from an account written the day after the interview, and not one written several years later by an author who could not quite remember the correct order of events.

passed as a positively friendly discussion of the state of the marriage of Mary's half-sister Jane and the Earl of Argyll. And finally Mary promised to do justice to the offending Catholics, which produced from Knox the remarkably benign response, 'I am assured then that ye shall please God, and enjoy rest and tranquillity within your Realm; which to your Majesty is more profitable than all the Pope's power can be'.[36]

That was a unique lowering of his sword, and he promptly recovered. The sentence immediately following that response reads:

> This conference we have inserted to let the world see how deeply Mary, Queen of Scotland, can dissemble; and how that she could cause men to think that she bore no indignation for any controversy in religion, while that yet in her heart was nothing but venom and destruction, as short after did appear.

What he meant was that, despite the fact that she honoured her promise and summoned the offenders in May, the Parliament held immediately afterwards was not godly enough. Since this was the Parliament which, for example, passed an act making adultery punishable by death, it is a little difficult to see what Knox actually wanted, when he complained that it was not harsh enough.[37] Again, we are seeing the obsession. Do what she would, Mary was the agent of Antichrist.

Thus at their last meeting, in June 1563, all was back to normal. The provocation this time was the sermon in which Knox exhorted the nobility to resist the Queen's marriage to a papist. In that sermon, Knox made his position devastatingly clear. He had, he claimed, been with the Protestant lords in their 'most desperate tentations' and 'most extreme dangers'. And after their survival of these trials and dangers, for which they should have thanked God, what had they done? Betrayed God's cause, 'when ye have it in your own hands to establish it. The Queen, say ye, will not agree with us. Ask ye of her that which by God's word ye may justly require, and if she will not agree with you in God, ye are not bound to agree with her in the Devil'. Nothing could better summarize Knox's unchangeable loathing for Mary, his refusal to compromise with the unthinkable idea that a Protestant Church might be – was being – established under the rule of a Catholic Queen. Summoned to Mary's presence, the Queen fruitlessly, if justifiably, pointed out that:

> I have borne with you in all your rigorous manner of speaking, both against myself and against my uncles; yea, I have sought your favours by all possible means. I offered you presence and audience whensoever it pleased you to admonish me; and yet I cannot be quit of you … .

---

[36] Knox, *History*, II, pp. 71–4.
[37] *APS*, II, p. 539; Knox, *History*, II, pp. 76–80.

This was the occasion of Knox's famous answer to Mary's question, 'What have ye to do with my marriage? Or what are ye within this Commonwealth?'

> A subject born within the same ... and albeit I neither be Earl, Lord or Baron within it, yet God hath made me (however abject I be in your eyes) a profitable member within the same ... And therefore, Madam ... whensoever that the Nobility of this Realm shall consent that ye be subject to an unfaithful husband, they do as much as in them lieth to renounce Christ, to banish his truth from them, to betray the freedom of this Realm, and perchance shall in the end do small comfort to yourself.[38]

This ringing reply – despite its rather feeble final phrase – is accompanied by a marginal note reading 'Let Papists judge this day. 1567'. In 1567, Mary fell from power. But neither in 1563 nor 1567 did the papists notably benefit from her presence nor suffer from her absence. Again, Knox was conjuring up a vision of a Protestant struggle which had no roots in reality. No wonder Moray and Lethington, like Mary herself, saw him not as the messenger of the Lord so much as a profound irritant, a huge and buzzing fly – a pest. But nothing, it seemed, would stop him. In October 1563, he gave his backing to those who had broken in to the Queen's chapel at Holyrood, where Mass was being said in her absence. For this, he was summoned in December before the Council. The Queen came in with pomp and ceremony. But, said Knox, 'her pomp lacked one principal point, to wit, womanly gravity. For when she saw John Knox standing at the other end of the table bare-headed, she first smiled and after gave a gawf [guffaw] of laughter', and went on to say, 'Yon man gart me greit and grat never tear himself; I will see if I can gar him greit'. The result was predictable. Far from 'greiting', Knox treated the Queen and her questions with contempt, making it clear with whom he was prepared to debate: 'I began, ' he said, 'to reason with the Secretary, whom I take to be a far better dialectician than your Grace is ... .'[39] Mary's persistent and no doubt infuriating interruptions of Lethington's questions spoiled his chance. For that, he had to wait until the inordinately lengthy debate between them in the General Assembly of June 1564, with which Book IV closes, when he defended himself against Lethington's assertion that 'by God's providence we had liberty of religion under the Queen's Majesty, albeit she was not persuaded in the same', and his accusation that Knox especially amongst the ministry was undermining her authority and her subjects' good opinion of her. It was a wonderful opportunity

---

[38] Knox, *History*, II, pp. 80–84.
[39] Ibid., II, pp. 87–8, 94, 96.

for Knox to portray himself in the mould of the prophets of old, and, of course, to revive the issues of female rule and the legitimacy of resistance. Not surprisingly in the course of all this – when, as usual, Knox's answers were far longer than the questions put to him – Lethington found himself 'weary'. Not surprisingly, it ended inconclusively, running down into confusion over the question of whether there should be a vote on the issue of taking the Queen's Mass from her, with the curious final scene when Knox refused to write to Calvin for his advice, and not only refused, but concealed the fact that in 1561 he had already done so. And so, on another shabby note, Knox concluded his account.[40]

I make no secret of the fact that I am not one of Queen Mary's foremost admirers. And it is difficult not to admire John Knox. Yet when writing about their confrontations, it is impossible not to sympathize with the Queen, and not only with her, but with the Protestant lords whom Knox harangued and bullied as he did her. For what end? It is not in any way to detract from the undoubted and utterly sincere zeal with which John Knox sought to serve his God to speculate about the extent to which his passion was fuelled not only by the frustration of failing to embue others with his ideas of how God should be served, but by personal pique. There is, in Knox's relationship with Mary and her principal advisers, so much 'sound and fury, signifying ... ' – certainly not nothing, for no one could ignore Knox, but in practice remarkably little. Knox's *History*, that brilliant and compelling work which is propaganda not only for the Protestant cause in Scotland but for himself, would certainly ensure his towering place in the history of the Scottish Reformation. But there is an extent to which his own career, in England, Scotland and even Frankfurt and Geneva, can be seen as the career of a man too often shouting to make himself heard by men and women who would really have preferred not to hear him; and nowhere, surely, was that more true than in Scotland in the first half of the 1560s. It was, for example, only after 1567 that his power was acknowledged in Reformation satirical literature; and even then, he gets remarkably little attention.[41]

---

[40] Ibid., II, pp. 106–34; Knox, *On Rebellion*, pp. 182–209. Knox, *Works*, VI, pp. 133–4: Knox to Calvin, 24 October 1561.

[41] Gregory Kratzmann, 'Political Satire and the Scottish Reformation', *Studies in Scottish Literature*, 26 (1991), pp. 423–37, especially pp. 429–30. There is an admiring reference, probably to Knox's sermon at Moray's funeral on the text 'Blessed are they that die in the Lord' in 'The Regentis Tragedie'; equally, there is a scathing attack on him in 'Ane Admonition to the Antichristian Ministers in the Deformit Kirk of Scotland', in J. Cranstoun (ed.), *Satirical Poems at the Time of the Reformation* (2 vols, STS, Edinburgh, 1889–93), I, pp. 103, 334; II, pp. 17–24.

Perhaps that was particularly galling, for there are striking flashes of Scottishness in Knox, despite his earlier preference for England and the fact that his *History* was written in Anglicized language. He showed remarkable tolerance for Mary's third husband, James Hepburn, Earl of Bothwell. As the man whom everyone believed had killed her second one, Darnley, Bothwell was not the obvious candidate for admiration by a man of God. But Knox explained it with some pride as almost natural, for his forbears had served the Hepburns; the 'abject' Knox – the word he used of Mary's view of him – was not above invoking family connections as well as the favour of God in showing that he was a man to be reckoned with. For a moment, we are in the familiar Scottish world of kinship and lordship, rather than the terrifying world of God's battle with Satan for the Scottish soul. When he came before the Council in December 1563, he himself tells us of how he was accompanied by the brethren of the Kirk 'in such number that the inner close was full, and all the stairs, even to the chamber door where the Queen and Council sat'.[42] How many Scottish nobles have been damned by historians for doing precisely that, bringing their followers and supporters with them to overawe courts? And his *Appellation to the Scottish Nobility* of 1558, in which he saw England as already the covenanted nation which Scotland was not (and would not become until after 1560), has an almost paradoxical air, despite the logic of his argument; for the idea of the covenant with the Lord was surely one which came easily to a man writing about a society – his Scottish society – which was utterly familiar with covenants. Before the Refor mation, they had been called bonds, the bonds made between nobles and lairds for mutual support in secular purposes; but already in 1557, the year before Knox was writing, they had moved into the religious sphere with the First Band of the Lords of the Congregation.[43]

Pro-English, international and yet sometimes very Scottish, politically unrealistic and yet sometimes even secular in outlook: that was John Knox. And in the end, therefore, it is not quite possible to believe in the John Knox of the *History*, nor in the Mary whom he had to construct as a sort of Best Supporting Actress, in order to justify and lend conviction

---

[42] Knox, *History*, II, pp. 37–8, 93.

[43] Dawson and Mason have argued strongly that in 1558 Knox distinguished between England and Scotland; the first was covenanted, the second not. See above, notes 9 and 34. Nevertheless, in the *Appellation*, Knox does invoke the language of covenant for Scotland: Knox, *On Rebellion*, pp. 102–3. Dawson, 'The Two John Knoxes', p. 571, calls this 'a slip of the mind and pen'. Indeed – not suprisingly so. Bearing in mind Knox's Scottishness, such a slip would come easily enough to him, and it is just possible that the passage reflects a certain desire to see Scotland as a covenanted nation, on a par with England.

to his own self-portrait. Knox could inflame; he could inspire; he could terrify. He is, without doubt, one of the big figures of Reformation history, and not only in Scotland, although it is there that his legacy has lasted. The paradox is that he came to achieve that position despite the fact that his role was not central, was indeed sometimes a distraction and irritant, and all his efforts to conceal that do not quite succeed. In the long term, largely because of his *History*, he has had rather more admiration as the architect of the Scottish Reformation than he deserves, although no doubt no less than he felt that he merited. In the short term, in his own day – and especially as long as the Scottish Jezebel sat on the Scottish throne – it was a very different matter. Poor John Knox.

CHAPTER TWELVE

John Knox, Minister of Edinburgh and Commissioner of the Kirk

Michael Lynch

Sometime early in January 1559, John Knox received:

> Horrifying and sure accounts concerning changes of religion in Scotland, to the effect that Christ and his beloved Gospel be publicly taught and preached throughout that same kingdom. The hearts of those people are smitten and seized by the power of the divine Word in such a fashion that they abstain resolutely in all fear and horror from the loathsome and ignominious ceremonies and abuses of the Antichrist, and they assemble in crowds there where Christian and Evangelical meetings are held, where people preach in their [native] language, where God is invoked, and where the Sacraments are ordained and used according to Christ's instructions.

This is an extract from a hitherto unnoticed, eight-page tract, published in Geneva, in Lower German, sometime in 1559.[1] The recipient of the letter was John Bale, Marian exile and, as refugee Bishop of Ossory, familiar with the reluctance of another Celtic people to accept the Gospel. Its tone is apocalyptic and excited, drawing together evidence from across Europe, including Scotland, England and northern Germany, for a renewed outburst of evangelical fervour. Not only is the Pope identified as the Antichrist but there is more than a hint of the

---

[1] *Warhafftige Tydinge vam Vpgange des Euangelij und Straffe der affgesechten dessüluigen Vienden der papistischen Papen in Schotlande* ... [Truthful tidings concerning the ascendancy of the Gospel and the punishment of its declared enemies, the papist priests in Scotland, from a letter in Latin by William Cole to the honourable and most learned Sir John Bale, sometime bishop in England, at the present time however an exile in Basle] (Geneva, 1559). William Cole was another Marian exile, who would have been a natural go-between of Bale and Knox; he moved from Frankfurt to Basle during the winter of 1556–57, but joined Knox's congregation in Geneva in June 1557: C.H. Garrett, *The Marian Exiles* (Cambridge, 1938), p. 123. I am grateful to Mr I.C. Cunningham of the National Library of Scotland for first drawing my attention to the tract and to both Mr Theo van Heijnsbergen of the Department of Scottish Literature, University of Glasgow, and Professor Niebaum of the Department of Lower Saxon Studies, University of Groningen, for a translation of it. I have also benefited from discussion with Dr John Durkan.

coming of the last days. The first and most detailed example which the tract cites of this change of atmosphere is the Protestant riot in Edinburgh on 1 September 1558 – the feast day of St Giles, the burgh's patron saint. The tract provides some new detail about the riot. It claims that 'many thousands' (*viele dutzend Menschen*) of Protestant protesters assembled in the 'main street' of the town, as a consequence of a procession through the streets of the town by a 'motley crowd of monks and priests [accompanied by] the Queen [Regent] herself, her servants and her crowd of women'; they tore the statue of St Giles 'with violence from the necks of the carriers' and broke it up into small pieces before casting it into the Nor' Loch, 'the drain into which the dirt of the whole town is thrown'. The 'cross and standard bearers took flight' along with the 'disgraceful priests and monks' into nearby 'narrow lanes', hiding the golden religious crosses under their habits but abandoning the poles on which they were stuck.

How great a difference does this tract make to previous impressions of the slow spread of Protestantism in the capital before Knox's appointment as its minister in July 1559?[2] Its claim that there were 'many thousands' of rioters is scarcely credible. There are three significant points which suggest otherwise. One of them lies within the tract itself, which, unlike Knox's version of the 'tragedy of St Giles' in Book I of his *History of the Reformation*, written some five years after this event,[3] confirms John Lesley's account which discloses that the highlight of the procession was to have been the public apostasy of a number of Protestant sympathizers at the market cross of the burgh in the presence of the Queen Regent. That is more likely to have provoked a Protestant counter-demonstration than a new-found outrage at the annual procession marking the burgh's patron saint.[4] The tract interestingly implies that Paul Methven, a preacher active in Dundee and elsewhere in the summer of 1558, was one of the apostatizers; threatened with a 'death sentence', he was saved by 'the jostling and clamour' of the crowd. Nevertheless, as Knox himself later admitted, there were also some 'temporisers' that day who did not approve of this brand of muscular Protestantism; it is likely that those with the greatest reservations about mob violence were, like David Forrest, Master of the Royal Mint and a teacher in the burgh's Privy Kirk of the 1550s whom Knox named, the

---

[2] Michael Lynch, *Edinburgh and the Reformation* (Edinburgh, 1981), pp. 38, 73–4, 81–6, 178–9.

[3] Knox, *History*, I, pp. 127–9; see Maurice Lee, 'John Knox and his History', *SHR*, 45 (1966), pp. 79–88, for the dating of Book I.

[4] John Lesley, *The Historie of Scotland* (2 vols, STS, Edinburgh, 1888–95), II, pp. 382–3; see also Knox, *Works*, I, p. 560.

Protestants closest to the court and royal administration.[5] Another may have been William Maitland of Lethington, secretary to Mary of Guise.[6]

Lastly, and most significantly, there is nothing of sufficient substance in the tract to change the view that Protestantism was in a distinct minority in Edinburgh before the Reformation crisis of 1559 and for some time after it. The first specific indicator of Protestant strength remains the estimate made by the English ambassador, Thomas Randolph, that '1300 and odde' who had made 'open protestation of their belief' celebrated Communion by the new Protestant rite at Easter 1561, after being examined and admitted by 'ministers and deacons'. This was fully 21 months after Knox was appointed minister of Edinburgh in July 1559 and some eight months after the Reformation Parliament met in Edinburgh to abolish the Mass; it was also five months before Mary Queen of Scots returned to complicate matters in the capital.[7] The number of Protestant communicants, out of a burgh population estimated at some 12 000,[8] represented approximately one adult in five or six. There had undoubtedly been a distinct rise in the number of Edinburgh's Protestants in the second half of the 1550s, perhaps stimulated by Knox's visit in the winter of 1555–56, when the two separate Privy Kirks joined forces. But it remains likely that, by late 1558, they were still, at best, to be counted in hundreds rather than in the 'thousands' claimed in the Bale tract. The sight of Protestant rioters tearing down and trampling the religious banners of the craft guilds was hardly likely to have promoted an enthusiasm amongst the town's craftsmen for the new ideas.

One small discovery has been made in this area, although its significance is unclear. A craft which would have been prominent in the St Giles procession, marching under the banner of St Eloi, was the hammermen or metalworkers, which was the second largest in the burgh, with 72 masters in 1560; it had its own chapel, dedicated to St Mary Magdalene, as well as an altar in St Giles's. James Kirk has claimed that the hammermen appointed a Protestant chaplain, William Barbour, as early as November 1559. The evidence produced for the man's religious leanings in 1559 is scarcely conclusive: he is said 'soon afterwards' to have taken up the post of minister of Lasswade.[9] In fact,

---

[5] Knox, *History*, I, p. 128; Lynch, *Edinburgh*, p. 278.

[6] See Mark Loughlin's important study, 'The Career of William Maitland of Lethington, *c.* 1526–73' (unpublished University of Edinburgh PhD thesis, 1991).

[7] *CSP Scot.*, I, no. 967.

[8] Lynch, *Edinburgh*, pp. 9–10; this involves the use of the standard multiplier of 1.7 to take account of children.

[9] James Kirk, *Patterns of Reform: Continuity and Change in the Reformation Kirk* (Edinburgh, 1989), pp. xi, 134, 283.

the first reference to his new charge is not until March 1565, by which time much had happened, both in Edinburgh and to the hammermen. Yet this account is confused. The first mention of Barbour as 'thair minister of the Magdalene Chapel and collector to the beidmen' was in October/November 1560, not in 1559.[10] There had been an attempted Protestant *coup* within the craft in the summer of 1559, but it had failed; George Small, a saddler who had held office in the Privy Kirk of the mid-1550s, launched an unsuccessful attack on the craft hierarchy. But in May 1560, after the return of the Congregation to the burgh, another militant Protestant, William Harlaw, whose father had also held office in the Privy Kirk, was elected deacon.[11] Barbour's appointment now falls into place, as part of the *coup* which took place after the Congregation reoccupied Edinburgh in the spring of 1560. Far from disproving the presence of Catholicism within this important guild, the Barbour incident confirms that, before and after 1559–60, there were sharp religious divisions within this craft. Barbour did not enjoy an untroubled period as a Protestant chaplain after 1560. The craft found itself pursued in the civil courts by its former Catholic chaplain, Thomas Williamson, who had been held prisoner in Roslin Castle for an undisclosed offence in 1559, for breach of contract. This was a case similar to that pursued against the burgh council by the dismissed master of the grammar school, William Roberton, and Williamson, too, won his case. Also, by May 1562, the Catholic masters were back in control of the craft, and remained so until after 1567.[12]

The Bale tract is one of half a dozen pieces of fresh evidence or new studies which have appeared since the publication of my *Edinburgh and the Reformation* in 1981; it is probably the most inconsequential of them. The book itself was intended as a collective biography of Knox's Edinburgh rather than an individual study of Knox himself. This chapter will try to assess and draw together these new findings and to revisit the argument that Knox and the Protestant regime brought to power in the burgh council through a *putsch* in 1559–60 encountered a series of difficulties in Edinburgh, stemming from the conservative nature of

---

[10] J. Smith, *The Hammermen of Edinburgh and their Altar in St Giles Church* (Edinburgh, 1906), pp. 170, 172–3.

[11] Lynch, *Edinburgh*, pp. 56–9, 279, 285. Harlaw was also a member of the kirk session of 1561–62; see below, note 44.

[12] Lynch, *Edinburgh*, pp. 100, 288 (under Brocas); T. Ross, 'The Magdalene Chapel and the Greyfriars Churches, Edinburgh', *Transactions of the Scottish Ecclesiological Society*, 4 (1912–13), pp. 96–101, at p. 98.

burgh society, its suspicion of rapid or fundamental change and its dislike of the cost of reform. The new work includes Michael Graham's wide-ranging study of the discipline of the new Kirk, placing Edinburgh's experience in the 1560s in a wider context, including that of other towns, large and small.[13] Theo van Heijnsbergen has excavated the intellectuals, professionals and bourgeoisie of Edinburgh, finding a close-knit network of family and other connections which promoted an irenic Protestantism but also harboured a distinctively Erasmian-style Catholicism.[14] Alasdair MacDonald and Alan MacDonald have explored different aspects of the very Protestant triumphal entry orchestrated by the burgh council for Mary Queen of Scots two weeks after her return to Scotland in August 1561.[15] James Kirk has rediscovered a kirk session list for 1561–62, which is unique before the early 1570s.[16] And Margaret Sanderson's recent study of the Reformation in Ayrshire sheds light on the role of Adam Fullarton, self-styled leader of the Congregation in Edinburgh in 1559, as well as on Knox's service as a commissioner of the Kirk in Ayrshire in 1562.[17]

Fullarton acted as spokesman for Edinburgh's Protestants in the summer of 1559, when, after the arrival of the army of the Lords of the Congregation, they were allowed public worship in the burgh Church of St Giles with Knox as their minister. He was, arguably, the most important lay figure in the history of Edinburgh Protestantism in its first generation. Fullarton's wife, Marjorie Roger, was one of Knox's 'dear sisters' of Edinburgh with whom he corresponded in the later 1550s. She died in 1583, and her testament revealed an impressive library of over 30 books which included works of major Edwardian reformers of the late 1540s and early 1550s; in some cases, these were

---

[13] Michael F. Graham, *The Uses of Reform: 'Godly Discipline' and Popular Behavior in Scotland and Beyond, 1560–1610* (Leiden, 1996), pp. 49–64, 73–125; see also Chapter 13 in this volume.

[14] Theo van Heijnsbergen, 'The Interaction between Literature and History in Queen Mary's Edinburgh: the Bannatyne Manuscript and its Prosopographical Context', in A.A. MacDonald, M. Lynch and I.B. Cowan (eds), *The Renaissance in Scotland: Studies in Literature, Religion, History and Culture offered to John Durkan* (Leiden, 1994), pp. 183–225.

[15] A.A. MacDonald, 'Mary Stewart's Entry to Edinburgh: An Ambiguous Triumph', *Innes Review*, 42 (1991), pp. 101–10; Alan MacDonald, 'The Triumph of Protestantism: The Burgh Council of Edinburgh and the Entry of Mary Queen of Scots, 2 September 1561', *Innes Review*, 48 (1997), pp. 73–82. See also P. Davidson, 'The Entry of Mary Stewart into Edinburgh, 1561, and Other Ambiguities', *Renaissance Studies*, 9 (1995), pp. 416–29.

[16] Kirk, *Patterns of Reform*, p. 110 and notes.

[17] Margaret Sanderson, *Ayrshire and the Reformation* (East Linton, 1997), pp. 46, 121–3.

in editions which were published then and not later, giving a rare specific instance of the potential impact of English Protestant literature before the Reformation of 1559–60.[18] What Sanderson has discovered is Fullarton's roots, which lay in Ayrshire. This is, in one sense, surprising, for Ayrshire was something of a geographical enclave, without well-trodden trade links with Edinburgh. Fullarton was either the brother or the cousin of the Protestant laird of Dreghorn in Kyle, perhaps the key focal point of early Scottish Protestantism, which makes the discovery both intriguing and more understandable.[19] It seems clear that he worked his way into the Edinburgh merchant establishment by the familiar route of marriage, gaining his burgess-ship and membership of the merchant guildry in 1549.

It is now possible to place what happened in the capital during Knox's ministry into a fuller context than was previously possible. A series of contrasting studies of other local reformations have appeared over the last ten years; they have charted the progress of Protestantism in Angus and the Mearns, the diocese of Dunkeld, the very different burghs of Aberdeen and St Andrews and, most recently, in Ayrshire. They have underlined the diversity and complexity of local, rural or urban reformations in a society which was still instinctively regional or civic in its mental horizons.[20]

The Reformation in Edinburgh is even less likely to have been typical. Yet now the hothouse atmosphere of Edinburgh, a capital with a resident royal court for a third of Mary's personal reign,[21] an entrepôt which dominated the bulk of Scotland's overseas trade, the centre of emerging professional classes and home of two printing-presses, is better understood. Much more is known, as a result of the labours of John

---

[18] Lynch, *Edinburgh*, pp. 74, 76, 84–5, 221, 282. Marjorie Roger's library included Cranmer's short catechism of 1548 (*STC* 5993) and Hooper's *Declaration of the Ten Holy Commandments* (1548, 1550; *STC* 13746–50). Not surprisingly, she also had the Lekprevik 1563 edition of the debate at Maybole in August 1562 between Knox and Quintin Kennedy on the Mass (*STC* 15074); see note 69, below. See John Lesley, *History of Scotland* (Bannatyne Club, 1830), p. 269, for the impact of English Protestant literature.

[19] Sanderson, *Ayrshire*, p. 46.

[20] Frank D. Bardgett, *Scotland Reformed: The Reformation in Angus and the Mearns* (Edinburgh, 1989); Michael Yellowlees, 'Dunkeld and the Reformation' (unpublished Edinburgh University PhD thesis, 1990); Alan White, 'Religion, Politics and Society in Aberdeen, 1543–1593' (unpublished Edinburgh University PhD thesis, 1985); Jane E.A. Dawson, '"The Face of ane Perfyt Reformed Kyrk": St Andrews and the Early Scottish Reformation', in James Kirk (ed.), *Humanism and Reform: The Church in Europe, England and Scotland, 1400–1643* (Oxford, 1991), pp. 413–35.

[21] Edward Furgol, 'The Scottish Itinerary of Mary Queen of Scots, 1542–8 and 1561–8', *Proceedings of the Society of Antiquaries of Scotland*, 117 (1987), pp. 219–31, and fiche, C.1–D.6.

Durkan, of the war of rival printing presses in the burgh after 1560. One was run by Robert Lekprevik, official printer to the General Assembly; his edition of the *Book of Common Order* in 1564 was financed by Alexander Clerk, a merchant and client of James Stewart, Earl of Moray, who also had links with other Protestant notables such as Lord Lindsay of the Byres and Knox's long-standing friend, Robert Campbell of Kinzeancleuch.[22] The other press, which seems to have had a connection with the royal court, was run initially by John Scott, who published the stinging pamphlet attacks on Knox of the Catholic schoolmaster and controversialist, Ninian Winzet; although Scott's printing-irons were seized in 1562, when Winzet and Mary's French confessor, Rene Benoist, fled abroad, they were by 1565 in the possession of his business partner, Thomas Bassenden, who would later be called to account for printing Marian tracts during the civil war of 1568–73.[23]

A good deal more is also known about the royal court itself. Knox certainly feared its impact. He repeatedly denounced 'courtiers' and the 'holy water of the court',[24] but there was until recently little means of quantifying the effect of its re-establishment in 1561 on Mary's return from France. It was the lack of a royal court, always a hotbed of gossip and often of both political and religious controversy, in the 19 years which followed the death of James V in 1542 which probably did as much as any other single factor to contribute to the inchoate nature of early Scottish Protestantism. Without a regular forum for anticlerical literature or a theatre for changing religious fashions, as the court was in France in the 1550s, Protestantism in Scotland had to rely on local initiatives and leadership. After Mary's return, novel forms of propaganda and iconography would be used to promote, not so much a Catholic Queen, as a conservative image of monarchy and royal power.[25] In a society where, it is usually accepted, kinship and sovereignty generally counted for more than religious loyalties, such an approach would have considerable appeal.[26] Theo van Heijnsbergen's ground-breaking

---

[22] John Durkan, 'Contract between Clerk and Lekpreuik for printing the Book of Common Order, 1564', *The Bibliotheck*, 11 (1983), pp. 129–35; P. Watry, 'Sixteenth Century Printing Types and Ornaments of Scotland with an Introductory Survey of the Scottish Book Trade' (unpublished Oxford University D.Phil. thesis, 1992), pp. 31, 33–4; Lynch, *Edinburgh*, p. 281.

[23] Michael Lynch (ed.), *Mary Stewart: Queen in Three Kingdoms* (Oxford, 1988), pp. 16, 88; Watry, 'Sixteenth Century Printing Types', pp. 23–5, 40.

[24] E.g. Knox, *History*, II, pp. 12, 64, 107.

[25] Michael Lynch, 'Queen Mary's Triumph: The Baptismal Celebrations at Stirling in December 1566', *SHR*, 69 (1990), pp. 1–21; see also A.A. MacDonald, 'The Bannatyne Manuscript: A Marian Anthology', *Innes Review*, 37 (1986), pp. 36–47.

[26] Gordon Donaldson, *All the Queen's Men: Power and Politics in Mary Stewart's Scotland* (London, 1983), pp. 48–69.

prosopographical study, which focused on the extended legal family of the Bannatynes, has demonstrated an urban version of that thesis; it has revealed the extent in the capital of a 'middling' sort of intellectuals, lawyers and merchants often attached either to the royal administration or the burgh establishment who viewed loyalty to the Crown as part of a wider, traditional political culture; not surprisingly, they reacted ambiguously as well as positively to the prospect of religious reform.[27]

The formal entry of Queen Mary into her capital took place on 2 September 1561, two weeks after her arrival. It was three years and a day after the St Giles Day riot and two days before the first interview between John Knox and his Queen. That fact, together with what has been called the rather 'tasteless sacrilege'[28] which formed part of the entry, may give extra poignancy to the well-known passage in their exchange where Mary challenged Knox: 'I perceive that my subjects shall obey you and not me; and shall do what they list, and not what I command: and so must I be subject to them and not they to me.'[29]

It seems likely that both parties – the capital's new Protestant council, brought to power in a *putsch* in the course of the Reformation crisis, as well as the royal entourage – would have wanted to avoid the anniversary of the St Giles Day riot.[30] The new Protestant regime in the burgh, which had been plagued with a series of craft riots over the previous ten months, would have been anxious not to risk another opportunity for popular disturbance; its initial thought, to levy a tax on the populace to pay for the entry, had been abandoned as likely to 'engender murmur'.[31] The entry itself was an odd mixture of familiar royal triumphalism, probably established as a template in the reign of James III, and a Protestant demonstration; the Queen was presented with the keys to her capital by a boy descending from the heavens but also with a Protestant Bible and Psalter to show her the 'perfeytt waye unto the heavenis hie'. Another ritual, enacted at the Salt Tron, was a playlet depicting the Old Testament story of Korah, Dathan and Abiram who had challenged the authority of Moses and been consumed by fire.[32] Little of this comes as a surprise. The organizers belonged to a council distinguished by a militant Protestantism; it had sought to go beyond the letter of the law as enacted by the Reformation Parliament of 1560, in effect making Catholicism a crime as distinct from attending the Mass or being involved in a baptism by the

---

[27] Van Heijnsbergen, 'Queen Mary's Edinburgh', pp. 207–10, 211–14.
[28] MacDonald, 'Ambiguous Triumph', p. 107.
[29] Knox, *History*, II, pp. 13–20, at p. 17.
[30] MacDonald, 'Triumph of Protestantism', p. 79.
[31] Lynch, *Edinburgh*, pp. 90–95; *Edin. Recs*, III, p. 120.
[32] MacDonald, 'Ambiguous Triumph', pp. 106–7.

old rites.[33] Yet the burgh put itself into debt for over two years in order to perform the rite of passage which traditionally forged a new, closer bond between monarch and capital; ironically, one of the financiers of the entry was Maitland, one of the courtiers most despised by Knox. It had also staged an event which its own minister condemned. Knox criticized the 'verses, masking and other prodigalities, faine would fools have counterfeited France'.[34] This was, so far as can be detected, probably the first time that John Knox disagreed with the Protestant régime brought to power in 1560; it certainly would not be the last.

The new detail of the entry of September 1561, and the crassness of some of its Protestant imagery, helps to explain more fully the intervention by the Queen in town council elections a month later, when she unsuccessfully attempted to dismiss the newly elected provost and bailies after they had provocatively reissued previous ordinances of marginal legality, which bracketed together priests and others from 'the wikit rable of the antechrist' with 'adulteraris, fornicatouris an all sic filthy personis'.[35] It was a mistake by the Queen – and one which she would not repeat. But it was also an error committed by the new Protestant regime, which would learn that a capital had to learn to live with the presence of the royal court so close to it.

The composition of the kirk session which was elected in October 1561, in the wake of the Queen's unsuccessful intervention in the burgh council election process, has recently come to light.[36] It is a find of some significance, since nothing is otherwise known of the membership of Edinburgh's session before 1573.[37] It shows that Knox regularly attended the session along with John Spottiswoode, superintendent of Lothian – a relationship which has, as yet, scarcely been explored – and the burgh's second minister, the ex-Dominican friar, John Craig, who was appointed mid-way through its term of office, in April 1562. Yet does the list of its members justify the claim that it shows the 'powerful friends of Protestantism within the burgh establishment'?[38] What follows is a fuller analysis, based on the experience of burgh government, status and wealth of its members.[39]

---

[33] Graham, *Uses of Reform*, pp. 51–4, 56 n.

[34] MacDonald, 'Triumph of Protestantism', pp. 77, 81; Knox, *History*, II, p. 21. Knox's account of the entry is confused and misdated.

[35] Lynch, *Edinburgh*, pp. 97–9; Graham, *Uses of Reform*, p. 52; *Edin. Recs*, III, p. 125.

[36] Kirk, *Patterns of Reform*, p. 110 n; William Fraser, *Memorials of the Montgomeries, Earls of Eglinton* (2 vols, Edinburgh, 1859), II, p. 185.

[37] See Lynch, *Edinburgh*, pp. 267–73, for the composition of the kirk sessions of 1573–76.

[38] Kirk, *Patterns of Reform*, p. 110.

[39] See Appendices 1 and 2.

The session had on it six members of the sitting town council, elected in controversial circumstances in October 1561. They were the Dean of Guild, Alexander Guthrie; a sitting bailie, John Marjoribanks; three merchant councillors – Robert Glen, Alexander Park and John Spens – and a craft councillor, John Weir. Guthrie was one of three lawyers on the session; the others were both advocates – Richard Strang and the better-known figure of Clement Little, whose donation of his library, on his death 20 years later, would make him a major benefactor of the town college of Edinburgh.[40] So far, the evidence does seem to suggest that these were men of standing. What of their financial status? Lawyers usually avoided paying tax in Edinburgh, but a forced loan to the Crown in 1565 included them. In it, all three of these lawyers make substantial payments, as did three of the merchants on the session – Glen, Park and John Marjoribanks. Each of this trio belonged to the élite of the top 40 merchants in the burgh. Yet it is at this point that the evidence begins to run thin; the remaining seven merchants on the session were small, insignificant men. Only one of them figured in the top half of the 357 merchants paying the 1565 tax. Although no details are available of individual payments of craftsmen, it is clear that, in terms of wealth, all three craftsmen on the session were also nonentities.

What of their experience of burgh government? In almost all Scottish burghs, the Reformation was carried through by the existing establishment but in Edinburgh events had taken a very different path. In the course of the Reformation crisis, the town council had twice been displaced and twice replaced by a regime put in power by the army of the Lords of the Congregation.[41] This session, interestingly, contains the only two members of the council of 1559 who had agreed to continue serving – Glen and Spens. Apart from them, there were only two others on the session, Alexander Park and Andrew Slater, who had experience of burgh government before 1560, and Slater's was confined to a single year. Others had appeared only after 1560, as part of the new Protestant regime. John Marjoribanks had emerged out of obscurity in 1561 suddenly, and very unusually, to become a bailie. Alex Guthrie, the powerful town clerk, known to his Catholic enemies as 'King Guthrie', sat on the council illegally, as had Strang in 1559–60; lawyers were not entitled to do so.[42] There was a very strong element of *arrivistes* in this session. At least ten of its 18 members could be classified as such.

---

[40] For Little, see James Kirk, 'Clement Little's Edinburgh', reprinted in Kirk, *Patterns of Reform*, pp. 16–69.

[41] Michael Lynch, 'The Two Edinburgh Town Councils of 1559–60', *SHR*, 54 (1975), pp. 117–39.

[42] It is possible that Guthrie also engaged in trade, since he appeared amongst the merchants in a muster roll of 1558, but he paid tax as a 'man of law' in 1565.

What of the three craftsmen? None had ever sat on the town council. Although the burgh had 14 incorporated crafts and it was practice
on the burgh council always to have representatives from different
guilds, two of the three sessioners, William Harlaw (a saddler) and
John Weir (a pewterer), were drawn from the same craft – the
hammermen. As we have seen, this was a craft in which there were
sharp religious differences. In August 1562, during the lifetime of this
session, William Brocas, a Catholic who had been elected hammerman
deacon three months before by no fewer than 40 craft masters – was
called before the Privy Council, where he refused to abjure his faith.[43]
There are curiosities about each of these Protestant hammermen.
Harlaw had been awarded his burgess-ship only in December 1560,
five months before being appointed deacon of his craft. His importance lay in his family. His father, a tailor of the same name, had held
office in the Privy Kirk in the mid-1550s. Weir was appointed a craft
councillor in October 1561 in defiance of established procedure and
in the face of protests made by the other craft deacons. Both Harlaw
and Weir show, not the strength of Protestantism amongst the craftsmen, but its weakness; the council had been forced to breach
long-standing rules to ensure Protestant representation on it from the
crafts.[44]

The other craft sessioner, John Freir, was a skinner. This was another
important guild which was probably still largely Catholic in its sympathies; one of its prominent masters, John Loch, who was elected deacon
of the craft in 1561–62 despite his religious convictions, had bought the
vestments and chalice of the craft when auctioned off in 1560. The
former chaplain, the deacon, chalice and vestments next surfaced in
1565, when the priest was caught saying Mass in a private house on
Palm Sunday, put through a show trial and tied with his chalice to the
market cross, where he was, in Knox's unpleasant phrase, 'served with
his Easter eggs' by a mob of some 300 or 400. This display of militant
Protestantism again proved counter-productive: it provoked a riot by
Catholics in the burgh and intervention by the Queen and her Privy
Council to restore the peace. Freir was likely to have been in a minority
within his craft but clearly was a significant, if minor figure in the story
of Edinburgh Protestantism. The brother (probably the younger brother)
of a lawyer, he was again on the session in 1573–74.[45]

---

[43] RPC, I, p. 216.

[44] See Lynch, Edinburgh, pp. 96, 278, 285.

[45] Ibid., pp. 107–8, 267 (Freir), 290 (Loch); Knox, History, II, pp. 140–41; Jane E.A.
Dawson, 'Mary, Queen of Scots, Lord Darnley and Anglo-Scottish Relations in 1565',
International History Review, 8 (1986), pp. 11–12, for a wider, international context.

Taken as a whole, does the session list of 1561–62 show that Protestantism had already reached a powerful position within the burgh establishment, only two to three years after Knox's appointment as minister of Edinburgh? The answer, as often in Reformation Edinburgh, is ambiguous, and it would take a determinedly one-eyed view of the facts that are available to argue otherwise. On the one hand, the list does show that there was support for Knox amongst the upper echelons of both the merchant oligarchy which controlled the town and its legal establishment. Yet the assertion, based on the example of Clement Little and a handful of others, that the majority at the bar 'conformed at the Reformation',[46] is a reckless leap into the dark. A recent, much fuller scrutiny of Edinburgh's legal fraternity, taking as its starting-point the influential Bannatyne family, has produced conclusions which are more ambiguous. In what is a model of careful and balanced analysis, it explores with new levels of sophistication the motivation which underpinned both conformity to Protestantism and the continuing hankering after reform-minded Catholic orthodoxy. It describes Edinburgh's legal fraternity as typically being made up of 'university graduates and reform minded jurists, anxious to reform society without irrevocably breaking the values which underpinned it'. Their sympathies were with 'progressive but non-radical men of the middle'. This was an intelligentsia 'which had merged Christian or Erasmian humanism containing Lutheran elements with a native tradition of learning that focused particularly on education and legal reform, a mixture which might be termed civic humanism'.[47]

Such men were hardly converts with a simple mission; their Protestantism conformed to their existing values, high among which was a deeply conservative desire to preserve Scotland's cultural heritage.[48] This is an urban version of what Frank Bardgett, in his study of rural Angus and the Mearns, called a deeply conservative 'lairdly culture': in it, both the authority and the belief system of a lairdly landed class were enhanced by a distinctly conservative brand of Protestantism, orchestrated by the minor laird and provost of the burgh of Montrose, John Erskine, who (despite his published thoughts on the need for a separation between the two 'regiments') became a superintendent in the reformed Church.[49] In Edinburgh, which was undergoing something of

---

[46] Kirk, *Patterns of Reform*, p. 42.

[47] Van Heijnsbergen, 'Queen Mary's Edinburgh', pp. 195–6, 214.

[48] It is hardly surprising that Knox's judgements on the members of the Bannatyne circle were distinctly mixed. It included, for example, John Bellenden of Auchnoull, and Simon Preston of Craigmillar, both the subject of vitriolic attacks by Knox; see *History*, I, pp. 113, 219; II, p. 23.

[49] Bardgett, *Scotland Reformed*, pp. 157–8.

a 'cultural revival' before and after 1560, the political culture and
conservatism of a royal capital and a restored royal court comple-
mented one another.[50] It was not easy territory for an uncompromising
preacher with radical leanings like Knox.

There remains a problem in any analysis of Edinburgh's Reformation, as with the Scottish Reformation as a whole; the word 'conformity'
is often used loosely or uncritically, conflating passive or even reluctant acquiescence in the new religion and positive, though less than
fulsome, acceptance of it. Studies of the motivation and double-edged
effects of conformity in other parts of both England and northern
Europe suggest the need for a more discriminating approach.[51] The
kirk session list of 1561–62 provides further illustrations of the phenomenon. One of the features of the period 1561–62 was the attempt
made by the town council to consolidate the work of its predecessor,
in pursuing offenders and trying to harry Catholic recusants or protesters. Two of the sessioners – Richard Strang and Andrew Armstrong
– sat on an assize of the Court of Justiciary which in December 1561
convicted William Balfour, a Catholic inhabitant of Leith, for interfer-
ing with the examination of intending communicants by Knox's deputy,
John Cairns, in St Giles's and denying that Protestantism was the Word
of God. The new information confirms the impression of a packed
jury; it also contained two Protestant town councillors and a baxter
activist, David Kinloch, as well as a kinsman of the superintendent of
Lothian.[52] This helps to suggest a definite tie-in between the kirk
session and the criminal courts, which has been detected before, though
only occasionally.[53] If this was so, the reasons for conforming multiply; nominal conformity, many may have thought, could provide a
sanctuary from the zealots who were prominent in both council chamber and kirk session in the first flush of victory between 1560 and
about 1562.

There can be little doubt, however, that there was a militant tendency
present in the session of 1561–62. Four of its members would themselves be tried in the criminal courts for murder or sedition in 1565 or
1566, involved either at the fringes of the Chaseabout conspiracy or in
the murders of David Riccio and the Dominican friar John Black on the

---

[50] Van Heijnsbergen, 'Queen Mary's Edinburgh', p. 207.

[51] See R. Whiting, *The Blind Devotion of the People* (Cambridge, 1989), pp. 171 ff.;
Euan Cameron, *The European Reformation* (Oxford, 1991), pp. 415–16.

[52] Robert Pitcairn (ed.), *Criminal Trials in Scotland, 1488–1624* (3 vols, Bannatyne
Club, Edinburgh, 1833), I, pp. 416–18; SRO, JC 1/11, 24 December 1561; Lynch,
Edinburgh, pp. 99, 287; Graham, *Uses of Reform*, p. 56.

[53] Lynch, *Edinburgh*, pp. 175–6.

same night in March 1566.[54] Yet matters in Reformation Edinburgh were seldom as straightforward as that. In the spring of 1562, John Marjoribanks, the sitting bailie on the kirk session, appeared amongst a group of over 20 professional men, merchants and other burgesses to make a formal protest against the efforts of his own council and kirk session to dismiss the Catholic master of the grammar school, William Roberton.[55] James Aikman, on the session in 1561–62 and on the burgh council in the previous year, had a Catholic wife; she was among the worshippers caught attending an illegal Catholic baptism in the Queen's chapel at Holyrood in 1563. Aikman had to bail her out.[56] John Spens, another of the sitting councillors on the session, was dismissed by Knox as 'not worthy' because he accepted burgh office as a nominee of the Queen in 1565; ironically, he was appointed a burgh commissioner to the General Assembly shortly afterwards.[57] Even William Harlaw, militant son of a member of the Privy Kirk and willing to become involved in the Riccio murder, did not go the full mile on some aspects of the reformers' programme; he had tried to defend another craft deacon, hauled before the session for adultery in 1560.[58] The individual examples given here and elsewhere are often inconsequential in themselves, but collectively they demonstrate that even committed members of the new Protestant regime were not immune from the irenicism, ambiguity and compromises which marked the years of John Knox's tenure of the ministry of Edinburgh. Yet these were Knox's right-hand men, on whom he had to rely to push forward his mission.

What of the militant tendency, detailed earlier? Men like Guthrie and Slater, who were both prepared to risk involvement in armed insurrection against the Crown in 1565, were key members of the radical party brought to power in the burgh in 1559–60 and gradually squeezed out of the council chamber in the course of the first half of the 1560s. Theirs was an act of desperation in July 1565, when they were caught drilling armed companies on the Crags, close to the royal Palace of Holyroodhouse. Still more hot-headed were the actions of Armstrong and Harlaw, both involved in the double murder of the Queen's servant, David Riccio, and the Dominican John Black on the same night in March 1566. It is hard to believe that Knox's influence, like that of his

---

[54] These were Andrew Armstrong, Alexander Guthrie, William Harlaw and Andrew Slater; see Lynch, *Edinburgh*, pp. 282, 284, 285.

[55] *Edin. Recs*, III, pp. 141–2; Lynch, *Edinburgh*, pp. 100–101.

[56] Lynch, *Edinburgh*, p. 288, under Isobel Curror. Since Aikman had been made burgess and guild in 1530, it is likely that both husband and wife were elderly.

[57] Knox, *History*, II, pp. 170–71; Lynch, *Edinburgh*, p. 112.

[58] Lynch, *Edinburgh*, pp. 91–2, 95; see also Graham, *Uses of Reform*, pp. 49–50, 54, 86–90, for Kirk Session treatment of sexual offences in general.

closest confidantes, did not also wane in 1565–66. Committed Protestant activists such as these would return to power, but only after the deposing of Mary in 1567. It was then and only then that Edinburgh's Reformation gained a second wind. Yet that is a period about which comparatively little is known, not least because Knox's *History* stops short of it.

One more discovery is worth considering before turning to the wider picture. It may help provide another reason why Edinburgh's merchant establishment was so cautious in lending full-blooded support to Knox's vision of a Reformation. What was the effect of what the later, Presbyterian historian David Calderwood, who was resident in Edinburgh in the late 1580s and 1590s and must have known its merchants well, caustically stigmatised as their real 'religion': love of 'their particular'?[59] *Edinburgh and the Reformation*, although it emphasized the fears of the town about losing its position as the foremost trading centre in the realm as a result of its jurisdictional wrangles with the port of Leith, avoided systematic analysis of its overseas trade, which underpinned its wealth. A clearer picture can now emerge. In the three-quarters of a century before 1550, Edinburgh had gradually claimed more and more of the export trade at a time when the Scottish economy was recovering from a long slump. By 1500, 60 per cent of Scottish exports were customed at Leith. By the end of the sixteenth century, the figure would rise to 72 per cent. The recovery had begun to accelerate in the late 1530s, but was sharply checked by the Rough Wooing of the 1540s.[60]

Within this broad picture, less attention has been paid to the pace of Edinburgh's recovery, either during the last years of the reign of James V or in the 1550s and 1560s. A closer scrutiny of the evidence of the *Exchequer Rolls* suggests that Edinburgh did not recover as quickly as may have been expected after the political crises of the 1540s. The overall totals of customs paid across a dozen commodities ranging from wool and skins to fish, coal and salt suggest that there was by the mid-1550s a growing recovery – the figure, for example, for 1556 is on a par with those for the mid-1530s. After 1560, however, there was an alarming slide downwards, which was accelerating by 1564–65. Unfortunately, no returns survive for 1566 or 1567, in itself perhaps an indicator of

---

[59] Alan MacDonald, 'David Calderwood: The Not So Hidden Years, 1590–1604', *SHR*, 74 (1995), pp. 69–74; Calderwood, *History*, V, pp. 177–8; Lynch, *Edinburgh*, pp. 7, 222.

[60] Isobel Guy, 'The Scottish Export Trade, 1460–1599', in T.C. Smout (ed.), *Scotland and Europe, 1200–1850* (Edinburgh, 1986), pp. 62–81; Michael Lynch, 'Continuity and Change in Urban Society, 1500–1700', in R.A. Houston and I.D. Whyte (eds), *Scottish Society, 1500–1800* (Cambridge, 1989), pp. 98–100; *Atlas of Scottish History to 1707*, eds P.G.B. McNeill and H.L. MacQueen (Edinburgh, 1997), pp. 240–41, 250–61.

the disruption in that period; but the returns for 1564–65 were worse than those for the civil war years of 1572–73, when the merchants of the King's Party exiled in Leith carried on regardless. What Edinburgh faced in the mid-1560s was no less than a trade crisis. Both its scale and its root causes are worth exploring.[61]

The six years between 1560 and 1565 saw a drop of some 15 per cent in the overall customs paid compared with levels in the second half of the 1550s. This was a further deterioration from what had been a painfully slow recovery in the 1550s from the severe crisis in trade inflicted by the Rough Wooing in the 1540s. The scale of the contraction is better measured when it is realized that Edinburgh's exports in the first half of the 1560s were running at only 52 per cent of what they had been in the last years of the reign of James V.

It does not seem to have been the case that Edinburgh was losing its market share to any other burgh. It was in the 1560s actually marginally strengthening its relative position in all four of the key commodities – wool, woollen cloth, fells and hides, which typically made up over 90 per cent of the total custom paid by the burgh. The problem seems rather to have lain in demand for the two commodities in which Edinburgh enjoyed the largest share of overseas markets: by the early 1560s the capital had over 88 per cent of the trade in hides, but its exports were running at only 65 per cent of the levels of the later 1550s. There was a further sharp drop between 1563 and 1565, when exports fell to 39 per cent of what they had been during the regency of Mary of Guise (1554–59). In wool, the situation was even starker: the burgh had a total domination of the export trade by 1560, but the volume of exports in the early 1560s stood at only 73 per cent of 1554–59. The scale of the disaster which had overtaken Edinburgh's exporting merchants is better appreciated if wool exports are measured against what they had been quarter of a century before: an average of 1 259 sacks of wool were exported each year between 1537 and 1542; in 1560–65 the average was 361 sacks – a fall of 71 per cent. Because of the size of its stranglehold over the Scottish export trade – 63.3 per cent in 1560–65 – a drop in exports meant that, while most towns caught a cold, the capital would develop a fever.

Wool and the leather trade were the basic foundations of both overseas trade and industry in the capital. Its future commercial prosperity would lie in the general recovery of the export trade from the mid-1570s onwards, its own development in commodities such as cloth and its growing control over areas such as the coal trade. In the early 1560s,

---

[61] See Appendix 3. All evidence is drawn from the *Exchequer Rolls*, vols XVI–XIX.

however, the economic climate would have been gloomy and the merchant establishment nervous. In the eyes of most in positions of influence, this would not have been a time for radical experiment, whether religious or political, which might further jeopardize the burgh's stability or hinder it from recovering from a steepening economic slump. Here is the classic scenario of urban decline, recognised in the later German urban Reformation, for a *Ratsreformation*, a 'top-down', conservative programme, which, nervous of the urban mob, tried to control the pace of religious reform.[62] Once again, though for different reasons, we arrive at the conclusion that civic humanism rather than religious radicalism was the keynote of this Reformation.

In her recent study of Ayr and Ayrshire, Margaret Sanderson has detected a number of key factors to help explain the early success of its Reformation and the consolidation after 1560. There seem to be four main points.[63] Protestantism in Ayrshire had a long provenance, going back to the Lollards of the 1490s, and Knox had early contacts with sympathetic local nobles and lairds – perhaps from 1547 or even before. Secondly, although Protestantism rested as elsewhere on a network of personal and family contacts, the movement in Ayrshire had a mixed leadership amongst its laity, ranging from nobles to local lairds and to some burgh office-holders; they had taken the initiative by the late 1550s and would hold on to it after 1560. This helped it escape the worst effects of the flight of intellectuals and clerics out of Scotland in the late 1530s and early 1540s, which seems to have had more serious effects elsewhere.[64] Allied to a decline in endowments and Catholic piety from the 1540s, if not before, there was also in Ayrshire, it is argued, a substantial withdrawal from orthodox public worship in the mid- to later 1550s. This was almost certainly one of the main purposes of Knox's key tracts of 1557 and 1558, the *Appellation* and the *Letter to the Commonalty*, which urged true believers into recusancy and withholding of teinds due to the Church. The extent of recusancy may help explain the confidence of local Protestant leaders, like Knox's old friend, Robert Campbell of Kinzeancleuch, in seeking from an indulgent Queen Regent the official permission to withdraw, on a local basis, from the services of the established Church.

---

[62] Kaspar von Greyerz, *The Late City Reformation in Germany; the Case of Colmar, 1522–1628* (Wiesbaden, 1980), pp. 196–205.

[63] Sanderson, *Ayrshire*, pp. 36–47, 79–82, 90–91, 96.

[64] John Durkan, 'Scottish Evangelicals in the Patronage of Thomas Cromwell', *RSCHS*, **21** (1982), pp. 127–56; John Durkan, 'Heresy in Scotland: The Second Phase', *RSCHS*, **24** (1991), pp. 320–65.

How does Edinburgh compare with this fourfold scenario for a local Reformation which was both early in its origins and quickly consolidated after 1560? There was some continuity between the generations of the late 1530s and the 1550s, but there can be no escaping the fact that the capital's early Protestants were to be counted in handfuls in the 1530s and remained dispersed until the mid-1550s. Secondly, the landed leadership around Edinburgh was much more mixed or ambiguous in its religious loyalties than that around Ayr. The major Protestant noble was the Earl of Morton, who subscribed the First Band of 1557; but he was offset by the figure of Lord Seton, who held land to the east and west of the burgh. It is significant that when Edinburgh's hard core of Protestant activists were arrested in 1565 for their involvement at the margins of the Moray conspiracy, they were pledged by a group of lairds who were not from the locality.[65] There is for Edinburgh no evidence of a decline of Catholic endowments by the 1550s and indeed there are some pointers in the accounts of the Dean of Guild to fresh investment in the mid- and later 1550s in the burgh Church, including new choristers and an organist, and to repair of the song school; this is part of what has recently been seen as a wider revival of cultural activities within the capital.[66] Was there a withdrawal from the Mass as the Privy Kirk grew in numbers in the mid-1550s? There is some evidence, for example amongst Knox's 'dear sisters' of Edinburgh, of a withdrawal from 'idolatry', but no indication that it was widespread. Yet where was it that the Regent, no doubt confident of the outcome, found the inspiration for a religious referendum for the capital in 1559, during the lull in hostilities after the Congregation reached the capital and Knox was appointed minister? Might it have been the request which had been made by Protestant lairds from areas such as Ayrshire? If so, there is a real irony here. The leader of Edinburgh's Protestants in July 1559, who publicly proclaimed that God's truth should not be subject to the 'voting of men', was none other than Adam Fullarton, kinsman of a Protestant Ayrshire laird.[67]

Although John Knox remained first minister of Edinburgh from his appointment in July 1559 until his death in 1572, he was frequently

---

[65] Those who stood surety for the captains of the four companies caught drilling on the Crags included Sir Andrew Ker of Cessford (Lanarkshire) and Sir James Hamilton of Crawfordjohn (Roxburghshire). SRO, JC/1/12, 26 July 1565; Lynch, *Edinburgh*, pp. 109–10, 281–4. See Donaldson, *Queen's Men*, pp. 19, 40, 46, 75, 107, 160, 163.

[66] Van Heijnsbergen, 'Queen Mary's Edinburgh', p. 223.

[67] *Edin. Recs*, III, pp. 46–8.

absent from the burgh. One reason for this was that he accepted half a dozen invitations, mostly in the period between 1562 and 1565, to act as a visitor or commissioner of the Kirk. The incomplete implementation of the system of oversight envisaged in the *First Book of Discipline* through ten or twelve superintendents – only five were ever appointed – made inevitable such demands on his time. In 1562, for example, he was away for four months in Ayrshire. He was absent again in the early part of 1563, when he was involved in the trial for adultery of the minister of Jedburgh, Paul Methven. In 1564 he was away for six weeks preaching 'in the south', while his colleague, John Craig, was doing the same in the north; they were replaced, on a temporary basis, by Christopher Goodman, the English minister of St Andrews. In late 1565, Knox took on another commission 'for so long as occasion might suffer'. Added to this were his enforced absences, including his flight, to Kyle again, in March 1566, eight days after the Riccio murder. He returned to Edinburgh only briefly, in December 1566, and promptly applied to the General Assembly for a six-month sabbatical leave to arrange for the education of his sons in England.[68]

The first of these appointments as commissioner was in 1562, when he spent the months between August and December in Ayrshire and other parts of the west. This was a difficult mission and there are perhaps three possible interpretations of why Knox should have been chosen for it. The first reason almost certainly lies in his already close connections with the leaders of Ayrshire Protestantism. Yet it is also likely that a charismatic and uncompromising figure was needed to combat the danger of a revival of Catholicism in the area. Characteristically, the threat was met head-on in the form of a theological confrontation – it was too crude and knock-about to be called a disputation – conducted at Maybole between Knox and Quintin Kennedy, Abbot of Crossraguel, in September 1562. Ironically, what the visit did result in was not only a Protestant bond – signed among others by Adam Fullarton's kinsman, John Fullarton of Dreghorn – but also a Catholic backlash, which resulted in widespread celebration of the Mass in the west during the following Easter, in 1563.[69]

There is a third possible explanation. It may be that Knox's connections were banked upon by the General Assembly to check and vet the progress of a parish reformation in Ayrshire, where there had been a marked degree of initiative taken by lay leaders to appoint a parish

---

[68] Knox, *Works*, VI, pp. 122, 142–3; *BUK*, I, pp. 51, 54, 57, 73, 84–5, 113, 130; Calderwood, *History*, II, pp. 282, 284, 306, 394; *CSP Scot.*, I, nos 1132, 1136, 1157.

[69] Knox, *History*, II, pp. 55–6, 57; Knox, *Works*, VI, pp. 169–220; Pitcairn, *Criminal Trials*, I, pp. 427–30.

ministry.[70] The pace at which ministers, exhorters and readers were hired was remarkable; it was a rate which worried the Assembly which wondered, as it did in the case of Angus and the Mearns which had parallels in terms of the initiative seized by its laity, if all the new incumbents were fit to hold godly office.[71] If this was the case, it was Knox in an unfamiliar role; the Assembly found a variety of terms to describe it, including 'overseer' and 'visitor'. In reality, Knox was acting as a quasi-superintendent, the agent of a centralist authority.

What were the effects of Knox's absences on his ministry in Edinburgh? Apart from the six-week period in 1564, when he and Craig were both replaced by Goodman, the burgh had no locum appointed during Knox's absences.[72] John Craig and a reader, John Cairns, who can be traced to the Privy Kirk of the 1550s, soldiered on alone to minister to a flock which was notionally some 7 000 strong and divided into four separate congregations.

The first of Knox's absences as a commissioner, in the last four months of 1562, should have served as a warning. It was in this period that there occurred the first serious split in Edinburgh's Protestant party, over the attitude it should take to the Queen's interference in burgh politics.[73] Worse came in 1565, though here the problem was not Knox's absence but his intransigence. In his *History*, he recounts how there was, just before Easter 1565, an organised hunt for Catholic worshippers in certain areas of the country; letters were sent from the 'brethren of Kyle' to Dundee, Fife, Angus, the Mearns and the 'brethren of Edinburgh' urging the rooting out of the idolatry of the Mass.[74] This was the authentic voice of the conventicle. Need it be wondered with what enthusiasm Knox and his Kyle-born ally, Adam Fullarton, took up the suggestion? The result in the more complex setting of Edinburgh, however, was nothing short of disastrous. It led to the Palm Sunday riot when an ex-chaplain of St Giles's and the skinner craft, James Tarbot, was caught saying Mass, tied to the market cross, bombarded with eggs and rubbish and systematically beaten up before and after his trial. It provoked a riot by the burgh's Catholics, which brought Edinburgh to the brink of a war of religion. Knox had provoked what might well have turned into a Catholic revival.

---

[70] Sanderson, *Ayrshire*, pp. 109–14.

[71] *BUK*, I, pp. 25–6 (December 1562); Bardgett, *Scotland Reformed*, pp. 87–94.

[72] Knox's absences anticipated a more widespread phenomenon of the next generation, when politically active radical ministers, such as James Melville, left their charges for prolonged periods to pursue the central affairs of the Kirk – in Melville's case leaving the local schoolmaster as a locum.

[73] Lynch, *Edinburgh*, pp. 101–3.

[74] Knox, *History*, II, pp. 140–41.

From this point onwards, Edinburgh's Catholics seem to have risked more open celebration of the Mass. Whether this became a more general phenomenon beyond the capital is difficult to say, but the General Assembly from this point onwards regularly complained of the spread of the pollution of the Mass.[75] The estimates of attendance by Catholics at Easter Masses have usually been treated with scepticism because they were so large – 9 000 in 1566 and 12 606 in 1567.[76] As such, they would represent considerably more than the adult population of Edinburgh. On the other hand, the ability of the royal chapel at Holyrood to accommodate such numbers need no longer be doubted, since exploration of the records of the Sacred Penitentiary in the Vatican have revealed a standard right of Scottish monarchs to use portable altars at such times. The precise numbers are probably less important than the contemporary impression that the number of Catholic worshippers was growing.

Where was Knox during these two Catholic Easter celebrations? In 1566, he was taking refuge in Kyle, having fled there a week after the Riccio murder. In 1567, he was in England. By then, his old militant allies on the town council had been eclipsed. A new, more moderate regime, made up of both Catholics and Protestants who were generally men of a more irenic stamp, had taken control from late 1565 onwards. The radical regime returned to power in late 1567, after Mary was deposed. It was then that Knox's old friend from Kyle, Adam Fullarton, returned as bailie along with other veterans of the *coup* of 1559. A reformed programme would regain some momentum, at both national and local levels; by 1569, the first large-scale excommunications took place in Edinburgh, following the General Assembly's publication of its *Ordoure of Excommunicatioun*. In fact, Edinburgh had again acted in advance of the letter of the law; a pulpit had been set up in St Giles's 'for preiching to the papists' seven months before the Assembly published the order.[77] Yet there still seems little reason to doubt that what finally turned Edinburgh Protestant was the traumatic impact of the civil war which took up much of the period between 1568 and 1573; the capital was the epicentre of the struggle between 1571 and 1573. We should not be surprised about the transition of a firmly

---

[75] *BUK*, I, pp. 72, 78, 87; *CSP Scot.*, II, nos 174, 203, 319, 403; see also Knox, *History*, II, p. 5.

[76] See Lynch, *Edinburgh*, p. 188.

[77] The *Ordoure* was published in July 1569 (not June as indicated in the printed text); the previous meeting of the Assembly, on 25 February, had indicated dissatisfaction with the effectiveness of the process of excommunication. Knox, *Works*, VI, pp. 447–70; *BUK*, I, pp. 139–40; *Edin. Recs*, III, pp. 259, 264; Lynch, *Edinburgh*, p. 192; Graham, *Uses of Reform*, p. 45.

Catholic town into a centre of radical Protestantism in two generations – Norwich is another good example. In the 1550s, almost all the indications still suggest that Protestantism in Edinburgh remained in a minority or muted, despite a good deal of anticlerical feeling. By the early 1580s, the capital was a hotbed of radical protest. The generation in between had seen a top-down magistrates' Reformation. John Knox's Reformation advanced only when he had the willing co-operation of those in power.

One very practical matter remains unclear. The single congregation which before the Reformation had worshipped in the great Church of St Giles, was split into four after 1560, reflecting the four quarters of the burgh. The north-east quarter was sent to worship in the separate Trinity College Kirk. The other quarters attended the new service in different parts of St Giles, which was physically divided by walls into three separate Churches to allow more easily a focus for Protestant preaching amidst the sprawling structure of a Catholic collegiate Kirk, with more than 40 altars, side-chapels, aisles and pillars, all dedicated to different saints. Knox had the services of a reader, but secured a second minister only in May 1562. What happened until then? Was Knox obliged to preach, one after another, to his four separate flocks? And even after Craig's arrival, how did he cope with his senior colleague's frequent absences? It would not be until the late 1570s that the burgh had a team ministry of four. The more one thinks about how the logistics of Edinburgh's Protestant Reformation worked, the more tempting becomes the thought that it worked only patchily. The 'trumpeter of God' had been given an almost impossible task in 1559; we should not be surprised if he found it so. Like the manuscript text of his *History*, which he left to the 'kirk and town of Edinburgh', Knox's work in the capital was still incomplete when he died, in November 1572.

Appendix 1: Council experience of kirk session, 1561–62

Experience before 1561	Council members	Experience after 1562
C60–61	Alex. Guthrie DG, lawyer, town clerk	DG62–54 C64–65
C59–60	Richard Strang, advocate	
	Clement Little, advocate	
T52–53, C54–55, T56–57, C57–58, 60–61	Alex. Park (C) mt	T63–64, DG64–66, C65–67, DG67–68
C57–58, B58–59, C/B 59–60, B60–61	John Spens (C) mt	B62–63
C59–60, B60–61	Robert Glen (C) mt	B63–64, T64–65, C65–66, B66–67, 67–68
	John Marjoribanks (B) mt	
C58–59	Andrew Slater mt	B62–63, C63–64, B67–68, C68–70
C60–61	James Aikman mt	
	Andrew Armstrong mt	
	Alex Hope mt	
	Robert Johnson mt	
	Alex Lyall mt	
	John Weir (CC) pewterer [hammerman]	
	William Harlaw saddler	
D hammermen 60–61	John Frier skinner	D skinners 63–64

Key: B bailie; C councillor; CC craft councillor; D craft deacon; DG dean of guild; T treasurer.

Note: Those in italics were members of the sitting council of 1561–62

Appendix 2: Wealth of kirk session, 1561–62

This analysis is based on the tax roll of September 1565, printed in Michael Lynch, *Edinburgh and the Reformation* (Edinburgh, 1981), pp. 373–7. There are 357 merchants or 'neighbours' on the roll, each paying between £60 and £2; 31 'men of law and scribes' also figured, paying between £100 and £10. Craftsmen paid corporately, as part of their guild. Also added, where available, are details from an unpublished muster roll of 1558 (MS Council Register, ii, fos 126v–137v); this details the number of servants of both merchants and craftsmen. Only half of the session, however, can be traced since one of the four burgh quarters is missing from the record, as is the skinner craft. The range for merchants was from seven servants to none; for craftsmen (apart from baxters) from five to none.

£40 LAW	Alex Guthrie DG, town clerk	5 servants
£40 LAW	Richard Strang, advocate	
£60 LAW	Clement Little, advocate	
£60 MT	Alex Park (C) mt	
£30 MT	Robert Glen (C) mt	
£30 MT	John Marjoribanks (B) mt	
£15 MT	Andrew Slater mt	
£10 MT	John Spens (C) mt	2 servants
£10 MT	James Aikman mt	no servants
£10 MT	Robert Johnson mt	
£8 MT	Alex Lyall mt	1 servant
£5 MT	Andrew Armstrong mt	1 servant
N/A	Alex Hope mt*	no servants
N/A	John Weir (CC) pewterer	1 servant
N/A	William Harlaw saddler	3 servants
N/A	John Frier skinner	

Key:
LAW   assessed amongst 'men of law and scribes'
MT   merchant
N/A   not assessed individually

Note: * Alex Hope did not appear, but was assessed at 10s in a 1583 tax roll, confirming him a very small merchant; he was the younger brother of the better known Protestant, Edward Hope, who was on the council of 1561–52.

Average legal assessment: £38 8s

Scale of legal assessments:

£100–£50	Top 9
£40–£20	Top 23

Average merchant assessment: £11 16s

Scale of merchant assessments:

£60–£30	Top 40
£60–£12	Top 110
£60–£10	Top 175
£8–£2	Lower 180

Appendix 3: Edinburgh's overseas exports

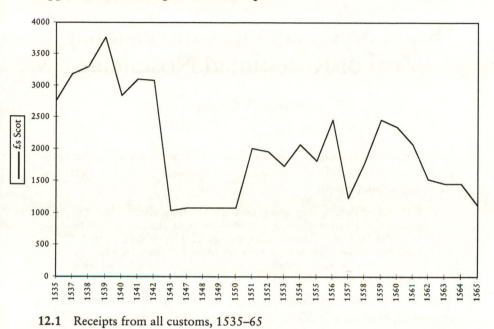

12.1   Receipts from all customs, 1535–65

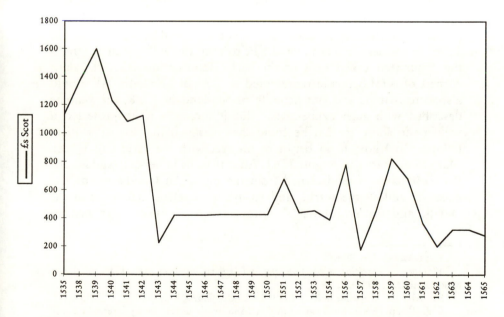

12.2   Receipts from wool, 1535–65

CHAPTER THIRTEEN

Knox on Discipline: Conversionary Zeal or Rose-tinted Nostalgia?

Michael F. Graham

John Knox the historian saw the Scottish Reformation, in its early years, as a swift spiritual renewal with dramatic social implications. Recalling 1558, he wrote:

> And this our weak begynnyng God did so bless, that within few monethis the hartes of many war so strenthned, that we sought to have the face of a Church amanges us, and open crymes to be punished without respect of persone. And for that purpose, by commoun electioun, war eldaris appointed, to whome the hole brethren promissed obedience ... .[1]

This rosy revolutionary nostalgia might be contrasted with the following report, made nearly 30 years later by a visitor to the parish of Port of Menteith, in rural Stirlingshire: 'Becaus thai heve not a pastor and also thair kirk [is] al[to]gether decayit, thair is na eldaris, deacones nor forme off disciplein in this congregatione quhairthrow sin and vyce grethe abundis amangis thame ... .'[2] What happened between 1558 and 1586? In fairness to Knox, we ought to note the gulf which separates the committed urban cells of the early Reformation from the dark corners of rural Scotland represented by Port of Menteith. We should also note that he was not actually in Scotland in 1558, the year he described with such exuberance.[3] But it looks as if he projected a winner too soon, so that he could then assign blame for subsequent failures. To Knox, it all began to unravel with the return of Queen Mary from France in August 1561. After that, he lamented, 'suddandlie the most parte of us declyned from the puritie of Goddis word, and began to follow the warld, and so again to schaik handis with the Devill, and with idolatrie'.[4] This version of events has proved

---

[1] Knox, *Works*, I, p. 300.

[2] *Visitation of the Diocese of Dunblane and Other Churches, 1586–1589*, ed. James Kirk (Edinburgh, 1984), p. 11.

[3] He arrived on the scene in May 1559. See Knox, *Works*, I, p. 318.

[4] Ibid., II, pp. 263–5. Knox wrote this in 1566, while in temporary internal exile in Kyle, after the Riccio murder.

influential.[5] But rather than shaking hands with the Devil, what Scottish reformers were really doing was encountering the problems inherent in the translation of the ideals of any revolutionary movement into the institutions of a wider society. Knox was presenting a historical thesis that would not get far in an undergraduate seminar today.

The construction of the reformed disciplinary apparatus was a central element in Knox's happy recollection of 1558. In writing of the election of elders and the punishment of 'open crymes ... without respect of persone', he was identifying the progress of the Scottish Reformation with the progress of a Calvinist-style reformation of manners, fostered by consistories, or kirk sessions, through the media of the pulpit and the penitent stool. Indeed, the *Scots Confession* of 1560, which Knox helped to write, went beyond Calvin himself by making discipline, properly administered, the third 'mark' of the true Church.[6] But behavioural reformation was an ambitious programme of cultural transformation which could only succeed after several decades, if it was to succeed at all. Nevertheless, Knox was certainly correct in his realization that the reformation of behaviour could be the most significant outcome of any Scottish Reformation which might take place. He probably came to this conclusion during his Genevan interlude; there is no mention of any disciplinary oversight in his recollection of the time he spent ministering to the group holed up in St Andrews Castle in 1546–47.[7] In Geneva, he would have observed at first hand a fully functioning disciplinary system, in which a consistory of ministers and lay elders closely scrutinized the behaviour of their neighbours, prominent and humble. In Geneva, by the late 1550s, even the traditional pastime of dancing was under fire (later, Mary Queen of Scots' dancing provided the subject-matter for several of Knox's rants), and Genevan authorities were willing to enforce Old Testament codes to the extent that adulterers were, in some cases, put to death.[8] This is the vision Knox had for post-Reformation

---

[5] Even some very recent work accepts the Knoxian notion of a swift, dramatic Reformation, with the enforcement of strict penalties for social misbehaviour. See, for example, Julian Goodare, 'Scotland', in Bob Scribner, Roy Porter and Mikulas Teich (eds), *The Reformation in National Context* (Cambridge, 1994), pp. 95–110, at pp. 102–3.

[6] *The Scots Confession, 1560 and the Negative Confession, 1581*, ed. G.D. Henderson (Edinburgh, 1937), p. 75.

[7] Knox, *Works*, I, pp. 182–205.

[8] E. William Monter, *Calvin's Geneva* (New York, 1967), pp. 152–3; E. William Monter, 'The Consistory of Geneva, 1559–1569,' *Bibliothèque d'Humanisme et Renaissance*, 38 (1976), pp. 467–84, at pp. 479, 483–4; Robert Kingdon, 'The Control of Morals in Calvin's Geneva,' in Lawrence Buck and Jonathan Zophy (eds), *The Social History of the Reformation* (Columbus, OH, 1972), pp. 3–16; André Biéler, *L'homme et la femme dans la morale calviniste* (Geneva, 1963), p. 125. The ongoing work by Robert Kingdon and his students to transcribe and publish the Genevan consistory register

Scotland; it would prove difficult to sell to his countrymen. When his critics opposed the naming of names in public admonitions – an essential aspect of Genevan-style discipline – in 1563–64, Knox predicted dire consequences for them: 'so lang as protestantis ar not eschameit manifestlie to do againis the evangill of Jueus Chryste, so lang can nocht the Mynisteries of God ceise to cry, that God wilbe revengit upon sik abusearis of his holie worde'.[9]

But the Genevan model was not the only possible source for a reformed disciplinary apparatus in Scotland. Most Scottish burghs had networks of courts with jurisdiction in matters of economic behaviour, and their bailiwicks could be extended to the enforcement of Christian brotherhood if a dispute obviously threatened to rend the fabric of civic harmony.[10] In fact, many of the urban kirk sessions which eventually emerged were alternate versions of burgh councils, nominated by councils and drawing members from the same pool of local notables.[11] There are also some scraps of evidence regarding the existence of reformed 'Privy Kirks' in Scottish burghs before 1560. A good deal of this evidence comes from Knox himself, who was probably dependent on the reports of others. Edinburgh had, according to Knox, a 'Privie Kirk', with an elected session, meeting during the 1550s in 'secreit and privie conventiounis in Houses, or in the Feilds'. Even in this voluntary, secret Church, he wrote, 'varietie of persones culd not be kept in gud obedience and honest fame, without oversiers, Elders and Deacones'.[12] Its reported leadership included John Willock, the ex-Dominican who later became superintendent of the west in the reformed Kirk; James Baron, a

---

should further illuminate the operation of the disciplinary regime in Geneva. For the Queen's dancing, see Knox, *Works*, II, pp. 393, 415–16.

[9] Knox, *Works*, II, p. 419.

[10] E.g. *The Gild Court Book of Dunfermline, 1433–1597*, ed. Elizabeth Torrie (Edinburgh, 1986), pp. 88, 93.

[11] For example, eight of the 14 elders elected to the St Andrews kirk session in October 1589 were elected to the burgh council that same month. See St Andrews University Muniments, B65/8/1, 125v, 130r; *Register of the Minister, Elders and Deacons of the Christian Congregation of St Andrews 1559–1600*, ed. D. Hay Fleming, (2 vols, Edinburgh, 1889–90) [hereafter *StAKS*], II, p. 650. Likewise, six of the 24 elders elected to Stirling's Holy Rude kirk session in November 1600 (for the 1600–1601 term) served as Stirling burgh councillors at the same time. See S[tirling] C[ouncil] A[rchives], CH2/1026/1, 20 November 1600; SCA, B66/20/2, 109. In Aberdeen, ten of 13 elders elected in 1575 were burgh councillors. See Allan White, 'Religion, Politics and Society in Aberdeen, 1543–1593' (unpublished University of Edinburgh PhD thesis, 1985), p. 298.

[12] Knox, *Works*, II, pp. 151–2; James Kirk, *Patterns of Reform: Continuity and Change in the Reformation Kirk* (Edinburgh, 1989), pp. 12–13. Kirk concludes that there were Privy Kirks elsewhere as well, due to the fact that public Kirks sprang to life so quickly in several burghs in 1559–60.

merchant and burgh councillor; Michael Christeson, Robert Watson and Alexander Hope, all merchants; Adam Craig, a goldsmith; James Gray, a mason; George Small, a saddler; William Harlaw, a Canongate tailor; and John Cairns, who later served the public Kirk as a reader.[13] Knox stressed that this was a group in which godliness mattered more than wealth and social standing. All communicants voted in session elections, he claimed, and the elders and deacons were named in descending order of vote totals, 'so that if a puir man exceid the riche man in votes, he preceids him in place'. Whether or not this is an idealized portrait, it is certainly true that the elders and deacons listed in the earliest extant public kirk session minutes for Edinburgh, those of 1574–75, were much more reflective of the burgh oligarchy than those listed above; the Privy Kirk may have been a revolutionary cell in more ways than one.[14] But since no records from this Privy Kirk have survived, we know nothing of its disciplinary activities.

So from the Genevan model, coupled with the institutional traditions of Scottish burghs, and possibly working on foundations laid by 'Privy Kirks', Knox and his fellow reformers sought to construct a system which could bring a behavioural reformation to the Scottish people. Many of the latter resented the increased scrutiny of their personal affairs which came with this form of evangelization, and Knox was enough of a public figure that critics associated his name with the new moral regime. The Edinburgh cook Ninian McCrechane was probably engaging more in wishful thinking than astute political commentary in the spring of 1562 when he said, 'Loving to God, my lord Arrane and my lord Boithuile ar aggreit now; Knox quarter is run, he is skurgeit throw the toun'. Edinburgh's burgh council ordered McCrechane scourged instead, and placed him in the branks as well. The widow Euphemia Dundas took a more direct approach the next year when she charged publicly that Knox had recently been caught with a prostitute and 'he had bene ane commoun harlot all his dayis'. Curiously, although the Edinburgh kirk session complained to the burgh council of her slander, the council dropped the case.[15] Knox could dish it out as well as he got it, though. In December 1570, after servants of William Kirkcaldy of Grange were involved in a killing and then rescued one of

---

[13] Calderwood, *History*, I, p. 304.

[14] Knox, *Works*, II, pp. 152–3; SRO, CH2/450/1, 23v–24v; Michael Lynch, *Edinburgh and the Reformation* (Edinburgh, 1981), pp. 38–40; Michael Lynch, 'From Privy Kirk to Burgh Church: An Alternative View of the Process of Protestantisation', in Norman Macdougall (ed.), *Church, Politics and Society: Scotland 1408–1929* (Edinburgh, 1983), pp. 85–96, at pp. 86–7, 93.

[15] *Edin. Recs*, III, pp. 132, 162, 164.

the alleged perpetrators out of Edinburgh's gaol, Knox denounced Kirk-caldy of Grange from St Giles's pulpit as 'a cruell murtherer, [and] open throat-cutter'. Kirkcaldy, sometime provost of Edinburgh and at that time captain of Edinburgh Castle, complained to the Edinburgh kirk session that Knox had slandered him. Kirkcaldy soon dropped the charge, but Knox would not let the matter drop, and called on the session publicly to admonish him in keeping with Knox's original de-nunciation.[16] The distribution of Easter Communion tokens in St Andrews in 1560 – an innovation necessitated by the new disciplinary system – was marred when John Law allegedly expressed his hope that 'the Divell knok owt Johne Knox barnes [brains], for, when he wald se him hanget, he wald gett his sacrament'. Law admitted to the local kirk session that he said 'God give Knox be hanget,' at least.[17] Critics of the new system like Law seem to have held Knox personally responsible for its creation. While this may have flattered the ego of the man himself (none who read Knox's *History* can fail to notice the starring role given to the author), it was not really accurate. But in the soundbite politics of the sixteenth-century market cross, Knox's name carried a lot of baggage.

While Knox served as a target for critics, ministers and lay elders spent the 1560s laying the institutional foundation of the public Kirk. Recent historiography has emphasized the regional nature of the Scot-tish Reformation,[18] and there appears to have been a geographic pattern to the spread of kirk sessions as well. All evidence of functioning sessions in the decade after 1560 comes from the coastal regions sur-rounding the Firths of Forth and Tay, in the south-east. Records survive for the St Andrews session beginning in 1559, Monifieth's from 1562 (although these are fragmentary until the late 1560s), and that of the Canongate for the period 1564–67.[19] Other evidence suggests the exist-ence of sessions elsewhere. Dundee apparently had one functioning

---

[16] Calderwood, *History*, III, pp. 20–29. The outcome of this case is unclear, although Knox did leave Edinburgh due to the Marian takeover of the town in the spring of 1571.

[17] No punishment for his offence was mentioned. See *StAKS*, I, p. 36.

[18] Ian Cowan, *Regional Aspects of the Scottish Reformation* (London, 1978); Michael Lynch, 'Calvinism in Scotland, 1559–1638', in Menna Prestwich (ed.), *International Calvinism, 1541–1715* (Oxford, 1985), pp. 225–55, at p. 229; Margaret H.B. Sander-son, *Ayrshire and the Reformation: People and Change, 1490–1600* (East Linton, 1997); Frank Bardgett, *Scotland Reformed: The Reformation in Angus and the Mearns* (Edin-burgh, 1989).

[19] *StAKS*; *The Buik of the Kirk of the Canagait, 1564–1567*, ed. A.B. Calderwood (Edinburgh, 1961) [hereafter *BKC*]; New Register House (Edinburgh), OPR 310/1. All quotations from manuscripts in the OPR (old parish registers) series are made with permission of the Controller of Her Britannic Majesty's Stationery Office.

from mid-1559, at least.[20] There is very little evidence from rural parishes (where the vast majority of the population lived), before the creation of the first presbyteries in 1581. Indeed, the failure of the parochial Reformation in rural areas was one of the justifications for the establishment of the presbyteries.[21] Only two pre-1581 kirk session registers from predominantly rural parishes have survived in any condition.[22] Of course, the paucity of surviving material may be evidence that few rural parishes even had sessions. A firm verdict is impossible, but there is no documentary evidence for widespread rural disciplinary practice before the advent of the presbyteries.

But since Knox spent most of his public career in urban settings and the Genevan model was certainly an urban one, the following examination of disciplinary practice is restricted to burghs. Given Knox's exuberant account of the early progress of discipline, and his disappointment at what followed, both noted earlier, it seems worth while to assess the functioning of Scottish reformed discipline at the time of his death. What had these changes, so closely identified in the public eye with Knox himself, wrought? We must avoid a literal interpretation of the phrase 'at the time of his death', because we only have records for one functioning urban kirk session, that of St Andrews, in 1572. If an extended mourning period is allowed following Knox's passing, thus delaying analysis to 1574–75, three burghs can be brought into comparison: Edinburgh and Aberdeen as well as St Andrews.[23]

The Reformations (the plural is used consciously) experienced in these three towns did not proceed at the same pace. St Andrews had joined the reformed camp early on, in June 1559 during an armed visit by the Lords of the Congregation which included public preaching by Knox himself. St Andrews's kirk session held its first recorded meeting the following month, and was in regular operation by the end of the

---

[20] Iain E.F. Flett, 'The Conflict of the Reformation and Democracy in the Geneva of Scotland, 1443–1610: An Introduction to Edited Texts of Documents Relating to the Burgh of Dundee' (unpublished St Andrews University MPhil thesis, 1981), pp. 83–6, 98.

[21] *The Second Book of Discipline*, ed. James Kirk (Edinburgh, 1980), p. 199.

[22] The registers are Monifieth (Angus), New Register House, OPR 310/1 and Anstruther Wester (Fife), New Register House, OPR 403/1. Anstruther Wester was, technically, a burgh, but it was tiny, and many of the parishioners came from the surrounding countryside or the equally tiny neighbouring burghs of Anstruther Easter, Pittenweem, or Kilrenny.

[23] The main documentary sources for what follows are: *StAKS* (St Andrews Kirk Session Register, 1559–1600); SRO, CH2/448/1 (Aberdeen St Nicholas Kirk Session Register, 1562–63, 1568, 1573–78); and SRO, CH2/450/1 (Edinburgh General Session Register, 1574–75), compared with its partial transcript, SRO, RH2/1/35.

year.[24] Edinburgh's Reformation was not so swift and dramatic, being marked by a sequence of coup and countercoup in 1559–60, with the last Catholic-dominated burgh council ousted in April 1560. The burgh was Protestant from that point on, but the political and geographic position of Edinburgh as the seat of Scotland's government and the centre of its economic life subjected the town to pressures that made consistency difficult.[25] For example, an act passed by the Edinburgh council in July 1562 limiting burgh office-holding to those who had joined the reformed Kirk was deleted the following January 'at the Quenis Maiesteis command'.[26] Later, during the civil war of 1568–73, the town was hotly contested, and occupied by the Queen's Men from spring 1571 until summer 1572. Even after that, William Kirkcaldy of Grange was able to harass (and occasionally bombard) the town from the ramparts of Edinburgh Castle, which he held in the Queen's name until May 1573.[27] This background of violence and destruction would profoundly influence disciplinary practices in the burgh, as we shall see. Aberdeen's Reformation came much later than St Andrews' or Edinburgh's. That northern town and its hinterlands were dominated by the Catholic Menzies and Gordon families,[28] respectively, and it was only in the early 1570s that Aberdeen's kirk session (with several Catholics as elders) even began functioning regularly, although it had made a couple of earlier, temporary appearances in response to political crises in the 1560s.[29] During the period under consideration here, Aberdeen's city fathers would receive a personal visit from the Regent Morton,

---

[24] Knox, *Works*, I, pp. 349–50, VI, p. 680; Jane E.A. Dawson, '"The Face of Ane Perfyt Reformed Kyrk": St Andrews and the Early Scottish Reformation', in James Kirk (ed.), *Humanism and Reform: The Church in Europe, England and Scotland, 1400–1643* (Oxford, 1991), pp. 413–36, esp. pp. 415–16; *StAKS*, I, pp. 1–3.

[25] Lynch, *Edinburgh and the Reformation*, pp. 8–9, 214–15.

[26] *Edin. Recs*, III, pp. 140–41.

[27] Lynch, *Edinburgh and the Reformation*, pp. 131–43; George Hewitt, *Scotland Under Morton, 1572–80* (Edinburgh, 1982), pp. 26–9.

[28] Provost Menzies and nine other burgh councillors vowed in December 1559 to defend the town's religious foundations against iconoclastic attacks launched 'under colour and pretence of godlie reformation', and refused to sign the reformed Kirk of Scotland's *Book of Discipline* in January 1561. *Extracts From the Records of the Burgh of Aberdeen, 1398–1625*, ed. John Stuart [hereafter *Aber. Recs*] (2 vols, Aberdeen, 1844, 1848), I, pp. 325–6; *The First Book of Discipline*, ed. James Cameron (Edinburgh, 1972), p. 12.

[29] SRO, CH2/448/1, pp. 1–20 (manuscript paginated rather than foliated); Allan White, 'The Impact of the Reformation on a Burgh Community: The Case of Aberdeen', in Michael Lynch (ed.), *The Early Modern Town in Scotland* (London, 1987), pp. 81–101; Bruce McLennan, 'The Reformation in the Burgh of Aberdeen,' *Northern Scotland*, 2 (1974–77), pp. 119–44.

accompanied by the Privy Council and the English ambassador, to ensure their commitment to the continuing cause of reform.[30]

The effect of these (mostly political) factors was that, while no disciplinary system could function in a holy vacuum, that of St Andrews could come closer to that Knoxian ideal than the others. But even there we must remember that many kirk elders were burgh magistrates as well. Whether or not Knox believed in a 'two kingdoms' theory, and however early one feels such an idea entered the Scots Kirk, ecclesiastical and civil jurisdictions were hopelessly mixed in the early modern Scottish burgh.[31] The question here is what these jurisdictions encompassed in the early to mid-1570s. Were 'open crymes ... punished without respect of persone'? Which open crimes? How were they punished? And, if Knox's egalitarian ideal was not being met, which persons were receiving special treatment?

St Andrews probably had a population of 3 000–4 000 in the late sixteenth century, and its burgh Kirk of Holy Trinity might have had 2 000 adult communicants.[32] In 1574, 63 of them found themselves summoned before the kirk session, and 26 did the following year, an average of 45 a year. This average is skewed by the high figure for 1574, a very busy year. For the whole decade of the 1570s, an average of only 36 people were summoned every year, or one out of every 56 communicants.[33] But in 1574, the kirk session decided to launch a frontal assault on what its members regarded as a relic of Catholicism: the celebration of Christmas, or 'superstitious keping of Zwil-day'. In January and February, 26 men were summoned for having celebrated this traditional holiday the previous December. Most of them were

---

[30] Privy Council meetings took place in Aberdeen from 9 August until 4 September 1574. See *RPC*, II, pp. 388–403. For descriptions of the visit, see Hewitt, *Morton*, pp. 39–40, and Allan White, 'The Regent Morton's Visitation: The Reformation of Aberdeen, 1574', in A.A. MacDonald, Michael Lynch and Ian Cowan (eds), *The Renaissance in Scotland: Studies in Literature, Religion, History and Culture Offered to John Durkan* (Leiden, 1994), pp. 246–63.

[31] For example, the Edinburgh kirk session in the mid-1570s would order those convicted of offences to pay fines to 'satisfy the magistrate' in addition to imposing public repentance in the Kirk. The fines would then often be collected on the spot by bailies sitting with the session. See SRO, CH2/450/1, 29v.

[32] Geoffrey Parker, 'The "Kirk by Law Established" and the Origins of "the Taming of Scotland": Saint Andrews 1559–1600', in Raymond Mentzer (ed.), *Sin and the Calvinists: Morals Control and the Consistory in the Reformed Tradition* (Kirksville, MO, 1994), pp. 158–97, at pp. 160–61.

[33] Michael F. Graham, *The Uses of Reform: 'Godly Discipline' and Popular Behavior in Scotland and Beyond, 1560–1610* (Leiden, 1996), p. 97.

privately admonished and promised not to repeat the offence, although four denied the charge and four others were forced to perform public repentance, sitting upon the penitent stool. One of the latter was Walter Younger, who predicted failure for the cultural revolution being attempted in the name of reformed Protestantism. Younger announced at a meeting-place of the St Andrews craftsmen that 'he [was] ane yowng man and saw Zuil-day kepit halyday, and that the tyme may cum that he may see the like yit'.[34] It is not clear that the local celebration of Christmas was stamped out as a result of this campaign, either. All the men summoned in 1574 were craftsmen, and two more craftsmen were summoned for the same offence a year later. By then, it was apparent that craftsmen were vulnerable to prosecution because the refusal to work on 25 December made their offence obvious.[35] Others may have found it easier to be discreet.

Intolerance of Yule observance was becoming a litmus test of reform elsewhere in Scotland as well. The Regent Morton admonished the politically suspect Aberdeen burgh council against 'the superstitious keping of festivall days usit of befor in tyme of ignorance & papistrie' in August 1574, and the council and kirk session there responded by summoning 15 offenders the following December and January, who also received private admonitions.[36] Catholic practices lingered in Aberdeen, but in St Andrews the effort to stamp them out may have been more successful. After 1574–75, cases of religious dissent or 'superstition' virtually disappear from the St Andrews kirk session register until the mid-1590s, when the Kirk at the national level became obsessed by fears of Catholic conspiracy.

Celebrating Christmas the traditional way was probably one of the 'open crymes' John Knox had in mind, although plenty of his countrymen (and women) would continue to regard it as a harmless pastime.[37] The open crimes the elders at St Andrews and elsewhere most commonly sought to punish were those of a sexual nature. If we remove the 28 cases related to the crackdown on Yule at St Andrews, we are left with 61 cases (38 male, 23 female), of which 42 (21 male, 21 female) were for adultery or fornication. The typical pattern, in St Andrews and elsewhere, was for an unmarried woman or widow to turn up pregnant, to be summoned before the kirk session, and there told to identify the father. Most complied readily, some of them alleging that the man in question had promised marriage. The male would then be summoned,

---

[34] StAKS, I, pp. 389–90.
[35] Ibid., I, p. 404.
[36] SRO, CH2/448/1, pp. 58–9, 61; Aber. Recs, II, pp. 25–6.
[37] Graham, Uses of Reform, pp. 118, 157, 277.

asked to admit or deny the charge (most admitted it), and urged to marry the woman if he was not already betrothed or married.[38] Regardless of whether they married, the couple would have to perform public repentance, and often pay a fine as well, before the child could be baptized. Perhaps most importantly from the perspective of local authorities, every illegitimate child would then have an identified father, who could be pressured to provide some support for his offspring. Thus the new disciplinary system became a useful tool for magistrates concerned as much with poverty and the expenses of poor relief as with the sinfulness of humanity.

The remainder of the offences pursued by the elders of St Andrews in 1574–75 need not concern us long. Three men were summoned for breaking the Sabbath (the session had campaigned vigorously on this issue in 1571–72, and would again in 1576). Two out of the three were admonished privately, but the third had ignored previous admonitions, so he was referred to the magistrates for punishment under a burgh regulation. Three men were charged with absence from Communion (one was fined), and two men and one woman for their involvement in disputes with neighbours. There were also two cases concerning the validity of marriages and one related to disobedience to the session. But sexuality was the primary and constant concern, and would remain so – 24 out of 34 cases in 1577, for example, and 19 out of 23 in 1578. In fact, sexual misdeeds made up the majority (55 per cent) of offences brought before kirk sessions in the first half-century of the Scottish Reformation.[39] Reformers and traditionalists might disagree as to whether celebrating Christmas, or even doing a bit of work on the Sabbath, was a sin, but nobody wanted to condone sexual licence, particularly when it produced illegitimate children.[40]

This concern over illegitimacy and paternity was also present in Edinburgh, bursting at the seams with 12 000 residents, but there political issues and the recent wounds of civil war overshadowed such mundane questions. In the 19.5 months covered by the surviving register (1 April 1574–17 November 1575), Edinburgh's kirk session handled 321 cases. This averages out to about 16.5 cases a month, or 198 a year. Given the

---

[38] If the alleged father was willing to deny his paternity with his hand on a Bible, however, the General Assembly had ruled in 1570 that he could not be held responsible for the child. See Calderwood, *History*, III, pp. 4–6.

[39] Sample of 4 594 cases. See Graham, *Uses of Reform*, p. 340.

[40] The first post-Reformation act of Parliament relating to the Sabbath was passed in 1579. See *APS*, III, p. 138.

typical age pyramid of an early modern town, Edinburgh would have had 7 000 adults, which means that one out of 35 of them would have been charged with some misdeed each year. This suggests a more intense level of disciplinary oversight than in St Andrews, which is particularly impressive considering that plague was present in Edinburgh in 1574.[41] In keeping with the national pattern, 172 of the citations, or 54 per cent, involved sexual misbehaviour. But similarities to the national pattern end there. First of all, the ministers and elders of Edinburgh seem to have held women primarily responsible for sexual misdeeds; 103 of the 172 charged were women. This prevalence of women among sexual offenders can also be found in the Canongate in the mid-1560s and (to a lesser extent) Aberdeen in the mid-1570s. In larger towns, single women were seen as posing a particular danger to public morality, while kirk sessions in smaller towns (like St Andrews) and rural parishes do not seem to have maintained any such double standard.[42]

But if the Edinburgh session put the sexual behaviour of women under a microscope, it did the same thing, even more dramatically, with the political behaviour of men. Early in 1573 Parliament mandated that those who had sided with the Queen in the civil war, then winding down, would have to acknowledge this offence before their ministers.[43] Parliament stipulated that this had to be done by 1 June 1573, but Edinburgh contained many stragglers, and much of the kirk session's business in the period under consideration was taken up with them. The authorities in Edinburgh had decided to make the reconciliation of the former rebels (some of whom had governed the town during the Marian occupation) a public spectacle; this is probably one reason why many of them were so slow to come in. Adherence to the Marian cause would be treated as a sin as well as a political offence. So when Thomas Elphinstone and Andrew Hay appeared in the spring of 1574, the session clerk recorded that their rebellion had been directed not only against the young king, but also 'against o[ur mr.] and salvator Christ'. They promised 'to forbeir ye societe and companie [of] ye wickit and to joyne w[i]t[h] ye godlie in all affection' in the future.

Twenty-eight men who confessed the same offence at that meeting were told to go to the Kirk on the following Wednesday at the sound of the second bell, and to stand bare-headed in black clothes by the door, confessing their sins. Then they were to sit in the place of public repentance for the length of the afternoon sermon.[44] The session made

---

[41] *Edin. Recs*, IV, pp. 29–30.
[42] Graham, *Uses of Reform*, pp. 287–9.
[43] *APS*, III, pp. 72–3.
[44] SRO, CH2/450/1, 1r–v. See also 9r.

it clear before three Communion celebrations in the following 14 months that nobody who had supported the Queen (if only by having remained in Edinburgh during the occupation) would get a Communion token until they performed this public repentance.[45] Those who had taken a more active role in the Queen's cause, such as four men who had participated in Kirkcaldy of Grange's bombardment of the town from Edinburgh Castle, would have to perform the ritual of repentance three times.[46]

Not surprisingly, some objected to this equation of incorrect political allegiance with sin. Thomas MacAlzeane, laird of Cliftonhall and a senator in the College of Justice, protested that he had been among the burgh's first Protestants, and yet the session was making no distinction 'betuixt me and [the] maist wilful murder[er]', (MacAlzeane had been ordered to make his repentance in sackcloth). He claimed he had remained in the town during the occupation primarily due to his fear of Archibald Ruthven, with whom he was at feud. The session was unmoved (MacAlzeane had served as an elder on a kirk session elected during the occupation), and told him he had to perform his repentance anyway. Ditto for the advocate John Moscrope, despite the fact that he had obtained a royal pardon for his activities during the civil war; the pardon might cover his rebellion against the King, but not his sin against the congregation.[47] The flesher James Fleming, who had been in the castle during the occupation, sought reconciliation early in June 1575 but was made to wait an extra three weeks 'be ressone of ye hevenes of his offense' before he was told to perform public repentance in sackcloth four times.[48] In all, Edinburgh's kirk session charged 92 men and two women (one of the latter actually a ten-year-old servant) with political sins during the period under consideration. Sexuality or politics together comprised 266 of the 321 cases handled by the session (83 per cent). There was little time for anything else.

This politicization of the disciplinary apparatus was the result of Edinburgh's central position in national politics and its experience in the recent civil war. Discipline was a versatile tool, and Knox favoured its political application.[49] It was also employed against the session elder

---

[45] SRO, CH2/450/1, 4r, 32v, 59v.

[46] SRO, CH2/450/1, 7v.

[47] SRO, CH2/450/1, 5v–6r, 26r, 28r–v, 46r–48r, 60r–61r, 65r–v, 67v, 68v, 71v–72v.

[48] SRO, CH2/450/1, 59r–v, 64r.

[49] In his 1559 letter to the nobility, Knox had warned nobles who had previously 'professed Chryst Jesus with us' that if they did not continue to provide political and ideological support, 'so shall ye be excommunicated from our societie, and from all participatioun with us in the administratioun of sacramentis … ' See Knox, *Works*, I, p. 333.

(and long-time King's supporter) Robert Gourlay and four other men who had been exporting corn from the city for profit in a time of dearth. One of them, William Horne, protested 'y[a]t he wes ye first y[a]t wes chargeit & ye lik wes nevir done to na uyer p[er]son ... befoir'. But this was futile; he and Gourlay were suspended from Communion (despite intervention on their behalf by the Regent Morton), while the others denied that they had been involved in the enterprise.[50] Other residents of Edinburgh ran afoul of the session for usury, for excessive banqueting at weddings, or for cross-dressing (a woman dressed as a man while dancing).[51] Such cases were rare, but they do demonstrate that session elders were at times willing to extend discipline into various aspects of popular culture, as some of their continental counterparts were.[52] As the burgh kirk session of Scotland's most important town, they seem to have been conscious of their place in the international Calvinist community. This was demonstrated in the summer of 1575 when they orchestrated a city-wide collection on behalf of the Huguenot exile Church in London.[53] Edinburgh had, after all, been Knox's Church through most of the 1560s. This feeling of connection to the wider cause of reform would be absent in Aberdeen.

In the first dozen or so years after 1560, Aberdeen's magistrates treated the Reformation as what they hoped would be a passing phenomenon, erecting a Potemkin-like facade of 'godly' zeal when political crises required it in 1562 and 1568, while generally governing the burgh as they always had.[54] But with the final defeat of Marian forces in 1572–73, it became clear that some form of Protestantism would be permanent, and burgh authorities set out for the third time to get a kirk session up and running. It is reflective of the peculiar religious *status quo* in Aberdeen that Catholicism was considered no impediment to membership on this session, provided one was of sufficient local importance. The leading Catholic elected in September 1573 was also the first elder listed: the burgh's Provost, Thomas Menzies of Pitfodels. In all, five of the 13 elders listed can be identified as men who had actively opposed

---

[50] SRO, CH2/450/1, 6r–7r; Calderwood, *History*, III, p. 328; Lynch, *Edinburgh and the Reformation*, pp. 153, 301.

[51] SRO, CH2/450/1, 14v, 15v, 23r, 34r.

[52] 'Le registre consistorial de Coutras, 1582–1584,' ed. Alfred Soman, *Bulletin de la société de l'histoire du protestantisme français*, 126 (1980), pp. 193–228.

[53] SRO, CH2/450/1, 51v, 56r, 61v, 70v.

[54] Graham, *Uses of Reform*, pp. 57–63; White, 'Impact of the Reformation on a Burgh Community'; White, 'Religion, Politics and Society', pp. 169–90.

the Reformation in 1559–60, and only one as a supporter.[55] While the opinions of some may have changed in the intervening 13 years, it is certain that several of these men's wives were still avowedly Catholic in 1574; the old faith still ruled their hearths if not their hearts.[56] Aberdeen also had a new minister starting in August 1573 – Knox's old Edinburgh colleague John Craig.[57] But it would take more than Craig's best efforts to bring this northern burgh in line with the Knoxian ideal.

Aberdeen was closer in size to St Andrews than Edinburgh. Like the former, and unlike the latter, it was also the seat of a bishop and a university. The combined population of Aberdeen and Auld Aberdeen, its smaller northern neighbour, was probably about 4 000, and the burgh Church of St Nicholas was Scotland's largest.[58] If Aberdeen proper had 3 000 residents, about 1 800 of them would have been adults. In 1574, the new kirk session handled the remarkable total of 207 cases, but only 87 the following year. Thus while more than one in ten adults received attention from the session in 1574, only one in 20 did so in 1575. In fact, numbers continued to decline thereafter until the session register ends in 1578. The average annual number of cases for 1574–77 (the complete years available) was 100. But by 1577 the annual figure had sunk to 41, meaning only one in 44 adults was charged that year. These imprecise calculations would place Aberdeen somewhere between Edinburgh (most intensive) and St Andrews (least intensive) on the disciplinary scale.

What was keeping Aberdeen's session so busy, particularly during its first full year of operations? The leading issues were, in descending order, sexuality (no surprise there), irregular marriage and Catholic practices. In 1574, 40 men and 62 women were charged with adultery or fornication (49 per cent of the caseload for that year), while 35 men and 25 women were charged the next year. Thus by 1575, sexuality had increased its market share of sin in Aberdeen to 70 per cent, an ascent which would continue, to 83 per cent in 1576, and 90 per cent in 1577.[59] This does not mean Aberdonians were becoming friskier; in fact

---

[55] The supporter was David Mar. Opponents were: Provost Menzies, Gilbert Menzies Sr., Alexander Chalmer Sr., George Middleton (bailie in 1573–74) and Andrew Hunter. See SRO, CH2/448/1, p. 19; *Aber. Recs*, I, pp. 315–19. For a discussion of lingering Catholicism in the burgh, see White, 'Impact of the Reformation on a Burgh Community', pp. 96–7.

[56] SRO, CH2/448/1, pp. 34, 38, 40, 47, 50–1.

[57] 'The Chronicle of Aberdeen, MCCCCXCI–MDXCV', in John Stuart (ed.), *Spalding Club Miscellany II* (Aberdeen, 1842), pp. 29–70, at p. 40. For Craig, see T. Angus Kerr, 'John Craig, Minister of Aberdeen and King's Chaplain', in Duncan Shaw (ed.), *Reformation and Revolution: Essays Presented to Hugh Watt* (Edinburgh, 1967), pp. 100–123.

[58] McLennan, 'Reformation in the Burgh of Aberdeen', p. 129.

[59] For details, see Graham, *Uses of Reform*, p. 120.

the absolute numbers of sexual offenders were declining – an indication, perhaps, of some success for the disciplinary programme. But the numbers of cases overall were sinking even faster. The peculiar concerns of Aberdeen's elders had kept them unusually busy in 1574–75, creating a statistical anomaly bound to frustrate attempts by modern historians to quantify early modern practices.

One of these concerns was irregular marriage. This issue received much more attention in Aberdeen than in any other community whose disciplinary practices I have studied. This was because 'handfast marriage' – a custom in which couples would seal alliances outdoors or at home, before witnesses but not necessarily clergy – appears to have been common in the area. The Church throughout western Europe had been trying to gain control over the institution of marriage since the eleventh century,[60] and in this respect Aberdeen's reformed Kirk was taking up a favoured cause of Catholic reformers. In 1562, Aberdeen's first (short-lived) kirk session had lamented the custom of handfasted couples to cohabit as long as seven years without formal marriage, ordered that all such couples marry within the Church, and stipulated that all future marriage promises be recorded by the session clerk.[61] Its (also short-lived) 1568 incarnation forbade ministers or readers to be present at handfastings, and declared that couples would not be considered legally married without the public reading of banns and a Church ceremony.[62] The kirk session of the 1570s continued this campaign. The year 1574 brought a round-up of couples – in some cases only represented by the male – who were living together without having formalized their marriages. There were 46 couples involved, and 57 individuals actually appeared before the session. Most were given a deadline to marry formally, and threatened with fines for failure. This dragnet spread widely, capturing two Menzies as well as many of their humbler neighbours. The fact that irregular marriages were accepted locally is verified by the session clerk's occasional tendency to refer to the woman in these couples as the 'wife'.[63] Clearly, local opinion regarded them as already married.

But the session wanted to change local marriage custom. It passed an order in June 1574 that all couples who wanted to marry had to give in their banns to be read and at the same time find caution that they would

---

[60] Georges Duby, *The Knight, the Lady and the Priest* (New York, 1983); John Bossy, *Christianity in the West, 1400–1700* (Oxford, 1984), pp. 21–4; John Gillis, *For Better, For Worse: British Marriages, 1600 to the Present* (Oxford, 1985), pp. 11–54.

[61] SRO, CH2/448/1, pp. 8–9.

[62] SRO, CH2/448/1, p. 16.

[63] SRO, CH2/448/1, pp. 31, 68.

remain celibate until formally marrying.[64] Unlike other sessional pronouncements, this one seems to have worked. It became quite common
for couples thereafter to appear before the session, request that their
banns be read, and find a cautioner to guarantee that they would not
'adheir together' until the formal ceremony.[65] Violators were fined and at
least told to perform public repentance as fornicators. In this area, the
dwindling caseload after 1574–75 is probably reflective of the Aberdeen
session's success rather than its flagging interest. Marriage was a legal
issue, with implications for property and family alliances. Children who
were officially legitimate could inherit whether or not their parents had
written wills. This was one issue on which the conservative Aberdonian
elders were happy to use the new apparatus of the reformed Kirk.

The burgh's Catholic past (and present), and its recent association
with the Marian cause – the Marian Earl of Huntly had only abandoned Aberdeen in October 1572[66] – meant that Catholicism would
also be an important disciplinary issue, at least in the short term, as
civic authorities sought to get back into the good graces of the young
King's government. As a result, 33 people – several of them burgh
officials or members of their families – were charged with maintaining
Catholic practices in 1574. This issue came to a head with the visit of
the Regent Morton in August, mentioned earlier. But once token compliance had been made, and the Regent had been paid off (after seeing
to the rearrangement of St Nicholas' Kirk in keeping with the needs of
reformed worship), this issue quickly faded, leading to only three cases
in 1575 and none in the following years.[67] This may be seen as analogous to the effort to make Marians perform public repentance in
Edinburgh, but there are significant differences. Edinburgh had been
deeply divided by the civil war; Aberdeen, with fewer supporters for the
King's cause, had not been. As a result, the healing process was much
quicker, despite the fact that the burgh had been on the losing side.

Otherwise, there is little sign that the behavioural ideology of the
reformed Kirk was having much effect in Aberdeen in the mid-1570s.
Sexual sinners paid fines, but many apparently did nothing more than
that. There would be scattered cases of Sabbath breach in 1576 and
1578, and elders were delegated in March 1576 to stroll on the links to
record the names of those playing golf during Sunday preaching.[68] But
offenders were only fined small amounts, or let off with a warning. The

---

[64] SRO, CH2/448/1, p. 41.
[65] E.g. SRO, CH2/448/1, pp. 42–3, 44–6, 60.
[66] *Aber. Recs*, II, p. 7.
[67] Graham, *Uses of Reform*, pp. 116–20.
[68] Ibid., pp. 88–9, 101, 129.

burgh council in October 1576 forbade the sale of fish or meat during Sunday preaching, but the rest of the day remained free for commerce, and the order had to be repeated four years later.[69] The session was very slow to order public admonitions against anyone, and only clearly did so on one occasion.[70] Only once did it resort to excommunication, and that was against an adulterous couple who refused to appear and answer charges in September 1573.[71]

While a strained Knoxian interpretation might see the pernicious influence of Queen Mary behind Aberdeen's slowness to embrace reformed discipline, Knox's tendency to blame the Queen for the Reformation's early failures is otherwise off the mark. As the reformer settled into his grave, elders and ministers in the burghs examined here were not yet showing much ability (or perhaps willingness) to enforce the full extent of the reformed disciplinary programme – Sabbath maintenance, Church attendance, catechizing, eradication of Catholic practices or the reform of popular culture. They wanted to curb illegitimacy, but this hardly distinguishes them from authorities anywhere else in Europe. They would use the disciplinary apparatus in the service of local concerns, such as shaming political losers in Edinburgh or regularizing marriage and appeasing the central government in Aberdeen, but this does not place them on any Calvinist vanguard either. And these were burghs, where Genevan-style neighbourly surveillance should have been easiest. Most of the population lived in villages and farm towns, which the long arm of discipline would be very slow to reach.[72]

---

[69] *Aber. Recs*, II, pp. 27–8, 38.

[70] Ibid., II, pp. 87, 117.

[71] Ibid., II, p. 21.

[72] Even in populous lowland regions, many communities still lacked working kirk sessions 25 to 50 years after the religious revolution of 1560 – e.g., Haddington in 1590, Newtown (near Edinburgh) in 1586, Crail (south coast of Fife) in 1605 (although this session had probably functioned earlier), Fossoway, Kincardine, Fowlis Wester, Tullibole, and Alva (all near Stirling) in 1586, Strowan (Clackmannanshire) in 1588, Falkirk and Tullibole (again) in 1591, Muckhart (Clackmannanshire) in 1592, Aberfoyle (Stirlingshire), and Port of Menteith (again) in 1593. See *Visitation of the Diocese of Dunblane*, ed. Kirk, pp. 15, 29, 33, 35, 43, 79; *The Records of the Synod of Lothian and Tweeddale, 1589–1596, 1640–1649*, ed. James Kirk (Edinburgh, 1977), pp. 27–8; Mark Smith, 'The Presbytery of St Andrews, 1586–1605: A Study and Annotated Edition of the Register of the Minutes of the Presbytery of St Andrews' (unpublished University of St Andrews PhD thesis, 1986), pp. 422–4; SRO CH2/121/1, 12v; SCA CH2/722/2, 22 June and 21 September 1591, 13 February 1592, 21 August 1593. As late as 1596, the General Assembly felt compelled to remind ministers that they were expected to form sessions in their parishes. See Thomas Thomson (ed.), *Acts and Proceedings of the General Assemblies of the Kirk of Scotland* (3 vols, Edinburgh, 1839–45), III, p. 865.

Appendix: Caseloads for three urban Scottish kirk sessions in the mid-1570s

Aberdeen

Year	Cases (M/F)	Sexuality (M/F)	Marriage (M/F)	Other (M/F)
1574	207 (109/98)	102 (40/62)	61 (49/12)	44 (20/24)*
1575	87 (49/38)	60 (35/25)	21 (12/9)	6 (2/4)
Average	147 (79/68)	81 (38/44)	41 (30/10)	25 (11/14)
1570s avg.	100 (52/48)	64 (29/35)	21 (16/5)	15 (7/8)

Note:* of the 44 cases classified as 'other' in 1574, 33 (10/23) involved religious practices.

Edinburgh

Year	Cases (M/F)	Sexuality (M/F)	Political actions (M/F)	Other (M/F)
1574*	203 (130/73)	105 (41/64)	68 (68/0)	30 (21/9)
1575*	118 (72/46)	67 (28/39)	26 (24/2)	25 (20/5)
Average	160 (101/59)	86 (34/52)	47 (46/1)	28 (20/8)

Note:* neither year is complete – the register begins in April 1574 and ends in November 1575.

St Andrews

Year	Cases (M/F)	Sexuality (M/F)	'Superstitious' practices (M/F)	Other (M/F)
1574	63 (50/13)	24 (12/12)	26 (26/0)	13 (12/1)
1575	26 (16/10)	18 (9/9)	2 (2/0)	6 (5/1)
Average	45 (34/11)	21 (10/10)	14 (14/0)	10 (9/1)
1570s avg.	36 (24/12)	19 (10/9)	3 (3/0)	14 (11/3)

Index

DATE DUE

NOV 1 7 03			
NOV 1 7 03			
DEC 7 04			
NOV 2 8			
DEC 0 4 2009			
MAY 0 3 2010			
DEC 0 3 2010			
DEC 0 4 2010			

FEB 02